CHILDREN'S
ENCYCLOPEDIA

CHILDREN'S ENCYCLOPEDIA

Edited by
Harold Boswell Taylor

GALLEY PRESS

How to use this book

The entries in this encyclopedia are arranged in alphabetical order. Throughout the book the use of capital letters indicates an entry elsewhere in its alphabetical position. The article on AMPHIBIAN, for example, directs you to a separate entry on FROGS AND TOADS. The last part of the book, pages 360-7, contains tables giving information on the solar system, the countries of the world, rivers, mountains, oceans and seas. On pages 352-3 is a map of the world, listing the countries in alphabetical order. More detailed maps will be found with the entries on the following: Australasia, Africa, Asia (Middle East and Far East), Europe, India, America (North and South).

First published in Great Britain in 1978
by Ward Lock Ltd under the title
Ward Lock's Encyclopedia

Published in Great Britain in 1982
by Treasure Press under the title
Children's Encyclopedia

This edition published in Great Britain in 1988
by Galley Press
in association with
Octopus Books
59 Grosvenor Street
London W1

ISBN 0 907407 56 0

Printed in Czechoslovakia

50451/5

A

AARD-VARK

African mammal with a tapering pig-like snout, donkey-like ears, a strong tail and sharp claws. It digs into termite nests and eats the insects with its long sticky tongue. The creature is about 2 m (6 ft) from tail to snout. The word means 'earth-pig'.

AARD-WOLF

Small mammal from southern and eastern Africa, related to the hyena, which feeds on ants and other insects. It has a distinctive mane which it erects when frightened. The word means 'earth-wolf'.

ABACUS

Ancient device, probably originating in the Middle East, used for arithmetical calculations. It consists of several rows of beads which can be moved to and fro along rods to represent units, tens, hundreds, and so on. Still widely used as a simple teaching aid in certain countries of the world.

ABÉLARD, Pierre (1079–1142)

French poet, philosopher and religious teacher who questioned many of the ideas and beliefs of his day and was often in serious trouble with the Church. Today he is best remembered for his love affair with Héloise, who became a nun after bearing his child.

ABERRATION

Term used in science, mainly to describe certain conditions of LIGHT; for example, the failure of light rays to meet at a point because they are refracted. Chromatic aberration is the failure of different colours in white light to meet at a focal point. In ASTRONOMY aberration means the apparent displacement of a heavenly body from its actual position caused by the refraction of its light by the Earth's atmosphere.

ABSOLUTE ZERO

Temperature of 0° Kelvin (−273.15 °C) and the lowest possible temperature, denoting a total absence of heat and therefore an absence of all molecular motion.

ACADEMY

Name given to many famous institutions in the fields of science, literature and the arts. The word goes back to the time of PLATO, who began teaching in an olive grove near Athens dedicated to a Greek warrior hero whose name was Academus.

ACID

Group of organic and inorganic chemical compounds. They combine with ALKALIS to form salts. Nearly all acids contain hydrogen and react with some metals by liberating hydrogen gas. They are corrosive and have a sour taste when dissolved in water. Among the inorganic acids are sulphuric acid (H_2SO_4), nitric acid (HNO_3) and hydrochloric acid (HC_1). Organic acids contain carbon atoms. Among them are acetic acid (vinegar), citric acid (in citrus fruit) and lactic acid (in milk). *See also* CHEMISTRY.

ACUPUNCTURE

Ancient Chinese medical treatment involving the insertion of metal needles in various parts of

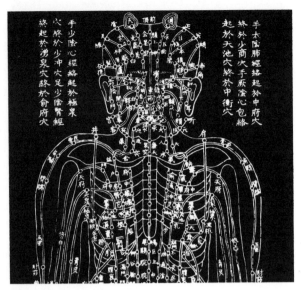

Chinese acupuncture chart

the body. Nobody knows why the treatment works, but it is thought that the needles direct, or re-direct, bodily forces and so restore a healthy internal balance. Acupuncture is still practised in China and now also in many Western countries.

ADAM, Robert (1720–92) and James (1730–94)

Scottish architects and interior designers whose work was modelled on the styles of classical Greece and Rome. Syon House and Osterley Park in Middlesex, and Kenwood House in Highgate, London, are fine examples of their work. The two men were brothers.

ADDISON, Joseph (1672–1719)

English essayist, poet and man of letters. With Richard Steele he was a regular contributor to *The Tatler* and *The Spectator* and a pioneer figure of modern journalism.

AEGEAN CIVILIZATIONS

BRONZE AGE civilizations which flourished on the islands and lands bordering the Aegean Sea between 3000 and 1000 BC. Most important of these were the Minoan civilization of Crete, named after the legendary King Minos; the Mycenaean civilization of mainland Greece; and the Cycladic civilization of the neighbouring Cyclades islands.

AENEID. *See* VIRGIL

AERODYNAMICS

The study of air in motion, as applied to the behaviour of air and other gases in engines and furnaces, air conditioning, the effect of wind on buildings and bridges, weather patterns (*see* METEOROLOGY) and AERONAUTICS (*see next entry*).

AERONAUTICS

The study and history of airborne flight. It includes BALLOONS, AIRSHIPS, GLIDERS and aeroplanes. Experts disagree on whether or not the term should also include rockets and space flight (astronautics). *See also* SPACE TRAVEL AND EXPLORATION.

A large part of the subject of aeronautics is concerned with the history and technological development of the aeroplane itself. The propeller or jet engine moves the aeroplane forward, so creating a flow of air over the wings. The shape of the wings in cross-section, and the angle at which they meet the flow of air, or airstream, are designed according to the principles of aerodynamics (*see above*). As the airstream passes over the wings it reduces normal atmospheric pressure on the upper wing surface. A second airstream passing under the wings increases air pressure from below. The combination of these two actions produces the required lift.

Other sections of the wing and of the tailplane control the aeroplane's direction and altitude. Also of great importance are the wing flaps for obstructing the airstream and reducing speed prior to landing.

Aeronautics: Otto Lilienthal with his glider

The following are significant events in the history of aeronautics:

1783 – First manned balloon ascent made by Pilâtre de Rozier and the Marquis d'Arlandes of France.

1784 – First balloon ascent in Britain made by James Tytler at Edinburgh.

1848 – John Stringfellow built and flew the first powered model aeroplane. Power came from a small steam-engine.

1852 – Henri Giffard of France made a flight in an elongated balloon steered by a rudder and propelled by a steam-engine driving a propeller.

1896 – Otto Lilienthal, known as 'the father of the aeroplane', killed in an accident after gliding experiments in Germany.

1900 – Count Ferdinand von Zeppelin's first airship made its trial flight.

1903 – Orville Wright made the world's first controlled, power-driven aeroplane flight at Kitty Hawk, North Carolina.

1905 – First officially recorded flight was made by Wilbur Wright at Dayton, Ohio. He flew 17.5 km (11 miles) in 18 minutes 9 seconds.

1906 – Santos Dumont of France made the first officially recorded aeroplane flight in Europe.

1909 – J.T.C. Moore-Brabazon (later Lord Brabazon of Tara) made first officially observed aeroplane flight in the British Isles.

Louis Blériot of France flew the Channel from les Baraques.

1919 – John Alcock and Arthur Whitten Brown made the first direct Atlantic crossing by air, flying from Newfoundland to Ireland, a distance of 3,024 km (1,890 miles).

1927 – Colonel Charles A. Lindbergh of the United States made first solo crossing of the Atlantic, flying from New York to Paris.

1928 – H.J. Hinkler flew from England to Australia: 19,600 km (12,250 miles) in 15½ days.

Southern Cross, a Fokker monoplane, with Captain C. Kingsford Smith and C. Ulm of Australia and H. W. Lyon and J. Warner of the United States, flew from Oakland, California, to Sydney, Australia.

1929 – Airship *Graf Zeppelin* made a world tour.

Flying-officer H.R.D. Waghorn of Great Britain won the Schneider Seaplane Trophy race: average speed 525.7 km/h (328.6 mph).

Squadron-Leader H. Orlebar of Great Britain set a world speed record of 575.5 km/h (357.7 mph) at Calshot, England.

1930 – Amy Johnson, Great Britain, completed 15,840 km (9,900 mile) flight from London to Australia in 19½ days.

1931 – Professor Auguste Piccard and Dr Paul Kipfer rose in a balloon to record height of 15,781 m (51,775 ft) at Augsburg, Germany.

Wiley Post of the United States and Harold Gatty of Australia encircled the globe in 8 days 15 hours 51 minutes, a record-breaking 24,900 km (15,470 miles).

1931 – Flight-Lieutenant G.H. Stainforth, Great Britain, set new seaplane speed record of 655 km/h (407 mph) at Calshot, England.

1932 – Miss Amelia Earheart of the United States flew from Newfoundland to Ireland in 13¼ hours, the first solo flight across the Atlantic by a woman.

Auguste Piccard and Max Cosyns set altitude record of 16,201 m (53,153 ft) in a balloon over Switzerland and Italy.

1934 – Major W.E. Kepner, Captain A.W. Stevens and Captain O.A. Anderson taking off from Rapid City, South Dakota, ascended to 18,184 m (60,613 ft) in a balloon.

Lieutenant Francesco Agello of Italy set new seaplane record of 709.2 km/h (440.7 mph) at Desenzano, Italy.

1938 – Two RAF single-engine Vickers Wellesley long-range bombers established new world's distance record for landplanes of 11,459 km (7,162 miles) by flying from Ismailia, Egypt, to Darwin, Australia.

1939 – First commercial trans-Atlantic service begun by Pan American Yankee Clipper, flying by way of New York, Bermuda, Azores, Lisbon, Bordeaux, Marseilles and Southampton.

British trans-Atlantic airmail service was inaugurated.

First jet plane, the German Heinkel He 178.

1941 – First flight by British jet plane, the Gloster E28/39.

1945 – H.F. Wilson raised speed record to 975 km/h (606 mph) in a Gloster Meteor.

1947 – Major Marion E. Carl, of the United States, flying a Douglas Skystreak jet plane, raised the world's speed record to 1,047.5 km/h (650.9 mph).

1947 – First flight faster than sound, when Captain Charles E. Yeager of the United States flew a Bell XS-1 rocket plane at a speed of 1,078 km/h (670 mph).

1948 – John Cunningham, Great Britain, set new altitude record for heavier-than-air craft in a de Haviland Vampire jet fighter: 18,119 m (59,445 ft) at Hatfield, Hertfordshire.

Major Richard L. Johnson, United States, set new world speed record of 1,079.8 km/h (671 mph).

1952 – BOAC Comet inaugurated world's first jet-liner service, London to Johannesburg.

1953 – Squadron-Leader Neville Duke set up new world speed record of 1,171 km/h (727.7 mph) in a Hawker Hunter at Tangmere, England.

1957 – USAF Stratojets made non-stop flight round world in 45 hours 19 minutes.

Captain J.W. Kittinger made record balloon altitude flight of 29,260 m (96,000 ft).

English Electric P.1 exceeded world speed record of 1,821 km/h (1,132 mph).

1969 – Anglo-French Concorde, supersonic airliner, made first successful test flights.

1970 – The first jumbo jet, the Boeing 747, entered airline service.

1976 – Anglo-French supersonic transport, the Concorde, began regular passenger services.

AESCHYLUS (525–456 BC)

First great Greek writer of tragic dramas and founder-figure of the theatre. Most of his plays are lost, but those which survive, whole or in part, include *Orestia*, *The Suppliants*, *The Persians*, *Seven Against Thebes* and *Prometheus Bound*.

AESOP (*c.* 650–560 BC)

Greek author of many famous fables, these being short stories about animals intended to highlight human follies and foibles. He is said to have been a slave, though freed later in life. The *Aesop's Fables* we know today are probably based on a version by a fourteenth-century monk, Maximus Planudes, and may contain some additional stories.

AFGHANISTAN

Independent nation in Asia to the north and north-west of PAKISTAN. It is a land of barren mountains. Its capital, Kabul, stands on the river of that name. Although the country is a little larger than France – 647,497 sq km (250,014 sq miles) – it has only about 15 million inhabitants, almost all of whom are Moslems. The people are of very mixed origins, the Pathans being among the most prominent. The Tajaks originated in Persia, and many speak that language. The Uzbeks are related to the people of Uzbekistan in the Soviet Union. Coal and natural gas are mined and cotton, fruit, natural gas and lamb skins are exported. A former monarchy, Afghanistan became a republic in 1973.

Africa

MADEIRA Is.

CANARY Is.

MEDITERRANEAN SEA

Tangier
Algiers
Tunis
Tripoli
Casablanca
Rabat
Maritime Atlas
TUNISIA

MOROCCO
Atlas
Sahara Atlas

WESTERN SAHARA

ALGERIA

LIBYA

U.A.R.
EGYPT

Alexandria
Cairo
Suez Canal

Arabian Desert

RED SEA

Tropic of Cancer

Dakhla

S A H A R A   D E S E R T

Ahaggar

Aswan Dam

Nubian Desert

GULF OF ADEN

MAURITANIA

Nouakchott

MALI

Niger

NIGER

Tibesti

CHAD

Khartoum

SUDAN

Blue Nile

Ethiopian Highlands

Djibouti

Dakar
SENEGAL
Banjul
9
10
Bissau
GUINEA
Conakry
Freetown
11

Senegal

Bamako
Ouagadougou
UPPER VOLTA

Niamey

Lake Chad

N'Djaména

Chari

White Nile

Addis Ababa

ETHIOPIA

SOMALI REP.

Mogadishu

IVORY COAST

LIBERIA

Monrovia

Abidjan

GHANA
Accra
TOGO
BENIN
Porto Novo

Volta

NIGERIA

Lagos

Bauchi Plateau

Benue

Niger

Adamaoua Highlands

CENTRAL AFRICAN REPUBLIC

Bangui

CAMEROON
Yaounde

Oubangui

Zaire

UGANDA
Kampala

KENYA

Mt Kenya
17058
Nairobi

GRAIN COAST
IVORY COAST
GOLD COAST
SLAVE COAST

GULF OF GUINEA

Equator

Libreville

8

GABON

CONGO

Brazzaville

Kinshasa

REP. OF ZAIRE

Congo Basin

Kasai

Lualaba

2
Kigali
1
Bujumbura

Lake Victoria

Lake Tanganyika

TANZANIA

Kilimanjaro
19340

ZANZIBAR

Dar es Salaam

Luanda

ANGOLA

Huambo

Bié Plateau

Lake Nyasa
(Malawi)

4
Lilongwe

MOZAMBIQUE

MADAGASCAR

Antananarivo

1	BURUNDI
2	RWANDA
3	DJIBOUTI
4	MALAWI
5	SWAZILAND
6	LESOTHO
7	CABINDA
8	EQUATORIAL GUINEA
9	THE GAMBIA
10	GUINEA-BISSAU
11	SIERRA LEONE

ZAMBIA

Lusaka
Dam
Victoria Falls

Lake Kariba

Zambezi

Salisbury

ZIMBABWE

Beira

MOZAMBIQUE CHANNEL

SOUTH

NAMIBIA
(South West Africa)

BOTSWANA

Matopo

Limpopo

Tropic of Capricorn

Namib Desert

Windhoek

Kalahari Desert

Gaborone

Johannesburg

Pretoria

Maputo

Mbabane
5

ATLANTIC

OCEAN

Orange

Vaal

Maseru
6

Drakensberg

Durban

INDIAN

REP. OF SOUTH AFRICA

Cape Town
Gt. Karoo
CAPE OF GOOD HOPE

OCEAN

0	500	1000	1500	2000 miles

0	1000	2000	3000 kilometres

Africa: Suk tribesman from Kenya

AFRICA

The second largest continent, Africa is three times larger than Europe and is occupied by about 450 million people. The total area is 30,319,000 sq km (11,707,000 sq miles). Until 1950 only four African countries were independent. The rest of the continent was governed by European countries. Six more countries gained independence in the 1950s. During the next ten years another twenty-four independent states were created. Now there are more than fifty, including island states.

Many of the African countries have rich natural resources which are not developed because of inadequate finances. Nearly all the world's store of diamonds comes from Africa and also much of its gold, uranium, copper, cobalt and manganese. There are deposits of oil, coal and iron. The land supplies cocoa, palm oil and sisal. Many of the trees in the vast forests are valuable hardwood such as ebony and mahogany. Africa also has the longest river in the world, the NILE, and the largest desert, the SAHARA.

AGINCOURT. *See* HUNDRED YEARS WAR

AGOUTI

Rodent native to South and Central America and the West Indies. About the size of a rabbit but tail-less, it feeds on leaves and fruit. The 'paca' is a close relative.

AGRICOLA, Gnaeus Julius (AD 37–93)

Roman general who conquered Britain as far north as the Scottish Highlands. His life was chronicled by his son-in-law, the historian TACITUS.

AIR

A mixture of gases that surrounds the earth. The most important gases are nitrogen (78%+) and oxygen (20%+). Air makes up the ATMOSPHERE. Compressed air is used for a variety of purposes such as inflating tyres, filling mattresses and helping in the buoyancy of submarines. The increase in the production of waste gases by transport and industry has led to worldwide anxiety about the effects of air pollution.

AIRPORT

Airports have grown in importance with the increase in air transport. At the world's busiest airports as many as 1,000 aircraft can land and take off in a day. This represents a daily flow of more than fifty, including island states. jet and supersonic aircraft need long runways, a large airport covers a vast area of land. Therefore most airports are outside towns.

The control tower is the nerve centre of an airport. Here the movement of every aircraft, on the runways, approaching the airport, and taking off, is plotted and controlled with the aid of advanced scientific equipment.

Chicago O'Hare International is the world's busiest airport with more than 34 million passenger departures and arrivals in the year. Other busy international airports are Heathrow (London), Charles de Gaulle (Paris), Kennedy (New York), Tokyo and Frankfurt.

AIRSHIP

Lighter-than-air aircraft with its own motive power. The Frenchman Henri Giffard developed the first balloon-with-engine in 1851; and early airships were called dirigibles (from the French) because, unlike BALLOONS, they could be directed, or steered, in flight. The German Zeppelin airships were used to bomb London during WORLD WAR I, but were also used in civil aviation after the war. Other famous airships were the British R-100 and R-101. In 1930 the latter crashed and burst into flames, killing 48 passengers, virtually ending airship design and development.

ALBANIA

Small mountainous agricultural country with an area of 28,748 sq km (11,100 sq miles) and 2,735,000 inhabitants, on the Adriatic coast. Its neighbours are Yugoslavia and Greece. The capital is Tirana. Since WORLD WAR II the country has had a Communist form of government. In 1961 Albania broke off relations with the Soviet Union and allied itself with China, but this special relationship was ended in 1977.

ALCHEMY

Ancient science, or pseudo-science, studied in many parts of Asia and the Middle East as well as Europe. It was a vast subject, concerned not just with a study of known natural substances, such as salt, mercury and sulphur, but with theology, mysticism and the secrets of human life and destiny. In this latter respect it shared many of the ideas and beliefs of ASTROLOGY. European alchemists of the Middle Ages and Renaissance periods were much concerned with the search for a mysterious substance, or

17th-century print of an alchemist's workshop

essence, called the Philosopher's Stone. With the aid of this they hoped to transmute, or change, 'base' metals into gold, and also to discover an elixir of life – something that would dramatically prolong life and health. Their theories and practices began to be discredited in the seventeenth century, with the foundation of the modern science of CHEMISTRY; though some people still study alchemy because of its attempts to link the natural world with mystical and spiritual ideas.

ALCOHOL

Commonly the word is used to mean ethyl alcohol or pure spirits; but in CHEMISTRY it describes a whole group of related compounds. Some alcohols are liquids, others solids. Alcohols are used as solvents, in the manufacture of varnishes, dyes, perfumes and certain pharmaceutical products. The alcohol in wine, beer and other intoxicating drinks is technically classed as a food.

Alexander the Great (left) in battle with Darius III

ALEXANDER the Great (356–323 BC)

King of Macedon who spread Greek civilization wherever he conquered and who had the
idea of forming a single community of the
whole known world. Alexander was educated
partially by the Greek philosopher ARISTOTLE.
He was only twenty when he succeeded his
father to the throne. He showed his military
skill as a young man by conquering in turn
Thebes, Persia, Syria and Phoenicia. In Egypt
he founded the city of Alexandria and he
established Greek colonies in India. He finally
returned to Babylon, intending to make it the
capital of his empire, but he caught a fever and
died only eleven days after his arrival, aged
thirty-two years.

ALFRED the Great (c. 849–900)

English king who fought many battles with the
invading Danes. After victory at the Battle of
Edington, Wiltshire, in 878, Alfred entered
into the Treaty of Wedmore with the Danish
king Guthrum. By this treaty Alfred ruled over
the kingdom of Wessex (mostly the south and
west of England) while the Danes controlled
most of the north and east (the DANELAW).
Alfred was also a notable administrator, laying
the foundations for a proper code of law, and
encouraging the spread of literacy among his
subjects.

ALGAE

Simple PLANT organisms that live in water and
moist soil. They vary considerably in size, from
large plants to microscopic single cells, and in
colour from yellow, green, blue-green and
green-brown to brown and red. All of them,
whatever their colour, contain the green pigment CHLOROPHYLL, which enables them to
make their food by PHOTOSYNTHESIS. Fish and
other water animals feed on algae. In many
countries certain species of algae are harvested
and even commercially grown for human food
and as fertilizer.

ALGEBRA

Branch of MATHEMATICS by which unknown quantities or factors are deduced from known quantities or factors. The general method of algebra is to present known and unknown quantities as parts of an equation (a mathematical statement of balance or equality) and then to isolate the unknown quantities by mathematical procedures which will reveal their value. A very simple example of an algebraic equation where x represents the unknown factor is:

$$10 = 17 - x$$
$$x = 17 - 10$$
$$= 7$$

The word algebra is of Arabic origin and derived from the title of a book written in AD 825: *Hisab al-jabr wal muqabala*, i.e. *The Science of Equations*. It was the Arabs who introduced algebra into Europe.

Early Egyptians and Greeks could cope with equations of the second and third degree, the products of which could be envisaged as representing areas and volumes respectively. But when it came to higher degrees, mathematicians could not think of a corresponding meaning. Arabic and Chinese mathematicians did not worry to the same extent about the concrete interpretations of their equations, and dealt with equations of the 6th degree.

In Europe, algebra was given its modern form in the sixteenth and seventeenth centuries, notably by René DESCARTES, who linked algebra with geometry by representing polynomial equations as curves. The power of algebraic method enabled NEWTON and LEIBNIZ to develop CALCULUS in the eighteenth century. By the nineteenth century the division of mathematics into 'pure' and 'applied' had developed.

ALGERIA

A republic in north Africa with an area of 2,381,741 sq km (919,646 sq miles), but with a population of 18.8 million, nearly all of them Arabs. A large area in the interior is part of the great Sahara Desert and uninhabited except by a handful of desert nomads. The capital is Algiers on the Mediterranean coast. For more than 100 years it was ruled by France and more than a million French people settled there and made it their home. After WORLD WAR II the native Algerians demanded independence, leading, in 1954, to war with France. In 1962 Algeria became independent. Ahmed Ben Bella became president in 1963 but he was overthrown by an army group led by Houari Boumédienne in 1967. When Boumédienne died in 1979, Benjedid Chadli became president.

ALKALI

Term in CHEMISTRY for the six metallic elements that form Group I of the periodic chart of ELEMENTS. More widely, the word is used to describe a large number of compound alkaline substances, mainly sodium and potassium alkalis and ammonia, produced in large quantities by the chemical industry. They are essential in many industrial processes, amongst others the making of glass, soap, paper, textile fibres and fertilizers.

Alkalis could be said to be the opposite of ACIDS. When an alkali and an acid are brought together, they neutralize each other and form a salt. *See also* PERIODIC LAW.

ALLEGORY

A story that uses its characters and events to convey a second and deeper meaning, usually of a moral or political nature. The parables of Jesus are a type of allegory. Other well known allegorical works are Aesop's *Fables* and Swift's *Gulliver's Travels*.

ALLOY

Blend of one metal with one or several other metals of non-metallic substances. The purpose is to obtain in the alloy both the positive qualities of the parent metal and certain improved qualities for a particular purpose, such as greater strength and hardness, greater resistance to rust, lower electrical conductivity, or lower melting point. Bronze was the first alloy to be discovered and consists of copper and tin. Brass is a hard alloy made from copper and zinc. Stainless steel is made up of about 74% steel, 18% chromium and 8% nickel.

ALMANAC

In its original sense an almanac is a form of calendar, giving advance information about such things as sunrise and sunset, tides, or religious events. Many almanacs today, however, also provide a summary of past events (e.g. in the fields of sport or politics), usually for the previous year. A few take the form of fortune-telling.

ALPACA

A close relative of the llama and a native of South America. It is smaller than the llama but has a fleece at least 60 cm (24 in) long from which the cloth known as 'alpaca' is woven.

ALPHABET

The word is made up from the first two letters of the Greek alphabet – *alpha* and *beta* – and describes any group of symbols (letters) intended to represent the sounds used in speech. The letters of an alphabet can be assembled in thousands of different combinations to form words, and are therefore much more flexible than other symbols such as pictograms or ideograms, each of which can only stand for one particular object or idea.

The origin of alphabets is obscure. Some scholars believe the first true alphabets developed from Egyptian HIEROGLYPHICS; others contend that the cuneiform scripts of the Sumerians, Babylonians and Assyrians hold the key.

Some of the principal alphabets in use today are Devanagari (Hindi), Bengali, Tamil, Arabic, Hebrew, Russian (or Cyrillic), Greek,

Arabic	Hebrew	Greek	Cyrillic (Russian)	Latin
ا	א	α	а	A
ب	ב	β	б	B
ك , س	כ,ס	κ,σ	к,с	C
د	ד	δ	д	D
ي	י	ε,η	е,э	E
ف	פ	φ	ф,е	F
ك	ג	γ	г	G
ح	ה	ʽ	г	H
ي	י	ι	и,й	I
ج	—	—	дж	J
د	כ	κ	к	K
ل	ל	λ	л	L
م	מ	μ	м	M
ن	נ	ν	н	N
و	ו	o,ω	о	O
ف	פ	π	п	P
ق	ק	ϙ	—	Q
ر	ר	ρ	р	R
س	ש,ס	σ,ς	с	S
ت , ط	ת,ט	τ	т	T
و	ו	υ	ы,ю	U
و	ו	υ	в	V
و	ו	F	—	VV
—	—	ξ	кс	X
ي	י	ι,υ	я	Y
ظ , ز	צ,ז	ζ	з	Z

Comparative table of alphabets

and the various versions of the Latin alphabet. The English language uses a version of the Latin alphabet, consisting of 26 letters, represented either in capitals or small letters (lower case). Five of these (a, e, i, o u) are classed as vowels, or letters standing for a sound of 'voice'. The remaining letters (b, c, d, f, g and so on) are consonants, intended to qualify the sound of a vowel.

Nearly all the other western European languages (e.g. French, German, Italian, Spanish, Dutch, Swedish) use versions of the Latin alphabet, modified to suit the sounds of the language by the addition of various accents, or by the addition of one or two extra letters. The German language is also sometimes still written or printed in a special form of the Latin alphabet known as the Gothic, Black Letter or Fractur script.

ALPS

Range of European mountains extending nearly 1,000 km (over 600 miles) from the Mediterranean coast between France and Italy, through Switzerland and Austria almost to the Danube at Vienna. The highest peak is Mont Blanc 4,810 m (15,781 ft) in France. Other famous Alpine mountains, all in Switzerland, are the Matterhorn, or Monte Cervino 4,477 m (14,688 ft), the Jungfrau 4,158 m (13,641 ft) and the Eiger 3,977 m (13,042 ft). Famous Alpine passes, for road or rail traffic, are Mont Cenis, Simplon, St Gotthard, Great St Bernard and Brenner. The Mont Blanc tunnel, opened in 1965, is 11.6 km (7¼ miles) long – at present the longest in Europe. Rivers rising in the Alps are the Rhine, the Rhône and the Po.

The Swiss Alps in winter

AMAZON

River of South America, approx. 6,400 km (4,000 miles) long, and greatest in the world for the volume of water carried and area of land it drains. The Amazon and many of its tributaries rise in the ANDES and flow eastwards, mainly through BRAZIL, to the ATLANTIC OCEAN. Almost the whole of the Amazon basin is dense tropical forest.

AMERICA

Name given jointly to two continents in the Western Hemisphere. They are connected by an isthmus through which is cut the PANAMA CANAL. The Panama isthmus and surrounding countries constitute Central America. North and Central America have an area of approx. 24,249,000 sq km (9,363,000 sq miles). South America has an area of approx. 17,832,000 sq km (6,885,000 sq miles). Mexico and most of Central and South America are often called Latin America because they were colonized by the Spanish and Portuguese and these two Latin languages are still spoken by the great majority of the people. The name 'America' is derived from that of the fifteenth-century Italian explorer Amerigo VESPUCCI.

Two great mountain chains run up the west coasts of South and North America – the ANDES and ROCKY MOUNTAINS respectively. In South America there is the River AMAZON. In North America there is the MISSISSIPPI River and the ST LAWRENCE River which is fed by the Great Lakes.

AMERICAN CIVIL WAR

War between the Federal States of the North, under President Abraham LINCOLN, and the Confederate States of the South, led by Jefferson Davis. The principal issue was whether or not the states of the South should break away from the Union and form an independent confederacy. Fighting started in 1861. The crucial battle was fought at Gettysburg, Pennsylvania in 1863; and the Confederate forces, under the command of General Robert E. LEE, finally surrendered to the Federal, or Union forces, commanded by General Ulysses S. GRANT, at Appomattox, Virginia, in April 1865. The American Civil War was the first to be extensively covered by war correspondents

CENTRAL
AMERICA
(see inset)

VENEZUELA

Orinoco

GUYANA

Georgetown
Paramaribo
Cayenne

SURINAM

FR.
GUIANA

COLOMBIA

Bogotá

Quito

ECUADOR

Magdalena

Putumayo

RIO
BRANCO

AMAPA

Branco

The mouths of
the Amazon

Belém

Marañon

Amazon

Manaus

Obidos

PARÁ

Fortaleza

P
E
R
U

Ucayali

Juruá

Purus

A M A Z O N A S

Madeira

Tapajós

Xingu

Araguaia

Recife

▲ Huascarán
22 211

ACRE

São Francisco

Lima

MONTANA

Madre de Dios

Guaporé

B R A Z I L

BAHIA

Salvador

Cuzco

Lake
Titicaca

BOLIVIA

▲ Illampu
21276
La Paz

Plateau of

Mato Grosso

Araguaia

Brasília

C
a
m
p
o

Arequipa

Oruro

Sucre

Santa Cruz

PARAGUAY

Paraguay

Paraná

SÃO PAULO

Brazil
Plateau

MINAS GERAIS

Belo Horizonte

Brazilian Highlands

PACIFIC

▲ Llullaillaco
22 057

Pilcomayo

Asunción

C
H
A
C
O

São Paulo

Rio de Janeiro

OCEAN

Tucuman

A
R
G
E
N
T
I
N
A

Paraná

P
a
m
p
a
s

URUGUAY

RIO GRANDE
DO SUL

Pôrto Alegre

Córdoba

Santa Fé

Uruguay

C
H
I
L
E

Valparaiso

▲ Aconcagua
22 834

Rosario

Santiago

Buenos Aires

Montevideo

Concepción

Bahía Blanca

Negro

Chonos
Archipelago

P
A
T
A
G
O
N
I
A

FALKLAND
ISLANDS
▲ Stanley

Straits of
Magellan

Tierra del Fuego

Cape
Horn

South and
Central America

500   1000 *miles*

500   1000   1500 *kilometres*

MEXICO

GUATEMALA

BELIZE

Belize

CARIBBEAN

Guatemala

HONDURAS

San Salvador

Tegucigalpa

SEA

EL
SALVADOR

NICARAGUA

Managua

COSTA
RICA

S. José

Panama Canal

P A N A M A

100 200 300 400 500 *miles*

250   500   750 *kilometres*

and photographers; and its use of artillery and trench warfare anticipated many twentieth-century developments.

AMERICAN WAR OF INDEPENDENCE

War between American colonists and British government forces. Originally the colonists only wanted a greater degree of local freedom, but on 4 July 1776 the Declaration of Independence committed them to complete self-government. The first serious clash of arms occurred at Concord, Massachusetts in 1774; British forces finally surrendered to General WASHINGTON at Yorktown, Virginia on 19 October 1781. A French force led by the Marquis de Lafayette had aided the Americans, and the peace treaty was signed in 1783.

AMINO-ACID

Type of organic acids that make up the proteins in living things. Sometimes called the 'building blocks of proteins'. Some contain sulphur but they all contain carbon, hydrogen, oxygen and nitrogen.

AMPÈRE, André Marie (1775–1836)

French scientist who did important work in the field of electro-magnetism. The electrical unit of current strength is also named after him, though it is usually shortened to 'amp'.

AMPHIBIAN

Cold-blooded vertebrate with smooth (i.e. not scaly) skin. Amphibia include newts and salamanders, FROGS AND TOADS. All are able to live both on land and in the water, breathing mainly by lungs when on land and through the skin when submerged in water. Most amphibia have four legs but some have lost the hind pair and others are legless. They are classified into the 'caecilians' with worm-like bodies and no legs, the tailed amphibia (newts and salamanders)

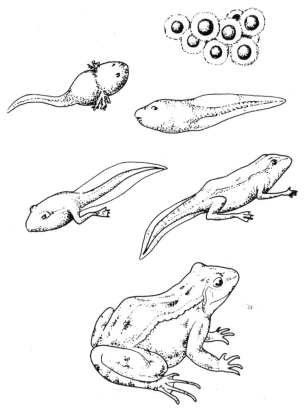

Amphibian: the life cycle of the frog

and the tail-less amphibia (frogs and toads). Caecilians are found only in the tropics. The eggs of amphibia are, with few exceptions, laid in water, and from them hatch the tadpoles which breathe by gills.

AMUNDSEN, Roald (1872–1928)

Norwegian explorer and the first man to reach the South Pole, on 17 December 1911. He and another team of explorers had previously been the first successfully to navigate the North-West Passage.

ANATOMY

Study of the structure and materials of living things, plants and animals, as distinct from PHYSIOLOGY, which is a study of their functions. Comparative anatomy deals with the differences in the anatomy of various plants or

Christ Glorified in Heaven by Fra Angelico

animals. Special anatomy concentrates on the anatomy of one particular organism. Within this branch of the subject comes human anatomy, which is itself divided into a number of subject areas: the skeleton, respiratory system, circulatory system (blood stream), alimentary system (digestion), reproductive system and nervous system. There is also practical anatomy, dealing with dissection, and what is called artistic anatomy, which is concerned with outward appearances as they relate to painting, sculpture and photography. *See also* PATHOLOGY.

ANDERSEN, Hans Christian (1805–75)

Danish writer. Among his many classic children's stories are *The Little Mermaid, The Tin Soldier* and *The Little Match Girl*. His story *The Ugly Duckling* is generally regarded as a fabled account of his own rather sad life. There is a commemorative statue of the Little Mermaid in the harbour at Copenhagen.

ANDES

Mountain range extending up the Pacific coast of South America for a distance of nearly 8,000 km (5,000 miles). The highest peak is Aconcagua, 6,960 m (22,830 ft) in Argentina. Many of the mountains are volcanoes, most famous of these being Cotopaxi, 5,897 m (19,342 ft) in ECUADOR.

ANDORRA

One of the smallest countries in the world, situated in the PYRENEES between France and Spain. Its area is only 453 sq km (175 sq miles), with a population of 26,000.

ANGELICO, Fra (1387–1455)

Italian painter of the Renaissance period. He was also a Dominican friar, and a fuller version of his name is Fra Giovanni Angelico, or Brother John the Angelic. He painted mainly FRESCOES, the most famous being in the church of San Marco, Florence.

ANGLO-SAXON

Name given to the peoples who crossed the North Sea and invaded Britain in the fifth century. They included Angles, Jutes and SAXONS. The Anglo-Saxon period in English history extends from about AD 450 to 1066, the year of the NORMAN CONQUEST. Many English titles and place names date from Anglo-Saxon times, e.g. Earl, Sherriff, Alderman, Brocklehurst, Sunderland.

ANGOLA

Independent African country since 1975, formerly an overseas province of Portugal, situated on the west coast of the continent and bordered by ZAMBIA, ZAÏRE and NAMIBIA (South-West Africa). It has an area of 1,246,700 sq km (481,380 sq miles) and a population of about 7 million. Angola exports petroleum, coffee and diamonds.

ANIMAL KINGDOM

The Animal Kingdom encompasses all creatures from the single-cell amoeba to ourselves as human beings. The biggest single distinction to be made among the huge variety of animal life is between those creatures with some type of backbone (vertebrates) and those without a backbone (invertebrates). The vertebrates include all types of fish, amphibians, reptiles, birds and mammals, including man. The invertebrates include insects and arachnids, crustaceans such as crabs and lobsters, and such humble creatures as worms, starfish and sponges.

The principal classifications of animal life, working from the general to the particular, are: phylum (plural phyla); class; order; family; genus (plural genera); species. *See also* ARACHNID; ARTHROPOD; BIRD; CRUSTACEAN; FISH, INSECT; MAMMAL; MOLLUSC; REPTILE.

ANT

Insect of more than 5,000 different varieties and an estimated population far exceeding that of any other animal. Some ants are hunters of other insects, some cultivate aphids for a kind of honey, some collect and store grain, others cultivate special fungi as food. Most will also scavenge and so help in the natural process of the removal of dead or decaying matter.

Ants live in colonies, creating nests either in the earth or in dead trees or plants. They lead a highly organized existence, each type of ant having a particular duty to perform, though experts disagree about whether or not this should be regarded as a mark of true intelligence. The queen is the most important member of an ant colony. She mates in flight and then returns to earth to lay her eggs, often establishing a new colony or nest in the process. *See also* TERMITE.

ANTARCTICA

Continent surrounding the South Pole, with an area of 8,000,000 sq km (5,000,000 sq miles). It is the coldest region in the world. Over 90% of the world's ice is estimated to be in Antarctica, and the lowest temperature, −88.3° centigrade (−126.9° Fahrenheit), has been recorded there. Nevertheless, there is abundant life round the coasts, including WHALES, SEALS, PENGUINS and many varieties of sea bird. There are also several permanent scientific stations on the continent. 1957–8 was International Geophysical Year and a major exploration of Antarctica was made. *See also* SCOTT.

A snocat at work in the Antarctic

Springboks, a species of South African antelope

ANTEATER

Animal belonging to a group of toothless mammals native to the tropical regions of America. The best-known member of this group is the giant anteater from South and Central America, about 2.4 m (8 ft) long from tail to snout. It has a strange, funnel-shaped head and a long sticky tongue which it uses to scoop up ants and termites. The spiny anteater is found in New Guinea through eastern Australia to Tasmania.

ANTELOPE

Even-toed, hoofed group of mammals native to Africa and India. Antelopes include the KUDU, nyala, ELAND, DUIKER and waterbuck. They vary in size from the tiny royal antelope to the large eland. All are herbivorous, cud-chewing animals, able to live in a wide variety of terrains, from plains to forests, deserts to mountains.

ANTHROPOLOGY

The full study of man in relation to his ways of life, human societies and environment.

Physical anthropology is the study of man's place in the natural world and of his relationship with other animals

Social anthropology is concerned with the different races of mankind, their physical features, ideas, beliefs and ways of life. *See also* ARCHAEOLOGY, FOLKLORE, GEOGRAPHY and SOCIOLOGY.

ANTIBIOTICS

Branch of medical science based on the fact that some BACTERIA can prevent the growth of other bacteria, and used in the treatment of many diseases and other infections. Penicillin, found naturally on decaying fruit and some cheeses, was the first antibiotic to be successfully isolated and manufactured, in 1941. Various strains of it are still the most widely used of all antibiotics. Another important antibiotic is streptomycin.

Antibiotics are used in agriculture as well as medicine, in the control of plant diseases. One problem connected with them, however, is that the bacteria they are intended to control may develop a new strain and so become resistant to treatment. Hence there is much research into the isolation and production of new antibiotics. *See also* Sir Alexander FLEMING.

APE

Apes or, more correctly, anthropoid apes, are a group of mammals bigger and stronger than monkeys and lacking a tail. They include the GORILLA, CHIMPANZEE, GIBBON and orangutan. They are mainly vegetarian, though sometimes they will eat small creatures like insects.

APOCRYPHA

Group of fourteen books which conclude the Old Testament of the BIBLE, but are omitted from many editions. The word in this context means 'hidden writings', and the Books of the Apocrypha deal mainly with ancient Hebrew history, legend and religious instruction.

APOSTLE

In the New Testament the name refers to the twelve disciples whom Jesus chose to be his companions. They were originally Simon Peter, James and John, Andrew, Philip and Bartholomew, Matthew, Thomas, James the son of Alphaeus, Thaddeus, Simon the Canaanite and Judas Iscariot. Matthias took the place of Judas, who hanged himself after betraying Jesus.

AQUARIUM

A container, either a pond or some form of tank, in which fish, reptiles and plants are kept. There are two types of aquaria, the 'cold water' type in which goldfish, minnows, sticklebacks, lizards, etc. can be kept and bred and the 'heated' aquarium for keeping tropical fish.

Before you start an aquarium the subject should be thoroughly studied as there is a lot to do and learn if the fish are to keep healthy and survive.

AQUEDUCT

Artificial channel or system of pipes designed to carry water over land. One of the most famous Roman monuments, the Pont du Gard in southern France, was part of a system of aqueducts which carried water to the town of Nîmes. A famous modern example is the Colorado Aqueduct in the United States designed to carry water from the Colorado river to the city of Los Angeles.

The Pont du Gard aqueduct, France

AQUINAS, St Thomas (1226–74)

Italian theologian. Born near Naples of noble descent, he studied at the monastery of Monte Cassino and at Naples University. He then became a Dominican friar (1243). After further study at Cologne and Paris he received his doctorate (1258). He spent the rest of his life teaching and writing and travelling in the service of his order. He died in 1274 and was canonized in 1323.

ARAB

Someone belonging to one of the races which inhabit most of the territories of the Middle East and North Africa. Present-day Arab countries include ALGERIA, EGYPT, IRAQ, JORDAN, KUWAIT, LEBANON, LIBYA, MOROCCO, SAUDI ARABIA and TUNISIA.

Arab history and culture are closely linked to the Islamic faith. The rapid spread of ISLAM during the seventh and eighth centuries established Arab culture from Baghdad in the east (where the rulers were called caliphs) right across Moorish North Africa (where the rulers were sultans) and into Spain. Many of the finest Arabic buildings are mosques, and the form of Arabic writing known as Arabesque is religious in character.

During the Middle Ages Arabic art and science flourished, our systems of ARITHMETIC and ALGEBRA being largely Arabic in origin.

Arab influence declined with the rise to power of the Turkish or OTTOMAN EMPIRE in the fourteenth century, and during the nineteenth century large areas of Arab territory came under European control.

Today the Arab nations are independent, and, largely because of oil, some of them play a major part in world affairs. The establishment of the state of ISRAEL soon after World War II began a movement towards Arab unity; at the same time the Arab-Israeli wars of 1948, 1967 and 1973 have had an unsettling political effect. The Peace Treaty between Egypt and Israel (1979) has also proved divisive.

ARABIA

Large desert peninsula in south-western Asia. With the exception of its Jordan-Iraq border on the north, Arabia is surrounded by sea – the Red Sea to the west, the Arabian Sea to the south and the Persian Gulf to the east. Arabia was the original home of the Islamic religion. Today it is known to have the largest oil reserves of any area of comparable size and is consequently one of the richest in the world.

ARACHNID

The name given to members of a class of small land animals. SPIDERS are the best known. Others are ticks, mites, SCORPIONS and daddy-long-legs. Although similar in some respects, they are not INSECTS. Arachnids have four pairs of legs but no antennae (feelers). Insects have antennae but only three pairs of legs.

ARCHAEOLOGY

Branch of science and scholarship concerned with discovering the societies and cultures of ancient man. During the past fifty years archaeology has considerably enlarged our understanding of man's pre-history and has, from material evidence, created a clear picture of his development during the last 40,000 years.

Modern archaeological research involves field archaeologists who excavate sites, historians to assess the evidence, geologists, zoologists and chemists who use scientific methods such as radio-carbon dating to determine the age of wooden remains and other materials.

Submarine archaeology, concerned mainly with the investigation of sunken ships and their contents, is now an exciting branch of archaeological research.

What is known as industrial archaeology is concerned with the preservation or restoration of factories and machines which were part of the more recent INDUSTRIAL REVOLUTION.

Archaeologists examine Tutankhamun's tomb in Egypt

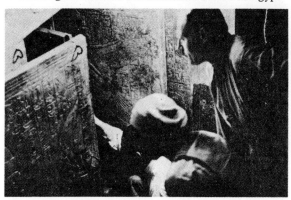

ARCHERY

Archery is the skill of using a bow and arrow, either in warfare or in sport (toxophily). Practically all the nations of the ancient world – the Babylonians, Assyrians, Persians, Greeks and Romans – used bows and arrows in war. During the Middle Ages the cross-bow, or arbalest, which fired arrows or bolts by means of a pulley and trigger mechanism, was widely used. But most famous was the English long-bow, approximately 2 m (6 ft) long, which played a decisive part in the English victories at Crécy and Agincourt, due to its flexibility and range. The long-bow was usually made of yew wood, and churchyards were traditionally planted with yews to ensure a regular supply.

Firearms brought about a decline in archery as a weapon of war. Today it is a sport, with world championship contests between national teams. Archers use a standard-size target 120 cm (48 in) in diameter. Bows are often made from fibreglass and equipped with calibrated sights, while arrows are constructed from some tubular metal alloy.

An archer with the bow full drawn

ARCHIMEDES of Syracuse (287–212 BC)

One of the world's greatest mathematicians and an outstanding engineer. His mathematical works included studies of spheres, cones, cylinders, spirals and irregular volumes. In mechanics he established the principles of levers and pulleys and invented a method of raising water by turning a tube with a screw running through it (Archimedes' Screw). He also discovered the law of flotation and the principle of specific gravity, which he used to test the purity of the gold in King Heiron's crown.

ARCHIPELAGO

Greek word meaning 'chief sea' and originally applied to the Aegean Sea between Greece and Turkey which is scattered with islands. Today the word describes any large group of islands.

ARCHITECTURE

The art or craft of building, especially when an original design of building or monument is involved. Architecture includes some of the principles of engineering.

The earliest human constructions, whether of huts for habitation or assemblages of large stones, are not generally classed as architecture. The history of the subject properly begins with the monumental buildings of the Egyptians (including the PYRAMIDS), the Babylonians and Assyrians, Indians and Chinese, dating from about 3000 BC.

The great age of European, or Western architecture commenced with the Greeks. The most famous monument to Greek architecture is the Parthenon in Athens, built in the Doric style, and dating from 500 BC. The Romans, renowned as engineers rather than architects, built many fine bridges and aqueducts, the arch being a special feature of their construction.

Arches and domes became a marked feature of Arabic or Moorish architecture, as they did of the Byzantine style – named after the city of

Byzantium, now Istanbul. The Byzantine style influenced many buildings in eastern Europe, including Russia.

The main architectural periods and styles of Western and Central Europe are as follows:

Romanesque (Norman) AD 600 to 1100	— Durham cathedral, England; the abbey of Vézelay, France
Gothic (Early English, Decorated, Perpendicular) 1100 to 1500	— Salisbury cathedral, England; Notre-Dame, Paris, and Chartres cathedral, France; Cologne cathedral, Germany; Burgos cathedral, Spain
Renaissance (Baroque, Rococo, English Renaissance) 1400–1750	— St Peter's basilica, Rome; Palace of Versailles, France; Banqueting Hall, Whitehall, London; St Paul's cathedral, London
Neo-Classical (Georgian and Regency) 1700–1800	— Kenwood House, London; The Royal Crescent, Bath

As the nineteenth century and the period of the Industrial Revolution progressed, some of the best design and construction work was applied to bridges and railway stations, and architects were generally content to copy earlier styles in their buildings. But in this century new methods of construction in steel and concrete have made possible exciting new developments in architecture. Notable twentieth-century buildings are the Empire State building, New York (1931); the Royal Festival Hall, London (1951); Coventry cathedral (1955); Sydney Opera House, Australia (1971).

Another aspect of architecture that has become increasingly important this century is

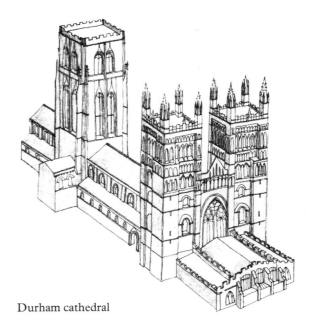

Durham cathedral

Town Planning, which is concerned with the distribution of buildings, open spaces, roads and railways within towns and cities. *See also* Robert ADAM; Filippo BRUNELLESCHI; Walter GROPIUS; LE CORBUSIER; MICHELANGELO; Christopher WREN.

ARCTIC OCEAN

Situated north of Canada, Greenland and Siberia, and extending to the North Pole itself. Much of it appears to be solid land simply because it consists of ice. In 1959 the nuclear-powered submarine USS *Skate* broke through the ice of the Arctic Ocean and surfaced at the Pole. *See also* Fridtjof NANSEN: Robert PEARY.

ARGENTINA

A Spanish-speaking republic and the second largest country in South AMERICA. It is 2,766,889 sq km (1,068,360 sq miles) in area, and has a population of about 27 million. It is a country of great plains called pampas, where cattle and wheat are produced, bordered by the ANDES mountains in the west. The capital is Buenos Aires.

Like many other countries of South America the country has seen a number of revolts which have led to changes in the government of the country. Between 1946 and 1955 the country was ruled by a dictator named Juan Perón. He was overthrown by the army and since then there have been other revolts. In 1973 Juan Perón returned from exile to Argentina. He was elected President but died a year later, and his wife, who was Vice-President, succeeded him as President. She was the first woman President in the Western Hemisphere, but was deposed in 1976 by a military junta.

ARISTOPHANES (448–385BC)

Greek comic playwright and poet. In Athens, where he lived, great freedom of expression was allowed to the satirist, and there were no bounds to Aristophanes's criticism and mockery of personalities. His plays, which include *The Birds*, *The Frogs* and *The Clouds*, combine satire and comedy.

ARISTOTLE (384–322 BC)

Greek philosopher, biologist and political thinker. He worked under PLATO in his philosophic school, the ACADEMY at Athens, and was later invited to study at the court of Philip of Macedon, where he taught the young ALEXANDER. After the death of Philip, Aristotle founded his own school called the Peripatos (Walk). His scholars were called the Peripatetics. In his writings Aristotle supplied many of the great topics which have fascinated scholars in succeeding generations, and the rules and terminology through which they could be discussed. His *Poetics* in particular set down important rules for tragic drama and have formed the basis of dramatic criticism ever since.

ARITHMETIC

The oldest and the most practical branch of MATHEMATICS, concerned only with numbers. As soon as early men learned how to write they developed a way of putting down numbers. The ancient Egyptians used a hieroglyphic (pictorial) method of representing numbers for counting, weighing and measuring.

The Greeks used an alphabetic system alpha for one, beta for two, and so on. The Romans used simple stroke marks for the first three numbers, but for five they used a 'V' sign which may originally have been represented by a hand; ten was two V's linked together as a cross. Since their number systems were very clumsy, the Greeks and also the Romans used an ABACUS to help them work out their accounts.

Primitive tribes of the present day still count by fives because there are five fingers on each hand; Eskimos still count in twenties. In the Middle Ages twenty (a score) was a much used number; in fact we still keep the word 'score' in such games as cricket, football, etc.

The Babylonians perfected a system of meauring time and angles. Instead of basing the numbers on ten as in the decimal system they took the number sixty as the base. Sixty has many factors, whereas ten is divisable by only two numbers – two and five. The Babylonian sexagesimal system, as it is called, survives in our measurements of time and angles. There are twelve months of the year, twenty-four (twice twelve) hours in the day, sixty minutes in an hour, and sixty seconds in the minute.

The decimal system as we know it today came to Europe through the Arabs, who in turn received it from the Hindus. It was the Arabs who first introduced the number zero, which was essential for the development of ALGEBRA. The use of the decimal point to indicate fractions was the contribution of John NAPIER, who also gave us LOGARITHMS.

The fundamental operations of arithmetic are addition, subtraction, multiplication and division. The sign + (plus) is used to indicate addition. Thus $5+7$ means 7 added to 5. The answer 12 is called the sum. Using equal signs we can write $5+7=12$. Subtraction is the reverse of addition. The sign for subtraction is − (minus). Thus $12-7=5$. The sign for multiplication is ×. Thus 7×5 means seven multiplied by five. The answer 35 is the product. Division is the reverse of multiplication and its sign is ÷. Thus $35 \div 7 = 5$.

Binary arithmetic is a simple numeration system used in digital computers. Only two symbols are used – 0 and 1. These symbols are represented by on/off electronic switches in COMPUTERS.

Chart comparing decimal and binary numerals

Decimal Numeral	Binary Numeral	Analysis of Binary Numeral
0	0	No 1
1	1	One 1
$2(2^1)$	10	One 2 + No 1
3	11	One 2 + One 1
$4(2^2)$	100	One 4 + No 2 + No 1
5	101	One 4 + No 2 + One 1
6	110	One 4 + One 2 + No 1
7	111	One 4 + One 2 + One 1

A great deal of arithmetic can be done mechanically, but it has been shown that some sentences of arithmetic can never be proved to be true or false by mechanical means.

ARKWRIGHT, Sir Richard (1732–92)

British inventor and manufacturer. He patented a spinning machine worked by water power and called the water frame. He also mechanized spinning processes. As it was convenient for the workers all to be in one building, Arkwright set up cotton mills, where machine carding, drawing, roving and spinning were carried out together. In spite of rivals copying his methods and machines, and the destruction of one of his mills by a mob, his business flourished.

Arkwright's spinning machine

ARMADA

The original Armada – the Spanish word for a battle fleet – was the one directed against England by Philip II of Spain in 1588. This was destroyed, partly by English naval tactics, and partly by severe storms which scattered the fleet all round the coasts of the British Isles. Since then 'armada' has been used to describe any large concentration of ships, and more recently, aircraft.

The Spanish Armada proceeding up the Channel

Armadillos – the nine-banded species

ARMADILLO

A family of small mammals native to South and Central America, distinctive because of the jointed bands of bony armour which extend from head to tail. Armadillos are nervous creatures and roll themselves into a ball or attempt to bury themselves in earth at the slightest sign of danger. They are mainly nocturnal and feed on insects and sometimes eggs, small snakes and small rodents. The most common species is the 'nine-banded' armadillo.

ARMOUR

Special forms of protection, usually of metal construction, against weapons of war. Throughout most of history, armour was worn by individuals as a protection against the swords, clubs or axes of opponents. Greek and Roman soldiers wore protective helmets and metal plates on parts of the body which still allowed them freedom of movement. Chain mail was the main type of armour at the time of the CRUSADES, followed by plate armour which covered the body from head to foot and made movement very difficult. Knights in plate armour often had their horses similarly protected. Body armour ceased to have much value with the introduction of guns and firearms in the sixteenth century. Since then armour has been applied mostly to weapons of war themselves, principally to ships (e.g. the so-called 'Iron-clads' of the late nineteenth and early twentieth centuries) and to tanks.

ARNE, Thomas Augustine (1710–78)

English composer of operas, oratorios, and songs, including 'Rule, Britannia'.

ARNOLD, Matthew (1822–88)

Distinguished English poet and critic and son of Thomas Arnold the famous headmaster of Rugby School. Among his poems are *Sohrab and Rustum* and *The Scholar Gypsy;* his prose works include *Essays in Criticism* and *Culture and Anarchy.*

Brass rubbing of a knight in armour, 14th century

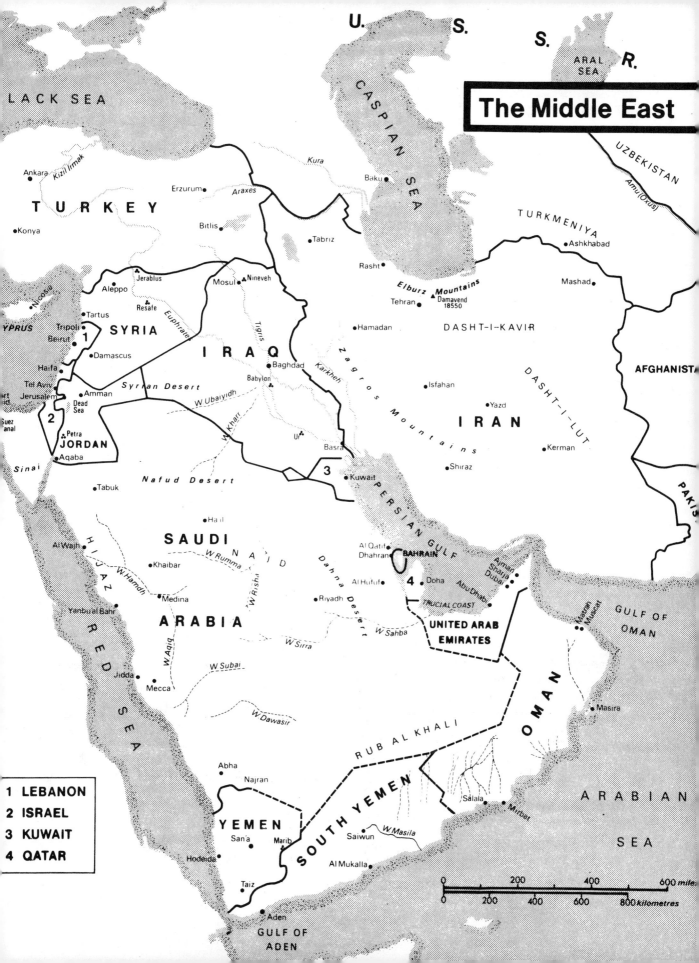

The Middle East

U. S. S. R.

ARAL SEA

LACK SEA

TURKEY

Ankara
Kizil Irmak
Erzurum
Araxes
Konya
Bitlis
Tabriz
Rasht
Baku

CASPIAN SEA

UZBEKISTAN
Amu (Oxus)

TURKMENIYA
Ashkhabad
Mashad

Nicosia
CYPRUS
Tripoli
Beirut
Tartus
Aleppo
Jerablus
Resafe
Mosul
Nineveh

Elburz Mountains
Damavend 18550
Tehran
Hamadan

AFGHANISTAN

SYRIA
Damascus
Euphrates
Tigris

IRAQ
Baghdad
Babylon

Karkheh

Zagros Mountains

DASHT-I-KAVIR

Isfahan
Yazd

DASHT-I-LUT

IRAN

Haifa
Tel Aviv
Jerusalem
Amman
Dead Sea

Syrian Desert
W. Ubaiyidh
W. Kharr

Ur
Basra

Kerman
Shiraz

Suez Canal
Sinai
Petra
JORDAN
Aqaba

Nafud Desert

Kuwait

PERSIAN GULF

PAKIS

Tabuk

Ha il

Al Qatif
Dhahran
BAHRAIN

Ajman
Sharja
Dubai

Al Wajh
HIJAZ
W. Hamdh
Khaibar
W. Rumma
NAJD

SAUDI

Dahna Desert

Al Hufuf

Doha
Abu Dhabi

Matrah
Muscat

GULF OF OMAN

RED SEA
Yanbu al Bahr
Medina
W. Risha

ARABIA

Riyadh

W. Sahba

TRUCIAL COAST

UNITED ARAB
EMIRATES

OMAN

W. Aqiq
Jidda
Mecca

W. Subai

W. Sirra

Masira

W. Dawasir

RUB AL KHALI

Abha
Najran

SOUTH YEMEN

Salala
Mirbat

ARABIAN

YEMEN
San'a
Marib

Saiwun
W. Masila

SEA

Hodeida

Al Mukalla

Taiz

1	LEBANON
2	ISRAEL
3	KUWAIT
4	QATAR

Aden
GULF OF
ADEN

| 0 | 200 | 400 | 600 miles |
| 0 | 200 | 400 | 600 | 800 kilometres |

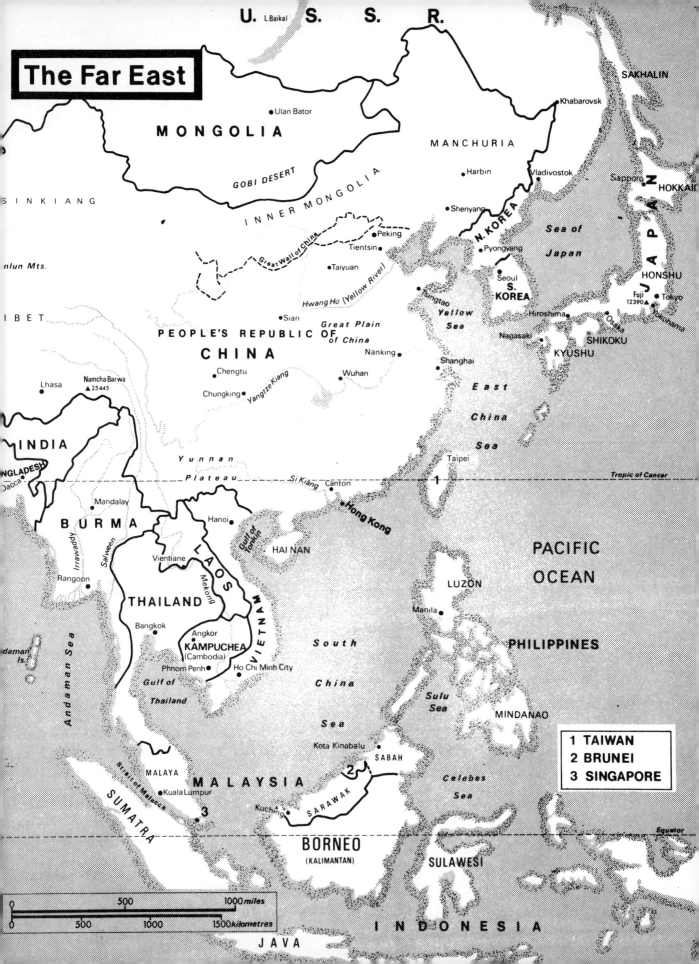

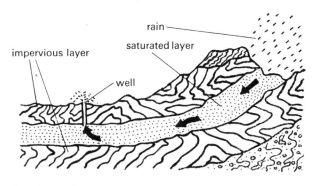

Artesian well

ARTESIAN WELL

Type of well where water is forced to the surface by natural pressure. Such wells occur when an inclined aquifer (water-bearing stratum) runs between layers of harder rock. The name is connected with the district of Artois in France.

ARTHROPOD

Any member of a large group of invertebrate (backboneless) animals having jointed feet and hollow, jointed parts such as antennae (feelers), wings and legs. Among the arthropods are insects such as BEETLE, BEE, BUTTERFLIES AND MOTHS, centipedes and millipedes, and CRUS-TACEANS such as crabs and lobsters.

ARTHUR, King

Legendary British hero whose life and adventures are closely linked with other Celtic myths and legends. He is taken as a symbol of Celtic British resistance to the Saxon invaders, which would place him historically somewhere between AD 500 and 1000. The Arthurian legends are centred upon Cornwall. Tintagel is taken to be Arthur's birth place, the mythical city of Camelot to be the seat of his kingdom, and Avalon his burial place. Guinevere was his queen and the magician Merlin his chief adviser. Objects associated with him are his sword Excalibur, drawn from a rock and returned upon his death to a lake, and the Round Table which represented equality among him and his Knights. The life and times of King Arthur have inspired many paintings, and poems, notably by Alfred, Lord Tennyson.

ARTILLERY

The word originally described all weapons of war, such as catapults, cross-bows and slings, which discharged some kind of missile. In its more usual sense, artillery deals with the subject of guns fired from some fixed or mounted position, as distinct from small-arms fired by the individual. Cannons and mortars were introduced in the fourteenth century, and artillery has played an important part in warfare right up to modern developments in ROCKETS and guided missiles.

ASIA

The largest continent, approximately 44,387,000 sq km (17,139,000 sq miles), containing some of the most desolate regions (the GOBI DESERT, the Siberian tundra), and the most populous countries – CHINA and INDIA. Asia also includes the HIMALAYAS, the most

King Arthur and the Knights of the Round Table

extensive and highest of all mountain ranges. It is divided from Europe by the Ural mountains, from Africa by the Red Sea, and from North America by the Bering Strait.

Asia has been the place of some of the world's earliest civilisations (China, Indus Valley, Sumer), and birth place of the greatest religious leaders – Gautama the Buddha in India, Confucius in China, Jesus of Nazareth in Palestine, and the Prophet Mohammed in Arabia.

ASS

Member of the horse family and when domesticated usually called 'donkey'. Asses are smaller than the horse, have long ears, an upright short mane and they 'bray' rather than 'neigh'. The four main species are the Somali wild ass or African wild donkey, the Kiang or Tibetan wild ass, the Onager or Persian wild ass and the Mongolian wild ass.

ASSYRIA

Kingdom of the ancient world situated in the Middle East in the region of the rivers Tigris and Euphrates. Two of its greatest rulers were Tiglath-Pileser I and Assurbanipal, commemorated on many surviving monuments. The Assyrian empire reached the height of its power in the seventh century BC, when it dominated Babylonia, Palestine and Upper Egypt. The chief city was Nineveh.

King Assurbanipal hunting on horseback

ASTROLOGY

Ancient belief that the sun, moon and planets (not the stars) influence a person's character and progress through life. Each year in astrology is divided into twelve sections, called the sun signs, these being symbolized by particular objects or animals (e.g. Libra, the scales; Taurus, the bull). This is the zodiac. A person's sun sign, plus the relative positions of the sun itself, the moon and planets at the exact place and time of birth can be represented by a special chart called a horoscope, and this is supposed to provide an insight into the subject's personality and destiny. On a broader scale, astrologers believe that the sun, moon and planets influence events on Earth.

ASTRONAUT. *See* SPACE TRAVEL

ASTRONOMY

Science of the nature and organization of all heavenly bodies and of the Earth itself treated as a planet. Some of the earliest scientific astronomical observations were made by the Babylonians, who recorded an eclipse in 2283 BC, and by the Chinese, who were among the first to map out the sky according to the constellations of stars. This aspect of astronomy – the observation and charting of stars in the night sky – has been used in navigation for thousands of years.

The history of astronomy is a fascinating account of man's gradually increasing knowledge of the relationship of our own planet to the solar system, and of the infinite extent of the universe. For more information *see* entries for the following astronomers: ARISTARCHUS; Tycho BRAHE; Nicolas COPERNICUS; John FLAMSTEED; Jean FOUCAULT; GALILEO Gallilei; Frederick HERSCHEL; Johann KEPLER; Isaac NEWTON; PTOLEMY. *See also* entries dealing with the following subject areas: COSMOLOGY; RADIO-ASTRONOMY; SOLAR SYSTEM; SPACE TRAVEL; STAR; TELESCOPE.

Astronomy: the 'Horse's Head' nebula in Orion

ATATURK, Kemal (*c.* 1880–1938)

He revolutionized Turkish politics after World War I, fought against the Greeks in Asia Minor and became the first President of the newly founded Turkish Republic. He then introduced many reforms designed to bring his country into line with Western-style customs and practices.

ATHLETICS

Athletics are competitive displays of running, jumping and throwing. They are organized into Track Events, which include the 100 m, 200 m, 1,500 m, 5,000 m and Marathon (just over 42,000 m) running events; and Field Events, which include the high jump, long jump, pole vault, putting the shot, discus and javelin throwing.

One of the outstanding events of modern athletics occurred on 6 May 1954 when Roger Bannister first ran a mile in less than four minutes (3 min 59·4 sec). The OLYMPIC GAMES have been the occasion for many other great athletic performances.

ATLANTIC

The ocean which divides the continents of Europe and Africa from North and South America. It is approx. 82,217,000 sq km (31,744,000 sq miles) in area, and is usually divided into the North and South Atlantic. A mountain range running north-south in the mid-Atlantic represents a plate edge along which new crustal material is being added, slowly widening the ocean. The deepest point, the Puerto Rico Trench, is 9,225 m (30,246 ft). *See also* CONTINENTAL DRIFT.

ATMOSPHERE

Blanket of air that surrounds our planet and is traceable at least 800 km (500 miles) into space. Its principal constituents are nitrogen, oxygen, carbon dioxide, and water-vapour, but other and rare gases exist in very small proportions, for example, argon, neon, helium, krypton, and xenon. The average pressure of the atmosphere at sea-level is 1.033 kg per sq cm ($14\frac{1}{2}$ lb per sq in). The density of the atmosphere, and so its pressure, decreases until it reaches zero at its diffuse perimeter. Its temperature, however, decreases up to about 8 km (5 miles) over the poles and 18 km (11 miles) on the equator, where it stays constant. Above this level (the *tropopause*) is the stratosphere, in the upper part of which temperatures fall again. The stratosphere ends at about 80 km (50 miles) up. In the ionosphere, temperatures rise again. Most gas molecules in the ionosphere are ionized, or electrically charged. *See also* WEATHER.

ATOM

The smallest particle of an ELEMENT that can possess the chemical properties of that element. Atoms are very small. Millions of them exist in the point of a needle, and they can only be observed through a powerful electron microscope. Nevertheless, an atom itself consists of different parts, these being a central nucleus (composed of particles called protons and neutrons) around which circulate electrons, the whole being roughly comparable in its organization to the movement of the planets round the sun in the SOLAR SYSTEM. Nuclei are tiny relative to the diameter of electron orbits. Of which element an atom is a part depends upon the number of protons and neutrons in its nucleus and the number of circulating electrons. Light elements have few electrons, protons and neutrons in each atom, while heavy elements have many. The *Atomic Number* of an element equals the number of protons in the nucleus of its atom. The *Atomic Weight* of an element is the weight of one of its atoms compared with the weight of one atom of oxygen (which itself has the atomic weight of 16).

Under normal conditions atoms do not, in fact, exist on their own but join with other atoms to form a MOLECULE of the element in question. Hydrogen, which is the simplest atom, with one electron circulating about a nucleus of one proton, forms the simplest molecule of two atoms. *See also* NUCLEAR ENERGY.

The structure of a helium atom

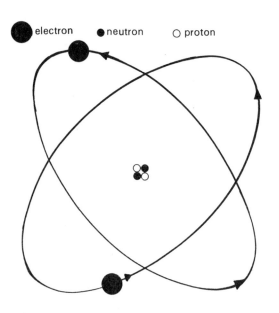

electron ● neutron ○ proton

ATTILA (AD 406–53)

Attila, the 'Scourge of God', was self-proclaimed king of the Huns – the great company of Barbarian races from eastern Europe and large tracts of Asia. Under his leadership the Huns attacked and devastated the eastern Roman Empire. Attila then led his forces westwards, but was defeated by a combined army of Romans and Visigoths at Châlons-sur-Marne in France in 451. The power of the Huns did not survive his death.

AUGUSTINE, St, Bishop of Hippo (354–430)

Born of a heathen father and a Christian mother, he studied philosophy at Carthage and was himself converted to Christianity by the Bishop of Milan, St Ambrose. His greatest work *De Civitate Dei* (City of God) is a powerful defence of the Christian Church.

AUGUSTINE OF CANTERBURY, St (died *c.* 604)

First Archbishop of Canterbury. Pope Gregory I despatched him from Rome to England where he was met by Ethelbert, King of the Jutes, on the island of Thanet. Augustine and his fellow missionaries converted thousands of English to Christianity, including the king.

AUGUSTUS CAESAR (63 BC–AD 14)

His full name was Gaius Julius Caesar Octavius (Octavian), nephew of JULIUS CAESAR, and the first and most illustrious of the Roman emperors. In 42 BC he and Mark Antony defeated the forces of Brutus and Cassius at Philippi; and in 31 BC he defeated the fleet of Antony and CLEOPATRA in the naval battle of Actium. From then until his death, Augustus Caesar restored order within the Roman Empire, while strengthening and extending its frontiers abroad. He was Roman emperor at the time of the birth of Christ.

Aurora Borealis seen in Arctic regions

AURORA BOREALIS

These are the so-called 'northern lights' (sometimes also known as aurora polaris), though the same phenomenon can be seen in the southern hemisphere, where it is called aurora australis. The aurora is only seen in Arctic or Antarctic regions, appearing as bands or curtains of coloured light. It is caused by the entry into the Earth's magnetic field of solar particles. These consist chiefly of electrons which ionize the atmospheric gases at a height of about 160 km (100 miles), the chemically excited atoms then discharge light rays of various colours.

AUSTEN, Jane (1775–1817)

English novelist born in Hampshire. Her completed novels, outwardly as quiet in character as her own life, are noted for their fine style and humour. These are *Pride and Prejudice, Sense and Sensibility, Mansfield Park, Emma, Persuasion* and *Northanger Abbey*.

AUSTRALASIA

Name given to lands in the Southern Hemisphere which include AUSTRALIA, NEW GUINEA, NEW ZEALAND and some islands in the PACIFIC OCEAN.

AUSTRALIA

A nation and continent of 7,686,848 sq km (2,968,070 sq miles) but with a vast desert region. The population of about 14½ million includes a majority of British origin, many from the mainland of Europe and about 50,000 aborigines.

Australia is an important farming country, and the foremost producer of sheep and wool in the world. It also exports large quantities of wheat and beef. However, Australia also has a large and growing steel industry and many other manufacturing industries. The country's industrial potential is great, with rich supplies of bauxite, iron ore, gold, copper, lead, silver and zinc.

Australia is made up of these states: New South Wales (cap. Sydney); Victoria (cap. Melbourne); Queensland (cap. Brisbane); South Australia (cap. Adelaide); Western Australia (cap. Perth); Tasmania (cap. Hobart). All these capital cities are ports, though Perth is served by the nearby port of Fremantle. The Federal capital is Canberra.

The Northern Territory is an area which is largely uninhabited. Its capital is Darwin. The Territory does not yet govern itself in the way that the states do.

One of the most important rivers is the Snowy in New South Wales and Victoria. A big new irrigation scheme was set up in Australia's great water conservation programme. This is the Snowy Mountains Scheme, established in 1949, which includes seven great dams. Tunnels and aqueducts carry water through the

Koala bear, an Australian marsupial

Australia and New Zealand

TIMOR SEA

CORAL SEA

Darwin

ARNHEM LAND

CAPE YORK PENINSULA

Gulf of Carpentaria

GREAT BARRIER REEF

KIMBERLEY

DAMPIER LAND

Fitzroy

Fitzroy

Port Hedland

BARKLY TABLELAND

NORTHERN TERRITORY

Cairns

Townsville

Great Sandy Desert

De Grey

Barrow Creek

Sandover

Mitchell

Flinders

Cloncurry

GREAT DIVIDING RANGE

Fortescue

Hamersley Range

Ashburton

Gibson Desert

Alice Springs

Macdonnell Ranges

Simpson Desert

Georgina

Diamantina

Rockhampton

Gascoyne

Carnarvon

WESTERN AUSTRALIA

Petermann Ranges

Musgrave Ranges

Alberga

Warburton

Coopers Creek

Thomson

QUEENSLAND

Great Victoria Desert

Stuart Range

L. Eyre

Flinders Range

Grey Range

Warrego

Toowoomba

Brisbane

Geraldton

NULLARBOR PLAIN

SOUTH AUSTRALIA

L. Torrens

Broken Hill

Darling

Lismore

NEW SOUTH WALES

Maitland

Kalgoorlie

L. Gairdner

Woomera

Port Augusta

Port Pirie

Bathurst

Blue Mts

Newcastle

Perth

Fremantle

Bunbury

Great Australian Bight

Lachlan

Wagga Wagga

Sydney

Wollongong

Adelaide

Murray

Canberra

SNOWY MTS

AUSTRALIAN ALPS

Albany

VICTORIA

Ballarat

Melbourne

BASS STRAIT

Tasmania

Hobart

TASMAN SEA

Auckland

NORTH ISLAND

Hamilton

BAY OF PLENTY

Waikato

New Plymouth

L. Taupo

Kaimanawa Mts

Napier

Mt Ruapehu 9175

Wanganui

Nelson

Wellington

Christchurch

Mt Cook 12349

Southern Alps

CANTERBURY PLAINS

Waitaki

Clutha

SOUTH ISLAND

FIORDLAND

Invercargill

Dunedin

FOVEAUX STRAIT

Stewart Island

500 miles
1000 miles
500
1000
1500 kilometres

100 200 300 miles
100 200 300 400 500 kilometres

Sydney Opera House, Australia

mountains. The Murray and the Murrumbidgee rivers are included in the scheme.

The first free immigrants arrived from Britain in 1793, the east coast of Australia having been discovered by Captain James COOK about twenty years before.

The first settled area in Australia was in New South Wales after 1788. In 1901 the six states were all united in a federation called the Commonwealth of Australia. The economy was based on farming, but mining and manufacturing are now the most valuable industries.

AUSTRIA

European republic, 83,849 sq km (32,376 sq miles) in area, bounded by Italy to the south, Switzerland to the west, Germany to the north and Hungary to the east. Much of the country is Alpine, while the DANUBE flows through plains in the east. The population is about 7½ million, the principal towns and cities being Vienna, the capital, Linz, Graz, Innsbruck and Salzburg.

Until the end of WORLD WAR I Austria was the central part of the great Austro-Hungarian Empire which had covered much of Central Europe for hundreds of years. The country was occupied by Germany in 1938 and fought with the Axis forces in WORLD WAR II. It was occupied by the Allies after the war, but regained its independence by a treaty of 1955 which guaranteed its political and military neutrality.

Austria is mainly an agricultural country, but tourism is an important industry.

AUTOMATION. *See* COMPUTER

AZTEC

The Aztec civilization flourished between AD 1200 and 1550. The people were descended from an Indian tribe, the Tenochcas. Their most famous kings or emperors were Itzcoatl (pronounced Eetz-co-atl), Montezuma, Axayactl (Ash-ay-ah-actl) and Ahuizotl (Ah-weetzotl), and the principal city was Tenochtitlan (Te-notch-ti-tlan).

The Aztecs built temples which very closely resembled the stepped, pyramid-shaped ziggurats of ancient BABYLONIA and ASSYRIA. They were also skilled in working gold, mosaic and such materials as rock crystal. The chief Aztec god was called Quetzalcoatl (Kwet-zalcoh-atl), the 'feathered serpent', and mass human sacrifice played a big part in their religion. They were completely subdued, and their civilization destroyed, by the Spanish conquistador Hernando Cortés. *See also* MEXICO.

Aztec temple at Technochtitlan

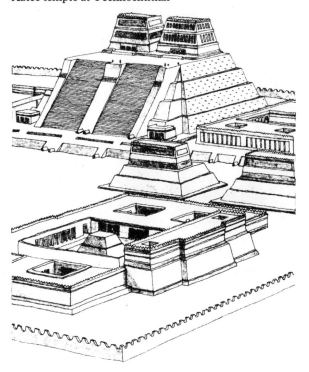

B

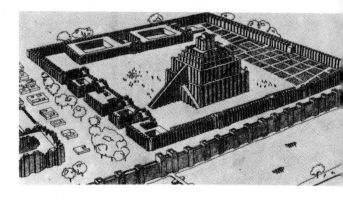

BABOON

Mammal belonging to the monkey family, native to Arabia and parts of Africa. Baboons live in groups or troops and are considered to be the most intelligent of the monkeys. They are also very strong and extremely dangerous when roused – even lions respect the male baboon. These animals were sacred to the ancient Egyptians.

Baboons – the most intelligent of the monkeys

BABYLONIA

Ancient kingdom of the Middle East, situated on the plain watered by the rivers Tigris and Euphrates; sometimes also called Chaldaea. Its principal cities were Babylon, Lagash, Nippur and Ur. For many centuries Babylonia was dominated by neighbouring ASSYRIA, but during the reign of one of its greatest kings, Nebuchadnezzar II (605–581 BC), it became one of the most powerful countries of the ancient world. *See also* SUMER.

BACH, Johann Sebastian (1685–1750)

The greatest member, both as organist and composer, of a famous German musical family. He was born in Eisenach (now in East Germany), and held several posts as court composer or church organist and choirmaster, the last and best known of these being at the church and school of St Thomas in Leipzig. His music can be divided into three main categories: compositions for organ, consisting of preludes and fugues, fantasias and toccatas; instrumental compositions, including the six Brandenburg Concertos; and choral works, comprising many cantatas, the *St John* and *St Matthew* Passions and the Mass in B minor. This great and varied output, together with the music of Bach's exact contemporary HANDEL, is regarded as the crowning glory to the many styles and forms of what is called in musical history the Age of Polyphony.

Two of J.S. Bach's sons, Carl Philipp Emanuel Bach and Johann Christian Bach (who settled in London), also became eminent composers, writing music (keyboard sonatas and symphonies) quite different in style from that of their father.

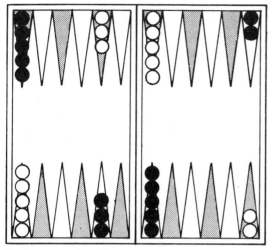

Backgammon board

BACKGAMMON

A game for two players, using a special board, counters and dice. The game is won when one player, by a succession of moves and strategems, determined by throws of the dice, is able to remove from the board, or 'bear off', all his counters. It can be played for money.

BACON, Francis, Lord Verulam and Viscount St Albans (1561–1626)

English statesman and philosopher. Born in London, he became, in turn, Attorney-General, Lord Keeper of the Great Seal and Lord Chancellor. In his *Essays, Novum Organum* and *Advancement of Learning,* Bacon emphasized the importance of experiment and observation in science, which made him one of the founders of modern scientific method.

BACON, Roger (*c.* 1214–94)

English philosopher and scientist, and one of the greatest scholars of the Middle Ages. He studied in Oxford and Paris, and at the invitation of Pope Clement II prepared an encyclopedia of learning. His methods of working and his special study of optics were far in advance of his time, though he shared many contemporary ideas, long since abandoned,

such as a belief in the Philosopher's Stone (see ALCHEMY). He was also a Franciscan friar.

BACTERIA

Microscopic organisms, consisting of one cell, and regarded as belonging to the plant world. Their various activities include the breaking down or building up of organic substances.

Bacteria reproduce by simple division and at an incredible rate. They are to be found in millions everywhere, including the human body. Some bacteria are infectious and spread harmful diseases; others are essential to the process of life itself, helping to break down dead materials, or convert nitrogen from the air into food. Different types of bacteria are given names according to their shape. Rod-shaped bacteria are 'bacilli'; bacteria with spherical shapes are 'cocci' and curved or spiral bacteria are 'spirilla'.

BADEN-POWELL, Robert, 1st Baron (1857–1941)

British soldier who commanded the defence of Mafeking (now Mafikeng) in the Boer War. In 1908 he founded the Boy Scout movement, which is now a world-wide organization. In 1910 he founded, with his sister, the Girl Guides. *See also* SCOUTS AND GUIDES.

Lord Baden-Powell, founder of the Boy Scouts

A badger emerging from his set at night

BADGER

Mammal, usually only seen at night, with very distinctive markings of white and black stripes on its face. Badgers live in burrows, or 'sets', feeding on roots, bulbs and other vegetable matter, also eggs, worms and other smaller mammals like mice or young rabbits. The American badger is generally similar to the European badger but with a dark brown face marked by a single narrow white stripe.

BADMINTON

A game similar to tennis but played with a shuttle (a half sphere of cork with feathers attached) instead of a ball.

BAHAMAS

A large group, or archipelago, of islands situated along the line of the Tropic of Cancer, east of Florida and north of Cuba. The total area is 13,935 sq km (5,381 sq miles). Most of the population of about 239,000 is concentrated on the two islands of Grand Bahama and New Providence, and the capital is Nassau. Tourism is the most important activity. The island of San Salvador was the place where Christopher COLUMBUS first landed in 1492. The Bahamas were a British Crown Colony until 1962. In 1973 they became a fully independent state.

BAHRAIN

An independent state and an island in the Persian Gulf which has an area of 622 sq km (240 sq miles) and a population of 407,000. Bahrain is mainly desert, but oil was discovered in 1932 and this has brought prosperity. The oil refinery at Sitrah is now one of the largest in the world.

BAIRD, John Logie (1888–1946)

Scottish inventor of a system of television which he first successfully demonstrated in 1928. His original method has since been superseded by the development of the cathode-ray tube, the basis of all modern television.

BAKER, Sir Samuel. *See* NILE

BALEARIC ISLANDS

A small group of islands off the east coast of Spain, forming a Spanish province, with a population of about 560,000. The main islands are Majorca, Ibiza, Minorca and Formentera, and tourism is now their main source of income.

BALKANS

A large, mountainous area of South-East Europe, in the shape of a peninsula, and comprising ALBANIA, BULGARIA, GREECE and YUGOSLAVIA. This territory was originally a part of the Roman Empire. Then in the sixth century AD began a series of invasions, mainly of slavic people, and from these emerged the various Balkan races: Serbs, Croats, Slovenes, Macedonians and Albanians. From the fifteenth until the nineteenth centuries most of the Balkan peninsula was part of the Turkish or OTTOMAN EMPIRE. After WORLD WAR I the largest single change was in the creation of Yugoslavia from the older states of Montenegro, Serbia and part of the disbanded Austro-Hungarian Empire.

Because of the great mixture of races, languages and religions, the Balkans have always been a politically unstable region, troubled by frequent wars and rebellions. The Balkan states remain divided, though now relatively peaceful. Greece is a member of NATO; Bulgaria exists within the Soviet Bloc; Yugoslavia and Albania are Communist states which pursue independent courses.

BALLAD

A type of poem or song recounting a story, often originating in folklore and therefore having no particular author. In the nineteenth century the word was sometimes used to describe a rather sentimental type of song. The French word *ballade* has been applied to pieces of music, usually for the piano, of a vaguely descriptive kind.

BALLET

One of the performing arts, based entirely upon dancing, and nearly always accompanied by music. Ballet as we think of it today started in the seventeenth century at the court of Louis XIV of France, and French has remained its

Scene from the ballet, *The Nutcracker*

official language. A very important person in the production of ballet is the choreographer, who plans the sequence of steps and dance routines. Some ballets are a part of larger works like an opera, e.g. the ballet music from Gounod's *Faust*. Others are complete stage works in themselves. Some are based on music not originally written for them, e.g. *Les Sylphides* (music by Chopin); most have specially written music, e.g. *Coppélia* (Delibes), *The Sleeping Beauty, Swan Lake, The Nutcracker* (Tchaikovsky), *The Firebird, Petrushka* (Stravinsky).

A famous ballet company was the Diaghilev Ballet (*Ballets Russes*) named after its founder and director, Sergei Diaghilev, who employed such celebrated dancers as Vaslav Nijinsky and Pavlova. Well known ballet companies today are the Bolshoi and Kirov Ballets in the Soviet Union; the Royal Ballet, Covent Garden, London; and the Australian Ballet.

BALLOON

A light container, usually spherical in shape, filled with a gas which will carry it into the air. The first successful balloon was designed by the Frenchman Joseph Michel Montgolfier and his brother Jacques Etienne. This was filled with hot air from a fire, and in 1783 it raised a man into the air for the first time. Since then balloons have been filled with some lighter-than-air gas – hydrogen or helium – thus allowing them to rise to greater heights and for a much longer period of time. In practice the filling of the balloon has to be carefully calculated to allow for changes in atmospheric pressure and temperature as this will affect the volume of the gas inside the balloon.

In WORLD WAR I balloons were used for observation, and in WORLD WAR II barrage balloons were flown as a protection against low-flying aircraft. Balloons called radiosondes are used for high-altitude studies of the atmosphere and weather conditions. *See also* AERONAUTICS and AIRSHIP.

BALLOT

A system of voting whereby each voter indicates his preference on a piece of paper which is then folded and placed in a ballot box, thus ensuring that his identity is kept secret. The word can be traced back to ancient Greece, when it meant 'little ball'. The system then was for voters to throw little coloured balls into a box to denote the preference.

BALZAC, Honoré de (1799–1850)

French novelist. He studied law, but against his parents' wishes, and with almost no money of his own, began to write. His chief work is the *Comédie Humaine,* a collection of many individual novels, intended to portray every aspect of life as he saw it.

BANDICOOT

A marsupial from Australia, similar to the KANGAROO but much smaller. The rat bandicoot is about 30 cm (12 in) from nose to tail, lives in hollows or ground burrows and eats roots, berries and insects.

BANGLADESH

Asian state, formerly East PAKISTAN, with an area of 143,998 sq km (55,601 sq miles). It gained independence in 1971 after a civil war between East and West Pakistan. The population of about 89 million people is mostly Moslem, and the capital city is Dacca. The country is almost entirely agricultural, the chief crops being rice, jute, tea and tobacco. But its position across the delta of the River GANGES makes it liable to frequent and disastrous flooding.

BANK OF ENGLAND

Nationally owned bank which keeps accounts for the government, handles negotiations, with its counterparts in other countries, and regulates the supply of money by such methods as the issue of currency and changes in the Bank Rate. It was established by Act of Parliament in 1694. *See also* MONEY.

BAPTISM

The word comes from the Greek, meaning 'to dip in water', and the Sacrament of Baptism is a part of almost every sect of the Christian Church. It is a sign that the baptised person has been admitted as a member of the Church.

Baptism of Christ, from a mosaic at Ravenna, Italy

BARBADOS

Island in the West Indies, part of the lesser Antilles island group. The total area is 431 sq km (166 sq miles). A former British colony, it became independent in 1966. The capital is Bridgetown. With 590 persons per sq km (1,536 per sq mile), it is one of the most densely populated places on earth. Sugar and tourism are the main sources of income.

BARBARY APE

Actually a type of monkey, but without a tail. Its natural home is North Africa, but a famous colony of the animals lives on the Rock of Gibraltar.

BARBARY SHEEP

Closely related to the goat family, with a long tail, large sweeping horns and a mane of long hair on the throat and forelegs. Found in parts of North Africa.

BARNARD, Christiaan Neethling (born 1922)

South African surgeon who performed the first heart transplant operation in the Groote Schuur Hospital, Cape Town in 1967.

BAROMETER

Instrument for measuring atmospheric pressure. Its simplest form is the Torricelli tube, named after Evangelista Torricelli who discovered in 1643 that air possessed weight and so exerted pressure. Far more widely used is the aneroid barometer which registers atmospheric pressure by means of a sensitive metal diaphragm. A barograph is a special type of aneroid barometer which keeps a continuous record of fluctuations in atmospheric pressure by means of the marking of a needle point upon graph paper attached to a revolving drum.

Domestic barometers are used to indicate changes in the weather (*see* METEOROLOGY). Other barometers are used in flying as an indication of altitude (*see* ATMOSPHERE). Blaise PASCAL used a barometer to measure the height of mountains above sea level.

BARRIE, Sir James M. (1860–1937)

Scottish author of many novels and plays, best remembered today for his play *Peter Pan* – about the boy blessed with eternal youth.

BARTÓK, Béla (1881–1945)

Hungarian composer. With his friend and fellow countryman Zoltán Kodály, he made an intensive study of Hungarian and Rumanian folk music, absorbing this into his own musical style. His compositions, including three piano concertos, the Music for Strings, Percussion and Celesta, a Concerto for Orchestra, the opera *Duke Bluebeard's Castle,* and six string quartets, have strongly influenced the course of twentieth-century music.

Aneroid barometer

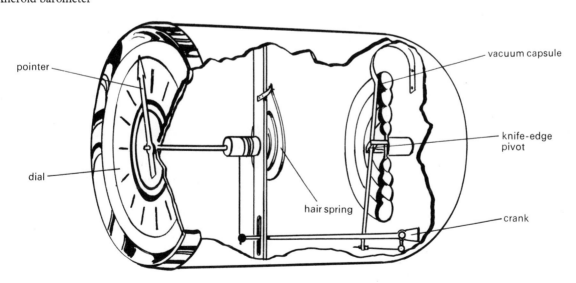

43

BASE

In chemistry a compound which will combine with an acid to form a salt. Some bases are formed when a metal oxide reacts with water. Then they taste bitter and turn red litmus paper blue. They break down (ionize) into positive and negative ions.

BASEBALL

American national game, similar to rounders. The main feature of the field is a square called the 'diamond'. The corners of this are 'bases' – home-base, from which the 'striker' (batter) does his hitting, then first, second and third base. Teams consist of nine players, and, as in cricket, when one team is batting the other is fielding. In fact, the bat is a form of club, and the ball is thrown by a 'pitcher'. The prime object for each side is to hit the ball, run from one base to the next, and so score as many complete runs between bases as possible.

Baseball field

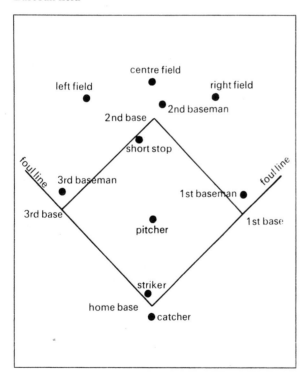

BASIC ENGLISH

A system by which the vocabulary of English is reduced to under 1,000 words. Thus if the words *dog* and *young* are included in the vocabulary there is no need for the word *puppy*, so it is left out. If you have *go* and *in,* there is no need for the word *enter.* The system was devised in principal by C. K. Ogden, and its purpose is to make English easily learned and understood. The word 'Basic' itself is made up like this: British, American, Scientific, International, Commercial.

BASKETBALL

The game requires two rings (the 'baskets'), 46 cm (18 in) in diameter to be positioned in front of two boards raised 3 m (10 ft) above the ground at each end of the court. It is played between two teams who compete for possession of a ball about the size and weight of a soccer ball and try to score goals by throwing the ball so that it falls through their opponents' ring from above. Players may bounce the ball and throw it to each other, but are not allowed to kick or run with the ball.

BASQUES

Race of people who live in the western region of the PYRENEES. More than two million live in Spain and half a million in France. They have retained their own language.

BAT

A small furry mammal with membranous wings. Bats are divided into two main groups: insect-eating bats and fruit-eating bats. There are also tropical vampire bats that extract blood from sleeping animals. Most bats are nocturnal, and also have poor eyesight. However, as they fly they emit very high-pitched sounds which are rapidly reflected back to them from all objects in their vicinity. In this way they effectively negotiate their flight.

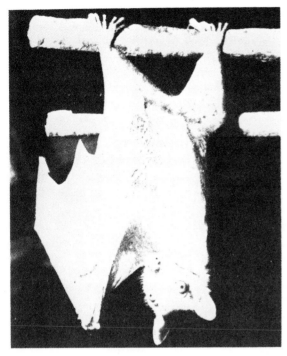

Bats are the only mammals that can really fly.

BATHYSCAPHE. *See* Auguste PICCARD

BATTERY

Device for producing ELECTRICITY through chemical action. Batteries consist of units called cells which are classed as either primary or secondary cells. *Primary Cells* only produce a certain amount of electricity, are than exhausted and cannot be re-charged. The Leclanché-type dry cell is one of these, widely used in transistor radios and torches. *Secondary Cells*, or accumulators, can be re-charged by passing an electric current through them. The lead-acid cell is a prime example, as used in cars. It produces current to start the engine and to supply power to the lights and other electrical components; at the same time, while the engine is running it is continuously being recharged from a generator which turns with the engine, but as it ages it will gradually lose its ability to hold a charge. *See also* Alessandro VOLTA.

BAUDELAIRE, Charles (1811–67)

French writer and author of a series of poems entitled *Les Fleurs du Mal* (Flowers of Evil) which is an important literary landmark. He was also an influential art critic.

BEAR

Group of MAMMALS found in many parts of the world. Most species hibernate during the winter. They are mainly vegetarian, with a real liking for honey; some eat ants and termites, and some are true carnivores. The principal types are the brown bear found in the mountainous regions of Europe and in parts of Asia; the American black bear and grizzly bear, the latter being a fierce hunter; the sloth bear of India and Sri Lanka; and the polar bear of Arctic regions, largest of the group at about 2.5 m (8 ft) in length. The Australian KOALA and the Chinese PANDA are not true bears. The koala is a MARSUPIAL, and although the panda is a plantigrade (walks on the sole), it is placed in a family of its own.

Polar bears in the Arctic region of Canada

The murder of Thomas à Becket

BEATITUDE

The word comes from the Latin *beatitudo* meaning 'blessedness'. It is especially applied to those sayings of Jesus contained in his Sermon on the Mount (Matthew, chapter 5). Perhaps the best-known of these beatitudes is 'Blessed are the meek: for they shall inherit the earth'.

BEAVER

Aquatic MAMMAL with a wide, scaly, paddle-like tail and fully webbed feet which it uses for swimming. The European beaver lives, like a water-rat, in burrows in the banks of streams. The American beaver makes dams of logs and branches, plastered with mud. These dams are to protect the beaver family from such animals as the coyote and cougar. Their food consists mainly of the bark of willow, poplars and other trees, but they also eat water-lilies, grass and roots.

BECKET, Thomas à (1118–70)

Chancellor of England and Archbishop of Canterbury. His early friendship with Henry II was followed by a serious dispute about the relationship between Church and state. Henry, in exasperation, is supposed to have said that he wished to be rid of 'this turbulent priest'. In the event four of the king's knights murdered Becket in Canterbury cathedral. He was canonized soon after.

BECQUEREL, Antoine Henri (1852–1908)

Most famous member of a French family of scientists, and one of the founders of modern physics. He studied the properties of uranium, also identified beta and cathode rays. He received the NOBEL Prize.

BEDE, the Venerable (*c.* 673–735)

English scholar, whose *Historia Ecclesiastica*, written in Latin, tells the story of Saxon times until 731. On it we depend for almost all our knowledge of early English history. It was translated into Anglo-Saxon by ALFRED THE GREAT.

BEDOUIN

Race of nomadic ARABS who inhabit the SAHARA desert and neighbouring regions, travelling from oasis to oasis with their camels and flocks of sheep and goats.

BEE

Very large group of insects found in the temperate and tropic regions. Most species of

Honey bee gathering nectar

bee are social insects, like ANTS, meaning that they lead highly organized lives in nests, or colonies (an average bee colony contains between 40,000 and 50,000 individuals). Also like ants, queen bees mate in flight and then create new colonies. In a colony there are male bees, called drones, whose job it is to fertilize the queen (and who have no sting). The female 'worker' bees are the ones who fly from flower to flower gathering nectar, which aids fertilization of the flowers themselves, and provides the bees with material for the construction of honeycombs. It is in these that the eggs laid by the queen are cared for until they finally emerge as new adult bees.

Bee-keeping involves the provision of special hives for the bees to live in and manufacture honeycombs.

A few species of bee, such as the familiar bumble bee, are solitary creatures.

BEETHOVEN, Ludwig van (1770–1827)

German composer, born in Bonn. As a young man he moved to Vienna and remained there for the rest of his life. His career as a pianist-composer was cut short by approaching deafness, and from then on he devoted himself to composition, leading a life of increasing solitude.

Beethoven inherited the forms of the SYMPHONY, CONCERTO, string quartet and SONATA from HAYDN, MOZART and other composers of the eighteenth century and dramatically enlarged them in terms of both form and expressive power. Thus he stands as a bridge between the classical period of the eighteenth century and the romantic period of the nineteenth century. Of his nine symphonies, the best known are the Third ('Eroica'), Fifth, Sixth ('Pastoral') and Ninth (Choral). He also wrote five piano concertos (the last of these being known as the 'Emperor' Concerto); the opera *Fidelio;* sixteen string quartets; and thirty-two piano sonatas, including the so-called 'Moonlight' Sonata.

BEETLE

One of the largest and most important groups of INSECT. Their Latin name (*Coleoptera*) means 'sheath-winged insects'. The word *beetle* means *biter,* and it is because of their eating habits that they are often considered a pest. The Deathwatch beetle eats its way through wood and can bring a roof down. The larva of the Colorado beetle is a pest in a potato crop. Some beetles, however, such as the ladybird, can be helpful by eating tiny aphids that attack plants.

Ludwig van Beethoven

The old city of Bruges, Belgium

BELGIUM

European kingdom between Holland and France with an area of 30,513 sq km (11,782 sq miles), which is about one-quarter of the area of England. But with a population of nearly 10 million it is one of the most densely populated nations in Europe. The capital is Brussels, also now the administrative centre of the EUROPEAN ECONOMIC COMMUNITY. Other major cities are Liège, a centre of heavy industry, and Antwerp, one of Europe's busiest ports.

Flemish and French are the official languages, but Flemish, a dialect of the Dutch language, is spoken in the Flanders region of Belgium, and French in Wallonia. In the past, Belgium was often called 'the cockpit of Europe', because of other nations' wars and battles fought on its soil. In the Napoleonic Wars the British, French and Prussians fought at Waterloo. In WORLD WAR I the British and French resisted the German advance across Belgium; and in WORLD WAR II it was again subjected to German invasion as part of that nation's attack on France.

In 1960 Belgium granted independence to its huge African colony the Congo now called ZAÏRE.

BELIZE

A country on the eastern coast of the Yucatán Peninsula in Central America, Belize has an area of 22,965 sq km (8,867 sq miles), with a population of about 132,000. It became independent from Britain in 1981 despite Guatemalan claims on it. Major products are sugar, citrus fruits and timber.

BELL, Alexander Graham (1847–1922)

Scottish-American inventor. As a teacher of deaf-mutes he invented many electrical deaf-aids for his pupils, and this work led, in 1876, to his invention of the telephone.

BELLINI, Giovanni (c. 1430-1516)

Venetian Renaissance painter and member of a distinguished family of artists. One of his pupils was TITIAN. His *Agony in the Garden* is in the National Gallery, London.

BELLINI, Vincenzo (1801–1835)

Italian composer of *I Puritani*, *Norma* and other operas, and master of the vocal style known, in Italian, as *bel canto*.

BELLOC, Hilaire (1870–1953)

Anglo-French writer of many travel and historical books, but best known for his nonsense verse for children – *The Bad Child's Book of Beasts* and *Cautionary Tales*.

BENELUX

Name derived from the three countries BELGIUM, the NETHERLANDS (Holland) and LUXEMBOURG when they formed a Customs Union in 1947.

BENEŠ, Eduard (1884–1948)

Co-founder of CZECHOSLOVAKIA in 1918, and President of the LEAGUE OF NATIONS. He was exiled from his country during WORLD WAR II and again, a few months before his death, in 1948 after the Communist take-over.

BEN-GURION, David (1886–1973)

Creator of the modern state of Israel. After the Turks expelled him from Palestine for pro-Allied activity during WORLD WAR I, he went to the United States to help raise the Jewish Legion.

In 1930 he became leader of the Jewish Labour Party, which came to power when the state of Israel was founded in 1948. He was Prime Minister from 1948 to 1953, and again from 1955 to 1963.

BENIN

West African republic on the Gulf of Guinea. It has an area of 112,622 sq km (43,486 sq miles), a population of about 3½ million and its capital is Porto Novo. Formerly a French colony known as Dahomey, it became independent in 1960.

Benin City in Nigeria was the centre of the powerful kingdom of Benin. During the fifteenth and sixteenth centuries this kingdom flourished.

16th-century ivory mask from Benin City, Nigeria

BENTHAM, Jeremy (1748–1832)

British philosopher and social reformer who held that the aim of the state should be to achieve the 'greatest happiness of the greatest number'. He helped to found University College, London, where his skeleton is preserved, dressed in a suit of his own clothes.

BENZ, Karl (1844–1929)

German engineer and pioneer in the development of the INTERNAL COMBUSTION ENGINE. In 1885 he built a motor vehicle powered by petrol; subsequently he did important work on systems of ignition and transmission.

BEOWULF

Anglo-Saxon epic poem, probably dating from the seventh century (though not written down until much later), and taken as the first important work of English literature. Beowulf is a mythical hero, like Hercules or Siegfried, though some of his adventures are based on historical events in Denmark.

BERBERS

Arab race of about 20 million people, inhabiting the north-western Sahara region of Africa. Their language is Berber, which is spoken by many Moroccans and Algerians.

BERLIOZ, Hector (1803–69)

French composer, born near Grenoble. Studied medicine, but took up music against his father's wishes. A pioneer figure in the art of orchestration and composer of many dramatic and colourful works in the romantic style, including the *Symphonie Fantastique,* the dramatic symphony *Romeo and Juliet,* the oratorio *La Damnation de Faust* (containing his version of the Rákóczi March), the opera *Les Troyens* (The Trojans), and concert-overtures *Le Carneval Romain* and *Le Corsair.*

BERMUDA

British colony and largest of a group of small islands, known as the Bermudas or Somers islands, in the western Atlantic. Its area is 53 sq km (20 sq miles). The capital is Hamilton. The island is a popular holiday centre.

BESSEMER, Sir Henry (1813–98)

Inventor of a process of making steel by removing the impurities (mainly silicon, manganese and phosphorus) from molten pig-iron. The Bessemer Convertor, in modified form, remains an important part of the steel-making process.

BEVAN, Aneurin (1897–1960)

British politician, Minister of Health in the Labour government of 1945–1950 and founder of the National Health Service.

BEVATRON

Machine known as an atom smasher. It can accelerate hydrogen nuclei to energy of more than 1 billion electron volts. Invented by Donald W. Kerst in 1940. The cosmotron is a similar device.

BEVERIDGE, William Henry (1879–1963)

British economist, whose *Beveridge Report,* published during WORLD WAR II, laid the foundations for the so-called Welfare State, which exists in a modified form in Britain today.

BHUTAN

Small kingdom of 47,000 sq km (18,148 sq miles) to the south-east of the Himalayas between India and Tibet, with a population of about 1¼ million. The capital is Thimphu. Bhutan enjoys close relations with India.

BIBLE

The title, taken from the Greek *biblia* ('books'), for a large collection of Hebrew and Christian sacred writings. It is divided into the Old Testament (39 books, not including the APOCRYPHA), and the New Testament (27 books).

The Old Testament can be divided into three principal sections: 1) a record of ancient Hebrew (Jewish) history and law-making (Genesis to Esther); 2) a collection of Hebrew poetry and drama (Job to the Song of Solomon); and 3) Hebrew preaching and prophecy (Isaiah to Malachi). The New Testament is an account of the principal Hebrew prophecy concerning the coming of a Messiah, as fulfilled in the life and teaching of Jesus of Nazareth; together with the teachings of early members of the Christian Church.

The earliest-known recorded parts of the Old Testament, cut into clay tablets, date from about 1000 BC (at the time of King David); and complete records of the Old Testament, written in Hebrew on parchment, probably date from the third or second centuries BC. The famous Dead Sea Scrolls, discovered in a cave in 1947, and including a complete version of the Book of Isaiah, date from this time.

The earliest parts of the New Testament are some of the Epistles (letters) of St Paul, though these now come after the four Gospel accounts of the life of Jesus (Matthew, Mark, Luke and John). Gospel is another Greek word, meaning 'good news'.

Medieval manuscript illustration of Noah's Ark

The first version of the complete Bible, written this time in Latin, and known as the Vulgate, dates from AD 405. Other important versions or editions of the Bible are: the first English version, translated by John Wycliffe (1384); the first printed edition, in Latin, by Johann Gutenberg (1454); William Tyndale's printed English New Testament (1526); Miles Coverdale's complete printed English edition (1535); the Anglican Authorized Version (King James Version) (1611); the New English Bible, rendered in modern English (1961); the Catholic Jerusalem Bible in modern English (1966).

The Bible, or parts of it, has been translated into over a thousand other languages.

See also CHRISTIANITY *and* JUDAISM.

BICYCLE

Lightweight vehicle with two wheels, and tractive power supplied by the rider. There is also the tricycle with three wheels, and the tandem designed for two riders. Ancestors of the modern bicycle include a type of two-wheeled scooter which a Frenchman, the Comte Mede de Sivrac, built in 1790; and the Penny Farthing, with a large front and a small rear wheel, dating from 1870.

Cycle racing is an event in the Olympic Games, but the most famous cycle race is the annual *Tour de France,* which covers a distance of up to 4,800 km (3,000 miles) in twenty-one days.

The velocipede, an early bicycle of 1862

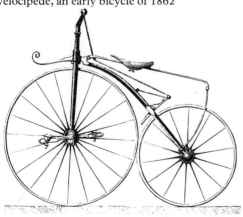

Big Ben

BIG BEN

Famous bell in the Clock Tower of the Houses of Parliament, London, installed in 1859, and nicknamed after the Commissioner of Works, Sir Benjamin Hall.

BILLIARDS

Indoor game for two people played on a large green baize-covered table, cushioned round the sides and with six 'pockets'. There are one red and two white balls, which are propelled by a long wooden pole called a cue. Points are scored by knocking the balls into the pockets, or by getting one ball to strike the two others (cannon). The name itself probably comes from the old French word *billard* meaning a stick with a curved end, and early versions of the game date back to the sixteenth century.

French billiards is played on a table without pockets, and consists only of scoring cannons. *See also* SNOOKER.

BIOGRAPHY

Word made up from the Greek *bios* (life) and *graphe* (writing), and name of the branch of literature dealing with accounts of the lives of men and women. Two famous biographical works are Plutarch's *Parallel Lives* of Greek and Roman heroes and Boswell's *Life of Dr Johnson*. Autobiography is an account of the writer's own life.

BIOLOGY

Name derived from the Greek words *bios* (life) and *logos* (discourse, or study), and describing the whole science of plant and animal life. Two of the first people to study life in a systematic, scientific way were the Greeks HIPPOCRATES and ARISTOTLE (fifth and fourth centuries BC). Today there are so many specialist branches of the subject, and so much of the work of one branch is related to the work of another, that clear distinctions are hard to make. There are also subject areas of biology that could equally well be treated as a branch of one of the other sciences. For example, biochemistry is the study of the chemistry of plants and animals. It is a subject which has grown enormously in the last hundred years, and has, by its investigation of such things as ENZYMES, HORMONES and VITAMINS, revolutionized much of the science of MEDICINE. Biophysics, in its turn, is that branch of biology which uses the techniques of the physical sciences, such as ELECTRONICS and certain aspects of NUCLEAR PHYSICS.

In this encyclopedia the many aspects of biology, ancient and modern, are treated in the following entries: ANATOMY; BOTANY; CYTOLOGY; ECOLOGY; EMBRYOLOGY; EVOLUTION; GENETICS; PALAEONTOLOGY; ZOOLOGY. There are also entries for many of the great scientists who have contributed to the subject, including Francis CRICK; Charles DARWIN; William HARVEY; Robert KOCH; Anton van LEEUWENHOEK; Carl LINNAEUS; Joseph LISTER; Gregor Johann MENDEL; Louis PASTEUR; Ivan PAVLOV; PLINY the Elder.

BIRD

Warm-blooded vertebrates, of the class *Aves*, distinguishable from all other forms of life by their feathers. Birds also lay eggs, have beaks, and scaly feet and claws or webbed feet, and are probably descended from REPTILES. The earliest known bird was Archaeopteryx of about 120 million years ago, and from this creature descended 8,600 main species of bird which exist today.

Most birds fly, and their skeletons are very light in relation to their size, the bones being hollow but strengthened by small internal struts. Flying birds also have highly developed muscles which raise and lower the wings, and these are attached to large breast bones shaped, for extra strength, rather like the keel of a boat.

Birds exist in a wide range of shapes, colours and sizes, and, as a class, are adapted to life in almost every kind of climate and terrain. They can be grouped as follows: *Perchers:* crow, jackdaw, sparrow, robin, and the song-birds like blackbird, thrush and NIGHTINGALE. *Peckers:* KINGFISHER, swift, HUMMINGBIRD. *Parrots:* parrot, mackaw, parakeet, budgerigar. *Birds of Prey:* OWL, FALCON, EAGLE, vulture, condor. *Waders:* stork, heron, crane, FLAMINGO. *Swimmers and Fishing Birds:* gull, DUCK, swan, pelican, cormorant, gannet. *Farmyard Birds:* hen, TURKEY, goose, pigeon, dove. *Game Birds:* pheasant, partridge, grouse. *Flightless Birds:* OSTRICH, kiwi, PENGUIN.

An arctic tern about to dive

BISMARCK, Otto von (1815–98)

Prussian-German statesman, known as the 'Iron Chancellor', and founder of a united GERMANY. Before Bismarck, Germany was a loose confederation of states, the largest of which was Prussia. As Prussian prime minister, Bismarck broke the hold of the Austrian Empire on other parts of Germany in the Austro-Prussian War of 1866. He then united the German states by leading them, with spectacular success, in war against France – the Franco-Prussian War of 1870–1. From then until his resignation as German Chancellor, Bismarck preserved peace and introduced many social reforms inside Germany.

BISON

Type of cattle, distinguished by its mane and the thick woolly hair over the front of its body and forelegs. There are two species, the European bison or wisent, and the American bison or buffalo.

BITUMEN

One of a number of substances mainly composed of hydrogen and carbon. They vary considerably in appearance and use. Naphtha, petrol, asphalt, and tar are all different kinds of bitumen. Some coal contains bitumen. They all burn with a great deal of smoke.

BIZET, Georges (1838–75)

French composer of several operas, including *The Pearl Fishers* and *Carmen,* and of incidental music to Alphonse Daudet's play *L'Arlésienne.*

BLACK DEATH

The worst of many outbreaks of plague during the Middle Ages, spreading from Asia to reach most of Europe by 1348. It was a form of bubonic plague, so called because it produced

Townsmen burying victims of the Black Death

black blotches under the skin. Between a third and a half of the population perished over a period of several years.

BLAKE, William (1757–1827)

English poet and artist. Born in London, he was inspired almost entirely by his own religious ideas and visions and produced poetry and illustrations absolutely unique in style and character. His poem starting with the words 'And did those feet in ancient time' is most familiar as the words to the hymn known as 'Jerusalem'. Two of his other groups of poems are the *Songs of Innocence* and *Songs of Experience.*

BLANK VERSE

Form of poetry with lines of equal length and rhythm but which do not rhyme. It is a type of verse specially suited for the stage, and has been used by many dramatists from SHAKESPEARE onwards.

BLENHEIM, Battle of. *See* MARLBOROUGH, John Churchill

BLIGH, William (*c.* 1753–1817)

British sea captain, set adrift with some others after a mutiny on board his ship HMS *Bounty*

William Bligh

in 1779. After a voyage of over 6,400 km (4,000 miles) in an open boat he and his companions landed in the East Indies.

BLOOD

Liquid that flows to and from the HEART through the bodies of all vertebrate animals. Arteries carry blood away from the heart, veins return blood to the heart. Blood consists of a type of plasma containing red corpuscles (haemoglobin) which carry oxygen from the lungs to the brain and other parts of the body, and white corpuscles which resist infection. Blood also removes waste products through the kidneys.

An adult human being has about 4.7 litres (8 pints) of blood. Severe loss of blood (about 1 litre) can be made good by a blood transfusion, once the patient's blood group has been established. The main blood groups are classified as Types A, B, AB and O, and these have to be matched in all cases of transfusion.

Anaemia is an illness caused by a lack of haemoglobin in the blood, leaving the patient pale and exhausted. Haemophilia is a blood condition which prevents normal healing of wounds. Haemorrhage is any escape of blood, but usually refers to cases of internal bleeding. *See also* William HARVEY.

BOADICEA (died AD 61)

British queen and leader of a revolt against the occupying Roman forces. She and her followers sacked the Roman towns of Camulodunum (Colchester), Verulamium (St Albans) and Londinium (London) before they were subdued. Her name can be spelt Boudicca.

BOCCACCIO, Giovanni (1313–75)

Italian writer, best remembered today for his work *Decameron*, a collection of one hundred short stories supposedly told by a group of Florentine noblemen who had fled to the country to escape the Black Death. Chaucer's *Canterbury Tales*, written some years later, is similarly constructed.

BOER WAR

South African war between Dutch farmers, or Boers, of the Transvaal and Orange Free State and the British in the territory round the Cape of Good Hope. Discovery of gold in the Transvaal brought ill feeling between the two sides to the point of conflict in 1899. The Boers besieged the British townships of Ladysmith, Kimberley and Mafeking, which were eventually relieved by reinforcements of British troops. After a period of guerilla fighting the Boers finally surrendered in 1902 and their territories were added to British South Africa, though they were granted self-government within the British Empire in 1907.

BOHR, Niels (1885–1962)

Danish scientist and leading figure in the investigations into the structure of the ATOM. In WORLD WAR II he joined the Allied team of scientists who produced the atomic bomb.

BOLIVIA

South American republic, 1,098,581 sq km (424,188 sq miles) in area – i.e. about eight times as large as England – with a population of about 5½ million. Sucre is the official capital, but La Paz is the seat of government and the principal city.

The country has no coastline, is largely mountainous and rather arid, and the economy is heavily dependent on mining, especially of tin. It derives its name from Simón Bolívar (1783–1830), the South American patriot who led successful revolts against Spanish colonial rule in VENEZUELA, COLUMBIA, ECUADOR, PERU and BOLIVIA itself.

BONE

Hard substance that makes up the skeleton of vertebrate animals. It consists of two kinds of tissue: compact tissue, which is the hard exterior, and cancellous tissue, which is the spongy inside, or marrow.

Long bones have three parts: the shaft, which is the long section; the metaphysis, being the flared part at the end of the shaft; and the epiphysis, or rounded end.

Rickets is a disease causing softening of the bones, usually due to a lack of vitamin D.

BORNEO

Large island lying across the line of the equator in south-east Asia, 743,000 sq km (287,000 sq miles) in area. It is divided politically between the Republic of INDONESIA, the Federation of MALAYSIA and the British protectorate of BRUNEI. Most of the people are DYAKS, many of whom still follow a tribal way of life. The remainder are of Chinese extraction.

BOSCH, Hieronymus (c. 1450–1516)

Dutch artist, noted for the fantastic and often nightmarish character of his paintings, prompted by the religious upheavals and abuses of his time. Among his works are *Earthly Paradise* and *Seven Deadly Sins* (both in the Prado, Madrid) and *The Ship of Fools* (Louvre, Paris).

BOSWELL, James (1740–95)

Scottish writer, and companion of Dr Samuel Johnson. His *Life of Johnson* is one of the most celebrated of all biographies.

BOTANY

The study of plant life. The principal classifications of plants are as follows: *Thallophytes* – algae, fungi and bacteria, and all seaweeds; *Bryophytes* – mosses and liverworts; *Pteridophytes* – all kinds of fern; *Spermatophytes* – seed-producing plants, which include trees, shrubs and all flowering plants.

Some of the first people to make a truly scientific study of plants were the ancient Greeks. Theophrastus (c. 372–286 BC), a pupil

The classification of plant life

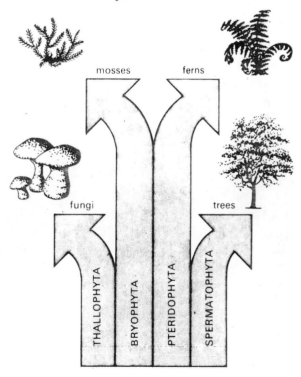

mosses ferns fungi trees

THALLOPHYTA BRYOPHYTA PTERIDOPHYTA SPERMATOPHYTA

of Aristotle, wrote a *History of Plants;* and Dioscorides compiled a list of herbal medicines. Modern studies of the subject date back to the seventeenth century. Robert Hooke (1635–1703) first identified plant cells through a microscope. In the next century Carl LINNAEUS produced the first systematic classification of plant life. And in the nineteenth century Gregor MENDEL investigated the process of plant reproduction and heredity.

Today, as with every other branch of science, botany is a vast subject, with many specialist fields of research. Morphology deals with the forms of plants. Developmental morphology (ontogeny) deals with the way plants grow. CYTOLOGY is the study of cell structure, and is itself a branch of the science of GENETICS. ECOLOGY is concerned with the relationship between plants and their environment. Economic botany is the study of plant life useful to mankind, and is closely related to many aspects of agriculture and to forestry. *See also* PHOTOSYNTHESIS; PLANT; TREE.

BOTSWANA

African state lying across the Tropic of Capricorn between NAMIBIA, ZIMBABWE and SOUTH AFRICA. Its area is 600,372 sq km (231,818 sq miles), but much of the land is the almost unin-

habited Kalahari, a semi-desert, and the population is only 788,000. Formerly the British protectorate of Bechuanaland, it gained independence in 1966. The capital is Gaborone.

BOTTICELLI, Sandro (*c.* 1444–1510)

Italian painter, one of the greatest of the Renaissance period belonging to the Florentine school. He is especially noted for his beautiful use of line. Botticelli's most famous paintings are *Primavera* and *The Birth of Venus,* both in the Uffizi Gallery, Florence. His *Mars and Venus* and *Nativity* are in the National Gallery, London.

BOUCHER, François (1703–70)

French artist of the Rococo period who produced many paintings for Madame de Pompadour at the Palace of Versailles. He was also director of the famous Gobelins tapestry factory.

BOULEZ, Pierre (born 1925)

French composer, noted for his work in the field of electronic music. Also a distinguished conductor.

Mars and Venus by Botticelli

BOURBON

Name of a French royal family that ruled in France itself, Spain and Naples. The first Bourbon king was Henry IV of France, crowned in 1589. With intervals the Bourbons retained the throne until 1848.

BOWLS

Game played on a specially prepared lawn, or 'green', and dating back to the 13th century. The object is to roll balls (bowls) about 12·5 cm (5 in) in diameter and weighing about 1·35 kg (3 lb) across the green and place them as close as possible to a small white target ball called the jack. The bowls are weighted on one side to give them directional bias as they roll.

BOXING

Sporting contest between two people using their fists to strike at each other. Boxing dates back to Greek and Roman times when a weighted leather glove called a cestus was used. It was a very popular sport in eighteenth-century England, known as pugilism or prize fighting, and was then fought with bare fists. The physical dangers of boxing were gradually controlled by sets of rules, the most important of these being laid down by the Marquess of Queensbury in 1865. Padded boxing gloves were introduced at that time. Today boxers, both professional and amateur, are classified according to their weight, as follows: Flyweight, up to 51 kg (8 st); Bantamweight, 54 kg (8 st 7 lb); Featherweight, 57 kg (9 st); Lightweight, 60 kg (9 st 7 lb); Welterweight, 67 kg (10 st 8 lb); Middleweight, 75 kg (11 st 11 lb); Light Heavyweight, 81 kg (12 st 10 lb); Heavyweight, over 81 kg (12 st 10 lb).

BOYLE, Robert (1627–91)

Irish scientist best remembered for his work on the physics of the atmosphere, and for his Law on the relation between the volume and pressure of gases. His other experiments on air under low pressure led to work on the nature of combustion.

Tycho Brahe observing the planets

BRAHE, Tycho (1546–1601)

Danish astronomer. He made important observations of the moon and some of the stars, but rejected the Copernican idea that the sun was the centre of the solar system in favour of the much older belief in the earth as the centre of the universe. His assistant was Johann KEPLER.

BRAHMS, Johannes (1833–97)

German composer, born in Hamburg, but worked for most of his life in Vienna. As a young man he was a great friend of Robert SCHUMANN and then of his widow Clara. Brahms combined in his work a deep respect for established musical forms with some of the drama and lyricism of the romantic period in which he lived. His works include four symphonies, four concertos for various instruments, many songs and instrumental pieces, and the choral *Ein deutsches Requiem* (A German Requiem).

BRAILLE, Louis (1809–52)

French inventor of the system, named after him, of a special reading code for the blind. It consists of raised dots on a page which are felt with the tips of the fingers. The system includes figures and music as well as words. Braille himself went blind in infancy.

BRAIN

Nerve centre controlling the functions and senses of many forms of animal life; and in human beings the centre also of the thinking processes. In anatomy the brain is divided into several sections: *cerebrum, cerebellum, pons vaolii* and *medulla oblongata*. The *cerebrum* is the thinking and reasoning part of the brain; the *cerebellum* controls posture, balance and movement; the *pons vaolii* relays messages

The human brain

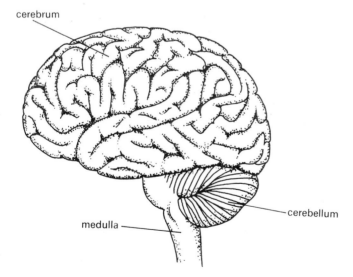

cerebrum

medulla

cerebellum

between the *cerebrum* and *cerebellum;* while the *medulla oblongata* is an extension of the spinal cord into the back of the brain, controlling the actions of the heart, lungs, digestion, and so on. The brain consists of millions of cells which operate by tiny electrical impulses, but exactly how and why it works remains a mystery.

An encephalograph (taken from the Greek word for brain) is an instrument designed to record its electrical activity.

BRAQUE, Georges (1882–1963)

French painter and one of the leading members of the 'Fauve' school of modern painters. He also worked closely with PICASSO and together they developed the 'Cubist' style of painting.

BRAZIL

Largest country of South America with an area of 8,511,965 sq km (3,286,668 sq miles), that is about the same size as the United States. The population is about 126 million. The largest city is São Paulo, the most famous is Rio de Janeiro, but the administrative capital is the new city of Brasília.

Brazil was colonized by the Portuguese during the sixteenth century and remained a Portuguese possession until 1820 when it became an independent state. Much of the country is drained by the hundreds of tributaries of the River AMAZON and large areas remain uninhabitable tropic jungle. But Brazil produces about one half of the entire world supply of coffee, and is also rich in minerals, notably manganese.

BRECHT, Berthold Eugen Friedrich (1898–1956)

German dramatist and poet, noted for his Marxist ideas. Before World War II he collaborated with the composer Kurt Weill to produce several operas, including *The Threepenny Opera*. His best-known play is *Mother Courage*.

BREZHNEV, Leonid Ilyich (born 1906)

Soviet statesman, first secretary of the Soviet Communist Party from 1964–66, then general secretary, in which capacities he has been effective political leader of the USSR.

BRITISH BROADCASTING CORPORATION (BBC)

Non-profitmaking organization, maintained by licence fees approved by Parliament, but free from any direct political control. Sound broadcasting began in Britain in 1922 when Parliament approved the setting up of the British Broadcasting Company. The creation of the British Broadcasting Corporation followed in 1927. In 1937 the BBC started the world's first television service. This was suspended during World War II, but resumed in 1946. During the war years the BBC was famous throughout Europe for its broadcasts to most of the occupied countries, which supplied resistance movements with military information, and helped to keep up civilian morale, thus being of great service to the Allied cause.

BRITISH COMMONWEALTH

Association of independent states which recognize the British monarch as their representative head. Some member states (e.g. Canada and Australia) accept the monarch as their own national Head of State. Others are republics, or have a monarchy of their own, and so their relationship to the British Crown is only an indirect one. Belize became the 45th member state in 1981.

The British Commonwealth of Nations emerged from the earlier British Empire, as former British territories assumed self-government.

In 1932 Dominion status was granted to such countries as Canada and Australia, giving them full status as independent nations within the Commonwealth. Since World War II nearly all other British colonies and protectorates have secured self-government, with the right to remain within the Commonwealth. Such membership has no bearing on the membership of other international organizations, such as the United Nations.

BRITTEN, Benjamin, Lord (1913–76)

English composer. He was born in Suffolk and returned there to found the Aldeburgh Music Festival. His best-known opera, *Peter Grimes,* was inspired by a story of the Suffolk coast; other operas include *Albert Herring, Billy Budd* and *Death in Venice.* Britten also wrote much music for children's voices or for their participation, such as the 'Spring' Symphony and the stage-entertainment *Let's Make An Opera!* For the orchestra he wrote the well-known Variations and Fugue on a Theme of Purcell, or *The Young Person's Guide to the Orchestra.*

BRONTË, Charlotte (1816–55); Emily (1818–48); Anne (1820–49)

Novelist daughters of a Yorkshire country parson. Charlotte wrote *Jane Eyre.* Emily Brontë's most famous novel was *Wuthering Heights,* which she first published under the pseudonym of Ellis Bell. Anne has not achieved the fame of her two sisters, though she was a talented writer.

Charlotte Brontë

Late Bronze Age swords from Austria, *c.* 1000 BC

BRONZE AGE

Period of history from about 5000 to 1000 BC, and characterized by the use of bronze for tools and weapons. It was preceded by the Stone Age and followed by the Iron Age.

BROWNING, Robert (1812–89) and Elizabeth Barrett (1806–61)

Robert Browning was one of the most eminent nineteenth-century English poets. His marriage to Elizabeth Barrett, herself a poetess, was a celebrated romance. After their marriage they lived mostly in Italy; and after Elizabeth's death Robert wrote his best-known work, the novel-in-verse *The Ring and the Book.*

BRUCE, Robert (1274–1329)

Scottish king and national hero. At first he supported Edward I of England in his conflict with Scotland, but later transferred his allegiance to William Wallace the Scottish patriot. In 1306 Robert Bruce crowned himself

Seal of Robert Bruce

king of Scotland, and in 1314 defeated a much larger England army at the Battle of Bannockburn. By the Treaty of Northampton in 1328 his title as King of Scotland was officially recognized.

BRUCKNER, Anton (1824–96)

Austrian composer of nine symphonies noted for their late romantic richness of sound; also several big choral works, including a *Te Deum.* One curiosity is an early symphony, known as Symphony no. 0.

BRUEGHEL, Pieter, the Elder (*c.* 1525–69)

Flemish painter, noted for his landscapes and colourful peasant scenes, and also for several paintings of religious fantasy and horror similar in character to those of Hieronymus BOSCH, and relating to the Spanish Inquisition in the Low Countries. Sometimes known as 'Peasant Brueghel'. His son, also Pieter, worked in a similar style.

BRUNEI

Sultanate under British protection on the north-west coast of Borneo. It has an area of 5,765 sq km (2,226 sq miles) and a population of about 220,000. The capital is Bandar Seri Begawan, and the chief products are oil, rubber and timber.

Brunel and the SS *Great Britian*

BRUNEL, Isambard Kingdom (1806–59)

Son of Marc Brunel, a French architect and engineer who settled in England. He designed a tunnel under the Thames and several bridges, including the Clifton Suspension Bridge at Bristol; planned and supervised construction of the railway line from London to Bristol and Plymouth, adopting the 7-foot (210 cm) gauge. He designed a series of equally remarkable steamships, including the *Great Britain*, first screw-propelled ship to cross the Atlantic, and the *Great Eastern,* largest ship to be built during the nineteenth century.

BRUNELLESCHI, Filippo (*c.* 1377–1446)

Italian sculptor and architect of the Renaissance. His masterpiece is the dome of the cathedral at Florence.

BUCHAN, John (1875–1940)

Scottish author and statesman. He served under Lloyd George during World War I, was a well-known MP, and Governor-General of Canada; but best remembered today for his adventure and thriller novels, including *The Thirty-nine Steps.*

BUDDHISM

Religion founded on the life and teachings of Prince Siddhartha, or Gautama the Buddha (Gautama the Enlightened One). He lived in India from about 560 to 480 BC, was born into a very rich family, but abandoned his wealth and station to seek spiritual enlightenment, attracting disciples who helped to spread his ideas after his death.

Buddhism is based on the far older beliefs of HINDUISM concerning REINCARNATION, or the progress of the soul through a series of earthly existences. It asserts that the cause of suffering is desire; that elimination of desire brings an end to suffering and an end also to the cycle of birth and re-birth (i.e. reincarnation). This fulfilment of the soul is called *nirvana.*

Buddhism did not become the major religion of its country of origin – India – but spread to many other parts of Asia, to Burma and Thailand, China and Japan. In the process Buddhist teachings became interpreted in different ways. In Tibet it had added to it many supernatural beliefs. In Japan, by contrast, there grew up the school of Zen Buddhism with its emphasis on strict personal discipline. Today it has about 170 million adherents.

BUDGET

A sum of money which it is expected will be needed for a certain purpose. It is a word used to describe the money which the nation is expected to need in order to carry on the work of government for a year. In Britain the nation's budget is presented to Parliament by the Chancellor of the Exchequer every year in

April and because of this the 'financial year' runs from April to April, instead of starting, as does the calendar year, on 1 January. In Australia, however, this 'financial year' runs from 1 July to 30 June.

BULGARIA

East European republic that borders the Black Sea. With an area of 110,912 sq km (42,826 sq miles) it is rather smaller than England, and has a population of about 9 million. The capital is Sofia. The people speak a form of the Slavonic language, similar to Russian, and Bulgaria itself is a part of the East European Communist Bloc. Its chief agricultural products are tobacco and wine, but such industries as coal and steel are developing.

BUNSEN, Robert Wilhelm (1811–99)

German scientist best known for the laboratory gas burner which still bears his name. But he also discovered the elements caesium and rubidium and devised an electrical battery, known as a 'Bunsen' cell.

BUNYAN, John (1628–88)

English writer, born near Bedford. He was a travelling tinker and fought in the Civil War with CROMWELL's forces. He then joined a nonconformist sect but was imprisoned in 1660 for twelve years as an unauthorized preacher. He was again imprisoned in 1673, during which time he began to write *The Pilgrim's Progress* (published 1678), the work by which he is still remembered.

BUOY

Anchored float used in marine navigation. They are of various shapes and colours, each being designed for a particular duty. *Channel buoys* mark the approach to the entrance of a channel and are usually pillar-shaped buoys. These are followed by a number of can-shaped

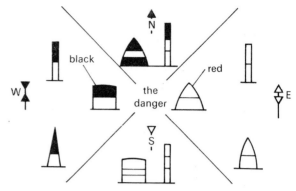

Cardinal buoyage system

buoys to port, and conical-shaped buoys to starboard. *Spherical buoys* usually denote the presence of an obstruction. *Special buoys* are used for marking wrecks, quarantine stations, telegraph cables, and as mooring buoys.

BURKE, Edmund (1729–97)

Anglo-Irish statesman and political essayist, a leading member of the Whig party and opponent of the war against the American colonists (American War of Independence). His speeches and essays on different aspects of policy and government are still highly regarded in political circles.

BURMA

Republic of South-East Asia with an area of 676,552 sq km (261,232 sq miles) which is more than five times as large as England. The population is about 34 million, and the two largest cities are Mandalay and the capital, Rangoon.

Burma was included as part of India within the British Empire up to World War II. During the war the country was occupied by the Japanese, and soon after Burmese leaders decided to leave the Empire and Commonwealth. In 1974 a new constitution made Burma a socialist republic.

Burma's tropical forests produce valuable woods, such as teak. Rice is the principal crop. The country is also rich in minerals, including precious stones and oil.

Robert Burns

BURNS, Robert (1759–96)

Scottish poet. He was the son of an Ayrshire farmer, but left the land in favour of a literary career. His duties as a government exciseman also gave him a regular income. Burns was a radical-minded man, an opponent of social injustice and hypocrisy and a supporter of the ideals of the French Revolution. He could write well in correct 18th century English, but composed his best-known poems in his native Lowlands Scots. These include the Scottish folk tale *Tam O'Shanter*, the satirical *Holy Willie's Prayer*, and the song *Auld Lang Syne*, now traditionally sung by people all over the world on New Year's Eve.

BURUNDI

African republic between Zaïre and Tanzania with an area of 27,834 sq km (10,747 sq miles) and a population of about 4 million. The capital is Bujumbura. Formerly part of the territory called Ruanda-Urundi. It produces coffee and some cattle.

BUTLER, Samuel (1835–1902)

English writer. His book *Erewhon* is a satirical attack on what he saw as the social abuses of his time; but he is best remembered today for his autobiographical novel *The Way of All Flesh*.

BUTTERFLIES AND MOTHS

Insects belonging to the order *Lepidoptera,* hence the name lepidopterist for a butterfly or moth collector. Butterflies usually fly by day and, like bees, visit flowers for nectar. Generally they have long, slim bodies and long, thin antennae with a thicker, club-like end. The wings of most species are beautifully coloured, and some large tropical varieties also have wing spans of as much as fifteen centimetres (nearly six inches). Many species of butterfly migrate. The Painted Lady, for example, travels each year from Africa to Britain.

Red admiral butterfly

Moths are mostly night fliers. They, too, can be beautifully patterned or coloured; but their bodies are generally thicker than those of butterflies and covered with a kind of soft fur, while their antennae end in a point and are often branched like fronds or feathers.

A notable characteristic of butterflies and moths is their life-cycle, or metamorphosis. They are born as eggs, which hatch into caterpillars. Then each caterpillar changes into a pupa or chrysalis, from which the butterfly or moth finally emerges.

BY-ELECTION

An election that has to be held unexpectedly because of the death or retirement of an MP or councillor.

BYELORUSSIA or WHITE RUSSIA

A major division of Russia and a charter member of the UNITED NATIONS. Also called Belorussia. Byelorussia was part of Lithuania for hundreds of years. It was incorporated into the Soviet Union in 1945.

BY-LAW

A rule which a local authority, or some other public body, is allowed by Parliament to make. People who break a by-law can be punished by a fine.

BYRD, Richard Evelyn (1888–1957)

American scientist and explorer. In 1926 he flew over the North Pole and two years later led an expedition to the Antarctic in the course of which he flew over the South Pole. He made further expeditions to the Antarctic, in 1933, 1939 and 1946, mainly to collect meteorological and other scientific information.

BYRD, William (1543–1623)

English composer who lived through the main period of struggle between English Catholics and Protestants. Byrd himself was a Catholic, but he wrote much church music (masses and motets) both for his own and for the newly established Anglican Church; also many madrigals. Elizabeth I granted to him and to his friend and colleague Thomas Tallis a monopoly of music printing.

BYRON, George Gordon, Lord (1788–1824)

English poet, and one of the most romantic figures of the early nineteenth century. He spent much of his life abroad, where he was admired more than in his own country, and died while fighting with the Greeks in their struggle for independence against the Ottoman Turks. Byron's chief poetic works are *Childe*

Harold and *Don Juan*. In fact, these are more in the eighteenth-century tradition of Pope than in the romantic style of Keats or Shelley.

BYZANTINE EMPIRE

Founded on the name of the ancient Greek city of Byzantium. In AD 330 the Roman Emperor CONSTANTINE adopted CHRISTIANITY, re-built the city, re-named it Constantinople, and made it his seat of government. The territories surrounding Constantinople then became known as the Byzantine Empire, or Byzantium. Through the reigns of JUSTINIAN and other Byzantine emperors, the Empire survived the Barbarian invasions which destroyed the ROMAN EMPIRE; and the onslaughts of the new religion of ISLAM, until Constantinople itself fell to the OTTOMAN Turks in 1453. It was re-named Istanbul in 1930.

Despite its stormy history of war and internal religious strife, commerce, art and learning flourished in Byzantium and strongly influenced the course of the Italian RENAISSANCE.

Below St Sophia, Istanbul, built by Justinian

Right Fulah woman with gold earrings, Mali, Africa

C

title 'Right Honourable', though the office is largely honorific.

The Cabinet dates back to the time of Charles II, who presided over meetings 'in cabinet' of selected members of the Privy Council. When George I, who could speak no English, came to the throne, he asked his Prime Minister, Sir Robert Walpole, to preside over the Cabinet in his place, and so set the pattern for future governments.

CABINET

Legislative body composed of chief government ministers, chosen by the PRIME MINISTER. The exact number of cabinet ministers varies according to the decision of the Prime Minister but is usually about twenty. Some ministers, such as the CHANCELLOR OF THE EXCHEQUER and the LORD CHANCELLOR, are always in the Cabinet, but otherwise there is no firm rule. All cabinet ministers are also members of the PRIVY COUNCIL and are given the

CABOT, John (1450–98) and Sebastian (1476–1557)

Italian navigators. In 1484 John Cabot came to England with plans to find a westerly route to the East. With the support of Henry VII he set out on a voyage of exploration and in 1497 reached Cape Breton Island and sailed along the coasts of Newfoundland and Nova Scotia. His son Sebastian explored the coast of Brazil in 1526 and later tried to find a North-East Passage to Asia round the coast of Russia and Siberia.

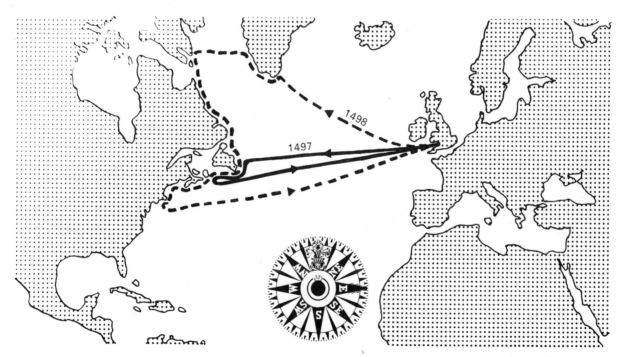

Left Battle of the Spanish Armada by Hilliard

Above John Cabot's voyages to North America

Cacti and succulent plants grown in a hothouse

CACTUS

Group of several hundred varieties of plant belonging to the *Cactaceae* family, found mostly in dry, hot regions. Most varieties consist only of a stem, or branches of stem, which can store water for long periods and is protected by prickles. Most cacti also produce highly coloured flowers at certain times.

CAEDMON

English poet who lived about AD 670. Very little is known about his life, but hymns attributed to him had a great influence on ANGLO-SAXON literature.

CALCULUS

A branch of higher mathematics discovered by NEWTON and LEIBNIZ. It includes the differential and integral calculus. The differential calculus is concerned with the rate of change of variable quantities; for example, velocity is the rate of change of position in relation to time. More formally it is expressed as:

$$\frac{\text{distance}}{\text{time}} = \frac{s}{t}$$

but with the differential calculus only infinitesimal increments of the quantities (known as variables in pure mathematics) are considered and are written by placing in front of the symbol d; thus ds means an increment of distance, dt an increment of time and $\frac{ds}{dt}$ an increment of velocity. From the diagram it will be seen that this is equivalent to the slope of the curve.

The integral calculus is concerned with determining the laws relating variables when the rate of change, that is, the differential, is known. The operation of integration is expressed by the symbol $\int$.

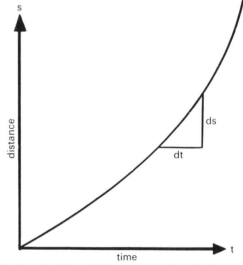

Calculus: the slope of the curve equals velocity

CALENDAR

Systematic division of the year into months, weeks and days, the year itself being determined by the progress of the sun. The ancient Egyptians and Chinese divided the year into thirteen months according to the phases of the moon (lunar months), the Egyptians later adopting the twelve-month system. The Romans gave the names to the months from which our own are derived (also giving us 'Calendar' from their word *Calends*, which was the first day of their month). JULIUS CAESAR reformed the calendar, making 1 January the start of the year, and the seventh month (July) is named after him. This Julian calendar was adjusted by AUGUSTUS CAESAR to take proper account of Leap Year (the extra day needed every fourth year to compensate for the fact that there are 365 days plus about six hours in a true solar year). In 1577 Pope Gregory XIII appointed astronomers to reform the calendar again, and this corrected Gregorian calendar was gradually adopted by most European countries, though not by Russia until after the Revolution of 1917. The Christian calendar, in terms of years, starts from the accepted birth date of Christ; though after the FRENCH REVOLUTION there was a short-lived attempt to create a new starting point for the calendar with new names for the months.

CALVIN, John (1509–64)

French-Swiss religious reformer, whose own conversion to the Protestant faith greatly in-

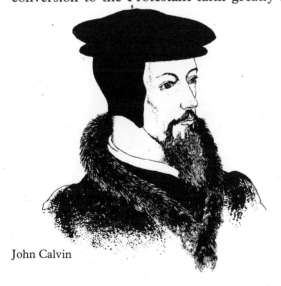

John Calvin

Ancient Mexican calendar

fluenced the Protestant churches in France (the Huguenots), Holland, England, Scotland and the American New England colonies. He gave his name to Calvinism, which describes a strict and simple way of life and religion.

CAMBODIA. *See* KAMPUCHEA, Democratic Republic of

CAMEL

Mammal, closely related to the LLAMA. There are two species of camel, the Bactrian of Central Asia and the Arabian, or dromedary, of the Arabian and Saharan desert regions. The Bactrian camel is a sturdy animal with long hair and two humps. The dromedary has only one hump and is slimmer and swifter. The humps are stores of a fatty substance which the animals draw on when food and water are scarce.

CAMEROON

Republic on the west coast of Africa with an area of 475,442 sq km (183,579 sq miles) and a population of 8,429,000. The capital is Yaoundé. The chief exports are coffee, cocoa and timber and oil production began in 1978. From 1884 to World War I, Germany ruled Cameroon. It was then partitioned between France and Britain. In 1961 Southern (British) Cameroon and East (French) Cameroon joined in an independent republic.

CAMPBELL, Sir Malcolm (1885–1948) and Donald (1921–67)

British racing drivers, father and son, who established land and water speed records. Donald beat his father's land speed record at 686 km/h (429 mph) and water speed record at 534 km/h (328 mph), and was then killed in a further attempt on his own water speed record.

CAMUS, Albert (1913–50)

French writer, and with Jean-Paul SARTRE considered a leading figure in the existential school of thought.

CANADA

Oldest Dominion within the BRITISH COMMONWEALTH, and the largest with an area of 9,976,139 sq km (3,852,019 sq miles). It is separated from the UNITED STATES for much of its length by the 49th parallel (the longest stretch of unprotected frontier in the world), then by the GREAT LAKES. The country extends northwards well beyond the Arctic Circle to the large group of islands including Baffin Island and the Queen Elizabeth Islands. In the west

are the Rocky Mountains, while a great plain (the prairies) stretches eastwards towards Hudson Bay and the Great Lakes.

The population is 23,992,000 and the chief cities are Toronto, Montreal, Vancouver, Ottawa, Winnipeg, Edmonton and Quebec.

Canada has a federal system of government, with the federal capital at Ottawa, and separate legislative assemblies for the provinces of Alberta, British Columbia, Manitoba, New Brunswick, Newfoundland (with Labrador), Nova Scotia, Ontario, Prince Edward Island, Quebec and Saskatchewan. There are also the vast, largely uninhabited regions of the Yukon and the North-West Territories.

Canada is the world's leading producer of timber and one of the chief producers of wheat. It is also very rich in minerals, especially nickel, aluminium, zinc and platinum. In co-operation with the United States, Canada has opened up the St Lawrence River to ocean-going ships (the ST LAWRENCE SEAWAY). The most famous tourist attractions are the Niagara Falls between Lakes Erie and Ontario, the Horseshoe Falls being part of Canada.

Parts of Labrador were probably explored by the VIKINGS, but the real discovery of Canada started with the voyage of John CABOT in 1497.

Rivermen poling logs in Quebec, Canada

During the next three centuries much of the country was disputed by the French and the British, and it was only in 1759 that British forces, under General WOLFE, finally gained control. Canada secured self-government from Britain in 1867; but much of Quebec province remains a French-speaking region, with some political movement towards complete independence.

CANALETTO, Antonio (1697–1768)

Italian painter, also known as Canale. He painted in a very clear, precise style, recording many contemporary scenes in Venice and later in London.

CANARY ISLANDS

Group of islands in the North Atlantic Ocean 96 km (60 miles) off the west coast of Africa, belonging to SPAIN. The total area is 7,270 sq km (2,810 sq miles). The largest island is Tenerife (capital Santa Cruz), followed by Gran Canaria (capital Las Palmas).

CAPE VERDE

Island republic in West Africa. The area is 4,033 sq km (1,557 sq miles), the population 312,000 and the capital is Praia.

CAPYBARA

Largest RODENT and a native of South America. It can measure over 1.2 m (4 ft) long and may weigh over 45 kg (100 lb). Capybaras are social animals, moving and feeding in troops. Their main foods are grass and water plants, and despite their size they are timid creatures.

CARACAL

A LYNX-like animal of the cat family, sometimes called the Persian lynx, found in Asia and Africa. It has short, tawny brown fur and tufted, blackish ears. The caracal preys on

The Supper at Emmaus by Caravaggio

small creatures like hares, and in India it is trained to hunt in the same way as the CHEETAH.

CARAVAGGIO (1573–1610)

Italian painter, born in Caravaggio, whose real name was Michelangelo Merisi. A revolutionary figure who brought a new realism to art by using in his paintings the costumes and attitudes of ordinary people.

CARBOHYDRATE

One of the three main classes of food used by the body. The others are PROTEINS and fats. Carbohydrates, as the name implies, contain carbon, hydrogen and oxygen. They comprise all sugars and starches.

CARBON

One of the most important and valuable ELEMENTS. Pure carbon exists as DIAMONDS and also as graphite, the 'black lead' in pencils. Minerals such as limestone contain carbon, and fuels such as coal and oil. A radioactive ISOTOPE (one form of carbon) called carbon 14 helps archaeologists to determine the age of some of their discoveries. Carbon 12 was adopted in 1961 as the standard for atomic weights.

CARIBOU. *See* REINDEER

CARLYLE, Thomas (1795–1881)

Scottish historian and author. Studied at Edinburgh University, but for most of his life lived in London, where he died. His best-known works are *History of the French Revolution* (1837), *Cromwell's Letters and Speeches* (1845), and *History of Frederick the Great of Prussia* (1858–65).

CARNEGIE, Andrew (1835–1919)

Scottish-American industrialist and philanthropist. Born in Scotland, he emigrated to America with his family in 1848. After a humble start to his career as a telegraph operator, he quickly made his way in industry, especially in iron and steel, amassing an immense fortune. On retiring in 1901 he founded many philanthropic trusts and funds. The Carnegie Hall in New York is named after him.

CARP

Originally native to the CASPIAN and Black Seas, this fish is now widely distributed. It has large scales, a long dorsal fin and barbels on the upper jaw. Normally it is about 30 cm (12 in) long, but some forms are over 1 m (3 ft) in length. The three most common kinds are *scale*, *mirror* and *leather* carp. The goldfish is a kind of carp.

CARROLL, Lewis (1832–90)

English writer, whose real name was Charles Dodgson. He was a mathematician by training, but in his fantasies *Alice's Adventures in Wonderland* and *Through the Looking-Glass* he created two of the great classics of children's literature.

CARTIER, Jacques (1491–1557)

French navigator whose pioneer exploration of Newfoundland and the St Lawrence River established early French claims in CANADA.

The real Alice, for whom Carroll wrote the stories

CASPIAN SEA

Largest inland sea, or salt lake, with an area of 272,000 sq km (170,000 sq miles), situated between Europe and Asia, mostly in the USSR. The river VOLGA flows into it, and the entire surrounding land is below sea level.

CASTLE

Fortified dwelling. The term 'castle' is most commonly applied to the fortresses belonging to Europen kings or important nobles during the Middle Ages. The first of this type were built by the Normans in France, during the eleventh century, and were then used by them to suppress the Saxons in England. The earliest castles were constructed of wood and consisted simply of a tower built on a mound and standing in a courtyard which was surrounded by a fence and a ditch. By the twelfth century the wooden tower had given way to a stone keep

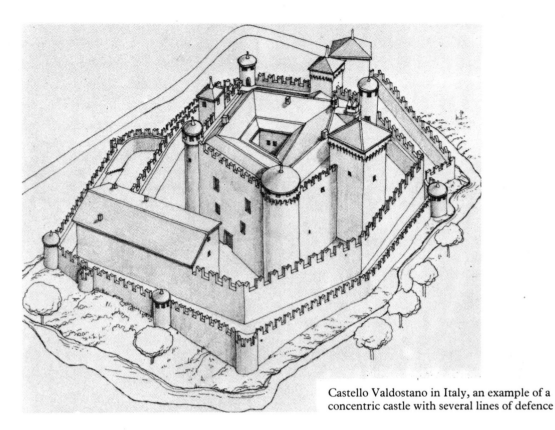

Castello Valdostano in Italy, an example of a concentric castle with several lines of defence

containing living accommodation for the whole household, centred around the Great Hall, and surrounded by a strong wall. As new methods of attack developed, the outer fortifications became more elaborate in order to withstand them. Second and third lines of defence were placed within the outer wall which was built higher and thicker than before and reinforced with towers and galleries where archers could position themselves to fend off enemies. The living quarters also became more comfortable and extended beyond the keep into further stone buildings constructed in the courtyard. By the middle of the seventeenth century, however, castles could be easily demolished by the powerful new artillery and so they gradually ceased to be used.

CAT

Large group of carnivorous MAMMALS distributed over many parts of the world, which includes the LION, TIGER, JAGUAR, LEOPARD, PANTHER, puma and CHEETAH. Most breeds of domestic cat are probably descended from a type of African wild cat. They were already very popular as domesticated pets with the ancient Egyptians.

CATHEDRAL

A church which is presided over by a bishop and is therefore the spiritual and administrative centre of a whole district or diocese. In the past some cathedrals served as palace churches, such as Aachen in West Germany. Others were abbey or monastery churches, such as Westminster Abbey in London.

CATHERINE the Great (1729–96)

Empress of Russia, German by birth but married to the weak and unpopular Tsar Peter III whom she overthrew. As Catherine II she introduced many social reforms and extended Russia's frontiers southwards and westwards to the Black Sea and into POLAND.

CATHODE RAY TUBE

This electronic apparatus consists essentially of an electronic gun which causes a thin beam of electrons to strike a fluorescent screen at the flattened end of a vacuum tube and so cause a spot of light. The intensity of the spot is controlled by a control grid. In the electrostatic type of CRT two pairs of deflector plates are placed in the line of the beam, and by applying suitable voltages to these the electron beam can be deflected as required. The magnetic type of CRT has an external system of coils which develop magnetic fields, and by applying electric currents to the deflection coils the electron beam's position, and hence the spot of light on the screen, can be changed. In TELEVISION the changing light signals are applied to the control grid so that the spot of light varies in intensity, while electromagnets bend the beam of electrons to cause the spot of light to trace a zig-zag pattern of light on the screen and make up a picture.

CAVENDISH, Henry (1731–1810)

English scientist who discovered hydrogen gas and the composition of water. The Cavendish Physical Laboratory in Cambridge is named after him.

CAVY

Group of South American rodents, including guinea pigs. They are timid creatures that live in burrows and eat plants.

CAXTON, William (c. 1422–91)

English printer. He started his career in commerce, then learned the new craft of printing from movable type in Germany. In 1476 he set up, in Westminster, London, the first British printing press. Among his achievements was the first printed edition of Chaucer's *The Canterbury Tales*.

CELL

The basic unit of all living matter, plant and animal. A cell consists of a nucleus containing CHROMOSOMES, a fluid called cytoplasm and a membrane. Plant cells also have a cell wall (cellulose) and CHLOROPHYLL. Individual cells themselves perform all the basic functions of life – digestion, respiration, reproduction. An adult human being has an estimated thousand million million cells in his or her body. *See also* GENETICS.

CELTS

Race of people who migrated westwards from central Europe to most parts of Italy, Spain, Gaul (France) and Britain, from about the

Celtic cross, Louth, Ireland

seventh to the fourth centuries BC. They were war-like people, but skilled craftsmen, good farmers, and gifted poets and musicians. Their priests were Druids. Many aspects of their culture have survived, including the old Celtic languages of Welsh, Gaelic, Irish, Manx, Cornish and Breton.

CENSUS

The counting of the people of a country. The first census in England, although not called by that name nor for that purpose, was William the Conqueror's survey of the country's people and property in 1085, which was entered in the Domesday Book. The first official census in Great Britain was taken in 1800. Since then a census has usually been taken every ten years.

CENTRAL AFRICAN REPUBLIC

Independent African state just north of the Equator. Formerly the French colony of Ubangi Shari. It is a little larger than France itself with an area of 622,984 sq km (240,549 sq miles) but has a population of only about 2 million. The capital is Bangui.

CERVANTES Saavedra, Miguel de (1547–1616)

Spanish author and dramatist. He led an adventurous life as a soldier, losing his left hand at the Battle of Lepanto. He wrote many books and plays, but his fame now rests on his classic novel *Don Quixote*, the satirical but also moving story of the deluded knight and his faithful servant Sancho Panza.

CÉZANNE, Paul (1839–1906)

French painter, born in Aix-en-Provence, and working there for much of his life. He was influenced by the work of the Impressionists (*see* IMPRESSIONISM), but developed a style which, in turn, influenced the development of CUBISM.

CHAD

Independent African state ruled by France from 1897 to 1960. It has an area of 1,284,000 sq km (495,782 sq miles), which is more than twice the size of France, but a population of only 4,513,000. The capital is N'Djaména. Much of Chad lies within the Sahara, including the Tibesti Mountains. Civil wars, which continued into the 1980s, have marred progress since 1965.

CHADWICK, Sir James (1891–1974)

British physicist who discovered the neutron, one of the particles of the atom.

CHAGALL, Marc (born 1887)

Russian painter, inspired largely by Russian-Jewish folk art and noted for the soft, dream-like quality of his work.

CHAMBERLAIN, Neville (1869–1940)

British statesman and member of a famous political family. He became prime minister in 1937 and entered into the 1938 Munich Agreement with HITLER in an unsuccessful attempt to avoid war, which broke out in September 1939. In 1940 he resigned and died the same year. *See also* WORLD WAR II.

CHAMBER MUSIC

Music written for performance in a chamber, or large room, by a small combination of instruments, as distinct from that written for performance in a big concert hall by a full orchestra. The most common forms of chamber music are the piano trio (piano, violin and cello) and the string quartet (two violins, viola and cello). Combinations of five, six, seven, eight or nine instruments are called quintets, sextets, septets, octets and nonets respectively; larger groupings of instruments are described as 'ensembles'.

The chameleon uses its long tail to grip its support

CHAMELEON

Group of REPTILES belonging to the lizard family, found mostly in Africa and the island of Madagascar. Special features are their eyes which can move independently of one another, their very long tongues which they use to catch insects, and a certain ability to change skin colour to blend in with their surroundings. They also have long tails, and the largest species can measure up to 60 cm (24 in) from head to tip·of tail, though most are much smaller than this.

CHAMOIS

Fleet-footed MAMMAL, native to the Alps, similar in many ways to both GOATS and ANTELOPES, but recognizable by its short, hooked horns. 'Chammy', a soft leather for cleaning, was at one time made from chamois skin.

CHAMPLAIN, Samuel de (c. 1567–1635)

French explorer who travelled up the St Lawrence river in Canada and charted much of the region of the Great Lakes. Also founder of the city of Quebec and first Governor of French Canada.

CHANCELLOR OF THE EXCHEQUER

The CABINET Minister who looks after the nation's money. It is the oldest office in the government and goes back to the days of Henry I. In those days the Chancellor sat at a table covered by a chequered cloth to receive the taxes which were at that time collected by the sheriffs. The Chancellor is regarded as the most important minister after the PRIME MINISTER and is the Second Lord of the Treasury, the Prime Minister being the First.

CHANCERY

One of the three divisions of the High Court of Justice. The LORD CHANCELLOR is its head, though he does not himself act as one of the judges. One of the chief duties of the Chancery Division is to act as guardian to children and young people who have inherited property, and who are called 'Wards in Chancery'.

CHARLEMAGNE (Charles the Great, 742–814)

King of the Franks who extended his kingdom eastwards from France into present-day Germany, Austria and Yugoslavia, and southwards into Italy and Spain. As a great champion of Christianity and a man of immense energy he built many churches, monasteries and places of learning, while trying to establish order and justice throughout his domains. Pope Leo III crowned him Emperor of the HOLY ROMAN EMPIRE, which he administered from his own palace at Aachen (now in West Germany).

Charles I

CHARLES I (1600–49)

King of Great Britain who succeeded his father James I in 1625. His marriage to the French Catholic Princess Henrietta Maria and his own bad judgments brought increasing religious and political opposition to his reign, especially from the Scots and from Parliament. His attempt to arrest five members of the Parliament was the starting point for the ENGLISH CIVIL WAR. His forces were defeated by those of Parliament under the command of Oliver CROMWELL, and he was executed.

CHARLES II (1630–85)

Son of Charles I *(see above)* and King of Great Britain. He attempted an invasion of England from Scotland after his father's execution but was defeated by CROMWELL at the Battle of Worcester (1651). After a period of exile in France he was restored to the throne in 1660.

CHARLES EDWARD STUART. *See* JACOBITES.

CHARTISM

British working-class political movement, based on a People's Charter (1838) which demanded such reforms as Household Suffrage (i.e. the right to vote for the head of every household); secret ballot; equal electoral districts; and payment of MPs. In 1848 – the Year of Revolution in many European countries – a great petition and march on Parliament were planned. The march was banned, troops were called out, and the Chartist Movement disintegrated. But much of its spirit survived in the rise of the modern Labour Movement.

CHAUCER, Geoffrey (*c.* 1345–1400)

First great English poet. He served as a royal courier in France and Italy, and later held official posts in London. Here he was able to write his poetry. His masterpiece is *The Canterbury Tales*, a series of stories told by pilgrims on their way from London to the shrine of Canterbury.

The Man of Law from Chaucer's *Canterbury Tales*

CHEETAH

Member of the cat family, very similar in appearance to a leopard, native to many parts of Africa, the Middle East and India. It is the swiftest animal on earth over short distances, capable of reaching a speed of about 100 km/h (just over 60 mph).

Two cheetahs or hunting leopards

CHEKHOV, Anton Pavlovich (1860-1904)

Russian novelist and dramatist, trained as a doctor but soon turned to writing. His four most famous plays are *The Seagull, Uncle Vanya, Three Sisters* and *The Cherry Orchard*. Although he is known chiefly for these plays, Chekhov also wrote novels and short stories, all with his brand of satirical humour.

CHEMISTRY

Scientific study of materials – solids, liquids, gases – their composition, structure and reaction to each other. Chemical reactions may all be described in terms of the exchange of electrons between ions, atoms and molecules; the exchange of nuclear material like neutrons and protons is nuclear physics. Chemistry recognizes that all matter consists either of ELEMENTS (substances that cannot be reduced to any other substances); or a combination of elements in fixed proportions, called compounds; or a combination of elements not in any fixed proportions, called mixtures. It also recognizes that elements are made up of minute particles of matter called ATOMS, and bases its methods of describing elements, compounds and reactions on this fact. Each element is represented by one or two letters, and the number of atoms of an element which combine with those of other elements to form one molecule of a compound is expressed accordingly. Thus 2 atoms of Hydrogen (H) combine with 1 atom of oxygen (O) to produce one molecule of water (H_2O). All chemical formulae are expressed in these terms, and these can then be applied to descriptions of chemical reactions. For example, calcium carbonate (chalk) has the formula ($CaCO_3$), meaning that each molecule consists of one atom of calcium (Ca), one atom of carbon (C) and three atoms of oxygen (O). If calcium carbonate is heated it breaks up into two other substances, carbon dioxide (CO_2) and lime (CaO). The reaction is expressed as a chemical equation:

$$CaCO_3 = CaO + Co_2$$

The big division within chemistry is between organic and inorganic chemistry. Organic chemistry is concerned primarily with the materials of living things or with materials which are in some way the product of living things, and has much to do with the many compounds involving the elements carbon, hydrogen, oxygen and nitrogen. Inorganic chemistry deals with non-living materials like metals and salts.

In this encyclopedia the discoveries which have led to the modern science of chemistry are discussed under the many individual entries devoted to the chemists who made them.

CHESS

Game for two players. The chess board has sixty-four alternately coloured squares, and the game is played with two opposing sets of pieces, comprising a king, queen, two rooks (castles), two bishops, two knights and eight pawns. Each type of piece has its own special moves, and can 'capture' (i.e. remove from the board) opposing pieces by moving on to their squares. The players make alternate moves (white always starting), and the object of the game is to place the opponent's king in such a position that it cannot avoid capture. This is checkmate. In fact, many games do not reach checkmate, one or other player choosing to resign when a decisive position has been reached.

Chess is a very ancient game, probably originating in India, though not in its present form. It was well established in Europe by the time of the Crusades, and has been played throughout the civilized world for hundreds of years. Some of the greatest world chess champions have been Wilhelm Steinitz (Austria), Emanuel Lasker (Germany), José Capablanca (Cuba), Alexander Alekhine (Russia), Mikhail Botvinnik (Russia), Bobby Fischer (USA).

CHILE

South American republic situated between the ANDES mountains and the PACIFIC OCEAN. It is a long narrow country, stretching from north to south for 4,480 km (2,800 miles), but at no point wider than 362 km (225 miles). Its total area is 756,945 sq km (292,274 sq miles), with a population of 11 million. The capital is Santiago and the chief port Valparaiso. The name 'Chile' comes from the Indian word *chilli* (place where the land ends), but the official language is Spanish.

Chile is a country of climatic extremes, ranging from the Atacama desert, where rain has never been recorded, to some of the wettest areas in the world. But the centre of the country has a warm, temperate climate, ideal for cereals and fruit. The country is also rich in mineral deposits, especially copper.

CHIMPANZEE

Most intelligent of the group of anthropoid APES, native to the tropical forests of central and west Africa. An adult male weighs about 200 kg (450 lb), though the 'pygmy' chimpanzees, found south of the Congo river, are much smaller.

CHINA

Asian republic with an area (including TAIWAN) of 9,596,961 sq km (3,705,610 sq miles) – the largest after the USSR and CANADA; and a population of 980 million – the largest. Leading cities include Peking, the capital, Shanghai, Nanking and Canton. The country extends from the Tropic of Cancer in the south to Mongolia and the USSR in the north, and from the PACIFIC in the east to the vast Sinkiang and Tibet regions, including much of the HIMALAYAS, in the west. The longest river is the YANGTZE KIANG.

China's recorded history goes back to about 2200 BC, by which time there were already well-established communities in the region of the Hwang Ho (Yellow River) and elsewhere. From that period until the twentieth century Chinese history is divided up into dynasties. It was during the Ch'in dynasty (3rd century BC) that the Great Wall of China was built. The most famous dynasties, noted for their beautiful arts and crafts, are the T'ang (AD 618–907), Sung (960–1279) and Ming (1378–1644). The Manchu dynasty, the last, was a time when China was increasingly exploited by European colonial powers, and by the United States. A republic was created in 1912 by Sun Yat-Sen. After WORLD WAR II Chiang Kai-Shek's leadership was challenged by the Communists

The Great Wall of China, built about 200 BC

under MAO TSE-TUNG, and in 1949 a Communist republic – the People's Republic of China – was declared. China is a mainly agricultural country, rice being the staple food, followed by wheat, barley and other cereals. Cotton and tea are two major cash crops. China also has large deposits of coal and some oil and, in the 1980s, the government encouraged industrialization and the production of consumer goods.

CHINCHILLA

RODENT noted for its fur, and native to certain parts of the Andes mountains of South America. It is about the size of a SQUIRREL.

CHIPMUNK

Name for the American ground SQUIRREL or striped gopher, also found in parts of Asia. Chipmunks differ from other species of squirrel by living in burrows.

CHIPPENDALE, Thomas (1718–79)

English cabinet-maker and wood carver who gave his name to one of the best-known of all furniture styles.

CHLOROPHYLL

Green pigment found in almost all plants. It is an essential requirement for the process of PHOTOSYNTHESIS, by which plants make their food. The name comes from two Greek words meaning 'green' and 'leaf'.

CHOPIN, Frédéric François (1810–49)

Polish-French composer, born near Warsaw, but living for most of his adult life in Paris. Composed almost exclusively for the piano, mainly in the form of short pieces – studies (*études*), preludes, nocturnes, impromptus, ballads, waltzes – creating an entirely new pianistic style. Two of his other sets of piano pieces – the mazurkas and polonaises – express his life-long devotion to the cause of Polish nationalism and liberty. Chopin was also a superb performer and revolutionized the technique of piano playing.

CHRISTIANITY

Religion based on the life and teachings of Jesus of Nazareth, and especially on the belief that he was an incarnation of God and that after his death by crucifixion he was restored to life and ascended to heaven. Thus he is known as the Christ, from the Greek *khristos* 'the anointed one', which is a translation of the Hebrew *masiah* or Messiah.

Jesus lived and died within the ROMAN EMPIRE, and it was within that empire that Christianity grew, first with the teachings of Jesus's own disciples (followers) and through the work of such apostles (messengers) as St Paul. Christians were persecuted by the Roman Empire up to the time of the Emperor CONSTANTINE (fourth century AD) who himself became a convert. He moved his capital to BYZANTIUM, which he re-named Constantinople, and for hundreds of years the

Christian Church became polarized around the administrative centres of Constantinople itself (from which grew the Eastern Orthodox Church) and Rome (from which grew the ROMAN CATHOLIC CHURCH). At the same time missionaries carried Christianity to the far corners of what were, or had been, parts of the Roman Empire, including Britain. There was a serious break between the Orthodox and Catholic Churches, called a Schism, in 1054. In the fifteenth century there was an even greater disruption, following the creation, by Martin LUTHER, of the Protestant Church, and for nearly three hundred years there was constant war and persecution throughout Europe between Catholics and members of the various Protestant churches. Only in this century have attempts been made to unify Christendom once more.

Nevertheless, Christianity has inspired many of the greatest works of art and architecture, books and musical compositions. It has also spread to many parts of the world, mainly during the period of European colonization of the Americas, Africa and the Far East. It has more adherents than any other religion, including an estimated 450 million Catholics, 230 million Protestants and 130 million Eastern Orthodox members.

The Christian calendar – now used by most countries – begins with the birth of Jesus, i.e. AD1, meaning *Anno Domini*, 'The Year of Our Lord', as distinct from BC, 'Before Christ'.

See also APOSTLE, BAPTISM, BIBLE, CHURCH OF ENGLAND, CHURCH OF IRELAND, CHURCH OF SCOTLAND, CONFIRMATION, CREED, LUTHER, MASS, POPE, PURITANS, REFORMATION, ROMAN CATHOLIC CHURCH.

Medieval carving of the flight into Egypt

CHROMATOGRAPHY

A method used in chemistry for separating mixtures. The mixture to be analysed is first made into a solution. This is poured on to some absorbent material, such as cellulose, in a glass tube. Some parts of the solution are absorbed. The rest remain, to be further analysed.

CHROMOSOME

A thread-like part of the nucleus of each plant and animal CELL. Each species (kind of plant or animal) has a characteristic number of chromosomes. Human beings have forty-six chromosomes set up as twenty-three pairs in most of their cells. Chromosomes are largely made up of DNA (deoxyribonucleic acid) and proteins. They consist of DNA units called genes. *See also* GENETICS.

CHURCHILL, Sir Winston Leonard Spencer (1874–1965)

British statesman, son of Lord Randolph Churchill and an American mother, Jennie Jerome. As a young man he joined the army and served in the Sudan; then became a newspaper correspondent, was captured during the BOER WAR, escaped and returned to England. He started his political career as a Conservative, then joined the Liberal Party and held several ministerial posts up to and including the early years of WORLD WAR I, after which he saw more war service. He returned to the Con-

Churchill demonstrates his famous victory sign

servatives after the war and became CHANCELLOR OF THE EXCHEQUER. In the years leading up to WORLD WAR II Churchill was an isolated figure politically, but in 1940 he became PRIME MINISTER and directed the British war effort and foreign policy until 1945, when he and his party were defeated at the General Election.

He served again as Prime Minister between 1951 and 1955. Sir Winston Churchill is best remembered today for the many famous speeches he made during World War II. He also wrote his war memoirs, *The Second World War*.

CHURCH OF ENGLAND

Its origins go back to the reign of HENRY VIII and his repudiation of the Pope's authority. Archbishop Cranmer began to create a separate church, and after a period of religious dispute between Catholics and Protestants, the Church of England, or Anglican Church, became established by law during the reign of CHARLES II. Its spiritual head is the Archbishop of Canterbury. The Anglican Communion consists of the Church of England itself and similar churches overseas, mostly in countries formerly part of the British Empire.

CHURCH OF IRELAND

Similar in many respects to the Church of England, confined mostly to Northern Ireland, and an independent body. Its head is the Archbishop of Armagh.

CHURCH OF SCOTLAND

Dates back to the REFORMATION and the figure of John Knox. He supported a form of church called Presbyterianism, from the Greek *presbyteros* ('Elder'), describing a type of governing body. In 1560 a Scottish Parliament accepted Knox's ideas, and the Presbyterian Church of Scotland was created. It is governed by a General Assembly under a President, or Moderator.

Right Scene from the ballet *Raymonda*

A scene from the film *King Kong*

Judy Garland in *The Wizard of Oz* (1939)

CICERO, Marcus Tullius (106–43 BC)

Roman orator, politician and writer. He led a stormy political life during the time of JULIUS CAESAR, which ended with his murder by soldiers commanded by Mark Antony and others. He is remembered for his brilliant speeches as a lawyer, and for such of his written works as *On the Republic* and *On the Laws*.

CINEMA

The invention of cinematography or motion pictures, like many other inventions, cannot be confidently attributed to one person. In England, probably in 1889, William Friese-Greene first produced moving pictures of a London street scene which could be projected back onto a screen. In France, at just about the same time, the brothers Louis and Auguste Lumière were perfecting a very similar method for photographing and then projecting a quick succession of still pictures that give the impression of continuous movement. In America Thomas Alva EDISON produced his kinetoscope, which contained a roll, or film, of successive photographic frames. The spectator could see these projected back through a small viewing panel, illuminated from within, similar to that of a mechanical penny-in-the-slot machine. The term 'motion pictures' is a little misleading for in fact in a cinema we see a rapid succession of

Left The kingfisher

still pictures (nowadays about 25 in a second) with darkness between them. The very first 'films' or 'movies' in the accepted sense of the word date from the 1890s, and were originally shown as novelty turns in music-hall shows. In 1902 the Frenchman Georges Méliès made the first film with a proper story, *Trip to the Moon,* which for its time created the most remarkable effects. In 1903 Edwin S. Porter's *The Great Train Robbery* was another landmark in the pioneering days of film-making. During WORLD WAR I, in the United States, actors and actresses were beginning to be known by their films, notably Charlie Chaplin and Mary Pickford. Also during that war the American D. W. Griffith made two of the first films to be taken seriously as artistic and technical creations, *The Birth of a Nation* and *Intolerance*. All these had been silent films. Dialogue, so far as it was needed, had to be interpolated into the film; music had to be provided 'live' by an orchestra or solo pianist. A way of recording sound simultaneously with the film was developed during the 1920s, and the first sound film, or 'talkie', *The Jazz Singer,* was produced in 1927. Soon after, Walt DISNEY perfected the craft of the animated cartoon with the creation of such characters as Mickey Mouse and Donald Duck; and colour was also introduced into films. Later technical developments, such as Cinerama, were largely in response to competition from television.

The Moscow circus, famous for its trained horses

CIRCUS

A type of spectacular entertainment involving performing animals, gymnasts and clowns, and in its present form dating from the eighteenth century. The word is inherited from Roman times, the Circus Maximus in Rome being a huge arena designed for chariot racing and gladiatorial contests. Circus can also describe a conjunction of roads, as in Piccadilly Circus in London.

CIVIL RIGHTS

The basic rights extended to the individual citizen within a larger community. They include freedom from persecution or discrimination on grounds of personal belief, religion or race, and access to the due processes of the law. They have become a major issue in world politics because in many countries they are shown not to exist, or to be open to abuse.

CIVIL SERVANTS

People who work for the government of a country, in helping to draw up legislation, or helping to administer the many departments or agencies of government, such as finance, health and social security, environment, and the armed forces.

CLAUDE LORRAIN (1600–82)

French artist, born in Lorraine, whose real name was Claude Gellée. Famous for his landscape paintings, which had a great influence on the work of other artists.

CLAUDIUS I (10 BC–AD 44)

Roman Emperor. He succeeded to the title after the assassination of Caligula. With his physical disabilities he was an unlikely man to head the ROMAN EMPIRE, but he showed unexpected abilities. He strengthened the administration of the Empire and completed the conquest of Britain, which he visited. He was poisoned, probably by his wife Agrippina.

CLAUSEWITZ, Karl von (1780–1831)

Prussian military historian and scholar, whose writings on the subject have been studied by many other generals and war leaders.

CLEMENCEAU, Georges (1841–1929)

French statesman. As Prime Minister and Minister of the Interior, he introduced many social reforms; but best remembered for his leadership of the nation during WORLD WAR I, and for his part in drawing up the peace treaty of Versailles. Popularly known as 'The Tiger'.

CLEOPATRA (69–30 BC)

Queen of Egypt. Her whole life was bound up with the fortunes of Rome. She was enthroned by JULIUS CAESAR, then entered into a fateful alliance with Mark Antony, which ended in their suicides after defeat at the hands of Octavian (AUGUSTUS CAESAR). She was noted for her great beauty.

CLIMATE

The general weather pattern of an area assessed over a long period, and based on calculations regarding temperature and precipitation (rainfall or snow). Climate depends on many things, including distance from the equator, altitude, distance from the sea, strength and direction of prevailing wind, direction and temperature of ocean currents. It largely determines the vegetation and general appearance of a region, and greatly affects the life-style of the people. The world's main climatic regions are classed as follows: equatorial, warm temperate, cool temperate, arctic. *See also* METEOROLOGY.

CLIVE, Robert (1725–74)

English soldier and administrator. He joined the East India Company as a young man and spent much of his life in that country. As an army officer he played a major part in the defeat of French forces in India. His greatest triumph was his subsequent defeat of a much larger Indian army at Plassey (1757), after which he became Governor of Bengal. Thus Clive laid the foundations for British rule in India. But charges of corruption laid before Parliament made him ill and depressed and he committed suicide.

CLOCKS AND WATCHES

A clock or watch is a device for indicating the passage of time by mechanical or electronic means. It is not known for certain who invented the mechanical clock, but it may have been a Benedictine monk named Gerbert who later became Pope Sylvester II. His clock was installed in the church at Magdeburg, Germany, in 996. The oldest existing clock in England is in Salisbury Cathedral, dating from 1386. For hundreds of years the motive power for clocks was supplied by heavy weights suspended beneath the clock itself. The invention of a mainspring within the clock then allowed timepieces to be much smaller, and led to the construction of watches which could be carried in a pocket or, much later, worn on the wrist.

Today many clocks are operated by electricity, and the most accurate of all are atomic clocks which are tuned to the vibration of atoms. They are reckoned to gain or lose only a few seconds every 100,000 years.

A recent development in clock and watch design is the substitution of figures (digits) for the traditional circular clock face marked out in hours, minutes and seconds.

The inside workings of a wrist watch

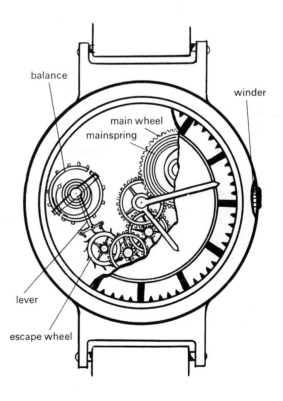

balance
winder
main wheel
mainspring
lever
escape wheel

Four different types of cloud:
(top left) *cumulus;* (top right) *alto-cumulus;* (bottom left) *cumulo-nimbus;* (bottom right); *strato-cumulus.*

CLOUD

Condensed water vapour floating in the air above the earth. The following are the principal cloud formations:

Upper Clouds: average altitude 9,000 m (30,000 ft).

   Cirrus: Detached, featherlike clouds

   Cirro-stratus: A thin, white cloud sheet

Intermediate Clouds: between 3,000 and 7,000 m (10,000 and 23,000 ft).

   Cirro-cumulus: Small rounded masses of white clouds (mackerel sky)

   Alto-cumulus: Larger rounded masses, arranged in groups

   Alto-stratus: Dense sheet of grey or bluish clouds

Lower Clouds: 2,000 m (6,550 ft).

   Stato-cumulus: Large masses of dull grey cloud

   Cumulo-nimbus: Dense layer of dark shapeless clouds (rain clouds)

Clouds of Diurnal ascending currents

   Cumulus: Apex 1,800 m (6,095 ft); base 1,400 m (4,500 ft). Thick cloud with flat base and dome-shaped upper part.

   Cumulo-nimbus: Apex 3,000 to 8,000 m (10,000 to 25,000 ft); base 1,400 m (4,500 ft). Great masses of cloud in the form of mountains

High fogs: under 1,000 m (3,000 ft).

   Stratus: A uniform, foglike cloud in the air

COAL

Black combustible mineral rock consisting chiefly of carbon, derived from the wood and foliage of dead and decayed trees. The coal forests flourished about 200 million years ago, and it was under the weight of deposits above them that they slowly turned to coal.

There are two main types of coal: anthracite, or hard coal, and bituminous, or soft coal. The latter burns with much more smoke than the former. Coal may be obtained by open-cast mining, but most deposits are fairly deep under the ground and pit shafts have to be sunk into them.

The INDUSTRIAL REVOLUTION depended

largely upon coal to power the steam-engine. Today the sources of power are more varied, with oil and gas (fossil fuels closely related in origin to coal), and nuclear energy. But coal remains an important source of power. It is also a source of many valuable by-products which contribute to the manufacture of detergents, antiseptics, drugs, dyes and insecticides.

The principal coal-producing countries are: USSR, USA, China, East Germany, West Germany, Poland and Great Britain.

COBBETT, William (1763–1835)

English politician and social reformer, especially concerned with agrarian reform. His book *Rural Rides* gives a vivid picture of early nineteenth-century English country life.

COBRA. *See* SNAKES

COCKCROFT, Sir John Douglas (1897–1967)

British nuclear physicist who was the first to split atoms artificially and so pioneered the development of nuclear energy.

COELACANTH

Lobe-finned fish from which four-legged land animals developed hundreds of millions of years ago. It was thought that all such creatures had been extinct for millions of years until one was caught off South Africa in 1938.

COLERIDGE, Samuel Taylor (1772–1834)

English poet of the romantic period. He wrote comparatively little, but *The Rime of the Ancient Mariner* is one of the best-known poems in the English language. Also collaborated with William WORDSWORTH on the *Lyrical Ballads*.

COLOMBIA

South American republic whose shores are washed by both the ATLANTIC and PACIFIC OCEANS. It is more than twice the size of France with an area of 1,138,914 sq km (439,761 sq miles), and has a population of about 26 million. The capital is Bogotá. Most of the country is a great grassy plain, but there is also tropical jungle. There are oil fields and gold mines.

Colombia takes its name from Christopher COLUMBUS, who sailed close to it, although the Spanish explorer Alonso de Ojedo had already landed on its shores. It remained under Spanish rule until 1824, when a revolution, led by Simón Bolívar, secured its independence.

A nucleonic probe detects coal at the working face

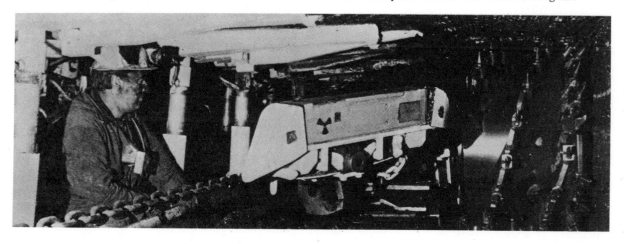

COLOUR

Sir Isaac NEWTON first began to develop the modern scientific theory of colour. Following his discovery of the spectrum it is possible to define any colour in terms of the wavelength of the light of which it is composed. Light consists of electro-magnetic waves. The wavelength, that is the distance from crest to crest of the wave, determines the colour of the light. The light of the shortest wavelength, which is 0.00004 cm, looks violet, while the light of the longest wavelength, which is 0.00007 cm, looks red. It is more convenient to express wavelength in Angström units, one such unit being a hundred-millionth of a cm. We can then say that the wavelengths of visible light range from about 4,000 Angström units at one end of the spectrum to about 7,000 Angström units at the other.

The colour of an object is caused by the fact that the material of the object absorbs some wavelengths from the light falling on it, and reflects others. For instance, a blade of grass, when white light falls on it, reflects only green and absorbs the rest. However, the green is not pure (monochromatic) but a mixture, to which we give the name of the chief, or dominant, wavelength present. Thus the dominant wavelength of the light from green grass could be 5,200 Angström units, or it might be 5,400 Angström units or in fact one of quite a number of wavelengths, all of which produce a green sensation. The only way to find out the actual dominant wavelength is to use scientific apparatus such as a colorimeter or a spectrophotometer.

Dominant wavelength is not the only fact by means of which we judge colour. For example, an orange reflects light with a dominant wavelength of about 5,900 Angström units. But if we take a paint of exactly the same hue and then mix black with it, the dominant wavelength is still the same, but the appearance has been changed. It looks darker and, if dark enough, may even be brown. So the lightness of a surface is an important factor in determining colour sensation. This is measured in terms of the proportion of light reflected. In other words the luminance factor of the surface has to be known. Furthermore, the colour depends on how much of the dominant wavelength is present. This quantity is called the purity. In addition to these factors there is the quality of the light being used. For instance, colours look different in electric light and in daylight.

There are thus four measurable factors in determining a colour in physics – dominant wavelength, purity, luminance factor, colour of the illuminant. *See also* SPECTRUM.

Christopher Columbus

COLUMBUS, Christopher (1451–1506)

Italian navigator, born in Genoa. Inspired by the travels of MARCO POLO, he sought a route to China and the East by travelling westwards round the world. He finally gained support for such a voyage from the King of Spain, and in

1492 sailed across the Atlantic in the *Santa Maria*. He first went ashore on an island in the BAHAMAS, which he named San Salvador. On that and subsequent voyages, Columbus explored Cuba, Jamaica, Trinidad and the mainland of South America. He retired to Spain, and died still convinced that he had at last reached Asia.

COMET

A comparatively light heavenly body with a luminous tail of gaseous matter which is ejected from the comet's body by the pressure of the sun's radiation as it approaches the solar system. The length of the tail varies but it can reach lengths exceeding the distance of the Earth from the sun. Comets follow either elliptic paths round the sun or parabolic paths towards or away from the sun. At one time it was thought that they came from outside our galactic system, but now it is known that many belong to it. Perhaps the best known is Halley's Comet which was first studied and predicted by Edmund Halley (1656–1742). This is visible from the Earth at intervals of about seventy-five years and should next appear in 1986.

COMMANDMENTS, The Ten

Probably the oldest part of Hebrew tradition. They are the foundation upon which the religion of Israel was built and developed; and they have profoundly influenced the ideals of many nations to this day. They are set out in the Old Testament (Exodus 20).

COMMUNISM

Political creed, put at its simplest as meaning 'From each according to his ability, to each according to his need'; practised or preached in a very broad sense by many people at different times and places. But especially associated with the nineteenth-century conflict between labour (those who produced goods and earned wages) and capital (those who invested in industry or secured profit), and the political thinking that this situation prompted. The principal thinker was Karl MARX, whose *Communist Manifesto* (1848), written in collaboration with Friedrich ENGELS, initiated much political action. By the turn of the century there were Communist parties in most industrial countries. In 1917 the RUSSIAN REVOLUTION brought about the creation of the first truly Communist state – the UNION OF SOVIET SOCIALIST REPUBLICS. After WORLD WAR II the victorious Soviet Union kept control of practically all the territories it had occupied, establishing Communist regimes in POLAND, CZECHOSLOVAKIA, HUNGARY, ROMANIA, BULGARIA and East GERMANY. In 1949 CHINA also turned to Communism, and since then there have been created several other Communist states.

COMOROS

An island republic in the northern part of the Mozambique Channel, it has an area of 2,171 sq km (838 sq miles) and a population of 414,000. A former French territory, the Comoros were declared independent in 1975.

COMPASS

The invention of the compass is usually credited to the Chinese round about the year 1200 BC. It was found that certain elongated stones had the property of turning round and pointing in the same direction when hung by a cord at their centre. These were lodestones – a type of iron ore which had become magnetized. This early type of compass was operated by placing one of these stones on a piece of wood which floated in a bowl of water.

The magnetic compass of today consists of a circular bowl suspended by two hinged rings in a box or binnacle. The bowl contains a paper compass card which is divided into degrees or points. Magnetic needles are attached to the card which are attracted to the Magnetic North. The card always points to the north, while the bowl turns around it.

COMPUTER

Automatic, electronic machine designed especially for the rapid solution of very complex and time-consuming mathematical problems. Also referred to as an 'electronic brain'. There are various types of which the two most important are the *digital* computer and the *analogue* computer. The digital is the larger, more expensive type used in science, business and industry. It handles figures (digits) in a similar way to that employed by an adding machine. It produces a special numerical result by breaking down a problem into a succession of the four arithmetical operations of addition, subtraction, multiplication and division, by any of the procedures known in numerical analysis.

The analogue computer uses physical quantities as 'analogues' to the variables being solved. It handles continuous data such as charts and curves. Each point on a curve is the analogue of the information plotted, just as distances along a slide rule are analogues of numbers. The analogue computer produces other charts or curves which are usually less precise than the digital results. This type of computer is used in technological studies.

CONCERTO

Type of musical composition, developed from the seventeenth-century Italian *concerto grosso* (or great concerto), which was a piece for a string orchestra, usually with passages for full orchestra interspersed with passages for a few instruments only. The true concerto, as a work for a solo instrument with orchestra, almost always in three movements, emerged during the eighteenth century. At this time there was also the *sinfonia concertante* for a small group of soloists with orchestra. Later, concertos for two or three solo instruments were often called 'double' or 'triple' concertos. There is also the concerto for orchestra, with special passages for various groups of instruments, which may in some ways be regarded as the descendant of the *concerto grosso*.

CONDOR

Type of VULTURE native to South America and especially the ANDES, with a big wingspan of about 3 m (10 ft). Its other main feature is its bald red head; the male also has a ruff round the base of the neck.

CONDUCTING

The art or technique of directing a musical performance. The idea of beating time, as a guide to musicians, goes back hundreds of years, to the time when most music was sung by choirs. With the rise of the orchestra in the seventeenth century, composers, who were almost always responsible for the performance of their own music, often beat time with a heavy staff upon the floor. Later they directed performances by giving a musical lead on a violin or at the harpsichord. Conducting as we think of it today started in the nineteenth century, when larger orchestras and more complex music required someone whose sole concern it was to co-ordinate the performance. Conductors also became more and more concerned with matters of interpretation, so that performances of a piece of music by one conductor or another became almost as significant as the music itself.

Colin Davis conducting the BBC Symphony Orchestra

Some outstanding conductors of the last one hundred years have been Hans von Bülow, Hans Richter, Gustav MAHLER, Arturo Toscanini, Wilhelm Furtwängler, Sir Thomas Beecham, Bruno Walter, Pierre Monteux, Sir John Barbirolli.

CONFEDERATION OF BRITISH INDUSTRY (CBI)

Association representing the views of managements in industry, as the Trade Unions represent the employees. It was formed in 1965 by an amalgamation of the British Employers' Confederation, the Federation of British Industries and the National Association of British Manufacturers.

CONFIRMATION

In the Anglican, Eastern Orthodox, Lutheran, Roman Catholic and some other churches, confirmation is the ceremony by which those baptized after birth 'confirm' the baptismal vows made for them by godparents, and so are admitted into full church membership.

CONFUCIUS (K'ung Ch'iu *c.* 551–479 BC)

Chinese philosopher whose doctrines of tolerance and simplicity profoundly influenced Chinese civilization. He taught his disciples what he considered to be the principles of good conduct in both personal terms and in government. His teachings are recorded in a book called the *Analects*.

CONGO, People's Republic of

Equatorial African state with an area of 342,000 sq km (132,054 sq miles) and a population of just over 1½ million. The capital is Brazzaville. Formerly part of French Equatorial Africa, it gained independence in 1960.

CONGO, Republic of. *See* ZAÏRE

CONGRESS

Name given to the national legislative body of the UNITED STATES OF AMERICA. It consists of two elected assemblies, the Senate and the House of Representatives. The House of Representatives is comparable to the British House of Commons in that its 435 members are elected according to the distribution of the population. The Senate, by contrast, is composed of two members from each of the fifty states, irrespective of population. Unlike the British PRIME MINISTER, the President of the United States is elected on a separate basis from either the House of Representatives or the Senate, and is not a member of either assembly.

CONGREVE, William (1670–1729)

English dramatist of the Restoration period. His most famous play is the comedy *The Way of the World*.

CONIFER or CONE-BEARING PLANT

A tree or plant that bears its seeds in cones. The leaves of conifers are usually evergreen and shaped like needles. The male flowers are catkins, but the female flowers develop into cones. The seeds fall to the ground from between the scales of these cones. Common conifers include pines, spruces, cedars, firs, junipers, larches, yews and cypresses.

CONRAD, Joseph (1857–1924)

British novelist of Polish birth, whose knowledge of life at sea provided the basis for most of his books, including *Lord Jim* and *Outcast of the Islands*.

CONSERVATIVE PARTY

British political party, developed out of the seventeenth and eighteenth-century Tory Party. It emerged as the Conservative Party during Benjamin DISRAELI's period of leadership – as a party prepared to accept change but regarding itself as the guardian of tradition and established values. Conservative Prime Ministers of this century include Stanley Baldwin, Neville CHAMBERLAIN, Winston CHURCHILL, Anthony Eden, Harold Macmillan, Edward Heath and Margaret Thatcher.

CONSTABLE, John (1776–1837)

English artist, best known for his large-scale landscapes such as *The Hay Wain* (National Gallery, London). He was among the first to paint out-of-doors straight on to his canvas, and the vibrant colours and freshness of his oil sketches display his fascination with the changing moods of nature and of the weather and light.

CONSTANTINE the Great. *See* BYZANTINE EMPIRE and CHRISTIANITY

CONTINENTAL DRIFT

The Earth's crust is split into rigid blocks or 'plates', which include the land masses. These plates are moved by convection currents in the Earth's mantle, causing the continents to drift, or change position.

The voyages of Captain Cook

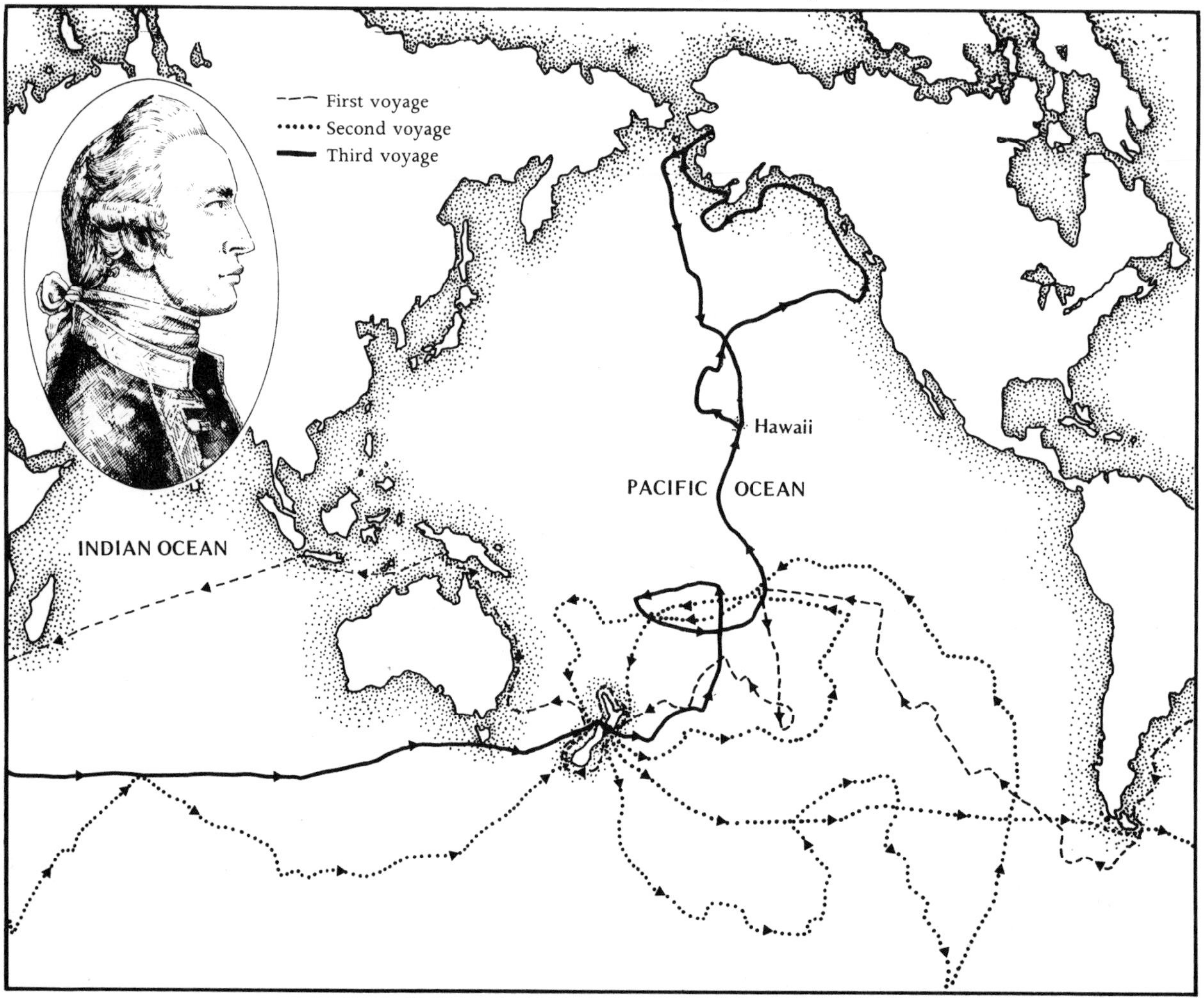

---- First voyage
····· Second voyage
——— Third voyage

INDIAN OCEAN

Hawaii

PACIFIC OCEAN

COOK, James (1728–79)

English naval captain and explorer. He made three voyages of discovery to the PACIFIC OCEAN, charting the coastline of NEW ZEALAND and the eastern coast of AUSTRALIA. He also sailed far into Antarctic waters.

COOPER, James Fenimore (1789–1851)

American novelist whose stories deal with the pioneering days of the American West. His best-known novel is *The Last of the Mohicans*.

COPERNICUS, Nicolas (1473–1543)

Polish astronomer, considered to be the father of modern ASTRONOMY. He rejected PTOLEMY's idea that the Earth was the centre of the SOLAR SYSTEM, reviving the notion of the Greek Aristarchus that the sun was the central body around which the planets, including Earth, revolved. He published his ideas in a work called *De Revolutionibus Orbitum Coelestium*, but they were not generally accepted for another hundred years.

Copernicus and a diagram of the solar system

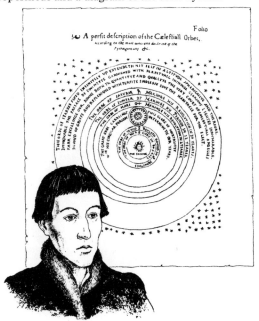

COPLAND, Aaron (born 1900)

American composer, many of whose works are inspired by JAZZ or other forms of American folk music. His compositions include the music for the ballets *Billy The Kid, Appalachian Spring* and *Rodeo*.

COPTIC CHURCH

A branch of the Christian Church centred in ETHIOPIA. The word *Copt* comes from the Greek for 'Egyptian', and the present Coptic Church has its origins in the early Christian communities that sprang up in Egypt and along the banks of the Nile.

CORAL

Limestone formations in the sea built up by millions of tiny animals. Coral reefs (ridges of coral near the sea surface) are only found in warm seas such as the South Pacific, because coral animals cannot live in cold water. There are three kinds of coral formation: fringing reefs which stretch from the shore into the sea; atolls which are small coral islands; and barrier reefs which are parallel to the coast but separated from it by fairly shallow water. The Great Barrier Reef of Australia, which is 2,012 km (1,250 miles) long, is the most extensive coral reef in the world.

CORELLI, Arcangelo (1653–1713)

Italian composer of the Baroque period who was one of the first to write important music for the VIOLIN and its related stringed instruments. the viola and cello.

CORMORANT

Sea bird which nests on coasts but is sometimes found on estuaries and rivers. It lives almost exclusively on fish for which it dives. The large kinds are more than 76 cm (30 in) long. They have webbed feet.

CORN LAWS

Laws intended to help British farmers by restricting the import of corn from abroad. There had been Corn Laws since 1361, but in the nineteenth century the inhabitants of the fast-growing towns demanded cheaper bread. The Anti Corn Law League was formed and the Corn Laws were repealed in 1846.

CORONA

Layer of gases that surrounds the surface of the SUN. They extend at least 13 million km (8 million miles) from the sun. The corona changes with sunspot activity.

CORONER

A person, usually a doctor or lawyer, who is appointed to inquire into cases of sudden or violent death, or where the cause of death is in doubt. The coroner holds a court with a jury, and if a verdict of murder or manslaughter is brought in, the matter is referred to the police.

COROT, Jean Baptiste Camille (1796–1875)

French artist, famous for his landscape paintings and for his treatment of light and tone.

CORSICA

French island in the MEDITERRANEAN Sea, close to the larger Italian island of Sardinia. Ajaccio, the chief town on the island, was Napoleon's birthplace.

CORTÉS, Hernando (1485–1547)

Spanish soldier. In 1519 he began the conquest of Mexico with a tiny force. He succeeded in carrying off the AZTEC king, Montezuma, but the people rose up against him, and the Spanish and their allies were routed. Later he returned with a much larger force, besieged the Aztec capital Tenochtitlan and destroyed it. MEXICO was renamed New Spain with Cortés as its governor. He also sent expeditions into GUATEMALA and HONDURAS.

The meeting of Cortés and Montezuma

COSMIC RAYS

Radiation particles that reach the Earth from outer space. Such radiations were unknown before 1910 and were not investigated satisfactorily until the American scientist R.A. Millikan started work in aeroplanes, on mountain-tops, and in balloons in 1923. There are two forms of cosmic radiation known as showers and penetrating radiation. The former consists of electrons. The latter consists of much heavier particles called mesons. These, at sea-level, are more penetrating than any known radiation from earthly sources.

Both the electron showers and the mesons are believed to be created by still other particles that come into the Earth's atmosphere from outside. The emission is continuous, and every minute, at sea level, approximately one ray passes through every square centimetre.

COSMOGONY

Branch of ASTRONOMY concerned with the origins of the universe. Today there are two rival theories. The 'Big Bang' theory suggests that everything started with a huge primordial explosion, as a result of which the universe is still expanding. The 'Steady State' theory argues that the destruction and creation of matter throughout the universe is a continuous process.

The spiral nebula 'M 74' in Pisces

COSMOLOGY

Branch of ASTRONOMY dealing with the structure and evolution of the universe. Modern thought on the subject started with Albert EINSTEIN's theories of RELATIVITY; the development of RADIO-ASTRONOMY has also revolutionized cosmological thinking. Much of this is concerned with speculation upon the origin of the universe, as discussed in the preceding entry.

COSTA RICA

Central American republic on the isthmus which joins North and South America. It has an area of 50,700 sq km (19,576 sq miles) and a population of about 2.2 million. The capital is San José. The country is quite prosperous, the main products being coffee, bananas and sugar cane.

COST OF LIVING

Term used for the amount of money needed to buy a standard quantity of goods and services. It includes foodstuffs, fuels, transport and other essentials of life. The Cost of Living Index relates changes in these costs to those at a given time in the past.

COULOMB, Charles (1736–1806)

French scientist who investigated many of the properties of electricity. Coulomb's Law states that the force between two electrical or magnetic charges varies inversely as the square of the distance between them. The unit of electrical charge is also named after him.

COUNCIL OF EUROPE

Organization created in 1949 to promote closer economic and political co-operation among the nations of western Europe. Its headquarters are in Strasbourg, France. It has a Consultative Assembly which brings together MPs from the parliaments of member nations. A smaller body, the Council of Ministers, brings together Foreign Ministers.

COUPERIN, François (1668–1733)

French composer, often called Couperin *le Grand* ('the Great') to distinguish him from other members of his large musical family. Employed at the court of LOUIS XIV at Versailles, and a very important figure in the development of Baroque keyboard music. His book *The Art of Playing the Harpsichord* is still widely studied though he also composed a certain amount of vocal music of great charm and beauty.

COURBET, Gustave (1819–77)

French artist, noted for the realism of his paintings, taking many of his themes from everyday life. Also active in revolutionary politics, taking part in the insurrections of 1848 and 1871 and imprisoned.

COUSTEAU, Jacques-Yves (born 1910)

French oceanographer. He helped to develop the aqualung as a means of allowing divers to breathe freely and independently under water, and has explored many parts of the ocean in his research ship *Calypso*.

COWARD, Sir Noël (1899–1973)

English actor and playwright. His plays and revues, including *Private Lives* and *Blithe Spirit*, are generally witty and satirical in character. Also wrote many songs in a similar vein.

COYOTE

Member of the WOLF family and native to North America. It lives mainly on small mammals, birds and reptiles. Also known as the 'prairie wolf' and the 'brush wolf'.

COYPU

Small mammal, native to part of South America; similar to a beaver, with webbed feet, but with a long, rat-like tail. Hence it is sometimes called the 'beaver rat'.

CRAB. *See* CRUSTACEANS

CRANACH, Lucas (1472–1553)

German artist of the Renaissance period who took his adopted name from the town of Cranach (now Kronach) in Bavaria. A friend of Martin Luther, he painted mainly religious subjects, and pictures taken from mythology.

CRANMER, Thomas (1489–1556)

First Protestant Archbishop of Canterbury. He promoted the English Reformation during the reigns of HENRY VIII and Edward VI, encouraged the translation of the Bible into English and made changes to the English prayer book. Burnt at the stake for treason and heresy during the reign of Queen Mary, who was a Catholic.

CREED

From the Latin *credo*, 'I believe'. A fixed statement of belief, especially applying to the Christian religion, and embodying such articles of faith as the Holy Trinity and the Resurrection of Christ. There are three versions of the Christian Creed in general use: 1) the Apostles' Creed, which is used by the Church of England during all normal services; 2) the Nicene Creed, formulated during the Council of Nicaea (325); and 3) the Athanasian Creed, which is a statement of Catholic doctrine and belief.

CRETE

Island province of GREECE, 8,300 sq km (3,200 sq miles) in area, and 130 km (81 m) south of the

Greek mainland. The population is about 500,000. Crete is of great interest historically as the place of the Minoan civilization, one of the most remarkable cultures of the ancient world.

CRICK, Francis H.C. (born 1916)

British biologist who, with Maurice Wilkins and James Watson, investigated the molecular structure of deoxyribonucleic acid (DNA), one of the basic materials of life. The molecular model of DNA is known as the Watson Crick model. *See also* GENETICS.

CRICKET

Game played with bat and ball between two teams of eleven players. In essence, each team takes turn at defending a wicket (three wooden stumps set in the ground and surmounted by small wooden bails) against the bowling of a member of the opposing team. The batsman in front of the wicket attempts to hit the ball hard enough, when it is bowled to him, to allow him to run the length of the cricket pitch (20 m, or 22 yds) before it can be retrieved by the bowler or any other member of his team and returned to the wicket. If he does this, he scores one 'run'. If he misses the ball and it strikes the

Australian Greg Chappell is bowled out.

wicket, or if he hits the ball and it is caught in the air by an opposing player, he is dismissed from the field ('out'), and his place is taken by another member of his own team. Runs continue to be scored until all the members of one team are dismissed, whereupon the opposing team starts to bat.

In practice, cricket is far more complex, and is a game involving a multitude of factors, such as the style of play of both batsmen and bowlers, the placing of the 'field', the condition of the ball, and of the pitch, and the factor of time related to the progress of an 'innings'.

The origins of cricket can be traced back to the thirteenth century, but in its present form it dates from the nineteenth century. The MCC (Marylebone Cricket Club) is the senior body for professional cricket in England, where teams are organized according to counties. The game is also played in most British Commonwealth countries, notably Australia. Test Matches between England and Australia are played for possession of a special trophy known as The Ashes.

CRIMEAN WAR

Fought between France and Britain on the one side and Imperial Russia on the other, the former two nations opposing Russian expansion towards the Mediterranean Sea. The war was fought out on the Crimean peninsula in the Black Sea. Hostilities started in 1854 and ended in 1856 with a token victory for France and Britain. It was more notable for its mismanagement, leading to such things as the disastrous charge of the Light Brigade at Balaclava. At the same time, it awoke British public opinion to prevailing army conditions, and drew attention to the work of Florence NIGHTINGALE, who went to the Crimea to tend the sick and wounded.

CROCODILE

Group of carnivorous REPTILES that live in or near water in many tropic or sub-tropical regions. Largest is the 'salt-water' crocodile of Australasia which can attain a length of over 9m (about 30 ft). Very closely related is the alligator. There are differences in the shape of their snouts and in the arrangement of the teeth. Other creatures related to the crocodile or alligator are the caimans, or caymans, of Central and South America, and the gavials of India, which have long, slender snouts.

Oliver Cromwell

CROMWELL, Oliver (1599–1658)

Lord Protector of England, born in Huntingdon and educated at Cambridge. He became an ardent Puritan, and at the same time a Parliamentary leader in the growing conflict between PARLIAMENT and CHARLES I. When the ENGLISH CIVIL WAR started in 1642, he created a Parliamentary force, well equipped and disciplined, known as the New Model Army, and so brought about the defeat of the Royalist forces. He had Charles I condemned and executed, and defeated Charles II's attempt at an invasion. As Lord Protector, Cromwell was then virtual dictator. He ruthlessly suppressed Catholicism in Ireland, while trying to create a coalition of Protestant European nations. The type of republic he had created depended on his own strength of character, and did not long survive his death.

CROMWELL, Thomas (c. 1485–1540)

English statesman. He became agent and secretary to Cardinal Wolsey, then chief adviser to HENRY VIII. He persuaded the King to deny the authority of the Pope, and declare himself head of the English Church. At the same time he persecuted those who opposed him or threatened his privileged position until he himself fell from grace and was executed.

CROOKES, Sir William (1832–1919)

English scientist who investigated the nature of cathode rays. He invented a type of electronic vacuum tube to study rays which are charged with particles of matter, and these Crookes Tubes were the forerunners of television picture tubes.

CROQUET

Ball game played by hitting, with a mallet, a ball through a series of hoops. Each player has a different coloured ball, and first through the hoops is the winner. Players may also deprive an opponent of any advantage by knocking the ball out of the way with a well-aimed shot.

CROWN JEWELS

Collection of royal regalia, of immense value, housed in the Tower of London. It includes the Imperial State Crown (which itself contains over 3,000 precious stones), St Edward's Crown, the Prince of Wales's Crown, and the Sword of State.

CRUSADES

A series of military expeditions intended to win back for Christendom from the forces of Islam the Holy Land (Jerusalem and the surrounding territories). Those taking part adopted as their emblem a red cross, and the Latin word *crux* (cross) bestowed upon them the name of Crusaders.

The First Crusade, inspired by the call to arms of Pope Urban II, was launched in 1096 and three years later the Crusaders captured Jerusalem. Further Crusades were organized, either to claim more lands for Christendom or to re-capture Jerusalem when it had again fallen to Islam. Most failed in their objectives, some ended in complete disaster, and the period of the Crusades finally ended when the great Crusader fortress of Acre fell in 1291.

Despite their military failure, the Crusades brought about a valuable cross-fertilization of the Christian and Islamic cultures. Arabic science, for example, had a great influence on European thought and practice. *See also* RICHARD I and SALADIN.

CRUSTACEAN

Group of invertebrate animals belonging to the phylum of ARTHROPODA, generally known as shellfish, and including crabs, lobsters, crayfish, shrimps and barnacles. One of the largest crustaceans is the giant spider crab of the Pacific Ocean, with legs up to one metre long (40 in). Strangest is the hermit crab, which has no shell of its own, and inhabits the shells of other dead creatures, moving from one shell to another as it grows. The largest lobster, the American lobster, can measure up to 90 cm (36 in).

Below Crustaceans

prawn

common crab

crayfish

goose barnacles

lobster

CRYOBIOLOGY

The study of how extremely low temperatures affect living things. Cryobiologists are mainly concerned with freezing living matter to preserve it for future use. This has proved of especial importance in preserving food and also in medicine for storing banks of skin, eye corneas and blood.

CRYOGENICS

The study and development of extremely low-temperature processes. The temperatures range from $-150°C$ ($-238°F$) to near absolute zero $-273.15°C$ ($-459.67°F$). Low temperatures were first produced by making liquid air in the 1870s. Extremely low temperatures are now usually obtained with liquid hydrogen, which gives a temperature of about $-253°C$ ($-423°F$), and liquid helium with $-269°C$ ($-452.2°F$).

CRYSTAL

Crystal structures are groups of molecules built up as units in a way that is roughly comparable to the use of bricks which are built up to form a larger structure. Many substances have crystal structures, from diamonds to sugar and salt. Snow and ice are crystalline forms of water. The geometric forms of various types of crystals are classed as follows: cubic, monoclinic, triclinic, orthorhombic, rhombohedral, hexagonal, tetragonal. The study of crystalline forms was much advanced by the use of X-RAYS, and more recently by electrons. X-ray crystallography is an important branch of physics.

CUBA

Caribbean island with an area of 114,524 sq km (44,220 sq miles) and a population of about 10 million. The capital is Havana. The chief products are sugar and tobacco. The island was discovered by Christopher COLUMBUS and it was a Spanish colony until 1898 when the United States of America, as the result of a war with Spain, gained control. Cuba finally achieved its independence in 1909. In 1959 the existing dictatorship was overthrown by a communist insurrection led by Dr Fidel Castro, who has governed the country since that time and who has made Cuba one of the most active nations, politically, among the underdeveloped countries of the world, both in Latin America and in Africa.

Seated Nude by Picasso

CUBISM

Style, or school, of painting that developed in the early years of the twentieth century, and which represented solid objects as seen simultaneously from different angles. This analysis of form often involved the use of geometric shapes like rectangles and cubes, hence the name. Pablo PICASSO and Georges BRAQUE were two of the leading Cubist painters.

CUCKOO

Large group of birds of over a hundred different species. The common cuckoo of Europe lays its eggs in the nests of other birds, and the young cuckoo then ejects the other eggs or chicks in the nest. But other varieties of cuckoo rear their own young in the normal way. They vary in size from the small, colourful cuckoos of Africa to the very large – almost pheasant-sized – 'channel-bill' cuckoo of Australasia.

CURIE, Marie Sklodowska (1867–1934)

Polish scientist who married the French physicist Pierre Curie (1859-1906). Together they first discovered polonium from pitchblende, then went on to isolate the radioactive element radium.

CYBERNETICS

Study of control and communication mechanisms in machines and animals. It covers all automatic control devices, selectors, relays, robots, and computers, and also the corresponding body mechanisms such as those of automatic balance, reflex action, and cerebral association. The application of cybernetics to electronic computers may throw light on the function of the brain.

Marie and Pierre Curie

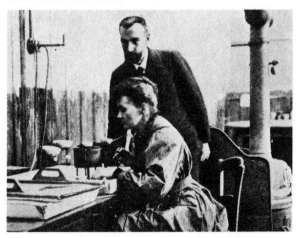

CYCLOTRON

Machine developed by the American physicist Ernest Lawrence and used in atomic research. It accelerates to tremendous speeds parts of the atom in order to 'bombard' and separate the parts of other atoms. Popularly known as an 'atom smasher'.

CYPRUS

Island republic in the eastern Mediterranean with an area of 9,251 sq km (3,572 sq miles) and a population of about 657,000. The capital is Nicosia. Cyprus was a British colony from 1918 to 1959, when it became independent, though remaining within the BRITISH COMMONWEALTH. Serious problems have resulted from disputes between Turkish and Greek Cypriots. After a war in 1974, Cyprus was partitioned into the Turkish north and Greek south.

CYTOLOGY

Science of the structure and organization of cells.

CZECHOSLOVAKIA

Republic of central Europe, with an area of 127,869 sq km (49,373 sq miles), which is a little smaller than England, and a population of 15 million. The capital is Prague, and other important cities are Brno, Bratislava and Plzen. The country is famous for its glass and china. It has other heavy industries and rich agricultural regions.

Czechoslovakia achieved its present existence after WORLD WAR I, bringing together the Czechs themselves from the regions of Bohemia and Moravia, and the Slovaks. It was occupied by Nazi Germany during WORLD WAR II, and soon after the war adopted a Communist form of government. It remains a member of the eastern European Soviet Bloc. *See also* Eduard BENEŠ.

D

DAGUERRE, Louis Jacques Mandé (1789-1851)

French inventor of an early type of photographic process. Prints made by this process were called daguerreotypes, and were among the earliest photographic portraits.

DAHOMEY. *See* BENIN

DALI, Salvador (born 1904)

Spanish artist, and one of the most celebrated of all Surrealist painters. *See also* SURREALISM.

DALTON, John (1766–1844)

English chemist best known for his atomic theory and classification of chemical compounds. But his scientific interests were many and varied, including the first scientific investigations into colour blindness, from which he himself suffered.

DAM

Barrier constructed across a river or lake to contain the flow or volume of water. The purpose of dams can be to store water for domestic or industrial use, or to control its flow for irrigation purposes. Dams can also be used as sources of hydro-electric power, and as such are of increasing value.

DANCE

Means of expression by bodily movement, usually to the accompaniment of music, especially of rhythm. Dancing is probably the oldest of all organized forms of human expression. Cave paintings dating back 20,000 years depict forms of ritual dance. Every community has developed a style of tribal or folk dancing, closely related to music, usually of a magical or religious nature. In this connection the hypnotic power of certain types of dancing has been demonstrated by, among others, the Dervishes of Moslem countries.

Court dances for social occasions largely developed during the RENAISSANCE and Baroque periods (fifteenth to seventeenth centuries). These included the minuet, bolero,

Traditional Hindu sword dance

pavane, gigue and sarabande. From these formalized dances, as performed at the court of Louis XIV at Versailles, grew the art of BALLET as we know it today. In the nineteenth century the waltz became the most popular of all social dance forms. The growth of JAZZ and of Latin American music in the twentieth century saw the rise of many new dance styles, notably the charleston, the rumba and the tango. Still based on early jazz forms were later twentieth-century dances, such as rock n' roll.

DANEGELD

'Danegeld' was originally the money or tribute which was paid to the invading Danes, particularly by Ethelred II 'the Unready' (978–1016), to buy them off and avoid fighting them. Later it became a tax paid to the King of England to pay war expenses.

DANELAW

That part of north-east England which the Danes occupied about AD 850. Town names ending in -by (Whitby), -wick (Runswick), and -toft (Lowestoft) are of Danish origin and are found in the former Danelaw. The division of Yorkshire into 'Ridings' is also a Danelaw survival.

DANTE Alighieri (1265–1321)

Italian poet, generally regarded as one of the greatest figures in world literature. His fame rests on *La Divina Commedia* (The Divine Comedy). This is divided into three parts – Inferno, Purgatory, Paradise – and takes the form of a vision in which Dante himself is led through these regions by the shade of the Latin poet Virgil. In its broadest sense the work is an allegory of the soul's search for God.

DANTON, Georges Jacques (1759–94)

One of the leaders of the FRENCH REVOLUTION. His leadership helped the people of Paris to

Portrait of Dante; on the right is Florence Cathedral

defend themselves against the Prussians and the Royalists in 1792. He voted for the death of the King and was an original member of the Committee of Public Safety and of the Revolutionary Tribunal that inaugurated the Terror. However he became one of its victims and was executed.

DANUBE

Major European river which rises in the Black Forest and flows eastwards through Germany, Austria, Hungary, Yugoslavia and Romania to the Black Sea for a distance of 2,858 km (1,776 miles). It serves three European capitals, Vienna, Budapest and Belgrade.

DARIUS

The name of three Persian kings of whom the most famous, known as Darius the Great, reigned from 521 until 486 BC. He was one of the greatest rulers of the East and built many inscribed monuments from which we know his history. He did much to bring about the civilization of his country and empire but he was eventually defeated by the Greeks at Marathon (490 BC).

DARWIN, Charles (1809–82)

English historian (his grandfather was Josiah WEDGWOOD). His journey on board HMS *Beagle* to regions of the Pacific Ocean inspired his thinking about the EVOLUTION of plant and animal life and led to his book *On the Origin of Species,* one of the most controversial and influential works of the nineteenth century.

DAUMIER, Honoré (1808–79)

French artist, celebrated for his drawings and lithographs, some political, many depicting social conditions in nineteenth-century France.

DAVID (died *c.* 1000 BC)

Second king of Israel, and the first to rule a united Israel in Palestine. The story of how David, the shepherd boy, killed Goliath, found favour at the court of Saul and founded a famous line of kings is told in the BIBLE (Samuel 1).

DAVID, Jacques Louis (1748–1825)

French artist. He started as a court painter to Louis XVI and eventually became official painter to NAPOLEON. Worked in the neo-classical style, his paintings including *The Death of Marat* and *The Death of Socrates.*

DAVY, Sir Humphry (1778–1829)

English scientist, noted for his investigations into various gases, for his discovery of the metals strontium, sodium and potassium, and especially for his invention of a safety lamp for miners, designed to detect the presence of the dangerously combustible gases.

DEAD SEA

Situated between the states of Israel and Jordan, it is the saltiest body of water in the world, practically devoid of life. Fresh water from the River Jordan flows into it, but evaporates quickly in the heat to leave behind salt deposits.

DEBUSSY, Claude-Achille (1862–1918)

French composer, born at St Germain-en-Laye, near Paris. He developed a highly original harmonic style and has exercised a strong influence on the course of twentieth-century music. His piano pieces, notably two sets of Preludes, are some of his most remarkable compositions. Other works include *Prélude à l'Après-midi d'un Faune* (Prelude to the Afternoon of a Faun) and *La Mer* (The Sea), for orchestra; and the opera *Pelléas et Mélisande.*

Claude Debussy

DEER

Name of a group of mammals which grow antlers and/or long, tusk-like upper teeth (canines). Belonging to this family are the red deer, wapiti, Indian sambar, chital, fallow deer, elk or moose and roebuck. Deer's antlers are true bones, which grow out from the frontal bones, and are renewed each year.

DEFOE, Daniel (c. 1659-1731)

English author, sometimes described as the first English journalist. He wrote on almost every subject, politics, religion, records of travels, translations and histories. His most famous work is *Robinson Crusoe*, while *Moll Flanders* is regarded as one of the landmarks in the growth of English fiction.

DEGAS, Edgar (1834–1917)

French artist, classed as one of the Impressionists. His paintings portray ballet-dancers, theatres, cafés and race-course scenes, and he also produced many bronzes of dancers and horses.

DELACROIX, Ferdinand Victor Eugène (1789-1863)

French artist, and one of the leading figures in the Romantic movement in painting.

DELIUS, Frederick (1862–1934)

English composer of German descent whose very personal style owes little to any other style or school of music. Works include *An English Rhapsody: Brigg Fair* and *On Hearing the First Cuckoo in Spring*, both for orchestra.

DEMOCRACY

Word used to describe a system of government which is intended to reflect the choice of the majority of the people through elections. It is derived from two Greek words, *demos* (people) and *krateo* (rule), since it was the city states of ancient Greece that first practised a form of democracy. However, it is only within the past two hundred years that the right to share in the choice of government through elections has

The Little Dancer aged Fourteen by Degas

gradually been extended to all adult citizens of a country.

DEMOCRATIC PARTY

One of the two major political parties of the UNITED STATES OF AMERICA. It is, in general terms, more liberal than the REPUBLICAN PARTY, receiving most of its support from the big cities, although traditionally it has also been supported by the conservative southern states. The most celebrated Democratic President has been Franklin D. ROOSEVELT.

The Little Mermaid, Copenhagen, Denmark

DENMARK

European kingdom forming part of the region of SCANDINAVIA. It has an area of 43,069 sq km (16,630 sq miles) and a population of 5 million. The main part of the country is the peninsula of Jutland, but the capital, Copenhagen, is on the island of Zealand. Denmark is famous for its butter, cheese, bacon, ham and other processed foods. It joined the EUROPEAN ECONOMIC COMMUNITY in 1973. *See also* GREENLAND.

DENSITY

Term in PHYSICS to describe the quantity of matter per unit volume of a substance. Numerically it is MASS per unit volume of the substance at a standard temperature and pressure.

DESCARTES, René (1596–1650)

French mathematician and philosopher. As a mathematician he founded a new form of geometry, called analytic geometry. As a philosopher he created a school of rationalist thought which he expounded in his book *Discourse on Method*. This contains the famous dictum *Cogito ergo sum*, 'I think, therefore I am'.

DETERGENT

Substance with cleansing properties; the word generally refers to substances made from petroleum and coal-tar by-products. Ordinary SOAP is made from edible fats, so that detergents represent a direct saving of food. Furthermore, for many purposes they are better than traditional soaps because of their penetrating and dispersing powers and their freedom from scum. They are instantly soluble and equally effective in hard, soft or salt water. On the other hand, petroleum-based detergents can cause pollution as they are not broken down by bacterial action.

DEW

Waterdrops deposited on exposed cool surfaces. This moisture is partly caused by condensation of water vapour in the air and partly by evaporation from warm ground (radiation). Plants also give out water vapour through their leaf pores. The level below which the temperature of a surface must be reduced in order to obtain water deposits is known as the 'dew point'.

DIAGHILEV, Sergei Pavlovich (1872–1929)

Russian impresario whose ballet company, the *Ballets Russes*, or Russian Ballet, became a focal point for the arts in the early years of this century. Diaghilev commissioned music or stage and costume designs from STRAVINSKY, FALLA, PROKOFIEV, RAVEL, and DEBUSSY; PICASSO, BRAQUE, Derain and MATISSE; and employed the greatest dancers of his time, including Pavlova, Nijinsky and Massine. He died in Venice.

Diamond mining at Kimberley, South Africa

DIAMOND

Precious stone of extreme hardness, a crystalline form of carbon. They are mined principally in Africa, India and South America. Their weight is measured in carats, and big stones are very valuable. Faceting is the process of splitting diamonds up into smaller sections. Many are sold as precious stones; many more are used in industry.

DIAZ, Bartholomew (*c.* 1455–1500)

Portuguese explorer who sailed down the west coast of Africa and discovered the Cape of Good Hope.

DICKENS, Charles (1812–70)

English novelist. He lived close to the poverty line as a boy, and though he became rich and famous, his sense of social injustice lived on in his novels. He created many of the most famous characters in English literature, notably Mr Pickwick, Fagin, Uriah Heep, Mr Snodgrass, Mr Pecksniff, Sarah Gamp and Mr Micawber. His books include *The Pickwick Papers, Oliver Twist, Nicholas Nickleby, Dombey and Son, Great Expectations, Bleak House* and *A Tale of Two Cities.*

DIDEROT, Denis (1713–84)

French writer and philosopher. His biggest work, produced in opposition to the Church and state, was his *Encyclopédie,* in which he tried to gather together all the new ideas and scientific techniques of his time.

DIESEL ENGINE. *See* INTERNAL COMBUSTION ENGINE

DINGO

Wild dog, native to Australia, rather like a large fox in appearance.

The Australian dingo

DINOSAUR

Large group of extinct REPTILES which lived during the Mesozoic period, roughly between 225 and 65 million years ago. The word *dinosaur* means 'terrible lizard', and while some were quite small, the most famous members of the group, as reconstructed from fossil remains, were very large and of fearsome appearance. Largest of all was Brontosaurus (meaning 'thunder lizard') which measured up to 30 metres (100 ft) from head to tail and may have weighed as much as 30,000 kg (30 tons). These huge creatures were vegetarian. Most ferocious was probably the carnivorous Tyrannosaurus Rex. The dinosaurs flourished for nearly 150 million years, and exactly why they became extinct remains a mystery. *See also* EVOLUTION and PALAEONTOLOGY.

Dinosaurs: the largest prehistoric animals

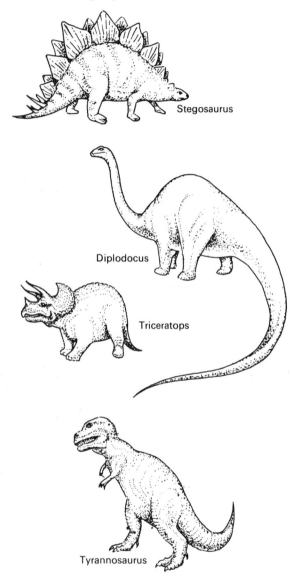

Stegosaurus

Diplodocus

Triceratops

Tyrannosaurus

Walt Disney's Mickey Mouse in *The Sorcerer's Apprentice*

DISNEY, Walt (1901–67)

American cartoonist and film producer. In the 1920s he revolutionized the form of the animated cartoon with the creation of Mickey Mouse, Donald Duck and other characters. Later produced full-length animated cartoon films, including *Snow White and the Seven Dwarfs*.

DISRAELI, Benjamin, Earl of Beaconsfield (1804–81)

British statesman. PRIME MINISTER in 1868 and again from 1874 to 1880, he pursued a policy of colonial expansion abroad while introducing social reforms at home. He is considered to be the founder of the modern CONSERVATIVE PARTY.

DJIBOUTI

An African republic facing the Red Sea. Formerly the French Territory of Afars and Issas, it has an area of 22,000 sq km (8,495 sq miles) and 340,000 people. The capital is Djibouti. It became independent in 1977.

DOG

Large group of carnivorous MAMMALS, mostly domesticated and kept as pets, though some

DIOGENES (412–323 BC)

Greek philosopher and member of the Cynic school, which taught that virtue was the highest good. He is supposed to have lived in an earthenware tub.

species of wild dog, such as the DINGO, remain. Very closely related to dogs are the WOLF, JACKAL and FOX.

DOLPHIN

Dolphins, like WHALES, are MAMMALS, although they live in the sea. They grow to a length of about 2 m (7 ft) and are considered to be highly intelligent. They communicate with each other by a series of clicks and whistles; and navigate by a system of echo-location.

DOMESDAY BOOK

This was compiled on the orders of WILLIAM the Conqueror, and is a detailed record of the distribution of population and of land throughout England in and around the year 1085.

DOMINICA

A republic in the West Indies, independent since 1978, Dominica has an area of 751 sq km (290 sq miles) and a population of 80,000. The capital is Roseau.

DOMINICAN REPUBLIC

Caribbean republic that occupies about two-thirds of the island of HISPANIOLA in the West Indies. It is 48,734 sq km (18,817 sq miles) in area and has a population of about 5½ million. The capital is Santo Domingo. The country was a Spanish colony until 1821.

DONATELLO (1386-1466)

Italian sculptor of the Florentine School and one of the most important artists of the RENAISSANCE period.

DONIZETTI, Gaetano (1797–1848)

Italian operatic composer and a master of the *bel canto* style of singing, designed to display the agility and tonal beauty of the voice. His operas include *Don Pasquale* and *Lucia di Lammermoor*, this being based on Sir Walter SCOTT's novel *The Bride of Lammermoor*.

DONNE, John (1573–1631)

English poet, classed as one of the so-called 'Metaphysical poets', combining in his work feelings of passion with deep and concentrated thought. He was also interested in THEOLOGY and became Dean of St Paul's, London.

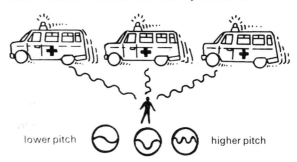

lower pitch   higher pitch

The Doppler effect

DOPPLER EFFECT

An apparent change in the frequency of SOUND, LIGHT or RADIO waves when either the source of the waves or the observer moves toward or away from the other. The sound of a car horn, for example, has a higher pitch as the car approaches and a lower pitch as it moves away. Astronomers use this effect to calculate the speed of a star. Named after Christian Doppler who first described the effect in 1842.

DORMOUSE

RODENT about the size of a house-mouse but fawn in colour and a creature of the countryside. Lives mainly on nuts and acorns and hibernates during the winter.

DOSTOEVSKY, Feodor Mikhailovich (1821–81)

Russian novelist, whose works portray many aspects of life in pre-revolutionary Russia and also examine patterns of human behaviour. His most celebrated novels are *Crime and Punishment*, *The Idiot* and *The Brothers Karamazov*.

DOWLAND, John (1563–1626)

English composer who was one of the first to write true songs (or 'ayres') and also composed much music for the lute.

DOYLE, Sir Arthur Conan (1859–1930)

British writer. In such stories as *The Hound of the Baskervilles* he created Sherlock Holmes, the most celebrated character in detective fiction. His other novels include *The Lost World*.

DRAKE, Sir Francis (1540–96)

Elizabethan sea captain and explorer. He made a fortune by plundering Spanish ports in the WEST INDIES, before becoming the first Englishman to sail round the world in his ship the *Golden Hind*. Later helped to scatter and destroy the Spanish ARMADA.

DRAMA

A performing art that depicts events or situations through the speech and actions of characters, as portrayed by actors and actresses in a play. Drama started with the ancient Greeks. Their productions included people called a 'chorus', who commented upon the progress of the play. There was often singing and dancing as well. The Greeks also created the two principal types of drama – tragedy and comedy – which still exist today. SOPHOCLES and ARISTOPHANES, respectively, were the two greatest exponents of Greek tragedy and comedy.

In the Middle Ages there were MIRACLE or Morality Plays, usually performed on the steps of a cathedral or church, and intended as a form of religious instruction. The RENAISSANCE brought about new developments in drama: in the type of popular dramatic entertainment known in Italy as the *Commedia dell'arte;* and above all, in the wonderfully dramatic and expressive plays of SHAKESPEARE. Later came the pure, 'classical' styles of French drama as contained in the work of CORNEILLE, RACINE and MOLIÈRE; and the English RESTORATION comedies of CONGREVE and others.

In the last hundred years dramatists of many countries have written great plays, expressing a wide variety of political and social ideas, including CHEKHOV, IBSEN, SHAW and Eugene O'NEILL.

Traditionally plays were written for performance upon a stage in a theatre, but in this century radio and television have inspired new forms and styles of drama. Another twentieth-century development has been the so-called 'Theatre (or Drama) of the Absurd', in which the situations and dialogues of the plays are intended to make audiences question all their normal ideas or beliefs. Eugene Ionesco and Samuel Beckett are two leading figures in this field.

DREYFUS AFFAIR

A serious political crisis in FRANCE, created by the conviction, in 1894, of a Jewish army officer, Captain Alfred Dreyfus, on charges of treason. The nation quickly divided between those who believed in his innocence and those who insisted on his guilt. In a broader context the affair became a conflict between the left- and right-wing forces of the country, and nearly provoked a civil war. Subsequently Dreyfus was found to be the victim of a plot, and pardoned. *See also* EMILE ZOLA.

DRUIDS

Body of priests and religious teachers of Celtic Gaul (France) and Britain who practised ASTRONOMY and possibly human sacrifice. Their religion did not survive the Roman occupation. *See also* CELTS.

A spotted redshank leading a flock of teal

DRYDEN, John (1631–1700)

English poet, playwright and man of letters, and a major figure of the RESTORATION period. His best known play is *All for Love*.

DUCCIO DI BUONINSEGNA (*c.* 1250–1319)

Italian painter from Siena who created a new style of painting (the Sienese School) using some of the techniques of Byzantine art. His finest work is the double altar in Siena cathedral, of which the citizens were so proud that they carried it to the cathedral in a procession.

DUCK

Group of aquatic birds which belong to the same family as swans and geese. They usually have small heads, fairly long necks, rather heavy bodies, short tails, short legs and webbed feet. Some species of duck do not differ much in plumage between male and female, but in most cases the males (drakes) are more brightly coloured. Best known member of the family in the Northern Hemisphere is the mallard.

DUFY, Raoul (1877–1953)

French artist who painted many scenes of sailing regattas and race meetings in a light and colourful style.

DUGONG

MAMMAL which inhabits the waters round the coasts of India and Australia, now rather rare. It is something like a walrus in appearance and may be the origin of some of the old legends about mermaids.

DUIKER

Member of the ANTELOPE family and native to central and southern Africa. The name *duiker,* which comes from the Dutch, means 'diver' and describes the behaviour of the animal which dives or plunges into the undergrowth when approached.

DUMAS, Alexandre, the Elder (1802–70) and the Younger (1824–95)

French writers, father and son. Alexandre Dumas *père* (the Elder) wrote many famous novels, including *The Three Musketeers, The Count of Monte Cristo* and *The Black Tulip.* Alexandre Dumas *fils* (the Younger) concentrated more on drama, his best-known play being *The Lady of the Camellias,* this providing the basis for VERDI's opera *La Traviata.*

DUNANT, Jean Henri (1828–1910)

Swiss banker who founded the international Red Cross organization after seeing the wounded at the Battle of Solferino in 1859. His book, *Recollections of Solferino* led to the Geneva Convention for the treatment of wounded and prisoners.

DUNLOP, John Boyd (1840–1921)

He was a Scottish veterinary surgeon, but is famous as the inventor of the rubber pneumatic tyre.

DÜRER, Albrecht (1471–1528)

German painter and engraver and one of the greatest figures of the RENAISSANCE period. He was born in Nuremberg, visited Italy as a young man, then became court painter to the Emperor Maximilian. However, it is for his copper engravings, etchings (a technique he perfected) and woodcuts that he is best remembered today.

DVORÁK, Antonin (1841–1904)

Czech composer. He was an ardent supporter of Czech political independence and wrote

Self-portrait at the age of thirteen by Dürer

operas, symphonic poems and many other pieces based on Czech folk dances and legends. Dvorák also composed other less nationalistic works for the concert hall, including one of the finest of all cello concertos and nine symphonies. The last of these he subtitled *From the New World,* as it was composed during his stay in the United States of America.

DYAK

Race of people who live in BORNEO and are famous for their special types of house which are raised from the ground by long poles.

DYNAMITE

Explosive containing nitro-glycerine, invented by the Swedish chemist Alfred NOBEL.

E

EAGLE

Bird of prey which belongs to the same family as the buzzard, kite, harrier, VULTURE and OSPREY. The Golden Eagle chiefly inhabits mountainous regions and in the British Isles it is mainly confined to the Highlands of Scotland. The nest is large and built of sticks in a tree or on a cliff ledge. The American Bald Eagle is a national emblem of the UNITED STATES OF AMERICA.

EAR

The organ of hearing. It extends deep into the skull and consists of three main parts: the outer ear, the middle ear and the inner ear. The visible outer ear is known as the auricle. It receives and concentrates sound waves and passes them on down the opening known as the external auditory canal. The sound waves then pass into the middle ear, through the eardrum and across the three bones – the hammer, the anvil and the stirrup. The eardrum vibrates in sympathy with the sound waves, and it is the inner ear which sends the sounds to the brain.

EARTH

One of the nine planets of the SOLAR SYSTEM, and the one upon which we live. The Earth revolves upon its own axis and moves round the sun in an orbit located between Mars and Venus. Its physical characteristics are: diameter at equator 12,756.32 km (7,926.61 miles);

The Earth seen from space

diameter at poles 12,713.54 km (7,899.83 miles); mean distance from sun 150 million km (93 million miles); weight or mass 6.0 sextilion metric tons (5.87×10^{21} tons); revolves on axis once every 23 hours 56 minutes 4.09 seconds; revolves round the sun once every 365 days 6 hours 9 minutes 9.54 seconds; length of orbit round the sun 958 million km (595 million miles); land surface 148,350,000 sq km (57,280,000 sq miles); water surface 361,563,400 sq km (139,660,400 sq miles); total surface area 509,917,870 sq km (196,940,400 sq miles).

EARTHQUAKE

A sudden movement in the EARTH'S crust (outer layer) which produces vibrations. These vibrations may be detectable only by sensitive instruments called seismographs, or they may destroy cities. Many earthquakes are caused when rocks move along faults (cracks). Severe earthquakes are most common near the edges of the 'plates' in the Earth's crust, such as around the PACIFIC Ocean, along the mid-ATLANTIC ridge and in the MEDITERRANEAN and south-west Asian regions. They occur when the plates move. Some earthquakes are caused by volcanic action, explosions and other factors. Earthquakes under the sea trigger off huge waves called tsunamis. *See also* CONTINENTAL DRIFT.

ECHIDNA

Egg-laying MAMMAL native to Australasia. Its body is covered with spines mingled with brownish grey hair and it is about 45 cm (18 in) long. The echidna, which has no teeth, has a beak-like muzzle which it uses to feed on ants and termites. It burrows rapidly into the earth with its spade-like claws when disturbed. Also known as the 'spiny anteater'.

ECLIPSE

Phenomenon that takes place when the the SUN, MOON and EARTH are in direct line (*see* diagram). The eclipse of the sun viewed from the umbra (completely shaded area) is said to be total, and partial when viewed from the penumbra (partially shaded area). The moon is eclipsed when the Earth is in direct line between the sun and the moon.

ECOLOGY

Scientific study of what is generally known as the Balance of Nature. All plants and animals depend on each other for their survival, and if the way of life of one kind of plant or animal is disturbed, this may affect the existence of many other forms of life. The activities of human beings, in industry and agriculture, can seriously upset the overall balance of life by, for example, the pollution of rivers or the atmosphere, the clearing of large areas of forest land for cultivation, or the widespread use of insecticides. Ecologists study these problems and suggest ways in which a reasonable balance of nature can be maintained for the benefit of all.

ECUADOR

South American republic situated on the PACIFIC coast. It has an area of 283,561 sq km (109,489 sq miles) and a population of 8⅓ million. The capital is Quito, which lies practically on the line of the equator (or *ecuador* in Spanish), but also stands more than 2,700 m (9,000 ft) above sea level high in the ANDES mountains. About one third of the people are descendants of the INCAS, and the remainder are of Spanish descent. Ecuador owns the GALAPAGOS ISLANDS.

Positions of Earth, sun and moon during a total eclipse

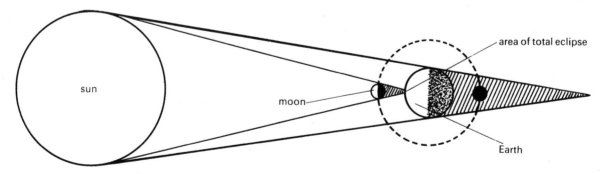

EDISON, Thomas Alva (1847–1931)

American scientist and inventor. He received very little formal education but made some of the most important contributions to twentieth-century technology, including the invention of the phonograph (forerunner of the gram-ophone) and the development of the electric light bulb and wireless telegraphy.

EEL

Group of FISH with a snake-like appearance. The common eel spawns in the ATLANTIC, in the region of the SARGASSO SEA, and when the young eels hatch they make their way across the Atlantic for a distance of nearly 5,000 km (3,000 miles) to fresh-water rivers and streams in Europe. Other types are the dangerous conger and moray eels, which can grow to a length of 3 m (10 ft); and the so-called 'electric eels' (actually related to the catfish), which can generate up to 400 volts – enough to stun a fully grown man.

EGYPT

North African ARAB republic with an area of 1,001,449 sq km (386,683 sq miles) and a population of nearly 42 million. The capital is Cairo; other important cities are Alexandria and Port Said. The most important natural feature of the country is the River NILE which flows northwards through arid desert. For thousands of years the Egyptians have de-pended entirely upon the waters of the Nile for their livelihood. In 1968 the Aswan Dam came into operation, controlling the river flow and providing all-year-round water for extensive irrigation as well as hydro-electric power. There is also the SUEZ CANAL which connects the Red Sea with the MEDITERRANEAN SEA. Egypt's major industry is cotton and textiles; there are also oil and sugar refineries.

Egypt has long been a tourist centre on account of the remains of its ancient civiliz-ation. This dates back to the fifth millennium

Egyptian relief of the Pharoah Akhnaten

BC, and for over three thousand years the Egyptian civilization flourished under a suc-cession of kings, or PHARAOHS. The surviving palaces and temples, wall paintings, tombs, jewelry and HIEROGLYPHIC inscriptions are a continuing source of wonder and fascination. Chief sites visited today are the PYRAMIDS and the SPHINX, just outside Cairo, and the Valley of the Kings further down the Nile valley.

In the first century BC Egypt came under

Roman control, despite the efforts of CLEO-PATRA to retain the nation's independence. The country was then overrun by the Arabs during the great period of ISLAMIC expansion. European interest in Egypt dates from NAPOLEON's campaigns in the 1790s. France and Britain continued to have a political and economic interest in the country until 1956, when the new President, Gamal Abdel Nasser, took over control of the Suez Canal. Recent Egyptian history has been marred by brief wars with ISRAEL in 1948, 1956, 1967 and 1973. In 1979 Anwar as-Sadat, who had been Egypt's president since 1970, agreed a Peace Treaty with Israel, but most Arab nations opposed his initiative. Sadat was assassinated in 1981.

EIFFEL, Alexandre Gustave (1832–1923)

French engineer who designed many bridges and other structures in iron and steel. His most enduring monument is the Eiffel Tower in Paris, built for the World Fair of 1889. With a height of 300 m (984 ft) it was for many years by far the tallest structure in the world.

EINSTEIN, Albert (1879–1955)

German-Jewish mathematician and scientist. He worked in Switzerland and then in Germany until the Nazi take-over, when he emigrated to the United States. In 1905 and 1910, respectively, he published his *Special Theory of Relativity* and *General Theory of Relativity,* which revolutionized scientific thinking about the nature of the universe, with special reference to concepts of time and space. His work also helped to make possible the development of nuclear physics.

EINTHOVEN, Willem (1860–1927)

Dutch physiologist who developed the electrocardiograph to record heart action.

EIRE. *See* IRELAND

The Eiffel Tower, Paris

EISENHOWER, Dwight David (1890–1969)

American soldier and statesman. During WORLD WAR II he commanded the American landings in North Africa in 1942, and in 1944, as Supreme Commander of the Allied Expeditionary Forces, directed the invasion of Normandy and the subsequent advance of the Allies into Germany. In 1952 he was elected REPUBLICAN President of the United States, and re-elected in 1956.

ELAND

Member of the ANTELOPE family, native to Africa, standing 1.8 m (6 ft) tall, with spirally twisted horns. There are two species: the common eland and the Derby eland.

ELECTRICITY

The study of electrons in motion. Electrons, which are negatively charged, are normally bound in orbits around the positively charged nuclei of ATOMS. In certain circumstances electrons can be detached from their atoms and made to flow in an electric current.

Materials are divided into three categories by their electrical properties: *insulators* are materials in which the electrons are so tightly bound to the nuclei of the atoms that electric currents cannot flow; *conductors* are materials (often metals) in which the electron binding is so weak that large currents can be made to flow very easily; *semiconductors* are materials (such as silicon and germanium) whose properties fall between those of insulators and conductors. Semiconductors are used to make transistors and integrated circuits. (*See also* ELECTRONICS.)

The concerted drift of free electrons which makes up an electric current will only happen if a force is applied. This force, which is called an electromotive force if supplied by a generator, and a potential difference if supplied by a battery, is measured in volts. Current is measured in amperes. Power is measured in watts. Electromotive force multiplied by current gives power: for example, a force of 250 volts and 4 amps of current gives 1000 watts, or one kilowatt of power. *See also* MAGNETISM.

ELECTROLYSIS

Using an electric current to alter the chemical structure of a compound in solution. Chemical compounds are held together by electrical forces, and currents flowing through a solution of such compounds can often cause the constituent elements to split up and recombine. The substance being split is called the electrolyte and is generally an acid or a salt dissolved in water.

The process of electrolysis has many applications in industry. Aluminium is obtained cheaply from its ores (before electrolysis was used for extraction, aluminium was a precious metal), copper is refined, electroplating is carried out, chlorine is obtained from sea water, and heavy water is prepared in bulk.

ELECTRO-MAGNET. *See*
MAGNETISM

ELECTRO-MAGNETIC WAVES

A form of radiant energy made up of an electric field and a magnetic field, which vary in such a way that the two fields tend to maintain each other. Electro-magnetic waves form an entire SPECTRUM, including RADIO WAVES, LIGHT, X-RAYS and gamma rays, depending on the frequency of the waves. All electro-magnetic waves travel at the speed of light, which is 2.997×10^8 metres per second, or 300,000 km (187,500 miles) per second.

Michael FARADAY proved experimentally the relation between magnetic and electric phenomena. James Clark MAXWELL, on the basis of this work and by applying mathematical methods, showed the existence of electro-magnetic waves and that they were of the same nature as light. Conversely, light waves were seen to be a form of electro-magnetic wave. Maxwell's theories were proved experimentally by Heinrich Hertz some eight years after Maxwell's death. These experiments formed the foundation of radio and TELEVISION technology. Maxwell's theories also formed an important part of the background of EINSTEIN's theory of relativity.

Electric and magnetic fields

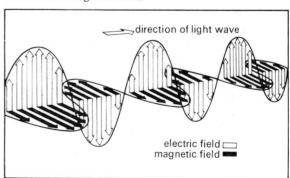

ELECTRON

Fundamental particle of electricity and matter. It was discovered by Sir J. J. Thomson in 1897. The electron carries a negative charge. Electrons exist in all atoms as particles revolving around the nucleus. These electrons can be ejected by heat, as a thermionic emission; by chemical action; and under the stress of high voltage, as in the cold-cathode discharge tube. An electron has a mass approximately 1/1840th that of a hydrogen atom, that is 9.1×10^{-31}/kg. The charge on it is approximately 16×10^{-20} coulombs. *See also* NUCLEAR ENERGY.

ELECTRONICS

The use of electricity for measurement, control, communications, computing and similar applications.

The first major discovery in this important branch of technology was made at the end of the last century by Thomas Alva EDISON, who discovered that he could make a current flow in

An integrated circuit for use in a computer

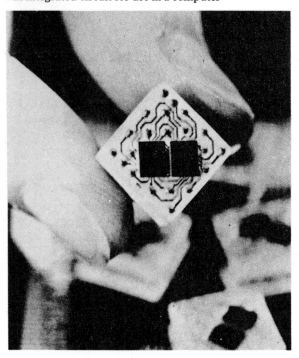

one direction only between the incandescent filament of a lamp and a metal plate enclosed in the same glass envelope. This was put to practical use in 1905 by Sir J. A. FLEMING in his valve for detecting wireless waves. In 1907, Lee de Forest invented the triode valve, with three internal electrodes, which allowed for the amplification of weak signals, like those received in early radio sets. Valve technology then developed, leading to radio and television, radar, and the very early forms of electronic computer.

The big revolution in electronics has been the development of solid state circuits, using semiconductor materials. The development of the transistor and later the integrated circuit has led to electronic components which are small, cheap, quick in operation and which draw very little current from the power supply. Integrated circuits combine thousands of transistors and their interconnections on a chip of silicon, and they are to be found in watches, washing machines and cameras, as well as full-sized computers, pocket calculators, radio and television sets and space satellites. *See also* RADAR, RADIO WAVES, TELEVISION.

ELECTRO-PLATING

Process of depositing by electrical means one metal upon another. An electric current is arranged to flow from immersed plates (the anodes) to the object to be plated through a metallic solution (the electrolyte). The anodes are of the same metal as that in the electrolyte and are slowly dissolved into it. The metal ions are attracted to the objects being plated and there give up their electric charges and deposit themselves on the surface. Silver, nickel, copper and zinc are the metals most commonly used in this process.

ELECTROSCOPE

Instrument used to detect the presence of electric charges. It is based on the fact that like charges repel each other.

ELEMENT, CHEMICAL

Substance that contains only one type of ATOM and that cannot be broken down chemically into simpler substances. By 1976, 105 known kinds of these basic chemical substances had been isolated. Fourteen of these were not originally found in nature but have been man-made.

Each element has a symbol consisting of one or two letters; for example, H is the symbol for hydrogen. These symbols are used when formulas are written for compounds.

ELEPHANT

A class of MAMMAL, the largest creature on land, also distinguished by its trunk. There are two species: the Indian, or Asiatic elephant, and the African elephant. The African species is larger – a fully grown bull can be 3.5 m (over 11 ft) tall and weigh up to 4,500 kg (10,000 lb) – and also has larger ears and tusks. Elephants live in herds and are herbivores; but a few live solitary lives and are known as 'rogue' elephants. Traditionally the Indian species has been used for domestic purposes whereas the African has not. However it is recorded that African elephants were tamed and used in warfare by the Carthaginians and the Romans.

African elephants

ELGAR, Sir Edward (1857–1934)

English composer, whose music is generally held to express something of the spirit of Edwardian England. He wrote mainly for the orchestra, including two symphonies, the *Enigma Variations*, and the *Pomp and Circumstance Marches* (the theme from the first of these being used for the patriotic hymn 'Land of Hope and Glory').

EL GRECO (*c.* 1547–1614)

Greek artist who spent most of his life in Spain (*El Greco* means 'The Greek'). His real name was Domenicos Theotocopulis. His paintings have a unique luminous quality to them, coupled with a sense of religious passion. Some of the finest of them are in the cathedral at Toledo, the city in which he lived and worked for many years.

ELIOT, George (1819–80)

English novelist, whose real name was Mary Anne Evans. Her best-known books are *The Mill on the Floss, Silas Marner* and *Middlemarch,* depicting in detail English rural life during the nineteenth century.

ELIOT, Thomas Stearns (1888–1965)

American-born poet and dramatist who settled in England and became a naturalized British subject. His poem *The Waste Land* is regarded as one of the most influential works of twentieth-century literature. Just as famous are his two poetic dramas *Murder in the Cathedral* (dealing with the death of Thomas à BECKET) and *The Cocktail Party.*

ELIZABETH I (1533–1603)

Queen of England from 1558 to 1603, the daughter of HENRY VIII and Anne Boleyn, and last of the Tudor monarchs. Religious dispute between Catholics and Protestants shaped

Elizabeth I: silver medal commemorating the Armada

some of the events of her reign, including the imprisonment and execution of MARY QUEEN OF SCOTS, and the dispersal of Philip II of Spain's ARMADA. More generally, Elizabeth's reign was marked by increasing prosperity at home and, through the exploits of Sir Francis DRAKE, Sir John Hawkins, Sir Martin Frobisher and Sir Walter RALEIGH, a big increase in English naval strength and prestige which laid the foundations of the British Empire. She also presided over one of the greatest periods of English literature and music, which included the achievements of William SHAKESPEARE, Christopher MARLOWE, Ben JONSON and Edmund SPENSER; and of Thomas TALLIS, William BYRD and John DOWLAND.

ELK

Largest member of the DEER family, also known as moose. There are two species, the American elk and the European elk, both types threatened with extinction.

EL SALVADOR

Central American republic with an area of 21,041 sq km (8,124 sq miles) and a population of about 4½ million. The capital is San Salvador. The principal crops are coffee, cotton and cane sugar.

EMBRYOLOGY

Branch of BIOLOGY concerned with the embryo – the growth of the fertilized egg in many forms of animal life up to a certain stage in its development.

EMU

Flightless BIRD, native to Australia. After the OSTRICH it is the largest of living birds, reaching a height of up to 150 cm (60 in), the female being the larger.

ENERGY

Capacity of a body to overcome resistance and do work. There are a number of forms of energy: kinetic energy of a body in motion; potential energy possessed by a body by virtue of its position, for example, a coiled spring or body placed above the earth's surface; atomic energy of fission. *See also* WORK.

A windmill uses the energy of the wind.

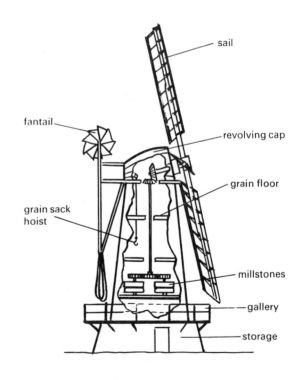

sail
fantail
revolving cap
grain floor
grain sack hoist
millstones
gallery
storage

The Tower of London

ENGELS, Friedrich (1820–95)

German political philosopher who collaborated with Karl MARX on publication of *The Communist Manifesto*. He wrote a number of books of his own, including *Landmarks of Scientific Socialism* and *Private Property and the State*. *See also* COMMUNISM.

ENGINE

An apparatus or device that can change energy into mechanical work. The steam-engine is a good example of an engine which changes heat energy into mechanical work. The hydraulic engine uses water pressure. The engine in the MOTOR CAR is an INTERNAL COMBUSTION ENGINE in which fuel burns in a confined space to produce high pressure.

ENGINEERING

Science or craft basically to do with the construction or maintenance of ENGINES, or, in a broader sense, to do with the transmission of ENERGY. Hence there are mechanical engineering, dealing with the operation of machinery; mining engineering; civil engineering, concerned with road or bridge construction, or such utilities as water works; electrical engineering; chemical engineering; RAILWAY, marine and aeronautical engineering.

ENGLAND

Largest part of Great Britain, with an area of 130,400 sq km (50,300 sq miles), and a population of 46.4 million (1979). The capital is London, itself with a population of nearly 7 million; other large cities are Birmingham (with a population of over 1 million), Manchester, Liverpool, Leeds, Sheffield, Newcastle, Bristol, Southampton and Portsmouth. The chief natural feature is the Pennine Chain of hills, often called the 'Backbone of England'. Important rivers are the Severn and the Trent, but most famous is the Thames because it flows through London. The principal industries are coal mining, iron and steel, motor and ship building, chemicals and electronics. North Sea oil is the newest factor in English (British) industry. English agriculture is highly mechanized, with the emphasis on dairy products. London is also a world centre of finance and banking.

Some of the first people to colonize England were the CELTS, but the earliest written records of the country's history date from the time of the Roman occupation, which lasted from about AD 40 to 440. Soon after the Romans came the invasions of the Angles (from which the name England is derived), Saxons and Jutes from other parts of north-west Europe; and later the Danes, who were opposed by King ALFRED but finally conquered the country at the time of King Canute (1017). The last military invasion was that of the NORMAN CONQUEST in 1066. English history thenceforth has been a gradual process of change from an Absolute Monarchy, with the king or queen as virtual dictator, to a Constitutional Monarchy, in which the monarch represents the nation while political power is controlled by a Parliament. (*See also* MAGNA CARTA, ENGLISH CIVIL WAR, OLIVER CROMWELL and RESTORATION).

English history has also been marked by the growth of naval power and the rise of the British Empire from the time of ELIZABETH I to the early years of the twentieth century; and by the INDUSTRIAL REVOLUTION, which made

England the first truly industrialized country. Since WORLD WAR I and more especially WORLD WAR II, England's position has radically changed. Many of England's (Britain's) industries have declined, and London is no longer capital of a world-wide empire. England's (Britain's) entry into the EUROPEAN ECONOMIC COMMUNITY represents a new chapter of the country's history.

ENGLISH CIVIL WAR

Fought between Royalists (those who supported CHARLES I) and PARLIAMENT, also known, respectively, as Cavaliers and Roundheads. Hostilities opened in 1642 and the first major engagement was at Edgehill. Royalist plans to capture London nearly succeeded until Oliver CROMWELL, in alliance with the Scots, won an important Parliamentary victory at Marston Moor (1644). Cromwell then reorganized the Parliamentary forces into the New Model Army and won an even more decisive victory at Naseby (1645). The next year Charles I fled to Scotland but was handed over to Parliament. After efforts to come to terms with the King, Cromwell, now in personal control of affairs, had him tried and executed in January 1649. The result of the Civil War was that the absolute power of the monarchy was destroyed. The monarchy was subsequently restored, in 1660, but thenceforth it was Parliament who increasingly controlled the nation's affairs.

ENTOMOLOGY

Scientific study of INSECTS in all their aspects, such as EVOLUTION, distribution and classification. The class of insects belongs to the phylum of ARTHROPODS and falls into twenty orders, comprising among others the BEETLE, bugs, lice, dragonflies, moths, BUTTERFLIES and BEES. The number of species of insect is enormous; nearly half a million are known, but it is estimated that there are about three million species in existence.

ENZYME

Agents of chemical change in living organisms. Animal digestive juices contain enzymes, such as pepsin and trypsin, which aid the conversion of foodstuffs into energy or body-building materials. In much the same way there are plant enzymes which convert starch into sugar as part of the process of PHOTOSYNTHESIS.

EPIC

Long, narrative poem usually recounting the exploits of some legendary hero. Two of the greatest epic poems are *The Iliad* and *The Odyssey* attributed to HOMER, dealing with the period of the TROJAN WAR and the adventures of the Greek hero Odysseus. Another famous epic poem, from the ANGLO-SAXON period, is *Beowulf*. In a broader sense the term can also be applied to novels, plays or films which encompass a broad sweep of historical events and which cover a long span of time.

EPICURUS (341–271 BC)

Greek philosopher who considered the pursuit of happiness and pleasure to be the greatest measure of good though not in the debased form in which it is often understood.

EQUATOR

Imaginary line encircling the EARTH mid-way between the North and South Poles. It divides the Earth into the Northern and Southern HEMISPHERES. It is marked as the zero line of latitude in navigation.

EQUATORIAL GUINEA

Small African republic on the Atlantic coast with an area of 28,051 sq km (10,831 sq miles) and a population of about 362,000. The capital is Malabo on Bioko Island. It was a Spanish colony until 1968. Cocoa, coffee and timber (from mainland Río Muni) are exported.

ERASMUS, Desiderius (*c.* 1466–1536)

Dutch scholar and humanist. He taught at Cambridge University for many years before finally settling in Basle, Switzerland. In a number of books, including *Praise of Folly,* he ridiculed religious superstition, but did not support the more direct attacks on the Church of men like Martin LUTHER.

ERIC THE RED

Norse explorer, probably the first man to voyage across the ATLANTIC OCEAN, reaching the coast of GREENLAND in 985. His son Leif Eriksson landed in 'Vinland', often identified as New England.

EROSION

The natural process by which the land surface of the Earth is gradually changed by the action of wind and water, with special regard to GLACIERS, rivers and the sea. There are some ways of stopping or slowing the processes of erosion, such as the construction of sea walls or groynes, or the planting of trees to bind together loose soil which might otherwise be blown away. On the other hand, the heedless cutting down of trees for timber or agricultural land, or the over-cultivation of land, can bring about soil erosion.

Erosion caused by the action of a river

Eskimos with their team of huskies

ESKIMO

Race of American INDIANS living in the far north of CANADA. Traditionally they constructed dwellings from ice or snow blocks, called igloos, travelled about on sledges or in a special type of canoe known as a kayak, and lived on the flesh and by-products of fish, seals and reindeer or caribous. Today most Eskimos live in normal houses, wear western-style clothes and travel about by car or aeroplane. Perhaps because of this more settled existence their population has doubled over the past twenty-five years from about 50,000 in 1950 to nearly 100,000 in 1977.

ESPERANTO

Specially invented language, by Dr L. Zamenhof of Poland, based on about 2,000 common words taken mainly from the Romance languages (Italian, Spanish, French), and intended to aid communication between nations. After some early success, it has largely fallen into neglect.

Europe

BARENTS SEA

Kola Peninsula

Kanin Peninsula

WHITE SEA

•Archangel

L Onega

L Ladoga

Gulf of Finland

•Leningrad

EUROPEAN PLAIN

UNION OF

SOVIET SOCIALIST

REPUBLICS

•Moscow

Volga

Kazan

•Kuybyshev

URAL MOUNTAINS

•Sverdlovsk

Smolensk•

Central Russian Uplands

Volga Heights

Ural

ARAL SEA

Vilnius

•Minsk

YELORUSSIA

Dnieper

Desna

Pripet

Pripet Marshes

Kiev

UKRAINE

Don

Volga

Astrakhan•

Rostov•

CASPIAN SEA

MOLDAVIA

Odessa•

Dnieper

Sea of Azov

Crimea

Caucasus Mountains

Elbrus 18480

GEORGIA

Tbilisi

AZERBAIJAN

Baku•

MANIA

Bucharest•

Danube

BLACK SEA

Sofiya•

ARMENIA

Yerevan•

Ararat 12945

BULGARIA

Istanbul•

Ankara•

Kizil Irmak

Sakaria

T U R K E Y

L Tuz

Erciyas 12850

L Van

•Tabriz

•Tehran

I R A N

ECE

Salonika•

Taurus Mts

•Aleppo

Tigris

Baghdad•

Athens•

AEGEAN SEA

•Nicosia

S Y R I A

Euphrates

RHODES

CYPRUS

I R A Q

CRETE

Basra•

1 GIBRALTAR
2 ANDORRA
3 BELGIUM
4 NETHERLANDS
5 NORTHERN IRELAND
6 LUXEMBOURG
7 SWITZERLAND
8 LIECHTENSTEIN
9 MONACO
10 ALBANIA

●●●●● = THE BOUNDARY BETWEEN EUROPE AND ASIA

ESTONIA

State on the Baltic Sea which became independent in 1918 but was absorbed into the UNION OF SOVIET SOCIALIST REPUBLICS in 1940. The principal city is Tallinn.

ETHIOPIA

African republic, formerly Abyssinia, east of SUDAN, with an area of 1,221,900 sq km (471,804 sq miles). The population is about 32 million, and the capital is Addis Ababa. The chief products are maize, cotton, coffee, citrus fruits and tobacco. Ethiopia is the home of the COPTIC CHURCH, one of the earliest Christian communities. Its most prominent figure this century has been the Emperor Haile Selassie, who was overthrown in 1974. Since then Ethiopia's military regime has struggled against secessionist forces in the east and south.

ETRUSCANS

Race of people who lived in Etruria (now Tuscany) on the west coast of ITALY from about the eighth to the first centuries BC. Little is known of their origins, but they created an impressive civilization, noted for its metalwork, sculpture and tomb decoration.

Etruscan terracotta, 2nd century BC

EUCLID (*c.* 300 BC)

Greek mathematician and philosopher. He created a system of geometry which is still taught today, and also wrote on such subjects as ASTRONOMY, MUSIC and OPTICS.

EUGENICS

The study of human GENETICS, especially with regard to theories about selective breeding and the possible improvement of human types.

EURIPIDES (*c.* 480–406 BC)

Greek dramatist, He specialized in tragedy, his plays including *Electra*, *Medea* and *Bacchae*.

EUROPE

Continent with an area of 10,532,000 sq km 4,067,000 sq miles), extending from the URAL mountains in the east to the ATLANTIC OCEAN in the west, and from the MEDITERRANEAN SEA in the south to beyond the Arctic Circle in the north. It includes ICELAND. Its greatest extent east to west is 6,400 km (4,000 miles) and from south to north 4,800 km (3,000 miles). Europe

can be regarded as a peninsula of the main land mass of ASIA with the addition of such groups of islands as GREAT BRITAIN and IRELAND. Its principal mountain ranges are the ALPS, the Caucasus and the PYRENEES. The principal rivers are the Volga, DANUBE, Don, Dnieper, RHINE, Elbe, Loire, Rhône and Po. The climate varies from arctic tundra in northern NORWAY and RUSSIA to sub-tropical in parts of southern SPAIN and ITALY; but generally it is temperate, with adequate rainfall all year round and few extremes of temperature.

Politically the continent is divided into a number of sovereign states, each with a proud history and traditions, though there are now movements towards some form of unification. The total population is about 686 million.

EUROPEAN ECONOMIC COMMUNITY (EEC)

Organization of European nations to promote the completely free movement between them of goods, services, capital and labour. Popularly known as the Common Market. It is the long-term intention to create a single currency, also to create new parliamentary institutions within the Community, and so to achieve a broad measure of economic and political union.

The first steps were taken in 1952 with the setting up of the European Coal and Steel Community, comprising the BENELUX countries (Belgium, the Netherlands and Luxembourg), FRANCE, ITALY and West GERMANY. These six countries formed the EEC when it was established, by the Treaty of Rome, in 1957. DENMARK, GREAT BRITAIN and IRELAND joined the Community in 1973 GREECE joined in 1981 and other countries have applied for membership. The affairs of the Community are largely administered from Brussels; while the first steps have been taken to create a form of European Parliament in Strasbourg. The European Atomic Energy Community (EURATOM) was also established in 1957 to promote co-operation between member states over the use of nuclear energy.

EUROPEAN FREE TRADE ASSOCIATION (EFTA)

Organization of European nations to promote trade among its members by forming a type of customs union. The member countries are AUSTRIA, NORWAY, PORTUGAL, SWEDEN, SWITZERLAND, FINLAND and ICELAND. Two other member countries, Great Britain and Denmark, resigned in 1972 prior to their entry into the EEC.

EVOLUTION

Scientific theories, mainly in the field of BIOLOGY, about the growth and development of plant and animal life, from its origins millions of years ago to the myriad forms of life existing today. Much thought and inquiry had gone into plant and animal life, as it was seen to exist, for thousands of years; but it was not until the nineteenth century that people started thinking seriously about how forms of life might have changed and evolved over periods of millions of years. The significance of fossil remains (*see* PALAEONTOLOGY) and the theories of Charles DARWIN had much to do with this. Today it is believed that life, in the form of simple cells, probably started about 3,100 million years ago. Initially evolutionary theory was seen as a threat to Christian orthodoxy, in that it conflicted with the possibility of a universe created by God, but today the two are not usually seen as opposing schools of thought.

EYE

The organ of sight. It is ball-shaped, only one small segment being visible. This visible part is the cornea, which acts something like the lens of a camera. Images are received on to the sensitive membrane at the back of the eye, the retina, and then transmitted by the optic nerves to the brain. Eyebrows, eyelashes, eyelids and the shape of the bones around the eye (eye sockets) are all designed to protect the delicate and exposed cornea.

F

FAEROE ISLANDS

Group of islands in the North ATLANTIC OCEAN, situated almost mid-way between the SHETLAND ISLANDS and ICELAND. Previously a province of DENMARK, granted self-government in 1948.

FAIR ISLE

Small island to the north of SCOTLAND, situated between SHETLAND and ORKNEY, famous for its brightly patterned knitted garments.

FALCON

Bird of prey closely related to the EAGLE and HAWK. Best known is the peregrine falcon used in the hunting sport of falconry.

A kestrel, a member of the falcon family

FALKLAND ISLANDS

British colony in the South ATLANTIC OCEAN, consisting of nearly a hundred islands, the two largest being East and West Falkland. The chief town is Stanley. Most of the inhabitants (only about 2,000) are of British descent. They raise sheep and export wool. South Georgia, an island 1,300 km (800 miles) to the east, is a dependency of the Falklands and acts as a whaling station.

FALLA, Manuel de (1876–1946)

Spanish composer. He was born in the region of Audalusia, home of flamenco singing and dancing, and his own music is full of its melodies and rhythms. His best-known works are the opera *La vida breve* ('Life is Short'), and the ballets *El amor brujo* ('Love, the Magician') and *The Three-Cornered Hat.*

FARADAY, Michael (1791–1867)

English scientist. Almost entirely self-taught, he became an assistant to Sir Humphry DAVY and went on to discover the principles of electro-magnetic induction which led directly to the development of the electric generator and the electric motor.

FAULKNER, William Harrison (1897–1962)

American novelist, whose books are mostly set in the MISSISSIPPI region of the American South. They include *The Sound and the Fury* and *Requiem for a Nun.*

FAURÉ, Gabriel Urbain (1845–1924)

French composer, noted especially for his songs *(chansons)* and for his setting of the Requiem Mass. He also composed fine chamber music.

FAWKES, Guy. *See* GUNPOWDER PLOT

The feudal system: villagers were allowed their own strip of land in return for working on the lord's land.

FEDERAL GOVERNMENT

Type of government organized on two levels: a central legislature which passes laws applying to the nation as a whole; and state or provincial legislatures which have the authority to make laws applying to their own particular region. The UNITED STATES OF AMERICA, CANADA and AUSTRALIA have federal forms of government.

FENCING

Swordsmanship organized as a sport. It is of French origin. Three types of weapon may be used – the foil, the épée, or the sabre. There is also a standard type of costume, partly designed as a form of protection, consisting of canvas jacket and breeches, gloves, and a face mask. It is included in the OLYMPIC GAMES.

FERMENTATION

Type of chemical change caused by the action of certain ENZYMES. The most familiar kind of fermentation is that produced by the enzyme YEAST which converts SUGAR into ALCOHOL, as in the production of wine and beer.

FERMI, Enrico (1901–54)

Italian physicist. He settled in the United States in 1938 and designed the first nuclear pile, which came into operation in 1942, thus pioneering nuclear physics.

FEUDAL SYSTEM

The way of life for most Europeans during the Middle Ages, whereby landowners (lords or barons) allowed their tenants (vassals or serfs) to cultivate sections of their land. In exchange the tenants were required to swear complete allegiance (or fealty) to their lord, which meant paying him such dues as he demanded, and, if required, taking up arms on his behalf. The Feudal System operated as a sort of pyramid of power, tenants owing allegiance to their lords, who in turn owed allegiance to the king. Feudalism started to decline during the twelfth century, as governments became more centralized and the mass of the people began to owe allegiance directly to the sovereign. In ENGLAND it was finally abolished in 1660, though most feudal practices had ceased long before that date.

FIBREGLASS

Glass stretched out into fine threads or fibres, which can then be woven into a kind of cloth. Reinforced fibreglass plastics are both strong and light and are widely used in construction of boats, motor cars and aircraft.

FIELDING, Henry (1707–54)

English writer, sometimes called the 'Father of the English Novel'. His best known work of this type is *Tom Jones*.

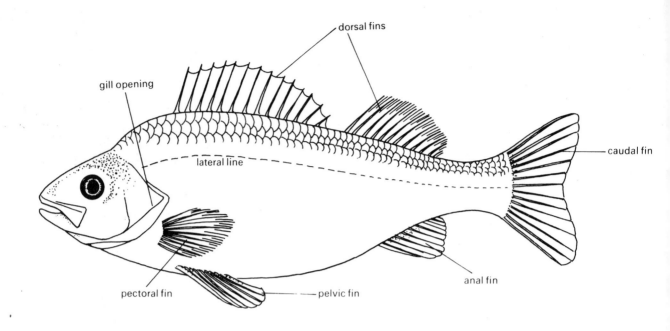

dorsal fins

gill opening

lateral line

caudal fin

pectoral fin

pelvic fin

anal fin

Above A typical bony fish

FIJI

Country consisting of a group of more than 500 islands in the South PACIFIC OCEAN, with a population of 630,000. The capital is Suva on the island of Viti Levu. Fiji was formerly a British crown colony. It became independent in 1970, but remains within the BRITISH COMMONWEALTH.

FINLAND

North European republic, included as part of SCANDINAVIA. It has an area of 337,009 sq km (130,127 sq miles) and a population of about 4.7 million. The capital is Helsinki. The landscape is noted for its hundreds of lakes, as well as for its extensive forests which make it one of the world's leading producers of timber. The northern part of the country is also a part of the region known as LAPLAND. Finland was a province of Imperial Russia until 1917. The language is not related either to the Scandinavian tongues or to Russian, but does have some connections with Magyar.

FISH

Large group of VERTEBRATE animals belonging to the class *Pisces,* living in either salt or fresh water, and very widely distributed throughout the regions of the world. They are distinguished by gills, through which they absorb oxygen from the water; by fins, which provide their means of propulsion and balance; and by the scales which comprise their skin. Fish, like REPTILES, also lay eggs, though in the case of some species, the female keeps the eggs inside her body until they have hatched. There are over 20,000 species of fish, ranging in size from the whale shark which grows up to 15 m (50 ft) to the goby, which is less than 1 cm ($\frac{1}{2}$ in) long.

FITZGERALD, Francis Scott Key (1896–1940)

American novelist, better known as F. Scott Fitzgerald: books include *The Great Gatsby, Tender is the Night* and *The Last Tycoon.*

Right Henry VII's Chapel, Westminster Abbey

ዮሴሶፎመዮ፡ቶለጥሪሱ፡ሀዋገ   ባቲ፡ሠጋሶ፡ተሰው፡ሰሶበአዘሪ
ቱሐፎቅበ፡ደእሒፎፎ፡ሊ፡ለዘ   ፨ፎሰው፡ልግፊ፡ቀቃጋ፨ቶንግለ፡ቱ
፡ባልለ፡ቱለ፡ጠሮመዬሶ፡መበሶ   ፤ዘዮሪ፤ዮጋ፡ደበ፡ቀልሐገ፡መሪ
      ፨ ሐ፡ጸሮ፡፡ሰለቡ   ሚቃ፡ለበሮፈዘ፡ኣሐመ፡ጋሐቡ

Above Lesser flamingoes at Lake Nakuru, Kenya

FLAMINGO

Group of BIRDS, distinguished by their very long legs, long necks and large, hooked beaks. They are classed as waders, and live in flocks or colonies in areas of shallow water in tropical or temperate regions. They feed by scooping up water or mud and sifting out edible matter. Most flamingoes have a delicate pink-white plumage.

FLAMSTEED, John (1646–1719)

English astronomer. First Astronomer-Royal at the time of the building of the Greenwich Observatory. His catalogue of the fixed stars was one of the first important landmarks of modern practical ASTRONOMY.

FLAUBERT, Gustave (1821–80)

French novelist noted for the care and precision of his style. His most famous book is *Madame Bovary*.

Left Noah's ark from a 17th-century Coptic manuscript

FLEMING, Sir Alexander (1881–1955)

Scottish chemist and bacteriologist who, with Sir Howard Florey and Ernst Chain, isolated the mould penicillin and prepared it as an effective ANTIBIOTIC medicine in the treatment of disease.

FLEMING, Sir John Ambrose (1849–1945)

English scientist, whose invention of the thermionic valve led to big improvements in RADIO transmission.

FLINT

Very hard, bluish-black stone surrounded by a white crust, derived from the FOSSIL remains of sponges or other marine life. They are found in chalk. Because of their sharp, pointed edges when broken, flints were often used as implements or weapons by prehistoric men. They were also used in some early firearms to help produce a spark which in turn ignited the charge of powder.

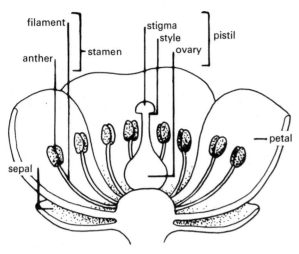

Cross-section through a flower

FLOWER

That part of some PLANTS concerned with reproduction. Flowers consist basically of a pistil, with ovaries at its base and stigma at its tip; stamens; sepals; and petals. For preproduction (i.e. the production of new seeds) to take place, pollen from the stamens must be transferred to the stigma. This is pollination. Sometimes plants can pollinate themselves. At other times they require pollen from the flowers of other plants (cross-pollination). One effective way of achieving this involves insects like BEES. They can be attracted to a flower by its bright petals, by its scent, and by the nectar contained within it. As they enter a flower, some pollen becomes attached to them, which they then carry to another flower. Human beings have cultivated flowers for hundreds of years, and by careful selection and cross-pollination of certain types of plant, have produced flowers of a size, colour and perfume which would never be found under normal conditions of nature. *See also* BOTANY and Gregor MENDEL.

FLY

An INSECT distinguished by having two wings. There are more than 5,000 species of fly,
ranging from midges no bigger than the head of a pin to craneflies (daddy-long-legs) with a wingspan of 62.5 mm ($2\frac{1}{2}$ in). The common housefly and bluebottle are the species most often encountered.

FOLKLORE AND FOLK MUSIC

The traditions, beliefs, legends and customs of a society or civilization that have been handed down from generation to generation. The most interesting parts of folklore are often contained in LEGENDS and MYTHS, usually transmitted by word of mouth and not written down until much later. Similarly the traditional songs and dances of different societies are learnt by imitation or repetition, usually changing slightly all the time and often existing simultaneously in several different versions. Some academic composers have taken a special interest in folk music, notably Béla BARTÓK and Zoltan KODALY in Hungary, and Ralph VAUGHAN WILLIAMS in England.

FOOD

The substances of nutrition needed by any PLANT or ANIMAL to make it grow and sustain its life. In human beings there are three types of food requirement: fats, carbohydrates and proteins. Fats are found primarily in dairy products; proteins in meat and cheese; and carbohydrates in bread, sugar and fruits. *See also* VITAMINS.

FOOTBALL

Association football is a game played with a fairly large, inflated ball on a marked pitch with a goalmouth placed at each end. There are two teams of eleven players, the object of the game being to project the ball into the opposing side's goalmouth (thus scoring a 'goal'). One member of each team (the goalkeeper) defends the goalmouth and may handle the ball as well as kick it. The remaining players may only kick the ball or propel it with their heads. Soccer became an organized game in England during the nineteenth century, and the controlling body today is the Football Association (FA). It is now also played in many other countries, and the international organizing body is the *Fédération Internationale de Football Association* (FIFA), which arranges the World Cup and other international competitions.

Rugby football is played with an oval-shaped ball and players may handle the ball as well as kick it. The rules differ from those of soccer in many other ways, including methods of scoring which are assessed in points rather than 'goals'. Rugby Union is played with fifteen members to each team. Rugby League has thirteen a side. American football (eleven a side) has developed from rugby.

FORD, Henry (1863–1947)

American industrialist. He founded the Ford Motor Company in 1903 and introduced many of the methods of assembly-line production now copied all over the world. The most famous result was the 'Model T' Ford, the first motor vehicle made for a mass market in 1908. It was cheaper and more reliable than any of its rivals and by 1925 Ford was producing 10,000 cars a day.

FORSTER, Edward Morgan (1879–1970)

British novelist, also an essayist and critic. He attacked the complacent and conventional attitudes of such institutions as the Church, the Civil Service and the Public Schools, as he saw them. His best-known book is *A Passage to India*.

FOSSIL

The shape or substance of a dead plant or animal transformed through chemical action, usually into rock or stone. COAL is a fossilized form of the remains of dead and decayed vegetation. Amber is fossilized plant resin.

Fossilized trilobite, an extinct marine anthropod

Much more dramatic are the fossil remains of some animals, which can be the most detailed and complete representation in stone of the shell or bones of the animal in question. Some fossil remains are over 500 million years old. They are most commonly found in limestones, clays and shales. *See also* EVOLUTION, GEOLOGY and PALAEONTOLOGY.

FOUCAULT, Jean Bernard Léon (1819–68)

French scientist who demonstrated the rotation of the EARTH by means of a 60 m (200 ft) pendulum suspended from the dome of the Panthéon in Paris. A similar pendulum can be seen in the Science Museum, London. Foucault also invented the GYROSCOPE.

FOX

Animal of the DOG family, distinguished by its pointed nose, long body and long bushy tail.

The European fox has a reddish-brown coat with a white underside. The Arctic fox has a white coat in winter which changes to brownish-grey in the summer months. There is also the fennec, smallest of the group but with large ears, which lives in the desert regions of AFRICA.

FOX, Charles James (1749–1806)

English statesman. A leading member of the Whig Party and twice Foreign Secretary, Fox championed many liberal causes. He opposed British use of force against the American colonies (*see* AMERICAN WAR OF INDEPENDENCE), supported the ideals of the FRENCH REVOLUTION and demanded reduction of the political powers of the King.

FRANCE

European republic and the largest country in Europe, apart from European RUSSIA, with an area of 547,026 sq km (211,219 sq miles). The population is over 53 million, and the capital is Paris. Other major towns and cities are Lyons, Marseilles, Bordeaux, Nice, Lille, Le Havre, Rouen and Nantes. France has extensive coastlines along the channel, the ATLANTIC OCEAN (including the Bay of Biscay) and the MEDITERRANEAN SEA. It is separated from Spain by the PYRENEES; from Italy by the ALPS; while the RHINE provides a natural frontier with West GERMANY for some of its length. The longest river is the Loire; other important rivers are the Rhône, the Seine and the Garonne.

The country is virtually self-supporting as far as agriculture is concerned; and it also produces and exports many of the world's finest wines. France also has many important industries, notably motor and aircraft manufacture, chemicals and textiles. It has many hydro-electric plants and a growing nuclear energy programme.

In Roman times the country was called Gaul. In the fifth century Gaul was overrun by various barbarian tribes, including the Franks,

Chateau de Chenonceaux, Loire, France

who bestowed upon it its present name. CHARLEMAGNE was king of the Franks, and under him the country formed part of the HOLY ROMAN EMPIRE. After his death the empire broke up and the power of the monarchy declined until the country was ruled by feudal lords. In the centuries that followed France entered a long period of conflict with ENGLAND (*see* HUNDRED YEARS WAR), whose kings laid claim to large areas of the country. JOAN OF ARC finally defeated the English and unified the nation. France was as much shaken by religious conflict between Catholics and Protestants (HUGUENOTS) as any other part of Europe, but entered one of its most illustrious periods with the reign of LOUIS XIV. The monarchy came to an end (except for one or two brief restorations) with the FRENCH REVOLUTION. This, in turn, brought about the rise of NAPOLEON and another period of French ascendency. During the nineteenth century France secured most of its overseas possessions, especially in North Africa, and gained in prosperity at home. It suffered badly in WORLD WAR I and was occupied for most of WORLD WAR II. Soon after there were bitter colonial wars fought in Indo-China (VIETNAM) and ALGERIA. These contributed to the downfall of the Fourth Republic and the return of Charles de GAULLE as President. The ending of these wars and entry into the EUROPEAN ECONOMIC COMMUNITY brought stability and prosperity to France. *See also* FRENCH COMMUNITY.

FRANCHISE

The right to vote. In GREAT BRITAIN this is extended to everyone over the age of eighteen, with a few special exceptions.

FRANCIS OF ASSISI, St (1182–1226)

Priest who founded the Franciscan order of friars of the ROMAN CATHOLIC CHURCH. His life was marked by simplicity and a deep respect for all living things.

St Francis of Assisi

FRANCK, Cesar Auguste (1822–90)

Belgian composer who spent most of his life as an organist in Paris. Wrote much for the organ and some instrumental and orchestral works, notably the Symphonic Variations for Piano and Orchestra, and the Symphony in D minor.

FRANCO, General Francisco (1892–1975)

Spanish soldier and statesman. In 1936 he led a right-wing insurrection against the existing government which was the start of the Spanish Civil War. With aid from HITLER and MUSSOLINI, Franco won the war for the Nationalists in 1939 and became dictator and chief of state from that year until his death. He kept SPAIN out of WORLD WAR II, and despite political repression, increased the country's prosperity.

FRANKLIN, Benjamin (1706–90)

American statesman, writer and scientist. As a statesman he was a diplomatic representative of his country in GREAT BRITAIN and FRANCE, and helped to draft both the Declaration of Independence and the Constitution of the UNITED STATES OF AMERICA. As a scientist he invented the lightning conductor. In addition, he was a popular journalist and innovator of many public services.

FREDERICK II, the Great (1712–86)

King of PRUSSIA. He successfully defended his country against a military alliance of AUSTRIA, FRANCE, RUSSIA and SWEDEN during the SEVEN YEARS WAR, winning several victories and carrying out some skilful retreats. After the war he revived Prussia's economy, introduced many social reforms and built her up into one of the great European powers. Frederick was also a lover of the arts and an enthusiastic musician.

FREE CHURCHES

Protestant Churches of ENGLAND and WALES, also sometimes called the Nonconformist Churches, not established by law like the CHURCH OF ENGLAND. They include the Baptists, Methodists, Congregationalists, Unitarians and the Society of Friends (Quakers).

FRENCH COMMUNITY

Economic and cultural association of states, chiefly in Africa, formerly part of the French Empire. Established in 1958 by President de GAULLE.

FRENCH GUIANA

French overseas territory on the north-east coast of South America. It has an area of 91,000 sq km (35,137 sq miles) and a population of 71,000. Most of the country is covered by huge forests with a wide variety of timber.

The execution of Louis XVI in 1793

FRENCH REVOLUTION

By 1789 France was almost bankrupt after a series of long and unsuccessful wars; royal extravagance had emptied the Treasury; the peasants suffered heavy and unjust taxes, while the middle classes resented having little or no say in the government. Discontent among the lower classes was aggravated by poor harvests and bad distribution of food. The main events of the Revolution were the setting up, in 1789, of a National Assembly, under the leadership of the Comte de Mirabeau, to prepare a new constitution; food riots in Paris and the Storming of the Bastille prison on 14 July 1789; the invasion of France by foreign royalist armies; the declaration of France as a republic and execution of King Louis XVI and Queen Marie Antoinette in 1793; the so-called Reign of Terror, intended to stamp out all opposition to the new regime; and the government of France by a small committee called the Directory until this was overthrown by General Bonaparte (NAPOLEON I) in 1799. The French Revolution was a momentous event in history. It was marked by much violence and confusion, but its ideas of 'Liberty, Equality, Fraternity', and the establishment of a strong republic affected events in every other country of the Western world. *See also* Georges DANTON and Maximilien ROBESPIERRE.

FRESCO

Method of painting on a plaster wall, usually while the plaster is still fresh so that the pigments of the paint combine with the plaster in a special way. Many great church paintings are frescoes.

FREUD, Sigmund (1856–1939)

Austrian doctor and pioneer figure of modern psychiatric medicine. He believed that the cause of much mental distress or abnormality is the effort of the conscious part of the mind to repress powerful but socially unacceptable feelings and impulses. His method of investigating mental distress is called PSYCHOANALYSIS. Freud's ideas about the different levels of conscious, subconscious and unconscious mental activity, and the interpretation of dreams, have also had a big influence on art, literature and education.

FRIENDLY SOCIETIES AND BUILDING SOCIETIES

Voluntary associations to which members pay contributions as an insurance against such things as sickness and unemployment. Their function is therefore much the same as that of an INSURANCE company. A special kind of friendly society is the building society. On the one hand, people can save money with a building society; on the other hand, they can borrow from the society in order to buy property, paying back the sum in instalments with an agreed rate of interest added. In GREAT BRITAIN the friendly and building societies play a big part in the domestic economy with the involvement of millions of pounds of investment.

FROEBEL, Friedrich Wilhelm August (1782–1852)

German educationalist and founder of the kindergarten system for teaching young children. Froebel Institutes of Education exist in many countries.

FROGS AND TOADS

Group of tail-less AMPHIBIAN animals, native to most tropical, sub-tropical and temperate regions. They lay eggs (spawn) and the young hatch as tadpoles which change shape as well as size as they grow to adulthood. Generally frogs spend more time in water than toads. Also they can jump, while toads usually only walk. The largest species of frog, the Goliath frog of Africa, is up to 30 cm (12 in) in length. Some types of frog are classed as edible; it is only the legs that are eaten.

FROISSART, Jean (c. 1333–1405)

French chronicler. His *Chronicles* trace the main events in ENGLAND, FRANCE, SCOTLAND, IRELAND and SPAIN from 1325 to 1400, and include eye-witness accounts of the battles of Crécy and Poitiers. They are the greatest of medieval histories.

FRY, Elizabeth Gurney (1780–1845)

English social reformer, especially concerned with improving prison conditions. She was a Quaker.

FUGUE

Type of musical composition in which a theme (or subject) is first played (or stated) on its own and then built upon itself in various ways. Each new entry on the theme is called a part; hence there are two-, three-, or four-part fugues. Double fugues contain two distinct themes, or subjects.

FULTON, Robert (1765–1815)

American engineer and inventor. With the support of the French and British governments he experimented with designing various projects, including a submarine. Returning to America in 1806, he built the first commercially successful steamboat, the *Clermont,* which plied between New York and Albany.

FUNGUS

The name of a group of PLANTS which have no green colouring matter (CHLOROPHYLL). They make up the lowest division of the plant kingdom and are known as thallophytes. Scientists who study fungi are called mycologists. There are over 75,000 species of fungi which grow everywhere. They have no stems, leaves or flowers and reproduce by means of spores scattered by the wind.

Structure and life cycle of the mushroom

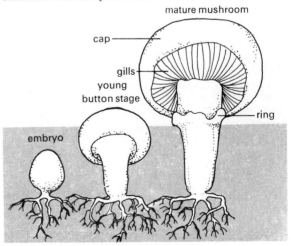

G

GABON

West African republic on the ATLANTIC coast and lying across the line of the EQUATOR. It has an area of 267,667 sq km (103,352 sq miles), which makes it larger than Great Britain, but a population of only about 652,000. The capital is Libreville.

GAELIC

The language of the Scots, Irish and Manx CELTS. In 1922 Irish Gaelic became the official language of the newly formed Republic of IRELAND. About 80,000 people still speak Gaelic in SCOTLAND.

GAGARIN, Colonel Yuri (1934–68)

Soviet cosmonaut. In 1961 he became the first man in space, circling the EARTH in his spacecraft *Vostok 1* in 108 minutes. He was later killed in an air crash.

GAINSBOROUGH, Thomas (1727–88)

English artist, noted for his portrait and landscape paintings, including *Blue Boy, Harvest Wagon* and *Watering Place*.

GALAPAGOS ISLANDS

Group of volcanic islands in the PACIFIC OCEAN about 1000 km (650 miles) from the South American mainland and owned by ECUADOR. They are famous for their unique forms of plant and animal life, which influenced Charles DARWIN and his theories about EVOLUTION when he visited the islands.

Giant tortoises on the Galapagos Islands

Galileo (right) explaining the solar system

GALILEO GALILEI (1564–1642)

Italian astronomer, mathematician and physicist. He invented a form of THERMOMETER, realized the value of the PENDULUM as a means of recording time, and investigated some of the properties of GRAVITY and motion. As an astronomer Galileo constructed the first true TELESCOPE and made important observations of the MOON, the SUN and some of the other planets. He also supported the notion of a SOLAR SYSTEM, with the EARTH and other planets revolving round the sun, as advanced by Copernicus. This was condemned as a heresy by the Church and he was made to recant in order to save himself from burning at the stake. After a brief imprisonment he was allowed to resume his other scientific studies.

GALLUP POLL

System devised by the American Dr George Gallup for assessing public opinion on various social or political issues by questioning a small sample of people and analysing their replies. Such polls are conducted particularly during election campaigns.

GALSWORTHY, John (1867–1933)

English novelist and dramatist. His best-known work is *The Forsyte Saga*, which provides an interesting picture of British upper-class life in the early years of this century.

GALTON, Sir Francis (1822–1911)

English scientist whose work on HEREDITY led to the study of EUGENICS. He also introduced a system of finger-print identification.

GALVANI, Luigi (1737–98)

Italian physiologist who investigated the relationship between certain electrical effects and animal tissue. The verb 'to galvanize' is derived from his name. So is the galvanometer, which is an instrument used to detect and measure electrical currents.

GAMBIA, THE

Small West African republic stretching inland from the ATLANTIC coast along the banks of the Gambia river for 290 km (180 miles). Its area is 11,295 sq km (4,361 sq miles) and the population is about 604,000. The capital is Banjul. Gambia is a former British colony. It became independent in 1965.

GANDHI, Mohandas Karamchand (1869–1948)

Indian national leader, widely known as the 'Mahatma' (Great Soul). In 1919 he first became involved in the Indian movement for independence from British rule. To this end he developed practices of non-violent civil disobedience and fasting. He gained a huge following among his fellow Indians and played a large role in the negotiations for Indian self-government soon after WORLD WAR II. He was assassinated by an extreme nationalist Hindu who opposed his plans for Hindu-Moslem unity.

GANGES

Principal river of India, rising in the Himalayas and flowing for about 2,490 km (1,550 miles) into the Bay of Bengal. By tradition it is a sacred river to the Hindus. Today it is used extensively for irrigation and to provide hydro-electric power.

GANNET

Large sea bird, about 90 cm (3 ft) in length, which breeds in large numbers along the coasts of the North Atlantic. They catch fish by diving straight down into the water.

GARIBALDI, Giuseppe (1807–82)

Italian soldier and patriot. In the cause of Italian unity he fought against the Austrians in the north, and conquered the regions of Naples and Sicily in the south with his small band of 'Redshirts'. Later he entered the Italian parliament as a deputy. Garibaldi was a world-famous figure in his own time and regarded as a hero by many working-class people, who saw him as a political liberator.

GAUGUIN, Paul (1848–1903)

French artist. He was a businessman up to the age of thirty-five. As a painter he worked in Brittany, then briefly with VAN GOGH in Provence, before travelling to Tahiti and the MARQUESAS ISLANDS in the PACIFIC OCEAN, where he produced most of his famous Post-Impressionist paintings.

GAULLE, Charles André Joseph Marie de (1890–1970)

French soldier and statesman. He became famous during WORLD WAR II as the leader of the Free French forces after the occupation of France by Nazi Germany. In 1944 he headed the liberation forces that entered Paris. After a period as head of the provisional government he retired from public life, but the political instability of the Fourth Republic and the

General de Gaulle in Paris, Liberation Day, 1944

conduct of the Algerian war brought him out of retirement. He then created a new constitution and became the first President of the Fifth Republic; concluded the Algerian war; granted independence to France's other overseas possessions; and pursued a policy of greater independence for France itself. In 1969 he was defeated in a referendum of his own calling, resigned from office and once more retired.

GAUSS, Karl Friedrich (1777–1855)

German mathematician who did important theoretical work in the fields of ASTRONOMY and ELECTRICITY. The *gauss* is a unit of electromagnetism.

GAY, John (1685–1732)

English dramatist. He wrote the libretto of *The Beggar's Opera,* the first opera to use English words. The music was taken from popular tunes of the day.

GAZELLE

Group of fairly small, sandy-coloured ANTELOPES native to parts of AFRICA and southern ASIA. They are noted for their speed.

GEARS. *See* MECHANICS

GECKO

Group of REPTILES belonging to the LIZARD family, native to tropical and sub-tropical regions. They have adhesive padded feet which enable them to position themselves on walls and ceilings and are often found in houses, usually at night.

GEIGER COUNTER

Device invented by Hans Geiger (1882–1947) and Sir Ernest RUTHERFORD (1871–1937) to detect and measure radioactivity, and widely used in nuclear physics. It can register radioactivity on a dial or as a series of clicks which accelerate with any increase in radiation.

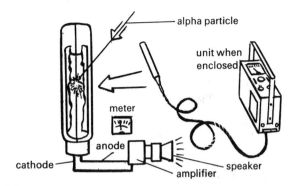

Geiger counter

GEISSLER TUBE

Special type of glass tube, named after Heinrich Geissler (1814–79), used to demonstrate the brilliant colours produced by electricity as it passes through gases and partial vacuums. NEON lights operate on a similar principle.

GEMSBOK

Member of the ANTELOPE family which belongs to the ORYX group, native to parts of Southern AFRICA. It is greyish-brown with black stripes and has long, rapier-like horns.

GENERAL AGREEMENT ON TARIFFS AND TRADE (GATT)

International agency, sponsored by the UNITED NATIONS, created to help world trade by reducing tariffs and other commercial barriers between nations.

GENERAL ELECTION. *See* PARLIAMENT

GENET

Small carnivorous MAMMALS, related to the civet. They are found in parts of AFRICA and southern EUROPE.

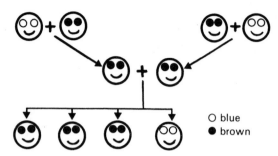

O blue
● brown

The gene for brown eyes is dominant

GENETICS

Science concerned with the study of the inherited resemblances and differences found in plants and animals related by descent. Genetics is closely linked with subjects like CYTOLOGY, REPRODUCTION, breeding and EVOLUTION.

The characteristics of individuals are determined by 'instructions' known as genes, which decide whether the offspring looks like the mother, the father, or possibly like neither. This genetic or instructional material has been passed on by each of the parents and is stored at the centre of every cell in the new creature's body. Genes are linked together in rod-like structures called CHROMOSOMES, which are too small to be seen with the naked eye but can be clearly distinguished under the microscope. In humans, most of them are roughly X-shaped, some are Y-shaped. There may be more than 1,000 genes in a single chromosome.

It has been found that chromosomes are arranged in pairs and that the cell centres or nuclei of each species contain a fixed number of chromosomes, which is typical of that particular species. Pigs, for example, have 60 chromosomes (30 pairs), while humans have 46 (23 pairs).

Reproductive cells, unlike body cells, do not contain pairs of chromosomes but a set of single chromosomes, which means they contain only half the normal number of chromosomes. When a human female egg cell and a human sperm cell unite to make a new individual, the 23 chromosomes from the egg cell and the 23

chromosomes from the sperm cell pair together to make the required number of 46. Each of the two paired chromosomes carries the same genes arranged in identical order.

All the physical and mental characteristics of an individual are determined by the combination of its genes and the environment in which is grows. We think that each gene governs certain particular characteristics such as colour of eyes, shape of nose, etc. The two genes in every pair inherited by a baby may be very different from each other, since one has been passed on by the father and the other by the mother. In such a case, one can completely suppress the other. If, for example, both the father and mother contribute a gene for blue eyes, the child will have blue eyes. But if one supplies a gene for blue eyes and the other a gene for brown eyes, the child will have brown eyes. This is so because in a pair of dissimilar genes one, in this case the one for brown eyes, can be 'dominant', while the other, in this case the one for blue eyes, is 'recessive'. The recessive character will reappear in future generations according to definite rules and in a definite ratio. Some of the rules of heredity were first laid down by MENDEL and are known as Mendel's Laws.

Recessiveness is one explanation for differences between parents and offspring. More rarely changes are brought about by genes actually being changed by the influence of chemicals, by radiation or, occasionally, just naturally. This is called mutation, and the best known example is probably the albino blackbird. In many cases the mutation is not beneficial to the species and is gradually bred out, but sometimes the mutant gene becomes established and then represents a step in the process of evolution.

It was discovered in the 1950s that genes are DNA molecules (that is, molecules of deoxyribonucleic acid) and that the information which genes carry is coded in strings of amino acids. DNA molecules are threadlike spiral structures which would be several centimetres long if they were unwound. *See also* BIOLOGY.

GENGHIS KHAN (1162–1227)

Mongol chieftain and warrior, whose title means 'Very Mighty Ruler'. His real name was Temujin. He conquered large tracts of ASIA extending from the Black Sea thousands of miles eastwards to CHINA, and so established the Mongol Empire. His grandson was KUBLAI KHAN, at whose court Marco Polo spent several years.

GEOGRAPHY

Science concerned with the surface area of the EARTH, especially as related to the distribution of land and water, physical features, climate population, agriculture, industry, communications and political boundaries. The name comes from the Greek *geo* meaning 'Earth'.

GEOLOGY

Science concerned with the EARTH'S crust, that is, with the composition, properties and age of rocks. Geology is of great importance in connection with mining or in the search for such materials as OIL and natural gas. It is of equal importance to PALAENTOLOGY. *See also* EARTHQUAKE, FOSSIL, GEOPHYSICS, MINERALS and PETROLOGY.

GEOMETRY

Mathematical study of space and those elements that comprise it, namely, points, lines, planes and volumes. Plane geometry deals with points and lines (two dimensional). Solid geometry deals with bodies possessing volume (three dimensional) and conic sections – the curves formed when a plane cuts a cone, namely, circle, ellipse, parabola and hyperbola. Analytical geometry, which was developed by René DESCARTES, consists essentially of defining and describing a point, line, plane or volume in terms of co-ordinates. *See also* EUCLID and PYTHAGORAS.

GEOPHYSICS

The application of science to the study of the EARTH and its ATMOSPHERE, with special reference to the physical properties of the structure of the Earth; the physical properties of seas and oceans and of the sea bed (OCEANOGRAPHY); weather and climate (METEOROLOGY and climatology); EARTHQUAKES (seismology); CONTINENTAL DRIFT (plate tectonics); and such matters as GRAVITY and Earth magnetism.

GERBIL

Small RODENT that looks like a mouse but uses its long hind legs to jump like a KANGAROO, sometimes called a sand rat. It lives in the desert regions of AFRICA and ASIA.

GERMANY

Country of central EUROPE divided into two independent states since WORLD WAR II.

The German Federal Republic (West Germany) has an area of 248,577 sq km (95,981 sq miles) and a population of 61 million. The

The wine-producing region of Mosel, West Germany

capital is Bonn, but much larger towns and cities are Hamburg, Essen, Düsseldorf, Köln (Cologne), München (Munich), Hannover, Frankfurt-am-Main, Nürnberg (Nuremberg) and Bremen. In the south the country is divided from AUSTRIA by the ALPS; in the north is the river Elbe and the large area of the north German plain; and in the west is the River RHINE. West Germany is highly industrialized, the centre of its heavy industries of coal, iron and steel being the Ruhr. Long stretches of the Rhine and the neighbouring river Mosel are an important wine-producing region.

The German Democratic Republic (East Germany) has an area of 108,178 sq km (41,770 sq miles) and a population of nearly 17 million. The capital is East Berlin, and other towns and cities include Leipzig, Dresden and Magdeburg. Agriculture plays a greater role in East Germany, but manufacturing now supplies over three-fifths of the nation's income.

Germany's recorded history began at the time of the ROMAN EMPIRE when the country was inhabited by a number of tribes, including the Goths, Franks, VANDALS and SAXONS. In the ninth century CHARLEMAGNE united the tribes of central Europe, but after his death Germany failed to become a single sovereign state. Instead it consisted of a number of separate kingdoms and principalities. The political division of the German people became more acute after the Protestant REFORMATION led by Martin LUTHER, their lands being fought over by Protestants and Catholics during the period of the THIRTY YEARS WAR. FREDERICK the Great and the rise of the kingdom of PRUSSIA during the eighteenth century saw the beginnings of German unity. This was achieved in the nineteenth century by BISMARCK, who established the German Empire under the leadership of Prussia. After their defeat in WORLD WAR I Germany became a republic, but economic and social problems led to the rise to power of Adolf HITLER and the Nazi dictatorship. Defeat in World War II left the nation occupied by the Allies – the United States, Britain and France in the west, and the Soviet

Union in the east. The existing capital, Berlin, situated in the Soviet zone, was itself occupied by the four Allied powers. In the western zone of the country elections to a newly created parliament (or *Bundestag*) in Bonn led to the establishment of the German Federal Republic in 1954. The first Chancellor, Konrad Adenauer, laid the foundations of future West German co-operation with other western European countries (*see* EUROPEAN ECONOMIC COMMUNITY) and a new prosperity. In the Soviet zone the communist German Democratic Republic was created in 1955. Berlin remains divided into East and West Berlin.

GERSHWIN, George (1898–1937)

Mostly in collaboration with his brother Ira, he wrote some of the best songs and musicals of the 1920s and 30s. As a largely self-taught composer he combined established musical forms with JAZZ styles in the *Rhapsody in Blue*, *An American in Paris*, the opera *Porgy and Bess* and other works.

GEYSER

Spring of naturally hot water or steam, usually gushing out of the ground for regular periods at a time. They are created by the heating of water under the ground by some form of volcanic action. ICELAND and parts of NEW ZEALAND are centres of geyser activity, but the most famous geyser, 'Old Faithful', is in the Yellowstone National Park, in the UNITED STATES.

GHANA

West African republic, formerly the British colony of the Gold Coast. It has an area of 238,537 sq km (92,104 sq miles) and a population of about 11½ million. The capital is Accra. The country is rich in minerals, including gold and bauxite. It is also one of the chief cocoa-producing countries. When the Gold Coast gained its independence in 1957 the former territory of British Togoland joined the new republic. It remains a member of the BRITISH COMMONWEALTH.

GIBBON

Smallest member of the APE family, lightly built with very long arms. They are extremely agile and swing from branch to branch and from tree to tree. They are the only apes which walk normally in an upright position. The gibbon is native to many tropical regions of south-east ASIA.

GIBBON, Edward (1737–94)

English writer and historian. His most famous work is *The Decline and Fall of the Roman Empire,* which is recognized as a great work of literature as well as of history.

GIBBONS, Orlando (1583–1625)

English composer. As organist at Westminster Abbey he wrote much church music, but is especially remembered as one of the great English composers of MADRIGALS.

Old Faithful geyser, Yellowstone Park, USA

GIBRALTAR

A small British territory off southern Spain. It has an area of 6 sq km (2 sq miles) and a population of about 30,000.

GILA MONSTER

A type of LIZARD, native to the desert regions of the UNITED STATES and MEXICO. It is one of the few lizards with a poisonous bite. It can survive for long periods on a store of fat in its tail.

GILBERT AND ELLICE ISLANDS
See KIRIBATI, TUVALU

GILBERT, Sir William Schwenk (1836–1911)

English playwright, best known for his long collaboration with Sir Arthur SULLIVAN over the production of comic operettas.

GILBERT, William (1540–1603)

English physician to Elizabeth I. He is best remembered today for his early investigations into MAGNETISM and ELECTRICITY. He first used the term 'electricity' to describe the property of amber for attracting other objects to it – the Greek word for amber being *electron.*

GIORGIONE, or Giorgio Barbarelli (*c.* 1478–1511)

Italian artist whose paintings are reckoned to mark the beginning of the so-called Venetian School of RENAISSANCE art.

GIOTTO DI BONDONE (*c.* 1267–1337)

Italian artist. He spent most of his life in Florence, and was one of the first to break away from the rather formal style of Byzantine painting, taking his inspiration from real people and scenes.

GIRAFFE

MAMMAL related to the OKAPI but very clearly distinguished by its long neck. Another feature is two short horns tipped with hair. Giraffes live in parts of AFRICA south of the SAHARA.

GLACIER

River of ice occurring in mountainous regions above the snow-line. Where great thicknesses of snow accumulate, the weight of the top snow compresses the lower layers into ice. When this mass rests on a slope, it begins to slide slowly downwards. As it moves the glacier scours out for itself a deep U-shaped valley. The rocks beneath it are ground to a fine powder which forms 'boulder-clay' or 'till'. Boulders and stones fall from the sides of the valley on to the ice and are carried along with it. When the snow-line (the lowest limit of permanent snow) is reached, the ice melts and the rocks resting on it are deposited in a heap which is called a moraine.

GLADSTONE, William Ewart (1809–98)

British statesman. He was Liberal PRIME MINISTER on four occasions, in 1868–74, 1880–5, 1886, and 1892–4. In foreign affairs he pursued a far less imperialist policy than his rival Benjamin DISRAELI, and his main achievements were in the field of social reform, especially with regard to education and extensions of the FRANCHISE. He also spent much time trying to give IRELAND a large measure of self-government, but in this venture he was not successful.

GLAND

Organ in the body which produces and uses substances extracted from the blood. There are two important kinds of glands, exocrine and endocrine. Exocrine glands discharge the substances through tubes which are known as ducts. Among the exocrine glands are the tear glands, the liver, kidneys and the sweat glands. Endocrine glands are sometimes called the 'ductless glands' because they do not use ducts. They discharge their substances directly into the blood stream. They produce HORMONES which affect growth. The hormones of the thyroid gland, for example, regulate metabolism, the rate at which the body uses oxygen and food.

GLASS

Hard transparent material obtained by the fusion (melting) of certain silicates and an ALKALI and cooled at a rate which avoids crystallization. The chief raw materials for glass are fine sand and limestone. Alkali is furnished by carbonates of potash and soda ash. The qualities and physical characteristics of glass are varied by the addition of certain substances, usually oxides; for example, cut glass contains lead oxide, glass of high refractive index barium oxide, and glass used in electrical and thermal apparatus boric oxide.

Glass blowers at work in the 19th century

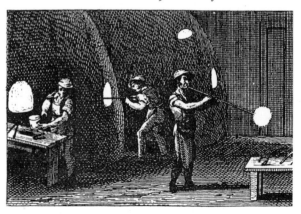

GLIDER

A glider is an aircraft which flies without an engine. The primary glider is made of open framework. The pilot has no protection. Sail planes or soaring planes are more expensive but

Right The mask of the mummy of King Tutankhamun

they are built to make full use of air currents. They are launched by power winch, car or an aeroplane. Once in the air the pilot finds rising air currents so that he can maintain height. Sir George Cayley (1773–1857) built the first bi-plane glider in England and the first successful glider in the world in 1810.

GLINKA, Mikhail Ivanovich (1803–57)

Russian composer. He created, in such works as his operas *A Life for the Tsar* and *Russlan and Ludmilla,* a distinctive Russian musical style which inspired nearly every other Russian composer who came after him. Hence he is often called the 'Father of Russian Music'.

GLOW-WORM

Not a worm but a type of INSECT, the female of which produces a pale greenish light in the region of her abdomen. Since she is wingless the glow is always seen on the ground.

GLUCK, Christoph Willibald von (1714–1787)

German composer of operas who worked for much of his life in Paris. He greatly streng-thened the dramatic content of opera and is therefore regarded as an important reformer in the operatic field. His works include *Alceste* and *Orpheus and Eurydice.*

GNU

Type of ANTELOPE native to parts of eastern and southern AFRICA, distinguished by buffalo-shaped head and horns.

GOAT

Group of cud-chewing (ruminant) MAMMALS, also distinguished by their hollow horns and, in the case of the males, a small beard on the chin. Domestic goats are found in communities all over the world, providing milk, meat and hides.

Left Gold ceremonial knife from Peru, *c.* 13th century

Species of wild goat include the IBEX and the markhor, found mainly in mountainous regions of EUROPE, ASIA and north AFRICA.

GOBI DESERT

Very large, arid desert region in MONGOLIA and northern CHINA about 1 million sq km (nearly 50,000 sq miles) in area. Traditionally the only people who inhabited the region were nomads; but the Mongolian People's Republic has recently irrigated some areas and opened them up to agriculture..

GODWIN, Mary Wollstonecraft (1759–97)

English writer and social reformer. She was almost a century ahead of her time with such publications as *Vindication of the Rights of Woman* and other works demanding women's rights. Her daughter was Mary SHELLEY, author of the novel *Frankenstein.*

GOETHE, Johann Wolfgang von (1749–1832)

German poet, dramatist and novelist, born in Frankfurt-am-Main, and generally regarded as the greatest figure in German literature. Goethe was a founder of the so-called *Stürm und Drang* (Storm and Stress) movement in literature, which led to the nineteenth-century Romantic movement in all the arts. Included among his works is the novel *Wilhelm Meister* and the play *Egmont.* His greatest achievement is the poetic drama *Faust,* the fullest treatment in literature of the legendary scholar and philo-sopher who sold his soul to the Devil for wisdom and knowledge.

GOG AND MAGOG

Symbolic figures from the BIBLE, but in Britain fondly regarded as the survivors of a legendary race of giants. They are depicted as two large sculptured figures in the Guildhall, London.

GOGOL, Nikolai Vasilyevich (1809–52)

Russian writer. He was a civil servant by profession, but wrote a number of highly original novels, including *Dead Souls*, which had a profound influence on the course of Russian literature.

GOLD

Valuable metal with the chemical symbol *Au*. From ancient times it has been highly valued, particularly for ornaments and decorations. Gold is to be found in minute quantities throughout the Earth's crust, even in the sea, but in this state is of little use to man. Worthwhile gold is mined from lodes (metal-bearing veins of rock) or from gravel deposits in river beds which have been washed out of gold-bearing rocks. The richest gold deposits are in the Transvaal (SOUTH AFRICA), the ROCKY MOUNTAINS in the USA and the Ural Mountains in the USSR.

GOLDSMITH, Oliver (1728–74)

Irish writer who eventually settled in London and was a close friend of Dr Samuel JOHNSON.

He is best remembered for his novel *The Vicar of Wakefield* and his play *She Stoops to Conquer*.

GOLF

Game played with a small white ball and a selection of long-handled clubs. It is played over a specially prepared course of about 5,500 m (6,000 yd), each player aiming to hit his own ball from a starting point (or tee) into a small hole in the fewest possible strokes. A standard golf course is divided into eighteen sections, each with its own starting point and concluding 'green' containing the hole. The players – usually two – may compete hole by hole (i.e. win the entire game by winning the largest number of 'holes'); or, as in most championship matches, the winner is the player who completes the whole course in the fewest strokes.

Golf originated in SCOTLAND, and the oldest club in the world is the Royal and Ancient Golf Club, St Andrews, Scotland, which was founded in 1764.

GOOSE

Group of BIRDS sharing many features in common with DUCKS and swans, including

Pink-footed geese in flight

webbed feet, and best suited to an aquatic life. There are twenty-five species, the best known being the greylag (from which the farmyard goose has been bred), the snow goose and the Canadian goose.

GORILLA

Largest member of the APE family, an adult male weighing about 200 kg (450 lb); native to the equatorial forests of AFRICA. They are vegetarian and generally inoffensive unless directly threatened.

Female gorilla with her ten-day-old baby

GORKY, Maxim (1868–1936)

Russian writer who became a leading figure in Soviet literature after the Revolution of 1917. His best known work is the play *The Lower Depths*.

GOUNOD, Charles François (1818–93)

French composer, mainly of operas, and especially of *Faust* which at one time was among the most popular of all operatic works.

GOYA Y LUCIENTES, Francisco José de (1746–1828)

Spanish artist. As painter to the Spanish royal court his portraits often captured with remarkable accuracy the character as well as the appearance of his subjects. During the period of the Peninsular Wars he painted some of the most graphic scenes of bloodshed and cruelty. He also produced many strikingly original etchings and drawings of Spanish life and legend. Goya had a great influence on the development of nineteenth-century art.

GRAMPUS

Largest member of the DOLPHIN family, but sometimes called the 'killer whale'. It feeds on sea birds, seals, porpoises and all kinds of fish.

GRANITE

Very hard, ancient rock, created by the cooling and crystallization of molten minerals deep beneath the ground. The three chief minerals in granite are quartz, mica and felspar, and the colour of the rock varies from grey to pink.

GRANT, Ulysses Simpson (1822–85)

American soldier and statesman. Commander-in-Chief of the victorious Union Army in the AMERICAN CIVIL WAR, then President of the newly restored UNITED STATES.

GRASS

Large group of PLANTS distributed throughout the world except for the polar regions. They include all the well-known cereals, such as wheat, barley and rice; also bamboo and sugar cane. Esparto grass is used in the manufacture of high-quality paper.

GRASSHOPPERS AND CRICKETS

Group of INSECTS, distinguished by their large hind legs, specially adapted for leaping. Crickets also produce a characteristic chirping sound by rubbing together parts of their forewings. Locusts are a large variety of grasshopper, native to parts of AFRICA and the Middle East. They will remain quiet and harmless for years. Then they will gather in enormous numbers, fly off in a huge swarm that can blot out the sun and, upon landing, devastate crops and other vegetation over a large area. Sometimes it is possible to anticipate their movements and destroy them, but locust swarms can still do immense damage.

GRAVITY

That force by which one object attacts another. In fact, every object attracts every other object, with a force that is a) directly proportional to the masses of any two objects, and b) is inversely proportional to the square of the distance between them. On or near the surface of the EARTH other objects fall downwards, or towards the Earth, simply because it has the greater gravitational attraction. Sir Isaac NEWTON formulated these laws and applied them to the organization of the SOLAR SYSTEM; the distances of the planets from the SUN and each other, and the orbits they follow.

GREAT BRITAIN

The more usual title given to the United Kingdom of Great Britain and Northern Ireland. It is a political title, and is not the same as

Great Britain's Queen: Elizabeth II and her consort

the British Isles which applies to the whole group of islands just off the mainland of north-western Europe, including the Republic of IRELAND. The U.K. comprises ENGLAND, Northern Ireland, SCOTLAND and WALES. It has an area of 244,046 sq km (94,232 sq miles).

By the Act of Union of 1707 Scotland united politically with England and Wales. In 1921 most of Ireland broke away from Great Britain, to form the Irish Free State. However, the flag of Great Britain, the Union Jack, continues to represent the three traditional symbols of the St George's Cross for England, St Patrick's Cross for Ireland, and St Andrew's Cross for Scotland.

From the eighteenth century onwards the creation of the British Empire overseas, and the development of the INDUSTRIAL REVOLUTION at home, were shared achievements, especially between England, Scotland and Wales. In this century Great Britain's entry into the EUROPEAN ECONOMIC COMMUNITY means greater unity between the different parts of the nation and the other European member states. On the other hand, there have been demands for a greater degree of regional self-government, especially in Scotland, and a reduction of the powers of the central government.

GREAT LAKES

Five freshwater lakes of North AMERICA situated between CANADA and the UNITED STATES with a total area of 246,000 sq km (95,000 sq miles). They are lakes Superior (the world's largest freshwater lake), Michigan, Huron, Erie and Ontario. Important cities and towns on their banks include Chicago, Detroit Toronto and Cleveland; and between lakes Erie and Ontario there are the Niagara Falls. Since 1959 the ST LAWRENCE SEAWAY has permitted ocean-going vessels to reach inland ports.

GREBE

Family of aquatic diving BIRDS distinguished by their long pointed beaks, abundant plumage

Great crested grebe

about the head and webbed feet set well back. They are found in many freshwater regions, and include the great crested grebe and the little grebe, or dabchick.

GREECE

South-east European republic with an area of 131,944 sq km (50,947 sq miles) and a population of about 9½ million. The capital is Athens and the second largest city is Salonika. The country comprises mainland Greece; the island of CRETE; and the many islands forming the Greek archipelago, including Rhodes, Lesbos, Lemnos and Naxos. Much of the terrain is mountainous and difficult to cultivate; but agriculture remains the main occupation. But the country is also very beautiful, and this, together with the many monuments to Greek antiquity, make it a world centre for tourism.

The Greek civilization was the principal foundation of Western civilization as a whole, especially concerning POLITICS, PHILOSOPHY, DRAMA, art and ARCHITECTURE. By 600 BC this civilization was well established, with the city state of Athens as its focal point. Under the rule of PERICLES Athenian culture reached its zenith, with the building of the PARTHENON and other celebrated monuments. At the same

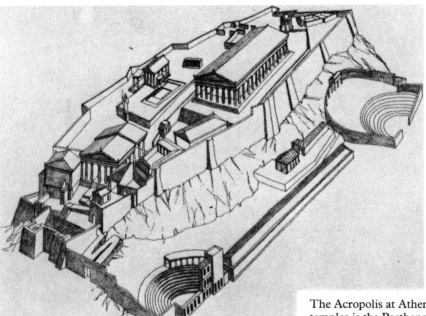

The Acropolis at Athens, Greece. The largest of the temples is the Parthenon, and at the foot of the hill are two theatres.

time there were the wars with Sparta, known as the Peloponnesian Wars. This period was followed by the rise to power of Philip of Macedon and his son ALEXANDER THE GREAT, who ruled Greece and created an empire stretching as far as India. The empire of Alexander did not long survive his death, and during the second century BC Greece was absorbed into the ROMAN EMPIRE. After the decline of Roman power the country formed an important part of the BYZANTINE EMPIRE up to the thirteenth century and was then conquered by the Ottoman Turks. Greece remained a part of the OTTOMAN EMPIRE until 1830, when it gained its independence after much bloodshed. During this century Greece has experienced several changes in its forms of government. It was occupied by the Germans in WORLD WAR II, and has been in conflict with TURKEY, mainly over the question of CYPRUS and the antagonisms between the Greek and Turkish sections of the population.

GREEK ORTHODOX CHURCH

Also known as the Eastern Orthodox Church. Today it claims about 91½ million adherents, in Greece itself and other countries of the eastern MEDITERRANEAN region; also in RUSSIA and some other parts of the Soviet Union. The official head of the Church is the Patriarch of Constantinople and the principal service, similar to the Catholic Mass, is the Eucharist (a word denoting Thanksgiving). *See also* CHRISTIANITY.

GREENLAND

Very large island territory in the North ATLANTIC OCEAN, mostly within the Arctic Circle, with an area of 2,175,600 sq km (840,050 sq miles). Most of this vast area is an icecap and virtually uninhabitable. Hence the population is only about 50,000, made up of ESKIMOS and some people of Danish ancestry. Greenland is a self-governing county of DENMARK.

GREGORY I, the Great, also
St Gregory (*c.* 540–604)

One of the first great Popes. He was an efficient church administrator, and sent missionaries to many different parts of Europe, including St AUGUSTINE to Britain. Pope Gregory also introduced a type of plainsong called the Gregorian Chant.

GRIEG, Edvard Hagerup (1843–1907)

Norwegian composer who expressed his country's FOLKLORE AND FOLK MUSIC in many of his compositions. His best-known works are the popular Piano Concerto in A minor and the incidental music to IBSEN's play *Peer Gynt*.

GRIMM, Jakob Ludwig Karl (1785–1863) and Wilhelm Karl (1786–1859)

German scholars, especially of FOLKLORE and LEGEND. Their volumes of collected fairy tales have been translated into many languages and so made the Brothers Grimm into household names all over the world.

GRENADA

A West Indian nation, Grenada became independent from Britain in 1974. It has an area of 344 sq km (133 sq miles), 110,000 people and the capital is St. George's.

GROPIUS, Walter (1883–1969)

German architect who has had a great influence on twentieth-century ARCHITECTURE. He founded the famous Bauhaus school of design.

GUADELOUPE

Group of islands in the WEST INDIES, formerly a French colony, now a French overseas department with a total area of 1,779 sq km (687 sq miles). The population is about 332,000, and the main products are sugar, coffee and cocoa.

GUAM

Island in the PACIFIC OCEAN, lying in the Mariana group of islands, administered by the UNITED STATES.

GUANACO

South American MAMMAL related to the CAMEL. These animals live in the mountainous regions of the continent and are noted for their thick coats of wool.

GUATEMALA

Central American republic which adjoins MEXICO and BELIZE. It has an area of 108,889 sq km (42,045 sq miles) and a population of just over 7 million. The capital is Guatemala City, and the chief products are sugar, coffee, cocoa and bananas.

6th-century painted bowl from Guatemala

GUERICKE, Otto von (1602–86)

German scientist. He invented the first air pump; also an apparatus called the thermoscope, which was an early device for measuring temperature.

GUILLOTINE

Device equipped with a heavy blade which is used for execution by beheading. It was perfected by Joseph-Ignace Guillotin and extensively used during the FRENCH REVOLUTION.

The word now also describes many paper-cutting machines.

GUINEA

West African republic, formerly part of French West Africa, with an area of 245,957 sq km (94,970 sq miles) and a population of about 5 million. The capital is Conakry. The country produces bauxite and iron ore.

GUINEA-BISSAU

West African republic, formerly an overseas province of Portugal, with an area of 36,125 sq km (13,949 sq miles) and a population of 791,000. It became independent in 1974 after a long guerrilla war.

GULF STREAM

Warm ocean current that flows north-eastwards across the North ATLANTIC OCEAN from the Gulf of Mexico to the countries of northern and western Europe, including the British Isles. The stream itself and the accompanying south-westerly air stream make the climate of much of EUROPE much more temperate than it would otherwise be.

GUNPOWDER

Probably invented in CHINA in the ninth century AD and introduced into EUROPE during the fourteenth century. It is a mixture of saltpetre, sulphur and carbon.

GUNPOWDER PLOT

A plan, supported by many English Catholics who were suffering from religious persecution at the time, to blow up James I and the English PARLIAMENT on 5 November 1605. One of the plotters, Guy Fawkes, had several barrels of gunpowder secretly stored beneath the Houses of Parliament in readiness. The plot was discovered and the ringleaders were executed.

GUTENBERG, Johann (c. 1395–1468)

German printer. He is considered to have been the first printer in Europe to print with movable type. In 1454 he published an edition of the BIBLE using metal type faces. The basic principles of his methods are still used today.

GUYANA

An independent South American republic, formerly British Guiana. It has an area of 214,969 sq km (83,005 sq miles) but a population of only about 857,000. The capital is Georgetown. Sugar, rice and coconuts are the chief products; but some GOLD and DIAMONDS are mined. The country became independent in 1966 but remains a member of the BRITISH COMMONWEALTH.

GYROSCOPE

An instrument invented by Jean FOUCAULT, widely used in navigation. Basically, it is a rapidly spinning wheel in a frame which only touches another surface at one point. This enables it to remain spinning in one plane however much its surroundings move from their original plane; that is, its centrifugal force overcomes GRAVITY. The gyro-compass and such other navigational aids as the automatic pilot are all based on the gyroscope.

Guy Fawkes, instigator of the Gunpowder Plot

H

HABEAS CORPUS

The term means 'you must have the body', and refers to the fundamental point of law that a suspected person must be brought before a magistrate or judge within a certain period after arrest. It protects the individual against custody or imprisonment without trial. The British *Habeas Corpus* Act was passed in 1679.

HABER-BOSCH PROCESS

A process for making synthetic ammonia named after two German chemists, Fritz Haber and Karl Bosch. Ammonia is an important ingredient in the manufacture of many drugs and of plastics.

HADRIAN (AD 76–138)

Roman emperor, best known for the defensive wall he had built in northern England as a protection against the Picts and Scots. Hadrian's wall originally went from Wallsend to Bowness, a distance of 117 km (73 miles). Sections of it still remain.

HAGGARD, Sir Henry Rider (1856–1925)

English writer, especially of colourful adventure novels, including *King Solomon's Mines*.

HAHN, Otto (1879–1968)

German scientist whose work on radioactive ELEMENTS led to the discovery of nuclear fission. *See also* NUCLEAR ENERGY.

HAIR

The substance that grows out of a MAMMAL's skin. In its broadest sense it includes fur, fleece, bristles and quills, which are spiny hairs. It gives warmth and protects the body against injury. Hair gets its colour from a pigment called melanin.

Hadrian and a mile-castle on his wall

HAITI

Caribbean republic on the island of Hispaniola, which it shares with the DOMINICAN REPUBLIC. It has an area of 27,750 sq km (10,715 sq miles) and a population of about 5 million. The capital is Port-au-Prince. The chief products are coffee, bananas, rubber and sugar.

HALLOWE'EN

All Hallows Eve, falling on 31 October of each year. Although it is now classed as a Christian festival, its origins go back to pagan times. In the old Celtic calendar Hallowe'en was the 'old year's night', when witches and spirits were said to be abroad.

HALOGENS

Halogen means 'salt producer', and is the name in chemistry for a group of non-metallic elements: astatine, fluorine, chlorine, bromine and iodine. The salts in the sea are compounds of halogens with metals.

HALS, Franz (*c.* 1580–1666)

Dutch artist. He was principally a portrait painter, his most famous work of this type being *The Laughing Cavalier*. It is in the Wallace Collection, London.

HAMSTER

Small group of RODENTS, native to some parts of EUROPE, and to western ASIA. The common hamster is grey or brown and looks very like a rat. The golden hamster is the type usually kept as a pet.

HANDEL, George Frideric (1685–1759)

Anglo-German composer. He was born in Halle in Germany, travelled to Italy, then became director of music to the Elector of Hanover (later George I of England). The main part of his career started with his arrival in London. For the London stage he wrote many operas in the prevailing Italian style, including *Berenice* and *Xerxes* (from which comes the famous 'Largo'. At the same time he adopted British nationality, the curious spelling of 'Frideric' being due to his unfamiliarity with English. Because of changes in public taste, Handel then started composing oratorios, most celebrated of these being *Messiah*. He also wrote much instrumental and orchestral music, including the *Water Music* and *Music For The Royal Fireworks*.

With J.S.Bach, Handel brought the Baroque period of music to a close. He was also one of the first composers largely to free himself of church or aristocratic patronage and make a commercial success of his music.

HANNIBAL (247–183 BC)

Carthaginian soldier, who led his armies against Rome in the Second Punic War. His

The Laughing Cavalier by Franz Hals

greatest achievement was to take his armies, which included elephants, up through SPAIN, across southern FRANCE and over the ALPS, to attack Rome from the north. His greatest victory was at Cannae (216). Returning to Carthage, he was finally defeated by the Roman general Scipio at the battle of Zama (202). He was later exiled from Carthage and took poison.

HANSARD

Popular name given to the Official Reports of the debates in both Houses of PARLIAMENT. Luke Hansard (1752–1828) published the *Journals of the House of Commons* from 1774 until his death. The Hansard reports were accepted as official from 1855. They are verbatim (word for word) reports, and are on sale to the public.

HARDIE, James Keir (1856–1915)

British labour leader, born in Ayrshire, Scotland. He had no schooling and taught himself to read and write. He worked in a coal-pit from the age of seven until he was twenty-four. After a period as a journalist, he founded the Independent Labour Party in 1893 and entered Parliament as member for West Ham. Later he became Chairman of the Parliamentary Labour Party. He opposed Britain's entry into WORLD WAR I.

HARDY, Thomas (1840–1928)

English novelist and poet. His novels are nearly all set in rural England, especially parts of Dorset and Devon, and are generally sad and pessimistic in spirit. They include *Far From the Madding Crowd*, *Under the Greenwood Tree* and *Tess of the D'Urbervilles*.

HARE

Mammal closely related to the rabbit, but larger in body and with longer ears and hind legs. Also, they do not burrow, like rabbits, but live in a kind of nest called a 'form'. They are found in many countries.

HARMONY

The sounding together of notes in a way that is musically significant. Until the seventeenth century the harmonies of Western music were mostly based on the scales of the Church modes. From then onward, harmony has been largely based on the twenty-four major and minor scales.

HARPSICHORD

Musical instrument belonging to the keyboard group of instruments, in which the strings are plucked by a type of quill instead of being hit by a hammer, as in the case of the PIANO. It dates from the sixteenth century, and remained the principal keyboard instrument until well into the eighteenth century, when it was superseded by the piano. However, harpsichords are still made, specifically for the performance of music originally written for them.

18th-century harpsichord

HARTEBEEST

Group of MAMMALS belonging to the ANTELOPE family, distinguished by their narrow faces and twisted horns with ridges across them. There are several species, all native to AFRICA.

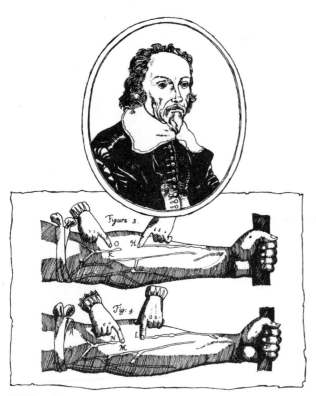

William Harvey

HARVEY, William (1578–1657)

English physician. His discovery of the circulation of the blood revolutionized MEDICINE and laid the foundations of the new science of physiology, the study of the functions and processes of living organisms.

HAWAII

Group of eight islands in the PACIFIC OCEAN, formerly the Sandwich Islands. The capital is Honolulu. The territory was annexed by the UNITED STATES OF AMERICA in 1898 and became the fiftieth state of the Union in 1959.

HAWK

Group of birds of prey. All have very keen eyes, powerful wings, hooked beaks and fierce talons (claws). Their nests are built of sticks high in a tree or on the ledge of a cliff. Hawks do not normally catch other birds on the wing but feed mostly on small mammals like mice and rats. They hover for long periods looking for prey and then dive very fast. The sparrow hawk is the most common species in Britain.

A sparrow hawk with its brood

HAYDN, Franz Joseph (1732–1809)

Austro-Hungarian composer. He was director of music for many years to Prince Nicholas Esterházy, a good patron of the arts who gave the composer plenty of opportunities to develop and perfect the new musical forms of the eighteenth-century Classical period – the sonata, piano trio, string quartet and symphony. After Haydn left his position at the Esterházy court, he paid two visits to London, writing his last twelve celebrated symphonies for these occasions. They are sometimes called the 'Salomon Symphonies' after the name of the man who arranged the visits. Haydn also wrote operas, masses and the oratorios *The Creation* and *The Seasons*. The tune of the West German national anthem, originally called the Emperor's Hymn, is also by Haydn.

HEART

Large hollow muscle that pumps blood to all parts of the body in many forms of animal life.

The human heart is divided into two halves, separated by a muscular wall. Each half is divided into two chambers, the upper atrium and the lower ventricle. The left pair pumps oxygenated blood to the body, and the right pair pumps blood to the lungs.

HEAT

Defined in PHYSICS as a form of ENERGY obtained from mechanical, electrical or chemical action. Heat energy can be converted into mechanical, electrical or chemical energy, and vice versa; but it is much easier to convert the other forms of energy to heat than vice versa. Heat is measured in terms of temperature. The *latent heat* of a substance is the amount of heat needed to change a given quantity of it from a solid to a liquid state, or from a liquid to a gaseous state, without any change in temperature (that is, just enough heat to bring about the change). The *specific heat* of a substance is the amount of heat needed to raise the temperature of a given mass of a substance by a given amount. Heat can be transmitted in three ways: by conduction (through solid objects, such as iron); by convection (through circulating currents in liquids and gases); or by radiation (electro-magnetic waves which can travel through a VACUUM). *See also* THERMODYNAMICS and THERMOMETER.

HEAT PUMP

Device for causing heat to flow from a low-temperature region to a higher-temperature region. A refrigerator is a type of heat pump, though today the term is more usually applied to machines which remove heat from the soil or rivers and use it to warm buildings. A liquid or gaseous cooling substance is alternately compressed by a pump, then expanded. The heat generated by the compression is transferred in a heat-exchanger to a convection system. The heat lost in expansion is made good by pumping the coolant through pipes buried in the soil or water.

HEBRIDES

Group of islands off the west coast of SCOTLAND, not all inhabited. Skye is the largest island of the Inner Hebrides; Lewis the largest of the Outer Hebrides group.

HEDGEHOG

Type of small MAMMAL noted for its spiny coat. As an added form of protection it can curl up into a ball. It is a nocturnal animal, living mainly on insects, slugs and worms. It hibernates during the winter.

A hibernating hedgehog

HEGEL, Georg Wilhelm Friedrich (1770–1831)

German philosopher whose ideas about the processes of history (called the historical dialectic) had a great influence on other philosophers, notably Karl MARX.

HEINE, Heinrich (1797–1856)

German poet who wrote in both a lyrical and a satirical style. His revolutionary political opinions led to his work being heavily censored in his own lifetime.

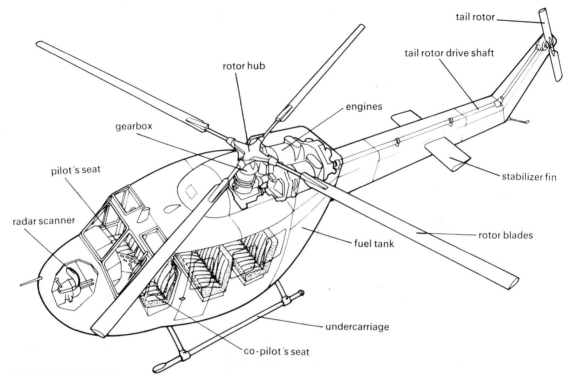

A passenger-carrying helicopter

HELICOPTER

Type of aircraft in which lift and thrust are provided by a power-driven horizontal rotor (usually three-bladed) located above the fuselage. Thus it can hover, ascend and descend vertically. Large designs have been built for passenger and military transport.

HELIOGRAPH

Means 'sun-writer' and consists of a mirror and shutter. It is used for signalling. Signals are controlled by the shutter and are made up of long and short flashes (Morse Code) of sunlight reflected by the mirror.

HELIUM

A lightweight gas and chemical element. It does not combine with other gases and is therefore called *inert* or *noble*. Sir Joseph Lockyer, a British astronomer, first found evidence of helium in the SUN in 1868. He named it helium from *helios,* the Greek for sun. Helium makes up nearly a quarter of the matter in the visible universe. Because of its lightness it is widely used in rockets.

HELMHOLTZ, Hermann Ludwig Ferdinand von (1821–94)

German scientist. Among his many discoveries and inventions were the Law of the Conservation of Energy; the opthalmoscope for examining eyes; and the measurement of nerve impulses.

HEMINGWAY, Ernest (1899–1961)

American novelist. His most famous book is *For Whom the Bell Tolls,* set in the period of the Spanish Civil War. Other novels include *A Farewell to Arms* and *The Old Man and the Sea.*

HEMISPHERE

Name given to any half of a globe, and especially to the EARTH. The word means 'half a sphere'. The Northern and Southern Hemispheres of the Earth are divided by the EQUATOR. The Eastern and Western Hemispheres are marked by the meridians of 20° West longitude and 180° East longitude.

HENRY VIII (1491–1547)

King of England from 1509 until his death. The first of his six marriages, to Catherine of Aragon, ended in divorce. This, in turn, brought about his quarrel with the POPE, which

Henry VIII

greatly helped the cause of the REFORMATION in England and led to the establishment of the CHURCH OF ENGLAND. In his younger days Henry was a fine scholar and patron of the arts. As he grew older his reign was marked by increasing tyranny, which included the execution of two of his other wives, Anne Boleyn and Catherine Howard.

HERACLITUS (c. 500 BC)

Greek philosopher who postulated that everything is made of fire and always changing into something else. He also taught that our senses mislead us and that by reason alone can we discover the truth. Because of his pessimistic views about his fellow men he is sometimes called the 'weeping philosopher'.

HERODOTUS (c. 485–425 BC)

Greek historian and geographer. His greatest historical work was an account of the struggles between the Greeks and the Persians, and for this he is sometimes called the 'Father of History'. He also made a map of the known world and was the first to distinguish between the continents of AFRICA, ASIA and EUROPE.

HERON

Wading BIRD, related to the bittern. It has a dagger-like beak, with which it catches fishes and other aquatic animals.

HERSCHEL, Sir William (1738–1822)

Anglo-German astronomer. In 1757 he came to England from Germany and began to build his own telescopes. In 1782 he became private astronomer to George III. He discovered the planet Uranus.

HIEROGLYPHICS

A special type of semi-pictorial writing (pictograms), used mainly by the ancient Egyptians.

The word *hieroglyph* is the Greek for 'sacred carving'; and most Egyptian hieroglyphic inscriptions are in tombs and have great religious significance. They were first deciphered by the French Egyptologist Jean-François Champollion.

HIMALAYA

Vast range of mountains in ASIA that extend for over 2,410 km (1,500 miles) across the northern frontier of INDIA. They include the highest mountain in the world, Everest, 8,850 m (29,030 ft). This was first climbed in 1953 by a team including the New Zealander Sir Edmund Hillary. Three of the greatest Asian rivers, the GANGES, Brahmaputra and INDUS, rise in the Himalayan range.

HINDENBURG, Paul von (1847–1934)

German soldier and statesman. He was a Field Marshal and Chief of the German General Staff in WORLD WAR I. He was elected President of the German Reich in 1925 and again in 1932. In 1933, as a result of elections, he appointed Adolf HITLER as German Chancellor, although he disliked the Nazi Party.

HINDUISM

Religion practised by the majority of the people in India. Its origins can be traced back nearly five thousand years, to the period of the Indus Valley civilization. It is founded upon a belief in REINCARNATION – the return of the soul to many earthly existences until spiritual purity and enlightenment are attained. This central belief lies behind the caste system, which splits up the population into strictly defined social groups; and the reverence extended towards some other forms of life. There are many forms of Hinduism, and many traditional deities, the principal ones being the trinity of Brahma, Vishnu and Shiva. The Brahmans are generally the most educated Hindus. There are also many systems of yoga, concerned with developing spiritual awareness. There are about 400 million adherents.

HIPPOCRATES (*c.* 460–377 BC)

Greek physician, often spoken of as the 'Father of Medicine'. The Hippocratic Oath is still the basis of the code of conduct or ethics within the medical profession.

HIPPOPOTAMUS

Large, stout MAMMAL, related to the PIG, and native to some of the rivers and lakes of AFRICA. It is an amphibious animal, equally at home on land or in the water; indeed, it can breathe, smell, see and hear while its body is almost completely immersed. One distinguishing feature is its smooth, hairless, dark hide. Another is the two tusk-like teeth in the lower jaw. Hippopotami feed on vegetation at night and sleep for most of each day.

Hippopotamus and offspring

HIROHITO (born 1901)

Emperor of JAPAN, now a constitutional monarch. He is descended from a dynasty that is believed to go back to the seventh century BC. After the Japanese defeat in WORLD WAR II, he repudiated his divinity and under the new constitution became a symbol of the state and not its sacred basis.

HISTORY

The recording and interpretation of past events. The term can be applied to the study of any particular subject, but generally it means an account of human social and political affairs from the time when records of one sort or another started to be kept, up to the present day. The four basic divisions of this type of history are as follows: Prehistory, before 3000 BC; Ancient History, 3000 BC to 450 AD; Medieval History, 450 AD to 1453 AD; and Modern History from 1453 AD to the present.

Adolf Hitler

HITLER, Adolf (1889–1945)

Austro-German political leader and dictator. He was born at Braunau in AUSTRIA, served in the German army in WORLD WAR I and was destitute for a time. The acute economic and social problems which faced GERMANY and Austria after the war helped to gain him support for his ultra right-wing National Socialist German Workers Party (Nazi Party). He was imprisoned after an attempt to seize power in Munich, during which time he wrote his political testament *Mein Kampf* (My Struggle). Upon his release, Hitler and such fellow party leaders as Hermann Göring and Dr Joseph Goebbels continued campaigning until the Nazi Party gained enough seats in the German *Reichstag* (Parliament) for Hitler himself to be appointed Chancellor (1933). Very quickly, he disbanded the existing political institutions, suppressed all opposition, started to persecute Jews, proclaimed himself *Führer* (Leader) and pursued an aggressive policy of uniting all German-speaking people in one nation or *Reich*. The annexation of Austria in 1938 (the *Anschluss*) and the partition of Czechoslovakia in 1939 led to the start of WORLD WAR II later that year. Hitler took control of the conduct of the war, which at first went extremely well for Germany. But the German people could not withstand the combined military strength of the Soviet Union, the United States and the British Commonwealth. Hitler refused to give in, dragged his country into total ruin and defeat and committed suicide in Berlin a few days before the final surrender.

HITTITES

Race of people who dominated Asia Minor and SYRIA during the period from about 2000 BC to 700 BC. They are mentioned many times in the Old Testament of the BIBLE. Scholars deciphered the cuneiform script of their records in the early 1900s, but the HIEROGLYPHIC script was not deciphered until 1947.

HOBBES, Thomas (1588–1679)

English philosopher whose book *Leviathan* was the first great English work on political philosophy.

HOCKEY

Game played between two teams of eleven players, on a marked pitch, with a ball and specially shaped bats, or sticks as they are called. In principle it is rather like soccer, the object of each side being to project the ball into the opposing side's goal. In CANADA ice hockey is the national sport.

HOGARTH, William (1697–1764)

English artist, whose paintings and engravings provide a vivid picture of eighteenth-century London life and morals. His most famous works are the two sets of paintings, *Marriage à la Mode* and *The Rake's Progress*.

HOHENZOLLERN

Powerful German royal family which took its name from the family castle at Zollern in Swabia. Starting as counts, they became electors of Brandenburg. They added PRUSSIA to their possessions in 1618 and from then on were closely connected with the rise and power of that country. The last Hohenzollern was Wilhelm II, King of Prussia and German Kaiser (1859–1941).

HOKUSAI KATSUSHIKA (1760–1849)

A famous Japanese colour print artist, born in Yedo (Tokyo). Among his prints are *Views of Fuji*. His work influenced GAUGUIN, VAN GOGH and TOULOUSE-LAUTREC.

The Wave by Hokusai

HOLBEIN, Hans the Younger (c. 1497–1543)

German portrait and religious painter. As a youth he became a friend of ERASMUS, of whom he produced many portraits. In about 1526 he came to England where he painted a number of magnificent portraits of Henry VIII and his wives. Holbein died of plague in London.

HOLST, Gustav (1874–1934)

English composer. He shared VAUGHAN WILLIAMS's love of English folk music; but also took an interest in such occult subjects as ASTROLOGY, which inspired his best-known work, the orchestral suite *The Planets*.

HOLLAND. *See* NETHERLANDS

HOLY COMMUNION. *See* MASS

HOLY GRAIL

According to medieval legend, either the cup used by Jesus Christ at the Last Supper or the cup which caught some drops of his blood while he was on the cross. Legends of its whereabouts and of those who went in search of it have inspired much later poetry, notably Alfred Lord Tennyson's *Idylls of the King*.

HOLY ROMAN EMPIRE

Founded by CHARLEMAGNE in 800. It emerged as a loose confederation of German and north Italian kingdoms and principalities. In the Middle Ages there was a long drawn-out struggle between the Empire and the Papacy over questions of power and authority. It was later mainly a collection of German states, but when NAPOLEON came to dominate Europe, he insisted on its absolution.

HOMER

Greek epic poet. Both the date and the place of his birth and death are not known precisely, but recent research suggests a date between 1050 and 800 BC. It has even been claimed that no such man as Homer existed and that the

Iliad and the *Odyssey* are collections of traditional ballads and not the work of one man. In any event they were known all over the Greek-speaking world before the sixth century BC. The *Iliad* is an epic poem dealing with the siege of Troy by the Greeks. The *Odyssey* describes the wandering of Odysseus, a Greek seafarer, on his way back to Ithaca after the fall of Troy.

HOMO SAPIENS

Scientific name for human beings. Anatomically, *homo sapiens* closely resembles the higher or anthropoid APES. Both are PRIMATES. The main differences are that *homo sapiens* has a larger brain (the title means 'humans with wisdom') and walks with a completely upright gait.

HONDURAS

Central American republic. It has an area of 112,088 sq km (43,280 sq miles) and a population of about 3½ million. The capital is Tegucigalpa. The main product is bananas; there are also silver mines.

HONG KONG

British crown colony in south-eastern CHINA. It consists chiefly of Hong Kong island and Kowloon peninsula attached to the Chinese mainland. The entire colony is only 1,045 sq km (403 sq miles) in area but has a population of 4,764,000. The capital is Victoria. It was founded in 1842 as a trading station.

HOOCH, Pieter de (1629–80)

Dutch artist who specialized in paintings of house interiors and developed very skilful effects of light and shade. His work is also a valuable source of reference to seventeenth-century domestic furnishings and decoration.

HORACE (Quintus Horatius Flaccus, 65 BC –8 BC)

Roman lyric poet. Although he wrote in many forms, he is perhaps best remembered for his odes. His work had a great influence on English poetry.

HORMONE

Substance produced within a plant or an animal. The word comes from the Greek and means 'set in motion'. Hormones are chemical messengers that help the body to function correctly. In animals they are produced by organs called endocrine or ductless GLANDS. Most human hormones, except for the sex

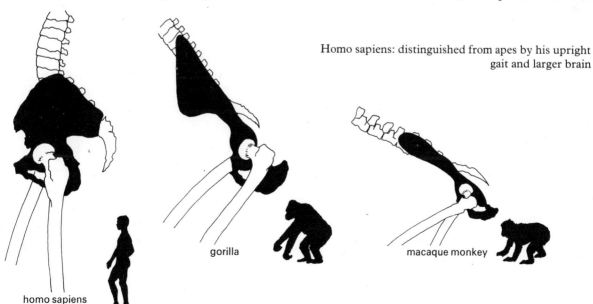

Homo sapiens: distinguished from apes by his upright gait and larger brain

homo sapiens

gorilla

macaque monkey

hormones which are known as steroids, contain some form of amino-acids, the building blocks of proteins.

HORSE

Animal belonging to the family *Equidae,* which includes the ASS and the ZEBRA. It evolved from a prehistoric animal, Eohippus, which was no larger than a terrier dog. It is probable that the horse was first tamed and domesticated in central Asia. The only real wild horse is Przhevalsky's horse.

The rider puts her horse over practice jumps

HORSEPOWER

A British measure of the rate of doing work. One horsepower is defined as 550 foot pounds of work per second (76.04 kilogramme-force metres a minute), or 33,000 foot pounds of work a minute. One foot-pound is the work needed to lift one pound one foot. 'Brake' horsepower is a measure of the useful work that can be performed by an engine. The term and its values were adopted by James WATT after conducting experiments with dray-horses to determine their pulling power. In terms of electrical power 1 horsepower equals 746 watts.

HOTTENTOT

Nomadic people of NAMIBIA (South-West Africa). They were the first people met by the Dutch in southern Africa. Many died from European diseases to which they had no resistance and, later, they interbred with other peoples so that pure Hottentots have become rare. The largest group is the Nama who number less than 40,000.

HOVERCRAFT

Type of craft which can operate on land or sea. The hovercraft is called an 'air cushion vehicle' in America because the main principle is that the flat-bottomed vehicle floats on a cushion of air. This is built up by sucking air through a funnel by means of a fan. Jets or propellers move the vehicle forward or backward easily because it is not in frictional contact with the surface it travels over. Sir Christopher Cockerell (b.1910) invented and pioneered development of the hovercraft.

HUDSON, Henry (died 1611)

British sea captain who explored the north-eastern coast of America including the Hudson Bay and Hudson Strait, which were named after him. He was also the first man to explore the Hudson river. On his fourth voyage his crew mutinied and he was set adrift in a small boat with his son and seven loyal sailors. He was never heard of again.

HUDSON'S BAY COMPANY

Formed in 1668 and received its charter in 1670. Its purpose was to open up trade, particularly in furs, and chart the North-West Passage. The company is still in existence.

HUGO, Victor Marie (1802–85)

French poet, dramatist and novelist. His poetry made him a leader of the Romantic movement in French literature. His best-known novels are *Notre Dame de Paris* and *Les Misérables.* Victor Hugo was also a gifted and highly original artist.

HUGUENOTS

French Protestants. Conflict between them and the Catholics started in the sixteenth century, and there was a general massacre of Huguenots throughout France, beginning in Paris on St Bartholomew's Eve, 1572. Henry IV gave them political and religious freedom with the Edict of Nantes (1598). But persecution was renewed by Cardinal RICHELIEU. LOUIS XIV organized *dragonnades* to convert Huguenots and other Protestants forcibly to Catholicism. He also revoked the Edict of Nantes, with the result that many of them fled abroad. Persecution finally ended with the FRENCH REVOLUTION and the publication of the *Rights of Man* that gave freedom of worship to everybody.

HUMAN BODY

In this encyclopedia the different systems and organs of the body are covered in a number of individual entries: ANATOMY, BLOOD, BRAIN, CELL, EAR, EYE, GENETICS, GLAND, HEART, HORMONE, LYMPH, MUSCLE, REPRODUCTION, SKELETON, SKIN, TEETH. The diagram on the right illustrates the main organs of the body.

HUMMINGBIRD

Large group of BIRDS, native to tropical and subtropical regions of the American continent. There are over 400 species. Some grow to a length of 22 cm (nearly 9 in), while the smallest of them is less than 5 cm (2 in) and is the smallest of all birds. They are all brightly coloured, and can beat their wings over 3,000 times a minute in order to hover in the air while extracting nectar from flowers with their long tongues.

HUMPERDINCK, Engelbert (1854–1921)

German composer, remembered today for his opera *Hänsel and Gretel* which is based on a famous fairy tale by the Brothers GRIMM.

The main organs of the human body

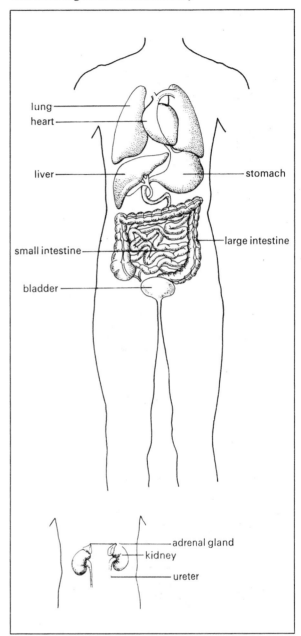

HUNDRED YEARS WAR

A long series of disputes and wars between the English and French kings, beginning with Edward III's claim to the French throne in 1337. The English victory at Crécy (1346) and siege of Calais were followed by a truce.

Edward's son, Edward, The Black Prince, re-opened hostilities and won another victory at Poitiers (1356). The crucial stage of the war started with Henry V's renewed claim to the French throne and his victory at Agincourt (1415). After lengthy negotiations JOAN OF ARC revitalized the French armies and defeated the English at Orleans (1429). She was then captured and burnt at the stake, but the French continued to gain the upper hand, pushing the English out of France until by 1453 only Calais was left in English hands.

HUNGARY

Central European republic with an area of 93,030 sq km (35,921 sq miles) and a population of over $10\frac{1}{2}$ million. The capital is Budapest. Nearly all the people are of Magyar descent, which gives them their distinctive language (not related to any Slavonic tongue) and their colourful folk music and dancing. Most of the country is a fertile plain, crossed by the River DANUBE, producing much wheat and other cereal crops; and wine. There are also deposits of coal, iron and bauxite.

Before WORLD WAR I Hungary was a part of the Austro-Hungarian Empire. After the war it lost territory to its neighbours, CZECHOSLOVAKIA, ROMANIA and YUGOSLAVIA; consequently it supported Nazi Germany in the hope of winning back its lost lands. During WORLD WAR II the country was occupied by the Soviet Union and in 1949 it became a Communist state. A revolt in 1956 was crushed, and Hungary remains a member of the Eastern European Communist Bloc.

HURRICANE

Violent storm in which winds of over 120 km/h (75 mph) blow in a circular pattern around a small central calm area, called the 'eye' of the storm. Hurricanes originate in tropical or subtropical regions. During the late summer and autumn they move up from the region of the Caribbean, often causing much damage along the eastern seaboard of the UNITED STATES. They are designated by people's names. In the PACIFIC region, such storms are called typhoons.

HUXLEY, Aldous Leonard (1894–1963)

English novelist, and grandson of T. H. Huxley. His most famous book is *Brave New World,* a bitterly satirical account of society as he thought it might develop.

HUXLEY, Thomas Henry (1825–95)

English biologist who strongly supported Charles DARWIN's ideas about plant and animal evolution and natural selection.

HUYGENS, Christiaan (1629–95)

Dutch scientist. He invented the pendulum clock, and also did much work in the field of OPTICS, maintaining that LIGHT is a form of wave motion.

HYDROCARBON

Important class of organic compounds which contain only the elements hydrogen and carbon. Hydrocarbons are obtained from crude oil and natural gas and used to manufacture plastics, synthetic fibres and solvents.

Aliphatic hydrocarbons contain the paraffin, olefin and acetylenic series. Among the alicyclics are terpenes.

HYDROCHLORIC ACID

Important industrial acid used in metallurgy and food processing.

HYDROFLUORIC ACID

Acid with important industrial and laboratory uses. Carl Scheele, the Swedish chemist, first prepared it in 1771. It is used to etch glass. Fluorides are the metal salts.

HYDROFOIL

Vessel with wings called 'hydrofoils' that lift the boat out of the water and enable it to skim over water at high speeds.

HYDROGEN

Chemical ELEMENT with the symbol H. The hydrogen atom is the lightest and simplest atom known. It is a good reducing agent. It is also excellent for use in balloons because of its lightness. Henry Cavendish, the British scientist, first studied the gas in 1766.

HYDROGENATION

Generally the term means treating a chemical substance with hydrogen with a resulting combination of the two. During recent years it has come more particularly to mean the production of petrol and other by-products from COAL.

HYDROGEN BOMB

The basis of the atomic bomb is a chain reaction (fission); but in the hydrogen bomb the process, although seated within the heart or nucleus of the atom, arises from the fusion or union of the nuclei (inner cores of atoms) of light atoms at enormously high temperatures. It is thought that this process of fusion, called by scientists a 'thermonuclear reaction', is similar to that which takes place in the sun to produce the great heat which it radiates. *See also* NUCLEAR ENERGY.

HYDROMECHANICS

Science of the physical properties of liquids, the name being derived from the Greek word *hydro* (water). Under this general heading comes hydrodynamics, the study of the properties and behaviour of liquids in motion. Hydraulics is the application of these studies to engineering. There is also hydrostatics, which is the study of liquids at rest or in equilibrium.

HYDROMETER

Specially designed glass tube calibrated to measure the density of a liquid in which it is immersed. It is used for testing batteries.

HYDROPONICS

Technique of plant cultivation in which the roots of a plant are immersed in a nutrient solution from which they draw their food. It is sometimes referred to as 'soilless' cultivation and is a very successful method of growing many greenhouse plants, such as carnations, tomatoes and cucumbers.

HYENA

Although this MAMMAL looks very much like a DOG, it really belongs to the CAT family. Hyenas are ungainly to look at because of their long neck and legs, short body, and sloping hindquarters. They eat small animals which they kill themselves or carrion left by other predators. They are native to regions of AFRICA and southern ASIA.

HYGROMETRY

That branch of METEOROLOGY concerned with the measurement and behaviour of water vapour in the atmosphere. The quantity of moisture or vapour is known as 'humidity' and is measured by means of an instrument called a hygrometer.

HYPNOTISM

Psychological method of inducing sleep, or a suggestive state of mind, by getting the subject to concentrate on one object or idea. An early practitioner was Dr Franz Anton Mesmer (*c.* 1733–1815), and from him is derived the term 'mesmerism'. There is nothing strange or abnormal about hypnotism. It cannot be imposed upon unwilling subjects. It can be an effective treatment for some nervous disorders.

I

IBEX

Wild species of GOAT, native to mountainous regions of EUROPE and ASIA, with long curving horns which are also ridged.

The ibex or wild goat

IBIS

Wading BIRD, closely related to the spoonbill, native to tropical or sub-tropical regions. There are twenty-six known species. Most famous is the 'sacred' Ibis of ancient EGYPT. Thoth, Egyptian god of wisdom, was portrayed with an ibis head. There is also the scarlet ibis of tropical South AMERICA.

Egyptian papyrus showing Thoth (right), god of wisdom

IBSEN, Henrik (1828–1906)

Norwegian dramatist. He started writing plays fairly late in his career, just at a time when such social and political issues as women's rights were claiming public attention. Such issues, and the hypocrisies of middle-class standards as he saw them, he very powerfully worked into such plays as *Pillars of Society*, *Ghosts*, *Rosmersholm* and *Hedda Gabler*. For these and other works Ibsen is regarded as one of the founder-figures of twentieth-century theatre.

ICE AGE

Period of the EARTH's history, lasting from about $1\frac{1}{4}$ million to 20,000 years ago, during which GLACIERS advanced from the North Pole to cover much of North AMERICA, EUROPE and ASIA. In geological terms it occurred during the **Pleistocene epoch**.

ICEBERG

A mass of floating ice, most of which is submerged, that has broken free from a GLAC-IER or ice shelf. In ARCTIC regions many icebergs come from the GREENLAND icecap and drift southwards into the North ATLANTIC OCEAN where they are a danger to shipping. It was such an iceberg that sank the passenger liner *Titanic* in 1912. Today the International Ice Patrol operates along the main North Atlantic shipping lanes.

An iceberg drifting south from Greenland

ICE HOCKEY. *See* HOCKEY

ICELAND

Island republic in the North ATLANTIC OCEAN, just below the ARCTIC Circle. It has an area of 103,000 sq km (39,771 sq miles) and a population of about 229,000. The capital is Reykjavik. Scenically Iceland is a place of dramatic contrasts. It has many GLACIERS; at the same time there are extensive hot springs and other forms of volcanic activity. The country's economy depends almost entirely upon fishing, and the successive extensions it has declared to its own fishing limits have brought it into conflict with other nations, including GREAT BRITAIN.

ICE SKATING

There are two kinds of competitive ice skating: figure skating and speed skating. Figure skating includes jumps, spirals and spins performed to music, while the free-skating event allows a much greater freedom of expression and interpretation. Speed skating involves races of various distances from 500 m to 10,000 m. Ice skating is included in the Winter Olympics.

IGUANA

Group of LIZARDS, native to the tropical regions of the American continent, the WEST INDIES and some PACIFIC islands. The largest members of the group can attain a length of 1.8 m (6ft).

IMHOTEP

Egyptian physician and vizier (chief adviser) to King Zoser, who lived during the third millenium BC. Also an engineer and architect who built the earliest PYRAMID. He was later worshipped as a god.

IMPRESSIONISM

Name given to an important style, or school, of painting, especially concerned with effects or impressions of light. It grew up during the nineteenth century, mainly in France, its principal exponents being Camille Pissarro, Auguste RENOIR, Édouard MANET and Claude MONET. Another group of painters followed, known as the Post-Impressionists, including Paul GAUGUIN, Paul CÉZANNE and Vincent VAN GOGH.

INCA

Empire founded about AD 1200 in PERU, and overthrown by Francisco Pizarro and other Spanish explorers in the sixteenth century. Its capital was at Cuzco. The Inca civilization was of a high order, as revealed by surviving examples of its arts and crafts. Especially impressive are the remains of the Temple of the Sun at Machu Picchu high in the ANDES mountains. The Inca culture has not been completely destroyed, and there are today more than 6 million people who speak Quechuan, the original Incan language.

INCOME TAX

A tax which people have to pay to the government on their wages or other sources of income. If people do not have to work, or do not get all their income through their work, they pay at a higher rate than do those whose only income is from working. Tax on earned income depends not only upon the amount of a person's wages but on such matters as whether he has to support only himself or a family as well. Income tax was first imposed in 1799 but it was withdrawn in 1816. In 1824 Sir Robert Peel reimposed it, and since then it has been an important part of the national revenue.

INDEPENDENT TELEVISION AUTHORITY (ITA)

Established by Act of Parliament in 1954 to provide an alternative television service to that already transmitted by the BRITISH BROADCASTING CORPORATION. The ITA owns and operates the transmitting stations. The actual programmes are supplied by fourteen other regional companies, whose source of income is derived from advertisements (commercials).

INDIA

Asian republic, much of it within the Tropic of Cancer, with an area of 3,287,590 sq km (1,269,415 sq miles) and a population of about 671 million. The capital is New Delhi and other important cities are Calcutta, Bombay and Madras. The majority of Indians are HINDU, but they speak a variety of languages, the principal one being Hindi. India produces much of the world's tea, also grows and produces cotton and jute. There is also coal and a growing steel industry. Economic problems remain because of the very high population, age-old customs which hinder increased productivity, and the intense summer heat and aridity of much of the country.

The origins of the Indian nation go right back to the Indus Valley civilization which flourished about 4000 BC. The first big change came during the second millenium BC when Vedic Aryans from the north gradually moved across the sub-continent, establishing a new pattern of life, including the Hindu caste system. About AD 700 Arab traders introduced the religion ISLAM into the country, and this was followed by large-scale Moslem invasions and the creation of the Mogul Empire. It was the power of the Moguls that British and French traders began to challenge in the eighteenth century; and it was largely due to Robert CLIVE and the British East India Company that India became a part of the British Empire. As the twentieth century progressed, there was increasing agitation for independence, as expressed by such men as the Mahatma GANDHI. This was achieved in 1947, PAKISTAN being created at the same time, as a separate Moslem state. India's first prime minister, Jawaharlal NEHRU, did much to consolidate democratic institutions and to preserve Indian neutrality, though there have been disputes with China, and, more seriously, with Pakistan.

INDIAN, AMERICAN

The races of people who inhibited the American continent before the arrival of European settlers. It is believed that they are related to some of the Asiatic peoples and at some time

Sitting Bull, war leader of the Hunkpapa Sioux tribe

made their way into the American continent by way of the Bering Strait. The North American Indians were organized into many separate tribes, speaking a variety of languages, and lived mostly in villages, with a chief at their head. They were skilful hunters and many practised simple farming. Their existence was a fairly simple one and some tribes, such as the Apaches, Sioux and Blackfeet, were nomadic. In Central and South America, however, they created such impressive civilizations as those of the Aztecs, Incas and Mayas. More than half the people of some Central and South American countries are still Indians or have some Indian ancestry.

INDONESIA

South-east Asian republic including the islands of Java, Sumatra, Celebes and most of BORNEO.

The total area is 2,042,012 sq km (788,468 sq miles), and the population is 141 million. The capital is Djakarta. The Indonesian islands are rich in minerals, including tin, coal and petroleum; and they produce rubber, tobacco and rice. Most of these territories were formerly a part of the Dutch East Indies. Indonesia was declared a republic in 1945.

INDUSTRIAL REVOLUTION

Name given to a period starting in the eighteenth century and continuing throughout the nineteenth century, during which new machines and manufacturing techniques, new forms of energy and new materials changed completely the economics and conditions of life of whole nations. The process started in GREAT BRITAIN due to the development of steam power by men like James WATT (coupled with an abundance of coal), the invention of machines like the spinning jenny, and the ability of British traders to create new overseas markets for manufactured goods. This turned Britain from an agricultural country into a predominantly industrial one; and though material prosperity increased it was not widely distributed, with the result that there was much squalor and hardship in new manufacturing towns like Manchester, Sheffield and Glasgow. New political and labour movements such as CHARTISM and then the TRADE UNIONS, date from this time. Much the same pattern of events was repeated in other European countries and in the UNITED STATES.

INERT GASES

Group of six chemical ELEMENTS so named to indicate their stability. They rarely combine with other elements. They are argon, HELIUM, krypton, NEON, radon and xenon.

INFRA-RED RAY

Beam of radiation just beyond the visible range of the red end of the SPECTRUM. Its wavelength is longer than 0.00007 cm (0.000028 in). Its physical effect is to produce heat.

INGRES, Jean Auguste Dominique (1780–1867)

French artist, and a leading painter of the neo-classical school. The invention of photography further influenced the very clear, cool style he had already developed.

INQUISITION

System established by the ROMAN CATHOLIC CHURCH to seek out heretics, that is, those who challenged or turned away from official Church teachings. It dates from the thirteenth century when Pope Gregory IX appointed inquisitors to seek out heresy. Those who voluntarily confessed to heresy before appointed inquisitors were usually treated lightly. Later, especially in SPAIN, the Inquisition became a much more fearsome institution, with frequent use of torture as a means of extracting confession. The Spanish Inquisition survived until the nineteenth century.

INSECT

Very large group of invertebrate animals, characterized by having three sections to the body – head, thorax, abdomen – and six legs. Many orders of insect are also distinguished by their life-cycle – egg, larva, pupa, adult. Many other species of insects have wings. Another notable feature of some insects is their large compound eyes, shaped like the cells of a honeycomb. Also, insects do not have lungs, but breathe through openings in the abdomen known as spiracles. There are about a million known species of insect, and the total insect population is estimated to be four times greater than the combined population of every other form of animal life. The principal groups of insects are: ANTS and TERMITES; BEES and WASPS; BEETLES; BUTTERFLIES AND MOTHS; GRASSHOPPERS AND CRICKETS, including locusts. Spiders and scorpions are ARACHNIDS, not insects.

The main features of an insect

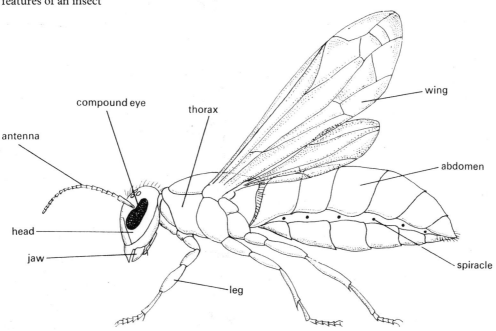

INSTINCT

Inherited patterns of behaviour requiring no instruction, common to all forms of animal life. In human beings instinct still reveals itself in such things as self-protection in the face of sudden attack. In other animals instinct plays a much larger role, as in the case of BIRDS. They build their nests entirely by instinct. More dramatic is the instinct which compels many species of bird to migrate. How this process works remains a mystery.

INSULIN

A HORMONE produced by the pancreas that regulates the body's use of sugar. Diabetes is an illness caused by a deficiency of insulin, now treated by injections of the hormone obtained from other mammals.

INSURANCE

A system of mutual protection against various contingencies, whereby many people pay regular sums of money (premiums) into a common fund and draw upon this fund if and when they need. The most usual forms of insurance are against such contingencies as fire, theft and accident. Maritime insurance is another important branch of the subject, as represented by Lloyd's of London. Some forms of personal insurance against accident and damage, such as motor insurance, are required by law. There are also state insurance schemes, notably the British National Health Insurance, which guarantees medical treatment to the entire population.

INTELLIGENCE QUOTIENT (IQ)

A measure of intelligence based upon a standard test. It is:

$$IQ = \frac{\text{Mental age}}{\text{Real age}} \times 100$$

that is, if a student of ten years reveals after test the same level of intelligence as an average student of twelve years, then the mental age of the ten-year-old student is twelve and his IQ 120.

INTERFEROMETER

A machine that divides a light ray into separate beams. Astronomers use the instrument to measure the direction, distance and size of distant stars.

INTER-GOVERNMENTAL MARITIME CONSULTATIVE ORGANIZATION (IMCO)

An agency of the UNITED NATIONS established in 1959. Its headquarters are in London. The main object is to encourage the use of the highest standards of safety in navigation. It has drawn up an International Code for the Carriage of Dangerous Goods at Sea, and in 1962 held an international conference on preventing the pollution of the sea by oil.

INTERNAL COMBUSTION ENGINE

Type of engine in which the combustion of the fuel acts directly upon the means of motion. Basically it consists of a piston inside a cylinder which is driven by the combustion of a fuel also within the cylinder. The engine was developed during the second half of the nineteenth century. The fact that the fuel is applied directly to the point of motion, and that the engine can be

Internal combustion engine

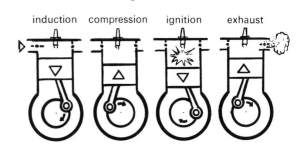

induction   compression   ignition   exhaust

switched on and off at will, make it far more mechanically efficient that the conventional STEAM ENGINE.

There are two main types of internal combustion engine. 1) The petrol engine. Here the fuel is a mixture (controlled by a carburettor) of petrol vapour and air, which is ignited by an electric spark. 2) The diesel engine (named after its inventor, the German scientist Dr Rudolf Diesel). This uses a type of fuel oil (without any air-mix) and ignites, not by an electric spark, but by the compression exerted upon it inside the cylinder. Petrol engines are largely confined to motor cars. Diesel engines have been widely adapted for use in lorries, buses, railway locomotives and ships. *See also* Karl BENZ.

INTERNATIONAL CIVIL AVIATION ORGANIZATION (ICAO)

A UNITED NATIONS inter-governmental agency, established in 1957 with headquarters in Montreal. Over a hundred countries belong to it. It helps governments to plan safe, regular flights along international air routes. A network of weather ships in the North ATLANTIC is one of the services to which ICAO contributes.

INTERNATIONAL COURT OF JUSTICE

This organization, sometimes called the World Court, meets at the Peace Palace at The Hague, Holland. It was first set up in 1922 in conjunction with the LEAGUE OF NATIONS. Under the UNITED NATIONS it was re-established with new rules. There are fifteen judges, elected by the General Assembly of the United Nations and by the Security Council.

INTERNATIONAL DATE LINE

An imaginary line internationally agreed to mark the place where each calendar day begins. It runs mainly along the 180th meridian in the

This clock shows how far each country's time is ahead of or behind Greenwich Mean Time.

PACIFIC OCEAN. For example, when it is Monday on the east of the date line it is Tuesday on the west of it.

INTERNATIONAL LABOUR (or LABOR) ORGANIZATION (ILO)

An agency of the UNITED NATIONS, originally established by the LEAGUE OF NATIONS in 1919. Its object is to improve the conditions of workers and seamen all over the world. Every year it holds a conference to which all the member countries send four delegates. In addition the ILO sends experts to countries which ask for help in such matters as the setting up of trade or technical schools where people can learn special skills. The headquarters are at Geneva.

INTERNATIONAL MONETARY FUND (IMF)

An agency of the UNITED NATIONS which aims to help member nations achieve better economic growth by the freer circulation of international currencies. It was established in 1944, with headquarters in Washington DC, USA.

INTERNATIONAL TELECOMMUNICATIONS UNION

The oldest inter-governmental agency. It was organized in 1865 and is now an agency of the UNITED NATIONS with headquarters in Geneva. Its most recent task has been to study space communication techniques and regulations.

INTERNATIONAL TRUST TERRITORIES

The name given to certain territories not yet prepared for self-government, which come under direct supervision of the UNITED NATIONS. When the United Nations was first set up, there were many such territories, but their number has now diminished.

INTERNATIONAL CRIMINAL POLICE ORGANIZATION (INTERPOL)

International organization involving the police forces of more than 100 nations, founded in 1923, with headquarters in Paris.

INVERTEBRATE

Animal without a backbone. This large section of the ANIMAL KINGDOM includes INSECTS, ARACHNIDS (spiders, scorpions, centipedes), CRUSTACEANS (crabs, lobsters), MOLLUSCS (squids, octopus, cuttlefish, snails); also such creatures as starfish, jellyfish, sea anemones, down to the simplest single-cell forms of animal life such as the amoeba. *See also* ARTHROPODS.

ION

An ATOM that has gained or lost electrons, so producing a positive or negative electrical charge.

Their existence was first identified by Michael FARADAY. He observed that electric currents break down (or decompose) chemical compounds in solution by causing individual atoms to become electrically charged and so to move in opposite directions. He called them ions, from the Greek word *ionos,* meaning 'wanderer'.

IONOSPHERE

Layer of the Earth's ATMOSPHERE at distances of between about 80 km (50 miles) and 320 km (200 miles) above sea level. It is so called because the air and other gases at that altitude are highly ionized (*see* ION) by the sun's ULTRA-VIOLET radiation. The ionosphere makes possible long-range radio communication as it reflects back to Earth radio waves which would otherwise be lost in space.

Invertebrates

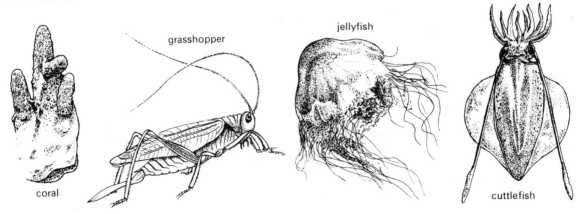

coral grasshopper jellyfish cuttlefish

IRAN

Islamic republic in south-western Asia, formerly called Persia, with an area of 1,648,000 sq km (636,331 sq miles), and a population of about 38 million. The capital is Tehran. Most of the nation is arid and mountainous, but some cotton is produced, and wool which goes into the manufacture of the famous Persian carpets. The chief source of income, however, is oil, shipped and exported from the Persian Gulf. The history of the nation goes back to the sixth century BC, when the original Persian tribes settled in the territory. They rose to a position of great power in the ancient world under such kings as Cyrus II and DARIUS I, before being defeated and subdued by ALEXANDER the Great. In the seventh century AD, Persia came under ARAB rule and was converted to Islam. In recent times Iran was a monarchy ruled by a Shah. But the Shah was deposed in 1979 and the people voted to make Iran an Islamic republic.

IRAQ

Republic of the Middle East (south-west ASIA), with an area of 434,924 sq km (167,934 sq miles) and a population of about 13 million. The capital is Baghdad. The chief export is oil, shipped mainly from the port of Basra on the Persian Gulf. Iraq lies along the course of the rivers Euphrates and Tigris which saw the rise of such great civilizations of the ancient world as those of SUMER and BABYLONIA, part of the kingdom of MESOPOTAMIA.

IRELAND

Name of the second largest island of the British Isles. Northern Ireland (Ulster) comprises six counties and is part of the United Kingdom (*see* GREAT BRITAIN). It has an area of 14,150 sq km (5,460 sq miles) and a population of 1½ million. The principal city is Belfast.

The Republic of Ireland (Eire) occupies the remainder of the island. It has an area of 70,283

An example of Early Christian art from Ireland

sq km (27,138 sq miles) and a population of about 3¼ million. The capital is Dublin. The country is popularly known as 'The Emerald Isle' because the moist climate keeps the countryside looking green. In fact, much of the land is poorly drained and hard to cultivate. Nevertheless, dairy produce, pork and bacon are important exports. Also, the government has attracted new industry through foreign investment.

The true history of Ireland began in the fifth century AD with the arrival of St Patrick and the conversion of the people to Christianity. Then followed a period when the Irish monasteries were among the most illustrious centres of Christian art and learning. Irish history thereafter has been less happy. It has been a long story of dispute with ENGLAND, usually to do with religion (Protestant England against Catholic Ireland), plus periods of famine. In 1800 an Act of Parliament created the Union of

Great Britain and Ireland, but agitation for independence from England increased.

In the nineteenth century the leader of this movement was Charles Stewart Parnell. As Prime Minister, W. E. GLADSTONE tried to grant self-rule to Ireland, but was opposed by English aristocrats in the House of Lords many of whom owned property in Ireland. During and just after WORLD WAR I there was armed rebellion in the country, and in 1921 the Irish Free State was at last established. Only the province of Ulster in the north remained within the United Kingdom, and a movement to unite it with the south has continued to cause troubles there. In 1949 the Irish Free State became the Republic of Ireland. It joined the EUROPEAN ECONOMIC COMMUNITY in 1973.

IRON

Silvery-white metal element, found in a variety of ores and mined in many countries. It gives its name to a general period of history, between about 2500 BC and 1200 BC, when it was first widely used and developed for tools and weapons. *See also* STEEL.

ISLAM

Religion based on the life and teaching of the Prophet Mohammed, who was born in ARABIA in AD 570. It is nearly six hundred years younger than CHRISTIANITY, and expresses many ideas and beliefs of both Christianity and JUDAISM, principally the belief in a single divine being, God or Allah. The sacred book is the Koran, containing the sayings of Mohammed, which Moslems (followers of Islam) believe to be the word of Allah. Mohammed himself, however, is not worshipped as a divine being. The principal place of worship is the mosque, and there is one major period of fasting each year called Ramadan. It lasts for a month, during which Moslems must not eat or drink between sunrise and sunset, except for the old, the very young or sick. Orthodox Moslems are known as Sunni. A more mystical sect, re-

Islamic tile showing the city of Medina

sponsible for much beautiful Islamic art, are the Sufis.

Very soon after the death of Mohammed in 632, Islam began to spread rapidly north and eastwards, across PALESTINE, SYRIA, Persia, and finally into INDIA; also westwards through EGYPT, right across North AFRICA and into SPAIN. Thus it became both a religion and an empire. It came into bloody conflict with Christianity at the time of the CRUSADES, and in Spain, from which country it was eventually banished. Today virtually the whole of North Africa, TURKEY and the Middle East, including PAKISTAN, remains a part of the Moslem world. INDONESIA and MALAYSIA are also largely Moslem countries. The total number of adherents is approaching 700 million.

ISOTOPE

Form of an ELEMENT created by adding or removing neutrons to or from the nucleus of its ATOMS. Some isotopes are radioactive. Radioactive isotopes are particularly useful because while they retain the normal chemical properties of the element, their radioactivity

Jerusalem, seen from the Mount of Olives

allows their presence to be detected in different chemical processes, and the processes can be better understood as a result. In agriculture, for example, the effectiveness of fertilizers on plants can be very closely monitored if the fertilizer in question contains isotopes. In medicine isotopes are widely used to destroy diseased cells in the body because the degree of their radioactivity can be accurately gauged. *See also* ATOM and NUCLEAR ENERGY.

ISRAEL

Middle East republic, the Jewish national state. It has an area of 20,770 sq km (8,020 sq miles), which is about the same size as WALES, and a population of 3,874,000. The official capital is Jerusalem, but Tel-Aviv/Jaffa and Haifa are also large cities. The chief products are citrus fruits and some mineral phosphates from the Dead Sea region.

Israel corresponds approximately to the an-cient Hebrew land of Canaan and then of Palestine, as described in the Old Testament of the BIBLE. A serious revolt against Roman occupation in AD 66 led to the destruction of Jerusalem and dispersal of the Jews from this homeland. Subsequently the region was absorbed into ISLAM, and it remained, for most of the time, an ARAB part of the world right into the twentieth century. An international Jewish movement, called Zionism, planned to create a new Jewish state in Palestine. In 1948 this was achieved with the creation of the modern state of Israel, but only in the face of bitter Arab resistance. Arab-Israeli wars occurred in 1948, 1956, 1967 and 1973, but Israel signed a Peace Treaty with Egypt in 1979.

ITALY

Republic of southern EUROPE, including the islands of Sicily and Sardinia. It has an area of 301,225 sq km (116,310 sq miles), with a

St Mark's, Venice, Italy

population of over 57 million. The capital is Rome.

Italy is largely a peninsula in the MEDITERRANEAN SEA, shaped rather like a boot. The ALPS provide natural frontiers with FRANCE, SWITZERLAND and AUSTRIA in the north-west and north. There is a fertile northern plain, created by the River Po, then another range of mountains running down the centre of the country, the Appenines. There are also volcanoes: Vesuvius, Etna in Sicily, and the island of Stromboli north of Sicily.

Italy produces large quantities of wine, also wheat, rice and other cereal crops, and many citrus fruits. Sicily and southern Italy remain under-developed regions, but in the north, especially around the cities of Milan and Turin, there is much industry. Genoa, Naples and Taranto are major ports. Other Italian towns and cities, apart from Rome itself, are world-famous because of their many beautiful buildings and other works of art, notably Florence, Venice and Ravenna.

The history of the country goes back to the ETRUSCANS and to the founding of Rome, some time in the sixth century BC. This led to the whole period of the ROMAN EMPIRE, which at its greatest extent stretched from Spain and the British Isles in the west almost to India in the east, encompassing the whole Mediterranean region. With the subsequent decline and fall of Roman power there emerged the important city-states of Venice, Florence and Genoa, which were centres of RENAISSANCE commerce and art. Italy remained politically divided until the nineteenth century, but it was Giuseppe Mazzini who aroused Italian nationalism, thus paving the way for the soldier and patriot Giuseppe GARIBALDI and the statesman Count Camillo Cavour to create a united country under King Victor Emanuel. Soon after WORLD WAR I Benito MUSSOLINI rose to power at the head of a right-wing fascist government. He took Italy into WORLD WAR II against the Allies and was deposed and finally shot by his own countrymen. After the war a democratic republic was established, and in 1957 Italy became one of the original six members of the EUROPEAN ECONOMIC COMMUNITY.

IVAN the Terrible (1530–84)

First Russian ruler to be crowned Tsar (Emperor). He waged successful campaigns of territorial expansion south-eastwards into Asia, and built up trade with western countries, both to the benefit of Russia. On the other hand, he grew into a tyrant who committed many atrocities against his own people.

IVES, Charles (1874–1954)

American composer. He was a businessman by profession, but wrote many pieces of music which were astonishingly advanced for their time. Many of these compositions were inspired by scenes and events in New England, where he lived.

IVORY COAST

West African republic with an area of 322,463 sq km (124,510 sq miles) and a population of about 8½ million. The capital is Abidjan. The chief exports are cocoa, coffee, timber and bananas. Formerly a French colony, it gained independence in 1958.

J

JACKAL

Member of the DOG family, looking rather like a cross between a FOX and a WOLF. Native to many parts of ASIA, AFRICA and south-eastern EUROPE. Also like a wolf, it hunts in packs during the night, in search of both carrion and living prey.

JACKSON, Thomas Jonathan (1824–63)

American Confederate general, and one of the outstanding military leaders of the AMERICAN CIVIL WAR. By his stubborn defence at the Battle of Bull Run he earned the nickname 'Stonewall'. He died soon after the Battle of Chancellorsville – his greatest victory – having been accidentally shot by one of his own men.

JACOBINS

A radical political society during the FRENCH REVOLUTION. The name came from its association with a monastery building in Rue St Jacques in Paris. The Jacobin leader Maximilien ROBESPIERRE ushered in the Reign of Terror.

JACOBITES

The supporters of James II and his descendants after the expulsion of the Stuarts by William III (1688–9) and after the accession of the Hanoverians (1714). The name was adapted from the Latin *Jacobus* for James. The Jacobites

Charles Edward Stuart, leader of the Jacobites

twice attempted to overthrow the monarchy. In 1715 they were led by the Earl of Mar and James II's son, called the Old Pretender. In 1745 an army led by CHARLES EDWARD STUART, and mainly composed of Highland chiefs and their men, won the Battles of Prestonpans (1745) and Falkirk (1746). They were, however, finally defeated by the Duke of Cumberland at Culloden Moor in 1746.

JADE

The name for two very hard minerals, nephrite and jadite, which are suitable for carving into delicate patterns. Although jade is generally associated with green, it can be any colour from black to white, yellow, brown and red. Nephrite is found mainly in AUSTRALIA and NEW ZEALAND. For centuries Chinese craftsmen have carved exquisite jade objects such as amulets, pendants, vases, bowls and figures.

JAGUAR

Powerful and dangerous member of the CAT family, native to Central and South AMERICA. It is like the LEOPARD in colour, pattern, voice and habit. The jaguar is a good climber and often lies in wait for deer, capybaras and peccaries, on which it feeds. It also catches fish.

JAINISM

Religion founded on the life and teaching of Vardhamana Mahavira, who lived in INDIA during the sixth century BC. It is similar in many respects to BUDDHISM. Enlightened beings are said to have become Jinas ('ones who have conquered'), and the name of the religion is derived from this. There are about 2 million Jains in India.

JAMAICA

Island republic in the WEST INDIES, with an area of 10,991 sq km (4,244 sq miles) and a population of about 2 million. The capital is Kingston. The chief products are sugar (from which rum is made) and bananas. The island is also the world's second largest producer of bauxite. It was discovered by Christopher COLUMBUS in 1494, and was a British colony from the seventeenth century until 1962, when it gained independence. It remains a member of the BRITISH COMMONWEALTH.

JAMES, Henry (1843–1916)

American writer who settled in England and became a British subject just before he died. He wrote several novels about British and American society, including *Portrait of a Lady* and *The Ambassadors,* but perhaps his best-known work is his ghost story *The Turn of the Screw.*

JANÁČEK, Leoš (1845–1928)

Czech composer. He used some Czech folk tunes and rhythms in his own music, but was especially interested in the inflections of Czech speech, which he incorporated into his own highly individual style. His works include the operas *Jenufa, Katya Kabanova* and *The Cunning Little Vixen,* and the orchestral Sinfonietta.

JAPAN

Group of islands in the north-western PACIFIC, with an elected parliament and a constitutional emperor. The four main islands are Hokkaido, Honshu, Kyushu and Sikoku. The total area of the nation is 372,313 sq km (143,759 sq miles), with a population of about 117 million. The capital is Tokyo (itself with a population of more than 11 million). Other large cities are Osaka, Nagoya, Kyoto and Yokohama. Japan is the most important industrial nation in Asia, and one of the leading industral nations of the world, with an enormous output of ships, motor vehicles, electronic equipment, glassware and chemicals. But much of the country remains unspoilt and beautiful, because it is mountainous.

Fujiyama, highest mountain in Japan

Buddhism entered Japan from China and Korea during the sixth century AD, but for another thousand years no other external factors had much influence on the traditional Japanese way of life, based on the SHINTO religion and a belief in the divinity of the emperor. European countries, and the United States, began to break into this isolation during the nineteenth century, and in a relatively short space of time Japan became not only a trading nation but a military power as well. In 1905 it waged a successful war against Imperial Russia, gaining territory on the Asian mainland. Further conquests in China led up to the attack on the American naval base at Pearl Harbor in 1941 and entry into WORLD WAR II. Japan surrendered after receiving atomic bombs on Hiroshima and Nagasaki. Democratic institutions were then established and the Emperor HIROHITO relinquished his time-honoured claim to divinity.

JAZZ

A branch of music. Its origins lie in the work songs and spirituals of the Negro slaves who worked on the cotton plantations in the southern states of the United States. The first recognizable jazz forms – blues and stomps – emerged in the early years of this century, partly as a result of the blending of Negro and Creole (French-Indian) musical styles. The principal feature of blues was a basic progression of harmonies. Stomps were characterized by snappy, syncopated rhythms. Improvisation was an important element of both. New Orleans was the place where many of the early jazz bands played in the period up to about 1920, and jazz musicians associated with this 'New Orleans' style include Ferdinand 'Jelly Roll' Morton, Joe 'King' Oliver and the young Louis Armstrong. During the 1920s jazz spread to the big American cities further north, to St Louis, Chicago and New York, and new styles developed, notably a piano style called boogie woogie. Larger, more professional-sounding bands were also formed, by such musicians as Edward 'Duke' Ellington and William 'Count' Basie. In the 1930s certain jazz rhythms and harmonies were taken up by many white Americans – Benny Goodman, Artie Shaw, Paul Whiteman, Glenn Miller – to create

Louis Armstrong

the immensely popular dance band style known as swing. Serious jazz musicians developed new styles of their own. In the 1940s Charlie Parker and Dizzy Gillespie created the style known as Bebop or Bop. Since then others (still mostly black men) have created styles which have taken jazz far from its simple origins and turned it into a highly intellectual art form.

Jazz has been, and remains, a largely (though not exclusively) American type of music. It has had a tremendous effect on the dance and popular music of this century. It has also influenced the work of many serious European composers, notably DEBUSSY, RAVEL and STRAVINSKY. Some American composers, especially GERSHWIN, have made use of jazz styles to create a distinctively American-sounding musical style of their own.

JEFFERSON, Thomas (1743–1826)

American statesman. He was principal author of the Declaration of Independence (*see* AMERICAN WAR OF INDEPENDENCE), and was then elected third President of the United States. In this capacity he bought from NAPOLEON a huge stretch of territory west of the MISSISSIPPI, known as Louisiana. This Louisiana Purchase, as it is called, was the biggest sale of land in history, and doubled the size of the United States.

JERBOA

RODENT about the size of a RAT, native to North Africa and parts of Asia. It has very long hind legs and can move at great speed by a series of leaps.

JET PROPULSION

This is based on the scientific principle, as expounded in one of Sir Isaac NEWTON's laws of motion, that to every action there is an equal and opposite reaction. A simple example of this is a balloon from which air is escaping. As the air rushes out at one end, so the balloon rushes forward in the opposite direction. In a jet engine air and fuel are burnt, and as the escaping gases of combustion rush out at one end of the engine, so the engine moves forward in the opposite direction with an equivalent force and speed. One form of jet propulsion is the ram jet (or the very similar pulse-jet). Here the engine has first to be set in motion (probably by some catapult device) so that air may enter and start combustion. The German V1

Jet engine: turbo-jet (top) and ram jet (bottom)

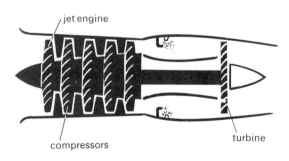

jet engine

compressors

turbine

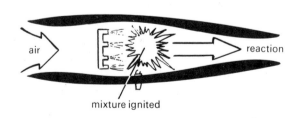

air

reaction

mixture ignited

Flying Bomb of WORLD WAR II operated like this. The far more common form of jet engine, used in nearly all jet-propelled aircraft, is the turbo-jet. A TURBINE within the engine draws air into the combustion chamber, so that combustion will start and the engine will develop thrust without the aid of any outside force.

Jet-propelled combat aircraft were built by both the British and the Germans during World War II. The first passenger jet airliner was the British *Comet*, which went into service in 1952. *See also* ROCKET and Sir Frank WHITTLE.

JOAN OF ARC, St (1412–31)

French patriot and national heroine. She was a peasant girl, born during the period of the HUNDRED YEARS WAR, who claimed she heard voices telling her to free her country from the English and have the Dauphin (heir to the throne) crowned king of a united France. Consequently she became a soldier and led a French army to victory at Orleans. Then she had the Dauphin duly crowned in the cathedral at Rheims. Soon after she was captured by the English, accused of heresy and burnt at the stake. She was canonized (made a saint) in 1920.

JODRELL BANK

Observatory, built near Manchester in 1957, with one of the world's largest radio telescopes. It has a dish-shaped antenna 76 m (250 ft) in diameter. From here astronomers have mapped cosmic radio sources and studied such phenomena as pulsars.

JOHNSON, Samuel (1709–84)

English lexicographer and writer. He was born at Lichfield, but spent most of his life in London. His greatest work of scholarship was his preparation of a dictionary of the English language, the first comprehensive dictionary of its kind. Dr Johnson, who typified what was best in eighteenth-century enlightenment and humanitarianism, wrote several books of his own, including the philosophical novel *Rasselas*. But most people know him best by the many sayings attributed to him by his biographer James BOSWELL.

JONSON, Ben (1573–1637)

English poet and dramatist. He wrote mainly satirical comedies, notably *Volpone, The Alchemist* and *Bartholomew Fair*. The first production of his early play *Every Man in his Humour* had SHAKESPEARE in the cast.

JORDAN

ARAB kingdom of the Middle East with an area of 97,740 sq km (37,740 sq miles) and a population of about 3 million. The capital is Amman. It shares a long stretch of frontier with ISRAEL and is the home of Palestinian refugees from that country. Jordan has therefore been drawn into the long-standing Arab-Israeli dispute, and in 1973 joined SYRIA and EGYPT in renewed war with Israel.

JOULE, James Prescott (1818–89)

English scientist who studied the relationship between heat and mechanical work. The unit of work, the joule, is named after him.

JOYCE, James (1882–1941)

He was born in Dublin, but made a living for many years teaching languages in Italy, Switzerland and France. In his two principal novels, *Ulysses* and *Finnegan's Wake,* he developed a style sometimes called 'stream of consciousness', representing a continuous flow of ideas and impressions as they flood into the mind of the characters. Through these two books, Joyce became one of the most influential writers of the twentieth century.

JUDAISM

Religion of the Jewish people based largely on the teachings of MOSES and other leaders and prophets as recounted in the Old Testament of the BIBLE. It is the oldest monotheistic religion

People praying at the Wailing Wall, Jerusalem

– belief in one supreme being, given various names by the Jews themselves, including Yahweh and Jehovah as well as God. Two other important sacred books are the *Talmud* and the *Torah,* containing the many laws and observances which orthodox Jews are supposed to keep. The principal festival is the Feast of the Passover, the principal place of worship is the Synagogue, and the priests are called Rabbis. Judaism is the religion from which both CHRISTIANITY and ISLAM have developed. There are about 14 million adherents; about 3 million in ISRAEL itself, and the remainder distributed among many other nations.

JUDO

Sport based on the ancient Japanese techniques of unarmed combat known as *ju-jitsu*. It is practised in many countries, and since 1964 has been an event of the OLYMPIC GAMES. It is important to distinguish between wrestling and judo. In the former, each contestant pits his strength against the other. In judo the art is to let one's adversary do all the work, using his strength, mistakenly applied, to bring about his own defeat. It requires great acrobatic skill. A coloured belt indicates a practitioner's level of skill, a black belt being the highest award.

JULIUS CAESAR (102–44 BC)

Roman soldier and statesman. Gaius Julius Caesar rose to political power with the help of his rich friend Crassus, and then formed a ruling triumvirate, or partnership, with Crassus and Pompey, a successful general. As a general himself, Caesar showed his military genius by conquering Gaul (France), and organizing two expeditions to Britain. With the death of Crassus, Caesar challenged Pompey for the position of supreme political power, pursuing his rival to Egypt where he fell in love with CLEOPATRA. Through further military triumphs Caesar ended as virtual dictator of the Roman Empire, but was murdered in the Senate in Rome by a group of conspirators,

Julius Caesar

including Brutus and Cassius, who feared his power. He was also a great orator and writer on military affairs.

JUNG, Carl Gustav (1875–1961)

Swiss psychiatrist who worked with Sigmund FREUD for some years on the causes and treatment of mental distress and abnormality. He later developed his own school of psychology, based on the idea of introvert and extrovert personalities.

JUPITER

Planet of the SOLAR SYSTEM with an equatorial diameter of 142,800 km (89,200 miles) and an average distance from the SUN of 777 million km (465 million miles). Jupiter is the largest planet and is about 1300 times more massive than the Earth. Its outer layer consists largely of turbulent clouds of gaseous hydrogen compounds like methane and ammonia. The most interesting surface feature is the so-called Great Red Spot which shifts back and forth across the surface, though its origin remains a mystery. Jupiter has four major satellites, two of which are about the size of our Moon and two

The Emperor Justinian with attendants, shown in a mosaic in the church of San Vitale, which he built at Ravenna

about as large as Mercury, and nine smaller ones. Ganymede and Callisto were photographed by Voyager spacecraft in 1981.

JURY

Group of people, usually twelve, who listen to the evidence in a court of law and then decide on a verdict – whether or not the person on trial is guilty of the crime as charged. Trial by jury is one of the safeguards on personal freedom, whereby the individual, charged with a crime, is judged by fellow citizens and not by officials of the state. In practice, only cases involving serious crimes are brought before a jury. If the defendant (the person charged) pleads guilty, then, of course, the jury has nothing to decide, since the actual sentence is decided by a judge.

JUSTINIAN (483–565)

Emperor of the BYZANTINE or eastern Roman Empire. He won back from the Vandals, Goths and other barbarian tribes many parts of the ROMAN EMPIRE previously conquered by them; strengthened the administration of the early Christian Church; and revived and improved the whole structure of Roman law. His wife Theodora played an important part in his government.

JUVENAL (c. AD 60–140)

Roman poet whose Satires represent attacks on the follies and vices of Roman life as he saw them. The famous phrase 'a healthy mind in a healthy body' is attributed to him.

K

KA'ABA

Sacred shrine of ISLAM in the city of Mecca, Saudi Arabia. It consists of a small building containing a black stone set in a silver ring, said to have been given to Abraham by the angel Gabriel. The Ka'aba is the principal place of pilgrimage for Moslems.

KAFKA, Franz (1883–1924)

Czech novelist, whose two most important books, *The Trial* and *The Castle,* deal with the theme of the individual as powerless before the workings of a vast and mysterious bureaucracy. He has been a very influential figure in modern literature.

KALEIDOSCOPE

Optical device which, if tapped or rotated, gives an endless number of geometrical patterns. It consists of a tube with an eyepiece at one end and at the other two mirrors set at an angle (60°) to each other, plus a glass compartment containing pieces of coloured glass.

KAMPUCHEA, Democratic Republic

South-east Asian republic, but until 1953 a part of French Indo-China. Formerly known as Cambodia, it became the Khmer Republic in 1970 and in 1976 adopted a new constitution and the name Democratic Kampuchea. It has an area of 181,035 sq km (69,902 sq miles) and a

The temple of Angkor-Vath, Kampuchea

population of about 9 million. The capital is Phnom Penh. Most of the country is a fertile plain watered by the Mekong River, and the chief products are rice and fish.

KANDINSKY, Wassily (1866–1944)

Russian artist, born in Moscow. He originally studied law but later turned to painting, working in Germany, Russia and France. He was one of the first European painters to work in a purely abstract style.

KANGAROO

Australian MAMMAL classed as a MARSUPIAL, distinguished by its strong back legs with which it advances by a series of long leaps. It also has a very large tail. The great grey kangaroo grows to a height of about 2.5 m (8 ft). A smaller variety is known as the wallaby. In the past kangaroos have been hunted, either for fur or because of damage they have done to crops. Today, because of decreasing numbers, they are protected by law in some areas.

KANT, Immanuel (1724–1804)

German philosopher. He never moved from his birthplace, Königsberg, although he became one of the most famous men of his time. In his book *The Critique of Pure Reason* he inquired into the whole of human knowledge and experience. In *The Critique of Practical Reason* he presented his ideas on ethics and human behaviour.

KARATE

Form of unarmed combat in which the contestants kick, strike or thrust with hands and feet. The word means 'empty hand', and the art originated in eastern countries such as Japan and Korea.

KEATS, John (1795–1821)

English poet. He trained as a doctor and surgeon, but became one of the greatest of the English Romantic poets. His works include the odes 'To a Nightingale' and 'On a Grecian Urn,' many famous sonnets, and the narrative poem 'The Eve of St Agnes'.

KELVIN, William Thomson, Lord (1824–1907)

British scientist who was active in many branches of science, including electricity and heat. His work helped to make possible the operation of transatlantic telephone cables. He also determined the 'absolute zero' of temperature (the ultimate state of coldness), and based the Kelvin temperature scale upon it, i.e. absolute zero is 0° Kelvin.

KENYA

East African republic that lies across the line of the Equator. It has an area of 582,646 sq km (224,973 sq miles) and a population of nearly 16 million. The capital is Nairobi. Coffee, tea and cotton are the principal exports. There are also famous national parks containing such wildlife as elephants, lions and zebras, which attract many foreign visitors. While the country was still a British colony there was serious political unrest involving a terrorist breakaway organization called the Mau Mau. Kenya became independent in 1963 and, under its presidents Jomo Kenyatta and Daniel Arap Moi, it has achieved political stability. It belongs to the BRITISH COMMONWEALTH.

KEPLER, Johannes (1571–1630)

German astronomer. COPERNICUS before him had asserted that it was the planets, including Earth, that moved round the sun, and not the sun that moved around the Earth. But he thought the planetary orbits were circular. Kepler proved by mathematics that the paths of the planets round the sun were not circular but elliptical, and so added significantly to our understanding of the SOLAR SYSTEM.

KEY

Musical term which describes a scale – a particular sequence of eight notes. There are twenty-four major and minor scales and keys, on which most Western music has been based during the last three hundred and fifty years. *See also* HARMONY.

KEYBOARD INSTRUMENT

Key is the word used to describe the levers on a PIANO which the player depresses with a finger in order to sound a note. The whole row of such keys is called a keyboard, and this word, in turn, is used to describe the group of instruments which operate on the same mechanical principle. The chief keyboard instruments are the piano itself and the older HARPSICHORD, clavichord and spinet. The ORGAN also has a keyboard, but because it is so different in other ways from instruments like the piano and harpsichord, it is not usually classed with them under this heading.

KIERKEGAARD, Sören Aabye (1813–55)

Danish philosopher. He criticized organized religion, claiming that religious experience was a matter for the individual, as the individual self or soul is the only reality. His ideas had an influence on the work of such writers as Jean-Paul SARTRE and Albert Camus.

KINETICS

Branch of MECHANICS concerned with the study of the relationship between objects in motion and the forces acting upon them. Kinetic energy is produced by a given amount of mechanical WORK. For example, when a man lifts a weight, the weight has potential energy, which is converted into kinetic energy when it falls. The kinetic energy of objects is related mathematically to their speed and MASS.

KINGFISHER

Group of BIRDS, comprising about eighty different species. Most are native to the tropics, but the common kingfisher, noted for its bright blue plumage, is found along many rivers and

The common kingfisher

streams of Great Britain. Another variety is the kookaburra, or 'laughing jackass' of Australia.

KIPLING, Rudyard (1865–1936)

English novelist who wrote many books, including *Kim* and *Plain Tales from the Hills*, about life in imperial INDIA.

KIRIBATI

Formerly the British Gilbert Islands, Kiribati became an independent republic in 1979. It has an area of 886 sq km (342 sq miles) and 58,000 people. The capital is Tarawa.

KNIGHTS OF ST JOHN (KNIGHTS HOSPITALLERS)

Order founded in the ninth century with the primary aim of treating and helping pilgrims. Later, members fought in the CRUSADES and were rivals of the KNIGHTS TEMPLARS. They were forced back by the Turks to Cyprus, then to Rhodes and finally to Malta. They found refuge there for hundreds of years until 1798.

KNIGHTS TEMPLARS

Military and religious order formed during the Middle Ages to fight and serve in the CRUSADES. Their original vow was to defend Christian pilgrims to the Holy Land, but they grew in power and acquired land all over Europe.

KNOX, John (1505–72)

Scottish reformer and preacher. He devoted his adult life, both in SCOTLAND and on the continent, to furthering the Protestant cause, especially in its Calvinist form.

KOALA

Australian MAMMAL which looks like a kind of bear, but it is classed as a MARSUPIAL. It lives off the leaves of eucalyptus trees.

KOCH, Robert (1843–1910)

German physician and bacteriologist who discovered the germs which cause tuberculosis, cholera and anthrax.

KODÁLY, Zoltán (1882–1967)

Hungarian composer. With his friend and compatriot Béla Bartók, he made an intense study of Hungarian and Romanian folk music, absorbing its rhythms and melodies into his own style. His best-known music is the suite from his opera *Háry János*. This starts with an orchestral 'sneeze' to indicate that the events which follow, recounted in the music, should not be taken too seriously.

KOOKABURRA. *See* KINGFISHER

KOREA

Country of eastern Asia forming a peninsula between the Yellow Sea and the Sea of Japan. It has an area of 219,022 sq km (84,569 sq miles). Korea has a very ancient civilization, but in this century its affairs have been dominated by foreign powers. It was occupied by JAPAN from 1910 until the end of WORLD WAR II. Then the country was divided between Soviet and American occupying forces. This led to the Korean War of 1950–3 and the establishment of two separate republics.

The Democratic People's Republic of North Korea is the larger of the two in area but has a population of nearly 18 million. The capital is Pyongyang. It is a Communist regime.

The Republic of South Korea has a population of about 38 million. The capital is Seoul. It has a republican form of government.

KUBLAI KHAN (1216–94)

Grandson of GENGHIS KHAN. He completed the conquest of CHINA and founded the Mongol dynasty that ruled the country for nearly a hundred years.

The kudu antelope

KUDU

Species of ANTELOPE native to south and east Africa. The male is distinguished by long twisted horns and a greyish coat with white vertical stripes.

KU KLUX KLAN

Secret society in the United States founded soon after the AMERICAN CIVIL WAR by defeated Confederates who feared that their states would be dominated by the black population. They dressed in white robes to represent the avenging ghosts of dead Confederate soldiers. They became a terrorist organization, persecuting Jews, Catholics and others, as well as black people.

KUWAIT

Independent ARAB sheikdom on the Persian Gulf. It has an area of only 17,818 sq km (6,880 sq miles) and a population of 1,344,000. It is one of the world's richest nations at present because of its oil exports.

L

LABOUR PARTY

Major British political party dedicated to the general principle of social equality and justice through such policies as the redistribution of wealth by taxation, extension of social services, and public ownership of certain industries and services. Whereas the CONSERVATIVE PARTY has traditionally been supported by landowners and business interests, the Labour Party has drawn its support from the TRADE UNIONS and working people generally. It emerged as a new force in British politics with the election to Parliament in 1892 of John Burns and Keir HARDIE. By 1922 it had replaced the LIBERAL PARTY as the largest party in opposition to the Conservatives. It formed minority governments in 1924 and 1929. The administrations from 1945 to 1951 created the basis of the Welfare State, including the NATIONAL HEALTH SERVICE; and also began the process of dismantling the British Empire, especially with the granting of independence to INDIA. There were further Labour administrations from 1964 to 1970. Labour Prime Ministers have included Ramsay MacDonald, Clement Attlee, Sir Harold Wilson and James Callaghan. There are similarly constituted Labour parties in other BRITISH COMMONWEALTH countries. *See also* Aneurin BEVAN.

LABRADOR

Part of the province of Newfoundland in CANADA. With an area of 292,000 sq km (113,000 sq miles) it extends north-eastwards from the mouth of the St Lawrence river, its long coastline washed by the cold Labrador current. The climate is severe and the population is only about 30,000, the main occupations being fishing and fur trapping.

Below Part of a new hydro-electric scheme in Labrador

LABYRINTH

The maze, in Greek mythology, that Daedalus built for King Minos of Crete as a prison for the monster Minotaur. Theseus killed the monster and found his way out of the maze by tracing the thread he unwound as he went in. A palace has been excavated at Knossos in CRETE that suggests a labyrinth of rooms and corridors.

LACE

An open fabric made by using cotton or silver and gold thread. Lace developed through the embroidery practised in Italy in the fifteenth century. In 1809 John Heathcoat patented a

Right Venice in the time of Marco Polo

Above Bobbin or pillow-lace, made by twisting threads

'bobbin net' lace-making machine, and modern machinery is a development of this.

LACQUER

A glossy protective coating used on metals, china and wood. Resin mixed with turpentine provides a spirit lacquer. Cellulose is a main constituent.

LACROSSE

Game played between two teams of twelve players with netted sticks and a small ball. The object is to throw or shoot the ball through the opposing side's goal. Lacrosse has fewer rules than almost any other ball game, those that do exist being intended to keep the game going and protect players from injury. The game was originally played by North American Indians, and is now widely played in CANADA.

LAFAYETTE, Marie-Joseph Paul, Marquis de (1757–1834)

French soldier and statesman. He commanded a French military force that fought with the American colonists against the British in the AMERICAN WAR OF INDEPENDENCE; and helped

Left Napoleon Bonaparte in his study, portrait by Jacques Louis David

to negotiate the peace that created the UNITED STATES OF AMERICA. During the FRENCH REVOLUTION he commanded the newly formed National Guard, before escaping from the Reign of Terror. After returning to France he commanded another National Guard during the Revolution of 1830 which unseated the unpopular Charles X.

17th-century illustration of a fable by La Fontaine

LA FONTAINE, Jean de (1621–95)

French poet and writer, famous for his *Fables* which he modelled on Aesop and other examples of this type of story-telling.

LAKE

A body of water surrounded by land. Some lakes are in fact called 'seas', such as the Sea of Galilee, the DEAD SEA, and the CASPIAN SEA, the largest inland body of water in the world.

LAMPREY

FISH with an EEL-like body. It is a parasite which attaches itself to other fish and feeds on their blood.

LANDSEER, Sir Edwin Henry (1802–73)

English artist, immensely popular during his own lifetime for such paintings as *The Monarch of the Glen*. He also designed the lions at the base of Nelson's Column in Trafalgar Square, London, which were among his last important works.

LANGUAGE

Means of communication by speech. Most, but not all, languages also have a written form, based on an ALPHABET or pictograms. The history and development of language is extremely involved, and many of today's languages are related to each other in some way or other. The following are the principal language groups:

Indo-European: Germanic (Dutch, English, German, Norwegian, Swedish); Romance (French, Italian, Portuguese, Romanian, Spanish); Slavonic (Czech, Polish, Russian, Serbo-Croat); Hellenic (Greek); Celtic (Breton, Gaelic, Welsh); Indo-Aryan (Hindi, Sanskrit, Sinhalese, Urdu).

Indi-Chinese: Burmese, Chinese, Siamese.

Semitic and Hamitic: Arabic, Berber, Ethiopian, Hebrew.

Finno-Ugric: Estonian, Finnish, Hungarian, Lapp.

Dravidian: Tamil, Telugu.

Bantu: Kafir, Zulu.

Turkic: Kirghiz, Turkish, Tartar, Uzbek.

A few languages, notably Basque and Japanese, do not come within any of the above classifications; while proper classification of the many Amero-Indian languages has still to be accomplished.

LANOLIN

Form of wax obtained from sheep's wool. It is widely used in medicines, ointments and cosmetics because it is easily absorbed by the skin and is partly antiseptic.

LAOS

Republic of south-east Asia, formerly a part of French Indo-China. It has an area of 236,800 sq km (91,434 sq miles) and a population of about 3.4 million. The capital is Vientiane. After WORLD WAR II Laos, with Democratic KAMPUCHEA (Cambodia) and VIETNAM, fought for their independence against France. This was achieved in 1954; but during the Vietnam War communist forces infiltrated Laos and this drew the country into the fighting, up to the time of the cease-fire in 1973. The monarchy was abolished in 1975 and the country was declared the Lao People's Democratic Republic.

LAO-TSE. *See* TAOISM

LAPLACE, Pierre-Simon, Marquis de (1749–1827)

French astronomer and mathematician. He wrote a very influential book, *Mécanique Céleste,* and contributed much other important thinking about the nature of the universe.

LAPLAND

Region that lies mostly above the ARCTIC Circle and comprises parts of northern FINLAND, NORWAY, SWEDEN and Soviet RUSSIA. It covers an area of nearly 390,000 sq km (150,000 sq miles), but the population is only about 34,000. These are the Lapps, a nomadic race who keep reindeer for food, clothing and transportation and still lead a largely traditional and independent way of life.

LASCAUX

Grotto near Montignac (south-west FRANCE) where some of the finest prehistoric cave paintings were discovered in 1940. They are estimated to be 20,000 years old, and are generally regarded as great works of art as well as important archaeological finds.

LASER

Word made up from the first letters of Light Amplification by Stimulated Emission of Radiation. A laser beam is an intense, narrow beam of light which is coherent; that is, all the crests of the waves are lined up together. Such beams can cut through strong, solid objects like steel plates, but they are used in science mainly for transmitting energy or speeding up chemical reactions. In navigation they can be used, like RADAR, for assessing the speed and distance of an object. The American scientist Theodore Maiman built the first laser device in 1960. Holographs are photographs taken in laser light; they have the remarkable property of being three-dimensional when viewed also in laser light.

LATITUDE

The distance north or south of the EQUATOR measured in degrees. Any point on the Equator itself is 0°. The latitude of the South Pole is 90° south and that of the North Pole 90° north.

LATVIA

Republic of the Union of Soviet Socialist Republics bordering the Baltic Sea. It has an area of 66,000 sq km (26,000 sq miles) and a population of over 2 million. The capital is Riga. It was incorporated into the Soviet Union in 1940, occupied by the Germans during WORLD WAR II and recaptured by Soviet forces in 1944.

LAVA

Molten rock that flows out of a volcano or crack in the earth. As the lava cools it becomes solid and forms igneous rocks. Lava flows still create new land, and volcanic soil is particularly rich and fertile. Sometimes the lava contains trapped gas in the form of bubbles. When solid, it forms a grey rock called pumice, which is so light that it floats on water. Pumice is a valuable scrubbing and polishing material. The islands of HAWAII are composed mainly of lava from volcanoes.

LAVOISIER, Antoine-Laurent de (1743–94)

French chemist. He investigated the processes of combustion, proved that AIR is a mixture of oxygen and nitrogen, that WATER is a compound of oxygen and hydrogen, and in these and other ways laid the foundations of modern chemistry. He was executed during the French Revolution.

LAW

The collection of rules by which any state maintains order within its society. In GREAT BRITAIN, the law-making process is conducted by PARLIAMENT. Proposed new laws are presented as Bills and if, after debate, they are accepted by a majority vote in the House of Commons, they duly become law. In Great Britain, as in most countries, there are also several distinct types of law. Constitutional law is concerned with the processes of government themselves, including such matters as changes in the FRANCHISE. Company law deals with the operation of many of the nation's commercial

Cave painting at Lascaux

and financial activities. These are branches of State law, that is, laws made by Act of Parliament. Common law, by contract, is based on past decisions taken by the courts on particular issues.

Today a clear distinction is made between courts of law that deal with civil actions, such as divorce, libel, or claims on property; and indictable or criminal offences, such as motoring offences, theft and murder. All indictable offences go first to a Magistrates' Court. MAGISTRATES have the power to pass judgment and sentence on defendants only within certain limits. Serious crimes are referred to a Crown Court where the accused, if he or she pleads innocence, is tried before a JURY. There are also courts of appeal for those who dispute any judgment made against them.

LAWRENCE, David Herbert (1885–1930)

English poet and novelist. In such novels as *Sons and Lovers* and *Women in Love* he explored men's and women's instinctive feelings and passions. The experiences of his own childhood in a Nottinghamshire mining village also find powerful expression in some of his work.

LAWRENCE, Thomas Edward (1888–1935)

British soldier and writer. During World War I he joined the Arabs in their fight against the Turks, becoming known as 'Lawrence of Arabia'. He completed his most famous book, *The Seven Pillars of Wisdom,* just before he was killed in a motor-cycle accident.

LEAD

Soft metallic ELEMENT, used in the manufacture of paints and glass, cable coverings, and as a protection against radio-activity. It was once widely used as a roof covering, but rising costs of the material have limited its use in this respect. Also, at one time it was widely used in water pipes, and plumbers are so called because the Latin for lead is *plumbum*. People working with lead are liable to an illness called lead poisoning, due to particles of the metal getting into their lungs or stomachs.

LEAF

The main food-producing part of a plant. Leaves are green because they contain CHLOROPHYLL. This manufactures carbohydrates, such as starch and sugar, from carbon dioxide and water in the presence of light; the process known as PHOTOSYNTHESIS.

Leaf: the process of photosynthesis

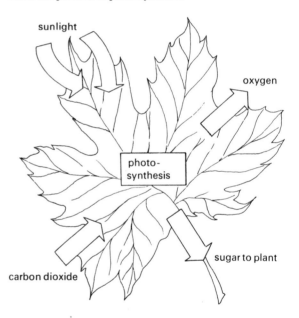

sunlight

oxygen

photo-synthesis

sugar to plant

carbon dioxide

LEAGUE OF NATIONS

International organization, with headquarters in Geneva, Switzerland, created just after WORLD WAR I with the object of preserving world peace through the collective action of member nations. The United States did not join the League, and it failed to prevent aggressive action by Benito MUSSOLINI and Adolf

HITLER, and the Japanese invasion of China. It came to an end with WORLD WAR II. After this war it was replaced by the UNITED NATIONS, created in 1945.

LEAP YEAR. *See* CALENDAR

LEAR, Edward (1812–88)

English writer and artist. He wrote many 'nonsense rhymes' and longer poems such as *The Owl and the Pussy Cat*. He illustrated much of his poetry, and during extensive travels produced many fine watercolours and drawings.

LEATHER

The tanned or dressed hide or skin of an animal. Tanning is a long and complex operation from the first removal of blood and hair from the skin to the finished product. The skins cleaned of all impurities are called pelts. They are then treated with tannin, a dark acidic compound present in some plants. This tanning process gives the pelts the colour, strength and consistency of leather. Various finishing waxes and polishes are then applied.

LEBANON

ARAB republic in the Middle East, bordering on the Mediterranean. It has an area of 10,400 sq km (4,016 sq km) and a population of about 3 million. The capital is Beirut. The Phoenicians built a great trading empire based on Lebanon 4,000 years ago, and the Cedars of Lebanon have been famous for hundreds of years, though not many remain today. In the late 1970s there was much fighting between Christian and Moslem Lebanese.

LE CORBUSIER (Charles Edouard Jeanneret, 1887–1965)

Swiss architect. By his work and his books he exerted a great influence on many aspects of

The church at Ronchamp by Le Corbusier

modern architecture, particularly on the construction of large blocks of flats. He designed Chandigarh, the new capital of the Punjab, and contributed to the design of the United Nations headquarters in New York.

LEE, Robert Edward (1807–1870)

Commander-in-Chief of the Confederate Army during the American Civil War. He won several important battles for the Confederates but was forced to surrender to General GRANT at Appomattox in 1865.

LEEUWENHOEK, Antony Van (1632–1723)

Dutch scientist and father of the science of microscopy. He was the first to see and describe bacteria with the MICROSCOPE he constructed and gave the first description of the red cells in the BLOOD.

LEEWARD ISLANDS

Group of islands in the WEST INDIES which are themselves a part of the group known as the Lesser Antilles. They are so called because they are sheltered from the Trade Winds by their position. They include the British VIRGIN ISLANDS and the French island of GUADELOUPE.

LEGEND

A story repeated from the past which many people have believed. Legends are often based on fact. The name comes from the Latin *legenda*, which means a story to be read aloud. Typical legends are the tales of King Arthur and his knights, William Tell, the Aboriginal legends about the rainbow snake and the stories of Paul Bunyan in America.

LEIBNIZ, Gottfried Wilhelm (1646–1716)

German philosopher and mathematician. As a philosopher he attempted to reconcile faith and reason with his concept of a universe composed of perfectly balanced and equal parts. As a mathematician he devised new forms of CALCULUS and invented a calculating machine.

LEMMING

Type of RODENT native to parts of SCANDINAVIA. What makes lemmings unique is their compulsion, at certain times, to head for the sea in their thousands, in a movement of mass self-destruction. The reason for this strange behaviour remains a mystery.

LEMUR

MAMMAL classed as a PRIMATE and similar to a type of monkey. It is found mainly in Madagascar and is usually nocturnal. The ring-tailed lemur lives up to its name with a long brown and white ringed tail.

LENIN (Vladimir Ilyich Ulyanov, 1870–1924)

Russian revolutionary. Born in Simbirsk, the son of a schoolteacher, he studied law at Kazan University before being expelled for political activities. He went to St Petersburg (now Leningrad), studied Marxism and founded a 'League for the Emancipation of the Working

Lenin addressing a meeting in Moscow, 1917

Class' from which the Russian Bolshevik party finally emerged. After a period of imprisonment and exile in Siberia (1896–8), Lenin left Russia and did not return until April 1917 when he took over command of the Bolsheviks. In October 1917 he led them to victory in the RUSSIAN REVOLUTION. Lenin became President of the Council of People's Commissars, as the new government was called. After four years of civil war (1917–21), his 'new economic policy' was proclaimed and helped to inaugurate some reconstruction of the devastated country. In 1922 his health began to fail and he died early in 1924. *See also* Karl MARX and LEON TROTSKY.

LEONARDO da Vinci (1452–1519)

Italian painter, sculptor, architect, musician, engineer and scientist, born in the village of Vinci near Florence. In 1466 he was placed under the tuition of Andrea del Verrocchio in Florence. BOTTICELLI was a fellow apprentice. He went to Milan in about 1482, where he remained for some sixteen years. During this time he produced his famous notebooks and many architectural plans and drawings. In 1483 he painted the *Virgin of the Rocks*, one version of which is in the National Gallery, London. His fresco *The Last Supper*, in the church of Santa Maria delle Grazie in Milan, was begun about 1485 and finished by 1498. In 1502 Leonardo entered the service of Cesare Borgia as a military engineer. Returning to

The Virgin of the Rocks by Leonardo

Florence in the following year, he painted the celebrated *Mona Lisa,* now in the Louvre, Paris. In 1506 he served the French King Louis XII in Milan as engineer and architect and also investigated problems of geology, botany, hydraulics and mechanics. In 1513 he undertook architectural and engineering commissions at the Vatican. He died in France while supervising the building of a canal. Leonardo's versatility and originality mark him out as the perfect RENAISSANCE man.

LEONCAVALLO, Ruggiero (1858–1919)

Italian composer. He wrote many operas, but only *Pagliacci* ('The Clowns') has been an enduring success.

LEOPARD

Member of the CAT family, sometimes called a panther, native to many parts of Africa and Asia. Distinguished by its black and yellow spotted coat and long tail. It is a resourceful hunter like the lion or tiger, but is also a good tree climber and often lies in branches to sleep or wait for its prey. Very similar is the JAGUAR of central and South America.

A leopard in Serengeti Park, Tanzania

LENS

Piece of glass or similar substance so shaped that it brings closer together, or deflects wider apart, rays of light passing through it. Lenses are either convex (thicker in the middle) or concave (thicker at the edges) according to their purpose. They are essential to optical MICRO-SCOPES and optical TELESCOPES: to cameras and film projectors. They are used in spectacles to adjust eyesight, though many people today use contact lenses which fit directly onto the eye and need no frames.

LEPIDOPTERA

Order of INSECTS covering all BUTTERFLIES AND MOTHS. They are distinguished by having four wings and proceeding through four stages of metamorphosis: egg, larva, chrysalis and adult.

LEPROSY

Bacterial disease that attacks the skin or the nerves or both. In severe cases the victim can lose limbs or become horribly disfigured. It is common to tropical and sub-tropical regions of

Africa, Asia and South America. The bacillus causing the disease was identified by the Norwegian physician A. A. Hansen in 1874 and today there are various treatments, though there are still millions of sufferers.

LESOTHO

Southern African kingdom surrounded by SOUTH AFRICA. It has an area of 30,355 sq km (11,721 sq miles) and a population of 1,340,000. The capital is Maseru. The Orange river, southern Africa's longest, rises in this mostly mountainous, farming country. Lesotho was formerly the British colony of Basutoland. It became independent in 1966, remaining in the BRITISH COMMONWEALTH.

LETT

Descendent of the Letgali, an ancient Nordic tribe. The Letts live in present-day Latvia, Lithuania, Estonia and northern Germany.

LIBERAL PARTY

British political party. It grew out of the older Whig Party of the seventeenth and eighteenth centuries, and during the nineteenth century became the main radical party in opposition to the Tory or CONSERVATIVE PARTY. W. E. GLADSTONE was Liberal Party leader and four times PRIME MINISTER, introducing many significant social reforms. The Liberal government that came to office in 1905 introduced further sweeping social reforms, including national insurance. Two Liberal Prime Ministers, Herbert Asquith and David LLOYD GEORGE, led Britain through WORLD WAR I, but soon after the war Liberal political power declined sharply, being replaced as the principal party of the left by the LABOUR PARTY. Since then the Liberal Party has been reduced to only a few seats in the House of Commons, sometimes still influencing events by holding the 'balance of power' between the two major parties.

LIBERIA

Independent republic on the west coast of Africa with an area of 111,369 sq km (43,002 sq miles) and a population of nearly 2 million. The capital is Monrovia, named after the American President James Monroe. The country was founded in 1822 as a home for American Negro slaves, with a constitution modelled on that of the UNITED STATES. It has rich deposits of iron ore, and also exports rubber, cocoa and coffee.

LIBRARY

Collection of books and other written matter. In the ancient world there was a famous library at Alexandria containing an estimated 500,000 hand-written papyrus scrolls. In Imperial Rome, at one time, there were about thirty libraries open to the public. In GREAT BRITAIN an Act of Parliament was passed in 1850 allowing towns to set up public libraries. The British Museum in London houses part of the British Library, the largest in the country. Other famous libraries are the Library of Congress in Washington DC, and the Bibliothèque Nationale in Paris.

LIBYA

Arab republic on the Mediterranean coast of North Africa. It has an area of 1,759,540 sq km (679,399 sq miles), but a population of less than 3 million. Tripoli is the capital. Most of Libya is desert, but revenue from oil has made it prosperous. Before World War II it was an Italian colony. It became an independent monarchy in 1951, but the monarchy was ended by an army coup in 1969.

LICHEN

Very simple and primitive PLANT form composed of ALGAE and FUNGI. It spreads over trees, stones and rocks, grey, green or brown in colour, and can be found from the tropics to places above the Arctic Circle.

LIECHTENSTEIN

Principality in the ALPS between AUSTRIA and SWITZERLAND, with an area of 157 sq km (61 sq miles) and a population of about 26,000. The capital is Vaduz.

LIED

The German word for song (pronounced 'leed'), plural *Lieder*. It is generally applied to the great song-writing tradition among German-speaking composers that started with SCHUBERT and continued with SCHUMANN, BRAHMS, Richard STRAUSS and others.

LIE DETECTOR (POLYGRAPH)

Instrument based on the assumption that when a person tells a lie his or her pulse rate automatically changes. The machine detects changes in both pulse rate and respiration. It was invented by the American John E. Reid in 1945 and is called the Reid Polygraph.

A Royal Navy Lifeboat

LIFEBOAT

Vessel designed to be launched from the shore and go to the rescue of other vessels in distress. In GREAT BRITAIN the Royal National Lifeboat Institution was formed in 1824 and today there are 150 such rescue vessels stationed round the coasts of the British Isles. They are designed to carry up to 100 people, are specially fitted with air tanks to give them extra buoyancy, and are painted white with a topside blue and red band.

LIGHT

Form of wave ENERGY which is the visible part of the electromagnetic SPECTRUM. Light from the sun is often called 'white light', though if it is passed through a prism it splits up into the seven basic colours of the visible spectrum. The speed of light is 300,000 km (187,500 miles) per second. In ASTRONOMY a Light Year is a measure of distance expressed as the distance covered by a light wave in one year. Though it has been proved that light waves do bend, in practice light can be considered to travel in straight lines; and a large part of the science of OPTICS is based on this assumption. Optics principally deals with the reflection and refraction of beams of light as applied to lenses and their use in MICROSCOPES, TELESCOPES and other optical devices. *See also* LASER and PHOTOGRAPHY.

Bishop Lighthouse, Scilly Isles

LIGHTHOUSE

Tower, usually positioned at some strategic point by the sea, and equipped with a powerful light as a guide or warning to passing ships. In the ancient world there was a famous stone tower at the entrance to the harbour at Alexandria with an open fire on its summit. The last such fire-beacon in GREAT BRITAIN, in the Bristol Channel, was dismantled in 1822. Today powerful electric filaments have their power intensified by a system of lenses and mirrors which can cast their beam many miles out to sea. Lighthouses in England and Wales come under the control of Trinity House.

LIMESTONE

Rock consisting almost entirely of carbonate of calcium. Some limestones are not more than beds of sea-shells or sea-lilies firmly compressed and cemented together. Others are formed from the skeletons of microscopic creatures that lived in the surface waters of great oceans. When these creatures died, their limy skeletons sank to the bottom and there formed an 'ooze' which eventually hardened into limestone. The material of some limestones is derived from seaweeds, while others are the remains of coral reefs. Others, again, owe their existence to chemical action or to the agency of bacteria which extract lime from sea-water.

LINCOLN, Abraham (1809–65)

Sixteenth President of the UNITED STATES. He was born in a log cabin in Kentucky and studied hard to be a lawyer. He first entered CONGRESS in 1846, and was elected Republican President in 1860. The AMERICAN CIVIL WAR broke out the following year, due to Lincoln's determination to hold the Union of States together in the face of Confederate demands for political separation. In 1862 Lincoln decreed the freedom of all Negro slaves. In 1863 he delivered his celebrated speech at the dedication of the national cemetery on the site of the Battle of Gettysburg. This Gettysburg Address concludes 'that this nation under God shall have a new birth of freedom, and that government of the people, by the people, for

Abraham Lincoln

the people, shall not perish from the earth'. He was assassinated by the fanatical Confederate John Wilkes Booth within a few days of the end of the war.

LINEAR ACCELERATOR

Type of atom smasher; the CYCLOTRON is the other. This kind of machine accelerates particles such as protons and electrons to high energies. The particles move in a straight line. In the cyclotron they have a circular path.

LINEN

A fabric made from flax and one of man's earliest fabrics. It has been found in the form of mummy wrappings in Egyptian tombs. Most of the flax for the Irish industry comes from Soviet Russia, which is the principal area in the world for flax growing.

LINNAEUS (Carl von Linné, 1707–78)

Swedish botanist who prepared the first truly scientific, systematic classification of plants.

LION

Largest member of the CAT family, native to Africa and parts of Asia. The lion is a tawny colour with a black tuft on the tip of the tail.

The male is distinguished by its mane around the head and neck. An adult male can weigh up to 225 kg (500 lb). Lions hunt by day and night, preying mainly on antelope, buffaloes and zebras.

LIPIDS

Animal fats and plant oils essential to good health. They contain vitamins A, D and E. Simple lipids contain only carbon, hydrogen and oxygen. Complex lipids also have phosphorus and nitrogen. One complex lipid group are known as sterols. Among these are cholesterol and sex hormones.

LIPPI, Fra Filippo (c. 1406–69)

Italian artist and Carmelite friar. His paintings, including his frescoes in the choir of Prato Cathedral, are noted for their colour and grace. One of his pupils was Botticelli.

LISTER, Joseph, 1st Baron (1827–1912)

English surgeon, and pioneer in the use of antiseptics. He introduced carbolic acid to prevent infection during operations, and discovered that instruments could be sterilized by heat.

LISZT, Franz (1811–86)

Hungarian pianist and composer, and one of the outstanding musical personalities of the nineteenth century. He was a pianist of phenomenal talent and one of the first to create the image of the virtuoso player—someone noted for his prodigious technique. Some of his own compositions, such as the *Hungarian Rhapsodies,* were intended primarily to display these features. However, Liszt was also a serious and original composer. He developed the form of the one-movement (or cyclic) symphony and sonata; and created a type of descriptive orchestral piece called the symphonic poem.

LITERATURE

The art of using words to convey a story or to express feelings, thoughts and impressions. The earliest literature was something memorized by people and passed on by the spoken word, being usually long accounts of fabulous adventures called EPICS. These were probably chanted or sung, thus creating a link with some of the earliest music. They were also usually recited as a type of poetry, this being easier to memorize than prose. This whole class of literature is said to be in the 'oral tradition'.

The origins of a written literature can be found in most of the civilizations of the ancient world; in India, China, and among the Jewish people whose great work of literature is the Old Testament of the BIBLE. However, it is the Greeks whose literature is taken to represent the start of Western literature. Their greatest single contribution was DRAMA, a form of literature that has continued undiminished to the present day. Other literary forms that developed from the time of the Greeks and Romans onwards have been POETRY in its many different styles and forms; the essay; BIOGRAPHY and autobiography; and the NOVEL. Other types of written work, dealing with such matters as HISTORY, PHILOSOPHY, POLITICS, RELIGION, science and criticism may also be classed as literature from the point of view of style. In this encyclopedia the work of dramatists, poets and novelists of different times and places is considered in individual entries.

LITHOGRAPHY

Process of image reproduction used by artists and printers and invented about 1769 by the German Aloys Senefelder. Basically it consists of drawing on a stone (limestone) with a special kind of greasy crayon or ink; the drawing is in reverse in order to be the right way round when printed. Next the stone is washed with a solution of turpentine and dried. Then it is sponged with water and inked with a roller. The parts of the stone carrying the drawing take the ink from the roller, while the remaining wet parts repel the ink. Finally paper is pressed on the stone and takes up the inked drawing. In commercial printing a metal plate is used in place of a stone, but the process is fundamentally the same.

LITHUANIA

Republic of the UNION OF SOVIET SOCIALIST REPUBLICS bordering the Baltic Sea. It has an area of 65,000 sq km (25,000 sq miles) and a population of about 3 million. The capital is Vilna. Like neighbouring LATVIA it was incorporated into the Soviet Union in 1940.

LITMUS

A simple indicator used in chemistry to detect the presence of acids and alkalis. It turns red when put into an acid and remains blue when put in to an alkali. It is also used as an indicator of the ion concentration in solutions. Litmus is obtained from lichen.

LIVINGSTONE, David (1813–73)

Scottish doctor and explorer. He went to AFRICA as a missionary and made many trips

Livingstone's journeys

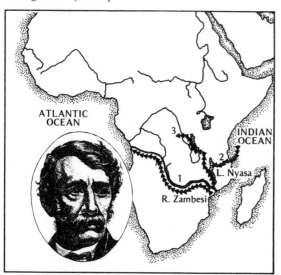

deep into unexplored territory during which he discovered the Victoria Falls (now in ZAMBIA) and Lake Nyasa (now in MALAWI). He was given up for lost during an expedition to discover the source of the river NILE, but was found by a relief expedition led by H. M. STANLEY. His travels and journals stimulated public interest in Africa, until then popularly known as the 'Dark Continent'.

LIVY (59 BC–AD 17)

Roman historian whose main work was a history of Rome itself in 142 books, although many of these are now lost. He is admired for his clear and confident style.

LIZARD

Large group of REPTILES, distributed throughout tropical and temperate regions of the world. Most species have legs, though some do not and are commonly mistaken for SNAKES. One big difference between the two types of reptile is that lizards can close their eyes while snakes cannot.

LLAMA

MAMMAL belonging to the same family as the CAMEL, but smaller and with no hump. Native to the region of the ANDES mountains of South America, and noted for its thick coat of wool to protect it against the cold on or above the mountain snow-line.

LLOYD GEORGE, David, 1st Earl (1863–1945)

British statesman. Though not born in WALES, his parents were Welsh and he spent most of his childhood in that country. He studied law, then entered PARLIAMENT as a Radical. He later became a leading member of the LIBERAL PARTY, and as CHANCELLOR OF THE EXCHEQUER introduced supertax and taxation of land values. This was strongly opposed by the

Lords, and led to the introduction in 1911 of legislation to limit their powers. In 1916 Lloyd George became PRIME MINISTER in place of Herbert Asquith; directed Britain's war effort up to the end of WORLD WAR I and helped to negotiate the peace treaty of Versailles. He resigned as Prime Minister in 1922 and held no further political posts.

LLOYD'S

British association of INSURANCE underwriters with headquarters in London, specializing in marine insurance. It derives its name from an eighteenth-century coffee house where such business was first transacted. An interesting feature of the premises is a ship's bell, rescued from a vessel named the *Lutine* which sank in 1799. This is rung to announce the loss of any other ship at sea.

LOBSTER

Group of CRUSTACEANS, distinguished by an oblong body and large pincer-like claws held in front of the face. Lobsters are found round most rocky coastlines. They are a greenish-blue when alive and red when cooked.

LOCKE, John (1632–1704)

English political philosopher who maintained that a ruler only had the right to govern with the approval of the people. His work had a big influence on the drawing up of the Constitution of the UNITED STATES and on the ideas of the FRENCH REVOLUTION.

LOGARITHM

System of arithmetic devised by the Scottish mathematician John NAPIER. Every number can be expressed by its logarithm, and the use of these greatly simplifies arithmetical calculations by reducing multiplication and division to addition and subtraction. The (Naperian) logarithm k of a number n is such that $n = e^k$ (e to the power of k) where e is approximately 2.718.

Naperian logarithms are called logarithms to the base e. Logarithms to the base 10 are more popular.

LONGFELLOW, Henry Wadsworth (1807–82)

American poet, most famous for his long narrative poem *The Song of Hiawatha* inspired by Red Indian folklore.

LONGITUDE

Imaginary lines, measured in degrees, which run north to south across the surface of the Earth, as distinct from LATITUDE lines, which run west to east. The prime meridian, 0°, passes through Greenwich. Any spot on Earth can be located by an intersection of latitude and longitude lines, measured in degrees, minutes and seconds.

LOOM

Frame machine used for weaving cloth. A power loom, introduced by Edmund Cartwright, played an important part in the development of the INDUSTRIAL REVOLUTION.

LORCA, Federico Garcia (1899–1936)

Spanish poet and dramatist whose work was largely inspired by gipsy themes and peasant life in the southern province of Andalusia.

LORD CHANCELLOR

CABINET minister and an experienced lawyer. He presides over the House of Lords and is head of the judiciary, which means that he appoints new judges. The Lord Chancellor is one of the chief members of the Judicial Committee of the Privy Council. When there is a change of government, there is also usually a change of Lord Chancellor.

LORD CHIEF JUSTICE

The judge who is President of the High Court of Justice, appointed by the PRIME MINISTER for life or until he retires. The Lord Chief Justice ranks next to the Lord Chancellor. Unlike him he cannot be a member of the Government or take part in politics.

LOTUS

Various kinds of water lily, growing mainly in tropical and sub-tropical regions, and in past ages sacred to the Egyptians, Indians and Chinese. In Greek mythology there was a land of lotus-eaters, visited by Odysseus and his men, where those who partook of the flower lost all memory and all care.

Louis XIV

LOUIS XIV (1638–1715)

Most illustrious of French kings, widely known as *Le Roi Soleil* ('The Sun King'). For over fifty years he was absolute ruler of France and the dominant personality of Europe. His ambition was to extend his country's natural boundaries to the RHINE, in which he was partially successful. For political reasons he also wished to have his grandson made king of SPAIN, but suffered defeat at the hands of the Duke of MARLBOROUGH in the War of the Spanish Succession. At home he had built the great Palace of Versailles just outside Paris, and attracted to his court some of Europe's most brilliant musicians, writers and scholars. But his extravagance and autocratic rule were to lead eventually to the FRENCH REVOLUTION

LOYOLA, St Ignatius (1491–1556)

Roman Catholic religious leader who founded the Society of Jesus, the Jesuits. He was a Spanish soldier who conceived the idea of his order while recovering from wounds in a monastery in 1521. Jesuits take vows of poverty and chastity. They promote religious education in schools and colleges.

LSD

A powerful drug with the full name lysergic acid diethylamide. First produced in 1938. The drug has serious hallucinatory effects.

LUCRETIUS (*c.* 99–55 BC)

Roman poet and philospher whose work *De Rerum Natura* ('On the Nature of Things') is especially interesting because it propounds an atomic theory which has proved to be remarkably close to the truth.

LUDDITES

Those who saw the introduction of machinery during the INDUSTRIAL REVOLUTION as a threat to their livelihood and sought to destroy it. There were Luddite riots in Nottinghamshire, Yorkshire and Lancashire between 1811 and 1818.

LULLY, Jean-Baptiste (1632–87)

Italian-born composer who spent most of his life in France as court musician to LOUIS XIV. He created a special type of French opera with much spectacle and dancing, and collaborated with such other famous men of his day as MOLIÈRE. He died of blood poisoning after banging his foot with a conducting staff.

LUTE

Musical instrument of Arabic origin, with strings plucked like those on a guitar. It was widely used as an accompaniment to songs or ayres during the sixteenth and seventeenth centuries.

LUTHER, Martin (1483–1546)

German priest and scholar who created the REFORMATION in Germany. He started life as

Martin Luther

an orthodox Catholic priest and a fine scholar who became Professor of Philosophy at Wittenberg University. But he was increasingly disturbed by what he saw as corruption within the Church, and in 1517 nailed to the church door at Wittenberg Castle his charges of corruption. He himself was then charged with heresy but refused to recant and was excommunicated. Under the protection of Frederick of Saxony he translated the New Testament of the Bible into German and set about the creation of a Protestant Church in Germany that still bears his name.

LUXEMBOURG

European state, called a Grand Duchy, that borders Belgium, France and West Germany. It has an area of 2,586 sq km (999 sq miles) and a population of about 356,000. The capital is also called Luxembourg. The Court of Justice of the EUROPEAN ECONOMIC COMMUNITY meets there.

LYMPH

Clear salty body fluid that carries nourishment to tissue cells and removes waste matter from them.

LYNX

Member of the CAT family and closely related to the wild cats. Best known is the common or northern lynx. It is a powerful animal, capable of killing sheep, but preying mostly on small animals and birds. It is now very rare in Europe, but a few survive in the Alps, Scandinavia and Russia. It is more plentiful in Central Asia.

LYREBIRD

Australian BIRD, so named because of the beautiful tail, shaped rather like the ancient harp called the lyre, which it displays during courtship.

MacARTHUR, General Douglas (1880–1964)

American soldier. During WORLD WAR II he won fame for his defence of the PHILIPPINES against the Japanese and then for his gradual re-conquest of the south-west PACIFIC area. He accepted the final Japanese surrender in 1945 and helped to draft their new constitution. He was appointed commander-in-chief of the UNITED NATIONS force in the Korean War but was later relieved of his command by President Harry Truman for political reasons, disregarding his ability as a leader.

MACH NUMBER

Speed of an aircraft or projectile measured in terms of the speed of sound as unity. The unit is named after the Austrian physicist Ernst Mach. Mach 0.5 is half the speed of sound, or sub-sonic. Mach 1 is the speed of sound, or transonic. Mach 2 is twice the speed of sound, or supersonic. For any given speed the Mach number varies according to the height, season and locality of the flight.

MACHIAVELLI, Niccolò (1469–1527)

Italian statesman and writer. His famous book, *The Prince,* is a detailed study of political power, based on his own experience of the complex and ruthless politics of Renaissance Florence.

Niccolò Machiavelli

MADAGASCAR

Island republic off the east coast of Africa, with an area of 587,041 sq km (226,670 sq miles) and a population of 8,726,000. The capital is Antananarivo. Formerly a French territory, Madagascar was proclaimed a republic in 1958. It exports cloves and clove oil and coffee.

MADEIRA ISLANDS

Group of islands off the north-west African coast forming a province of PORTUGAL. The total population is about 250,000 and the capital is Funchal. The islands give their name to a famous sweet wine.

MADRIGAL

Type of SONG for several voices, which originated in Italy during the fifteenth century and spread to most parts of western Europe, especially to England, where some of the finest madrigals were composed during the reign of ELIZABETH I. The chief composers in England include William BYRD and Orlando GIBBONS, and in Italy Claudio MONTEVERDI.

Right The cheese market at Alkmaar, Netherlands

MAGELLAN, Ferdinand
(c. 1480–1521)

Portuguese navigator who shared the idea of Christopher COLUMBUS and others that the Far East could be reached by sailing westwards. He embarked from Spain in August 1519 with a fleet of five ships, sailed southwards down the coast of South America and reached the Pacific Ocean through the Strait named after him. He then gave the Pacific its name, because his first impression of it was one of peace and calm. Magellan was killed by warring tribesmen in the Philippines, but one of his ships finally arrived back in Spain in September 1522 via the Indian and Atlantic Oceans, the first to have circumnavigated the world.

MAGISTRATE

Magistrates serve in the lower courts of law which hear minor offences. Most magistrates are invited to serve at the local Magistrates' Court although they may have no legal training. Such people receive the title Justice of the Peace (JP). In some cases the magistrates are qualified lawyers and theirs is a professional, full-time appointment. These are Stipendiary Magistrates. *See also* LAW.

MAGNA CARTA

A charter imposed upon King John by rebellious barons, limiting the sovereign's power in some respects and providing a code of civil rights. It was signed by the King at Runnymede on the Thames in 1215. He soon repudiated it, and for hundreds more years English monarchs exercised absolute rule. But Magna Carta nevertheless became a symbol of the rights of the individual, and it bound the king to rule according to law.

The charter contains sixty-one clauses providing for the liberty of the Church, protection against abuses of royal power, protection of life, liberty and property and the upholding of various feudal rights.

Left Les Parapluies by Pierre Auguste Renoir

MAGNESIUM

Silver-white metallic ELEMENT which burns with a brilliant flame. It is light, malleable and an ingredient of many metal ALLOYS. It is also used in photographic flashbulbs. Magnesia, which is an oxidized form of magnesium, has a very high melting point and is widely used as a heat insulator.

MAGNETISM

Force of attraction between iron-made or iron-containing substances. The exact nature of magnetism has still not been established, but its properties have long been known. A magnetized iron bar has what are called a north pole and a south pole, and from these poles proceed magnetic lines of force creating what is called a magnetic field. The existence of these lines of force can easily be proved by placing a sheet of paper over the magnet and sprinkling iron filings on to the paper. These will immediately arrange themselves along the magnet's lines of force. Two magnets will attract each other by their opposite poles, and repel by their like poles. The EARTH is a giant magnet with a north and south magnetic pole, although the geographical North Pole is a magnetic south pole, and vice versa! The positions of these

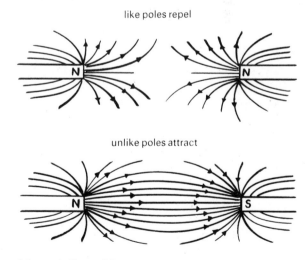

Magnetic lines of force

magnetic poles move slightly all the time in relation to each other, and have actually swopped places with each other many times in the Earth's history. It is the Earth's own magnetic field which makes a freely suspended or supported magnetized bar of iron swing round until its own north pole faces the direction of the Earth's geographical North Pole, and vice versa. The old lodestone, a form of magnetic iron oxide, and the modern compass, operate on this principle.

The connection between magnetism and electricity is very close. A coil of wire carrying an electric current creates its own magnetic field. A coil of wire round an iron bar thus forms an electro-magnet. At the same time, as Michael FARADAY first discovered, if a loop of wire is turned between the poles of a magnet an electric current is induced into it. This close interaction between magnetism and electricity enables mechanical energy to be converted into electrical energy (the electric dynamo or generator) and electrical energy to be converted back into mechanical energy (the electric motor). The same principles are applied to many other devices, including the telephone, loudspeaker and electric bell.

MAHLER, Gustav (1860–1911)

Austrian composer and conductor. In his own lifetime Mahler was most famous as a conductor, and for several years was director of the Vienna Opera. He nevertheless found time to complete nine symphonies of great length and complexity, plus several substantial song-cycles with orchestra, including *Das Lied von der Erde* ('The Song of the Earth'). His music makes an interesting transition between the styles of the nineteenth and twentieth centuries.

MALARIA

Fever caused by a parasite injected into the bloodstream by the females of a tropical species of MOSQUITO. Bouts of fever can return years after the original infection, but the sickness can be treated with various synthetic drugs, or with quinine.

MALAWI

East African republic, formerly Nyasaland, with an area of 118,484 sq km (44,205 sq miles) and a population of about 6 million. The capital is Lilongwe. For more than fifty years the country was a British Protectorate. In 1953 it became a part of the Federation of Rhodesia and Nyasaland, and in 1966 it was declared an independent republic, though remaining within the BRITISH COMMONWEALTH.

MALAYSIA

South-east Asian federation of thirteen states, including those on the Malay peninsula and Sarawak and Sabah (formerly British North Borneo). The total area is 329,749 sq km (127,324 sq miles), with a population of about 14 million. The capital is Kuala Lumpur. The country is the world's largest producer of rubber and tin. Malaya was formerly a part of the British Empire. It was occupied by the Japanese during WORLD WAR II, and in 1957 gained its independence. It changed its name to Malaysia in 1963 when Sarawak and Sabah joined the federation. It remains within the BRITISH COMMONWEALTH.

A street in Georgetown, Pinang, Malaysia

MALDIVES

Republic consisting of a chain of over 2,000 coral islands and atolls in the Indian Ocean, south-west of Sri Lanka. Most of the islands are uninhabited. The capital is Malé.

MALI

West African republic with an area of 1,240,000 sq km (478,793 sq miles) but a population of only 6.6 million. The capital is Bamako. Most people live in the river Niger valley, but much of Mali is desert. It became independent from France in 1960.

MALLARMÉ, Stéphane (1842–98)

French poet, and founder of the important group of poets called the Symbolists. His poem *L'Après-midi d'un faune* (Afternoon of a Faun) inspired one of DEBUSSY's best-known compositions.

The harbour at Gozo, an island off Malta

MALTA

Group of small islands in the Mediterranean Sea south of Sicily, of which Malta itself is the largest. They form an independent republic. The total area is 316 sq km (122 sq miles). The population is about 337,000 and the capital is Valletta. Malta has had a long and colourful history. The Phoenicians colonized the islands, St Paul was shipwrecked there, and during the sixteenth century the KNIGHTS OF THE ORDER OF ST JOHN defended the territory against Turkish attack. The Grand Harbour of Valletta became the headquarters of the British Mediterranean Fleet during the nineteenth century. During WORLD WAR II it was heavily bombed by the Germans and Italians, for which the people of Malta were awarded the George Cross for bravery. It gained independence in 1964 but remains within the BRITISH COMMONWEALTH.

MALTHUS, Thomas Robert (1766–1834)

English economist. He was one of the first to make a serious study of population, believing that population increases would outstrip food supplies unless held in check by famine, disease and war.

MAMMAL

Group of warm-blooded vertebrates, including the most advanced forms of life in the ANIMAL KINGDOM. The word 'mammal' comes from the Latin *mamma* meaning 'breast', and the one special feature shared by all mammals is that they suckle their young. Most also have hair and produce the young from the egg inside the body of the mother. They are classed as follows: MARSUPIALS (KANGAROOS, KOALAS, WOMBAT); RODENTS (RATS, mice, voles, BEAVERS); lagomorphs (RABBITS and HARES); carnivores (LIONS, TIGERS, LEOPARDS, DOGS, FOXES, BEARS); UNGULATES (COWS, HORSES, DEER, ANTELOPE, REINDEER, ELEPHANTS, HIPPOPOTAMI); PRIMATES (MONKEYS, APES and MAN). There are also WHALES, DOLPHINS, PORPOISES and SEALS that live mainly or entirely in the sea; the many species of BATS that spend much of their time flying; and such curiosities as the Australian duckbilled PLATYPUS, which lays eggs but is none the less classed as a mammal.

MAN

MAMMAL classed among the PRIMATES and distinguished by a higher intelligence which has led to speech, the use of fire, invention of tools and domination over almost all other forms of life. The technical name for man as a genus is *Homo sapiens* (man of wisdom); modern man is classed as a species of this genus.

MAN, ISLE OF

Island in the Irish Sea, 588 sq km (227 sq miles) in area, and about half-way between England and Ireland. The population is about 61,000, and the people, who are called Manx, are CELTIC in origin. Great Britain bought the island in 1765. It has its own legislature, the 1,000 year old Tynwald, which consists of a Legislative Council and the House of Keys.

MANATEE

Aquatic MAMMAL some 4 m (14 ft) long, and weighing about 680 kg (1,500 lb). Manatees have broad flat tails, and their forelimbs have become modified into flippers. They are found in the coastal waters of West Africa, the Caribbean and Central America and may have given rise to some of the legends about mermaids.

MANCHURIA

Large region of north-eastern CHINA with abundant coal and iron ore and much heavy industry. From 1931 to the end of WORLD WAR II the region was occupied by Japan.

MANET, Édouard (1832–83)

French artist and leading member of the Impressionist school of painting. His most famous painting, *Déjeuner sur l'herbe,* was violently attacked on grounds of indecency when first shown.

MANGANESE

Metallic element used in industry to strengthen steel and to remove impurities from it.

MANN, Thomas (1875–1955)

German novelist whose works include *Buddenbrooks, The Magic Mountain* and the short story *Death in Venice.*

MANTEGNA, Andrea (1431–1506)

Italian artist. He made a special study of perspective and combined techniques with his interest in Roman antiquities to produce paintings which greatly influenced the work of other RENAISSANCE artists.

MAO TSE-TUNG (1893–1976)

Chinese revolutionary leader and statesman. He joined the Chinese Communist Party when it was founded in 1921. He organized a peasant rising, and when this failed withdrew to the

The Bar at the Folies-Bergère by Manet

Mao Tse Tung in 1966

mountains of south-east China where he founded the Kiangsi Soviet and held out against the Nationalist forces of Chiang Kai-Shek. In 1934 Mao led the famous Long March of his followers from Kiangsi to Shensi province in the north-west of the country, patiently built up his organization and in the Civil War of 1946–9 drove the Nationalists from mainland China. He was elected first Chairman of the People's Republic of China and presided over the creation of a new Communist society.

MARATHON

A plain some 40 km (25 miles) north-east of Athens where the Persians were decisively defeated by the Athenians in 490 BC. News of the victory was carried by a runner. It is from this that the 'marathon race' is derived. The official distance for such an event is 42.2 km (26 miles 385 yd).

MARBLE

Sparkling form of limestone consisting entirely of fine crystals. Pure marble is white and the ornamental veins in some marbles are stains caused by traces of other minerals. Sometimes the fossils in ordinary limestones show up when the rock is polished. Such ornamental stones may be called 'marble' by masons. Some of the finest marble comes from Carrara in Italy.

MARCONI, Guglielmo (1874–1937)

Italian scientist and pioneer of radio communication. He took out his first patent for wireless telegraphy in 1896. He continued his experiments in Britain and succeeded in sending a signal from Cornwall to Newfoundland in 1901. From this time on wireless developed rapidly to become the quickest and most widely used means of communication.

MARCO POLO (c. 1254–1324)

Venetian traveller and explorer. As a youth he travelled with his father and uncle to the court of the Great Khan, the Chinese emperor. They reached the court in 1275, where Marco was appointed one of the Khan's envoys. He travelled in this capacity to Burma, India and Indo-China. The party finally left China for Venice, travelling via Sumatra, Ceylon (now Sri Lanka) and Persia. They arrived back at their native city in 1295, having been away twenty-four years. Marco Polo dictated the record of his travels when he was taken prisoner after a sea-battle between Venice and Genoa in 1298.

MARCUS AURELIUS Antoninus (AD 121–180)

Roman emperor and Stoic philosopher. Much of his reign was spent in defending the boundaries of the empire, but he established new

Statue of Marcus Aurelius in Rome

schools of philosophy and rhetoric in Athens and introduced legal reforms in Rome. He is said to have come nearer than any other man to ARISTOTLE's ideal of the 'philosopher-king'.

MARGARINE

Substitute butter made from vegetable oils or animal fats. Unlike butter, it is low in cholesterol content, a fatty substance said to be injurious to the heart.

MARIANAS

Group of volcanic islands in the western Pacific Ocean. The largest island, Guam, was the scene of bitter fighting between the Japanese and the Americans in WORLD WAR II. The islands are under UNITED NATIONS trusteeship, except for Guam which has been ceded to the United States.

MARIE ANTIONETTE. *See* FRENCH REVOLUTION

MARLBOROUGH, John Churchill, 1st Duke of (1650–1722)

English soldier. His involvement in British domestic politics led to a period of imprisonment, but when Queen Anne came to the throne in 1702 he was promoted to Captain-General with considerable powers at home and abroad. His greatest triumphs came with the War of the Spanish Succession. This was fought by an alliance of Britain, the Netherlands and Austria against LOUIS XIV of France, who claimed the Spanish crown for his grandson in order to secure Spain's vast overseas possessions. Marlborough led the alliance to spectacular victory at Blenheim (1704), followed by further victories at Ramillies, Oudenarde and Malplaquet.

MARLOWE, Christopher (1564–93)

English dramatist and poet. His plays include *Tamburlaine the Great, Dr Faustus* and *The Jew of Malta,* which influenced the early work of his exact contemporary, SHAKESPEARE. He was killed in a tavern brawl at the age of twenty-nine.

MARMOSET

Small squirrel-like MONKEY, native to the tropical forest of South America.

MARQUESAS ISLANDS

Group of volcanic islands in the South Pacific Ocean within the French Community. The two largest islands are Nuku Hiva and Hiva Oa.

MARS

PLANET of the SOLAR SYSTEM with an equatorial diameter of 6,759 km (4,224 miles) and an average distance from the SUN of 228 million km (142 million miles). Mars appears in the sky for brief periods with a distinct orange-red colour. Mars has two tiny moons. It has a very thin atmosphere which consists mainly of carbon dioxide, but which generates very fast winds which scour the surface and create dust storms. It has two white caps at its poles, but these are probably solid carbon dioxide and not frozen ice. In 1969 pictures relayed from American space probes revealed a surface pitted with craters, similar to that of the MOON, but it also has deep canyons, possibly cut by running water long ago. There is no evidence of life on Mars.

MARSHALL ISLANDS

Group of coral islands and atolls in the Pacific Ocean. The main island is Kwajalein. Perhaps the best known is the Bikini atoll where American atom-bomb tests were carried out after WORLD WAR II. The group is a United States Trust Territory.

MARSUPIAL

Group of MAMMALS which nourish and carry their imperfectly born young in a ventral pouch where they feed until they are more developed. The home of these animals, including the kangaroo, is Australia.

Kangaroos in New South Wales, Australia

MARX, Karl (1818–83)

German philosopher and economist, and founder of the international communist movement. With his friend and disciple, Friedrich ENGELS, he wrote the *Communist Manifesto,* which ends with the celebrated phrase 'Workers of the world unite! You have nothing to lose but your chains!' In London, where he finally settled, Marx wrote his principal work of political philosophy, *Das Kapital,* in which he argued that there was an inevitable pattern to history, leading to the break-down of capitalism and the creation of a new society of the working class (the proletariat). He also founded the International Working Men's Association, later known as the First Communist International. He is buried in Highgate Cemetery, London. *See also* COMMUNISM, LENIN and RUSSIAN REVOLUTION.

Mary Queen of Scots

MARY QUEEN OF SCOTS (1542–87)

Roman Catholic daugher of James V of SCOTLAND, and one of the most tragic figures in history. She became queen when only a week old, but lived for many years in France. Her first husband was the French Dauphin, who

227

Communion given at a Catholic Mass

died. Her second husband, Lord Darnley, was weak and cruel and was murdered. Her third husband, the Earl of Bothwell, was unpopular. She fled from Scotland to seek the protection of her cousin ELIZABETH I, who saw her as the focus of Catholic hopes and had her imprisoned. Finally she was accused of agreeing to a plot to assassinate Elizabeth, was tried, condemned to death, and executed.

MASER

An electronic device that amplifies or generates electro-magnetic waves. These are microwaves which operate at near absolute zero temperature ($-273.15°C$) with great stability and accuracy. Another advantage of the maser is its low noise level. It is used mainly in radar and radio astronomy reception. The word MASER stands for *Microwave Amplification by Stimulated Emission of Radiation*.

MASS

Term in PHYSICS to describe the total amount of matter of an object. It is not the same as the weight of an object, which varies according to gravitational force; whereas its mass will be the same anywhere in the universe. For all practical purposes, therefore, the mass of an object is constant, though according to Albert EINSTEIN's theories of RELATIVITY it increases with speed.

MASS

The principal service of the ROMAN CATHOLIC CHURCH, in which bread and wine are consecrated as the body and blood of Jesus Christ. Low Mass is spoken; High Mass is a more elaborate service, and is sung. Similar is the Eucharist of the Eastern Orthodox Church and Holy Communion of the Anglican Church.

The service of the Mass has also been set to music by many great composers, and is looked upon almost as a musical form. The usual five parts of the Mass, when set to music, are: *Kyrie, Gloria, Credo, Sanctus with Benedictus* and *Agnus Dei*. There are also some notable settings in music of the Requiem Mass, a commemorative mass for the dead. *See also* CHRISTIANITY.

MATHEMATICS

Systematic study of relationships between quantities and magnitudes, and the basic 'language' of all the sciences. In this encyclopedia mathematics is considered as ALGEBRA, ARITHMETIC, GEOMETRY and TRIGONOMETRY.

MATISSE, Henri (1869–1954)

French artist. He was a leading member of the 'Fauvist' movement in painting, and his own bold use of colour made him one of the most influental artists of the twentieth century.

MAUPASSANT, Guy de (1850–93)

French writer. Almost his whole output is in the form of short stories, noted for their psychological insight into human behaviour. His work has influenced many other writers.

MAURITANIA

West African Islamic republic with an area of 1,030,700 sq km (397,977 sq miles), but a population of only 1,632,000. The capital is Nouakchott. It is mostly desert, but it has huge iron ore reserves and iron is the leading export. Formerly French, it became fully independent in 1960.

MAURITIUS

Island state in the Indian Ocean, with an area of 2,045 sq km (790 sq miles) and a population of about 1 million. The capital is Port Louis. It is an independent member of the BRITISH COMMONWEALTH.

MAXWELL, James Clerk (1831–79)

Scottish mathematician and scientist who correctly predicted by mathematics the existence and nature of radio waves. He also did other valuable research into the nature of LIGHT.

MAYA

Civilization in Central America that collapsed with the Spanish Conquest. The Maya built magnificent cities (Copán, Chichén, Itzá, Mayapán). Perhaps their greatest achievement was building in stone which was richly and beautifully decorated. They were also skilled in

Mayan stone relief

astronomy and mathematics, and were the only Indians in America to develop an advanced form of writing.

MAYER, Julius Robert von (1814–78)

A German physicist who, with James Joule, discovered the first law of thermodynamics, which is the universal law of conservation of energy.

MAYOR

The first citizen of a city or borough who presides over the council. A mayor is elected by the councillors and serves for a year.

MECHANICS

Branch of PHYSICS concerned with the effect of forces acting on objects. The subject is divided basically into statics and dynamics. The first of these two categories, statics, examines objects which are at rest (i.e. in a state of equilibrium) due to the balance of forces acting upon them. A book resting on a table is in a state of equilibrium because the force of gravity pulling it downward is balanced or cancelled out by the upward supporting force of the table. An electric light bulb remains hanging motionless because the downward force of gravity is balanced by the upward force of tension in the supporting flex. In structures such as buildings and bridges the forces acting upon them to maintain their state of equilibrium are applied from many directions; but they can be represented diagramatically as 'lines of force' and calculated accordingly.

The second main category of mechanics, dynamics, examines the relationship between forces and moving objects. A simple example of dynamics is the action of a door on a hinge. If the door is pushed at its further distance from the hinge it will rotate about the hinge without much effort. If it is pushed close to the hinge, much greater effort will be needed to start its rotation. Two factors contribute to this rotation: the amount of force and the point of its application. These are known as the 'moments of force' and are fundamental to dynamics as applied to levers, pulleys and gears. *See also* HYDROMECHANICS, KINETICS, PNEUMATICS and WORK.

MEDICI FAMILY

Italian family who exerted a great influence on the politics of Florence in particular, and

Lorenzo de Medici

Western Europe in general, during the RENAISSANCE period. The two most famous members of the family are Lorenzo de Medici and Catherine de Medici, who became queen of France. They are especially remembered as patrons of the arts, employing many of the finest Renaissance artists and architects, including MICHELANGELO.

MEDICINE

The science of the treatment or prevention of disease. The beginnings of medicine date from the time of the Greek HIPPOCRATES. In this encyclopedia, significant advances in medical science are traced through the many individual entries on famous physicians and chemists.

Surgeons at work in an operating theatre

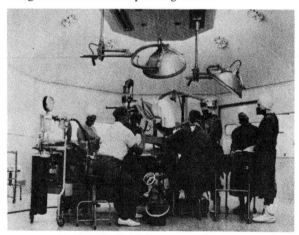

MEDITERRANEAN SEA

Large inland sea, connected to the Atlantic Ocean by the Straits of Gibraltar, with an area of 2,512,000 sq km (970,000 sq miles). The name means 'Middle of the Earth', and during a period of thousands of years the great civilizations of the ancient world – those of Egypt, Greece, Rome and Carthage – were centred upon it. It also gives its name to a type of climate, enjoyed by most of the surrounding countries, characterized by mild, wet winters and warm, dry summers.

MELVILLE, Herman (1819–91)

American writer. He went to sea as a youth, and worked his experiences into his novels. Best-known of these is *Moby Dick*, a story of whaling in the days of sail and of one man's obsessive pursuit of a great white whale.

MENDEL, Gregor Johann (1822–84)

Austrian priest and botanist. He experimented for many years with plant selection and breeding, his records of these experiments marking an important stage in the history and study of GENETICS.

MENDELEYEV, Dmitri Ivanovitch (1834–1907)

Russian scientist. His great contribution to science was the discovery that characteristic properties of the chemical elements recur in regular cycles in a table starting with the element of lowest atomic weight and progressing consecutively in order of weight. *See also* CHEMISTRY and PERIODIC LAW.

MENDELSSOHN-BARTHOLDY, Felix (1809–47)

German composer, usually known simply as Mendelssohn. At seventeen he wrote an overture to *A Midsummer Night's Dream*, which is one of the finest pieces of descriptive music for the orchestra. Another famous descriptive piece is the *Hebrides* overture (also called 'Fingal's Cave'). He also composed symphonies, concertos, many piano pieces called *Lieder Ohne Worte* ('Songs Without Words'), and, especially for English audiences, the oratorio *Elijah*. As a conductor, Mendelssohn did much to revive the music of J. S. BACH.

MERCURY

PLANET of the SOLAR SYSTEM with an equatorial diameter of 4,989 km (3,118 miles) and an average distance from the SUN of 57 million km (35.5 million miles). Because it is so small, and so near the sun, Mercury's gravity is probably not strong enough to retain an atmosphere. And because it is so close to the sun the sunlit face is extremely hot (about 400°C), while the far side, away from the sun, is extremely cold. The surface of Mercury is pitted with craters, like the moon.

MESMER, Franz Anton (1734–1815)

Austrian physician who practised a form of hypnotism which he attributed to something called 'animal magnetism'. His theories have been discredited, but he has lent his name to the verb 'mesmerize'.

MESON

Elementary nuclear particle that is unstable and is found in COSMIC RAYS. It has a mass between that of a PROTON and an ELECTRON. Mesons are usually produced by bombarding nuclei with very high energy particles. *See also* NUCLEAR ENERGY.

MESOPOTAMIA

Region between the Tigris and Euphrates rivers – the word means 'between the rivers'. It covers the present-day territories of Iraq, eastern Syria and south-eastern Turkey. Many civilizations have existed in this area, but since the break-up of the OTTOMAN EMPIRE in 1919, the name is not often used, except in historical and archaeological contexts.

MESSIAEN, Olivier (born 1908)

French composer. He has written much distinctive organ music, mostly religious and mystical in character. His fascination with bird song and with oriental rhythms and tone intervals have inspired other works for the piano or orchestra, technically complex but very expressive.

METABOLISM

Process by which all living things transform food into energy and living tissue. This is done mainly by digestion. ENZYMES break up the food molecules which are drawn into the bloodstream. In the process of respiration oxygen helps to break down the food molecules.

METALS

Group of chemical elements, such as iron, copper and lead, which have a high SPECIFIC GRAVITY. Metals in the electrolysis test show a positive charge. Combinations of metals are known as alloys. They are usually extracted from ores.

METEORITE

Piece of solid matter from outer space which enters the Earth's atmosphere and reaches the surface. Those which burn to incandescence are known as meteors or shooting stars. Most meteorites are no larger than pebbles but some much bigger than this have fallen to Earth.

METEOROLOGY

Scientific study of the Earth's weather. The principal factors which shape the weather at any given moment are temperature, degree of humidity in the air, atmospheric pressure, and wind force and direction. A large part of meteorology is concerned with weather forecasting. In Great Britain much advance information about weather conditions comes from weather ships in the ATLANTIC OCEAN. Today there are also weather satellites in orbit above the Earth which send back pictures of cloud formations over large areas and so provide valuable information about changing weather patterns. The average rainfall and temperature for a region, and how these vary from month to month throughout the year, provide information about its CLIMATE. *See also* ATMOSPHERE and CLOUD.

METRIC SYSTEM

System of weight and measures based on units in multiples of ten. The two basic units are the metre (for length) and the gramme (for weight). It was introduced in France during Napoleonic times, and is now used in many countries. Great Britain's conversion to metric weights and measures has largely coincided with entry into the EUROPEAN ECONOMIC COMMUNITY. In Britain's case it has also brought a change in the currency, and in the use of the centigrade scale instead of the fahrenheit scale for temperature readings.

MEXICO

Central American federal republic with an area of 1,972,547 sq km (761,646 sq miles) and a population of about 70 million. The capital is Mexico City. Much of the country is mountainous, and some of it is semi-desert. However, the land is rich in such minerals as silver, gold, lead and petroleum. Other important products are cotton, tobacco and coffee. Mexico was conquered by the Spanish explorer Hernando Cortés in the sixteenth century, and remained a Spanish possession until 1821, when a rebellion achieved independence. Spanish remains the official language, but many Mexicans are descended from the AZTECS, TOLTECS and MAYAS, who has established civilizations in the country before the Spanish Conquest.

MICA

Group of minerals which are widely used for heat-resisting purposes. They are also used in the manufacture of paper and paint.

MICHELANGELO Buonarroti (1475–1564)

Italian artist, architect and poet. One of his patrons was Lorenzo de Medici, and for the MEDICI family he designed a chapel in Florence

Michelangelo's *Pietà*

which includes some of his most famous sculptures. Another celebrated piece of sculpture, also in Florence, is the figure of David. Michelangelo regarded himself above all as a sculptor, but it is for his fresco paintings of the *Last Judgment* in the Sistine Chapel, Rome, that he is most widely known. He also designed and supervised the construction of the huge dome of St Peter's Basilica. In his work Michelangelo summed up many of the achievements of the whole RENAISSANCE period, and also exercised an enormous influence on the future course of art and architecture.

MICROMETER

Instrument for measuring small dimensions. A micrometer caliper has a micrometer screw attached, which is tightened onto the object to be measured. This is scaled to show how far it has turned. It can measure accurately to 0.0025 millimetre.

MICROSCOPE

Optical instrument used for viewing objects too small to be accurately observed by the eye, or too small to be seen at all with the naked eye. The electron microscope uses electromagnetic fields to scan objects and has magnifying powers thousands of times greater than an optical microscope. *See also* Antony van LEEUWENHOEK and OPTICS.

MILKY WAY

Galaxy of about 100,000 million stars, of which our sun is a member. From Earth it appears as a faint belt of light running across the night sky, though our planet and all the stars more distinctly seen are a part of it.

The Milky Way

MILL, John Stuart (1806–73)

English economist, philosopher and political thinker who supported efforts to improve social justice and advocated more civil liberties, including votes for women. His most important political work was *Essay on Liberty*.

MILTON, John (1608–74)

English poet. During the Civil War he sided with the Parliamentarians and served as Oliver CROMWELL's secretary. His greatest work is

Paradise Lost, a religious epic poem in blank verse, much of which he dictated to his daughters after he had gone blind.

MINERAL

The materials of which rocks are made, and which are often found in comparatively pure forms. Minerals include precious stones and the ores of metals, as well as such substances as calcite, quartz, sulphur, gypsum and rock salt. They may occur in 'massive' beds which can be mined or dug out, or in the form of crystals lining hollows in the rocks. The crystalline minerals are grouped according to the forms of their CRYSTALS.

Blue-and-white Ming vase

MING DYNASTY

This dynasty, famous for its porcelain, lacquerware and bronze, ruled CHINA between 1368 and 1644. Many famous buildings were completed in this period, including the Imperial Palace in the Forbidden City of Peking.

MINK

Small MAMMAL of the WEASEL family, specially bred for its white fur.

MINSTREL

Poet-musician of the Middle Ages who moved from town to town or from court to court. In different parts of Europe minstrels were known by different names. In Britain they were called bards. In France they were either troubadours (in the region of Provence) or trouvères. In Germany they were known as minnesingers (singers of love). Often they gathered together to hold contests of poetry and song. The Welsh *Eisteddfods* are a survival of this tradition.

MIRACLE PLAY

A kind of religious drama, based on the lives of the saints, that was popular during the Middle Ages. At first they were performed in churches. Later, they were given by trade guild members in the streets.

MIRAGE

Optical illusion caused by the refraction and reflection of LIGHT which occurs in very hot climates, particularly desert regions.

MISSISSIPPI

River in the United States which, with its principal tributary the Missouri, has a length of 6,080 km (3,800 miles), making it the world's third longest. With its many other tributaries, including the Ohio river, it flows southwards into the Gulf of Mexico.

MITHRAISM

Sun-religion, centred on Mithras, god of light and truth. It had many parallels with CHRISTIANITY, including belief in a miraculous birth and resurrection, and the idea of heaven and hell. Sunday was Mithras' holy day, too. His birth was also celebrated on 25 December, and both religions held Easter sacred. Mithraism was a rival of early Christianity in the West, with a strong following in the Roman army.

MOGUL

Moslem empire established in INDIA from about 1526 to 1857. The founder was Babar, a direct descendant of TAMERLANE, himself a descendant of GENGHIS KHAN. One of the greatest rulers was Akbar. The Moguls were generous patrons of the arts. Perhaps their most important contribution to India's culture was in the arts of Painting and architecture

MOHAMMED. *See* ISLAM

MOLE

Small MAMMAL with smooth fur. It spends most of its life digging burrows underground. Its pointed nose burrows forward and its strong paddle-shaped forelegs shovel the earth away. Its presence is indicated by the mole hills it leaves above the ground.

MOLECULE

Combination of two or more ATOMS. The simplest molecule is that of hydrogen, which contains just two hydrogen atoms. And since individual atoms do not exist under normal conditions, so one molecule of hydrogen, or one molecule of any other substance, is the smallest possible particle of that substance.

MOLIÈRE (Jean-Baptiste Poquelin, 1622–73)

French dramatist and actor. He joined a company of actors which later became the celebrated *Comédie Française*. Under the patronage of LOUIS XIV he wrote his best-known plays, comedies often directed against pretence and hypocrisy, including *Tartuffe*, *Le Misanthrope*, and *Le Bourgeois gentilhomme*.

MOLLUSC

Large group of INVERTEBRATE animals. They are distinguised by their soft, unsegmented bodies, and most species grow a protective shell. The group includes squid, cuttlefish, OCTOPUS, SNAIL, OYSTER and slug.

MONACO

Small Mediterranean principality which exists as an enclave of France. It has a permanent population of about 25,000, but the town of Monte Carlo is an international holiday centre.

MONASTERY

Dwelling place for monks to live and worship. The first Christian monasteries consisted of simple huts grouped near a wooden church. In the sixth century the Italian St Benedict founded the Benedictine Order, establishing a set of rules of conduct which have been observed since that time in monasteries throughout Europe. During the Middle Ages further Orders of monks and nuns were founded, and the monasteries and nunneries belonging to the strictest of these were built in very remote places.

Since monks were almost the only people who could read and write during the Middle Ages, monasteries were important for keeping alive the arts of writing, painting and music and were closely linked with the early development of universities. They also played a significant part in providing alms for the poor, tending the sick and giving shelter to travellers.

At the time of the Reformation in England

Ruins of Tintern Abbey, once a Cistercian monastery

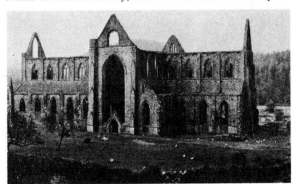

under HENRY VIII, the vast majority of English and Scottish monasteries were closed down and their lands and riches confiscated. *See also* CHRISTIANITY and REFORMATION.

MONET, Claude (1840–1926)

French artist, whose paintings, often depicting mist and hazy sunlight, are regarded by many as the finest examples of IMPRESSIONISM. Indeed, one of his paintings, *Impression: soleil levant,* gave its name to the whole artistic movement.

MONEY

Tokens used in the exchange of goods and services. Originally men made direct exchanges of their goods; for example, two goats for five sacks of grain. This was barter. The introduction of money brought far greater freedom and flexibility to trading and a general increase in wealth. The earliest money tokens were in the form of some substance that everybody valued equally. Salt was one such commodity. Then came precious metals, soon conveniently made into small coins. The city states of the Italian RENAISSANCE saw the start of modern banking and the introduction of paper banknotes – originally issued as receipts for coinage. The circulation of money in a community, how this should be controlled, distributed and invested, is all part of the studies of economics and finance. International finance has to take into account the relative purchasing power of different currencies.

MONGOLIAN PEOPLE'S REPUBLIC

Asian republic to the north of China, 1,565,000 sq km (604,283 sq miles) in area, but with a population of only about 1½ million. The capital is Ulan Bator. Practically the whole country lies within the region of the GOBI DESERT, and many of the people still follow the traditional nomadic way of life.

MONGOOSE

Small MAMMAL, fierce by nature but sometimes tamed as a pet. The Indian mongoose is famous for the way it can attack and kill large snakes like the cobra.

MONKEY

Group of PRIMATES which includes the BABOON, marmoset and mandrill. Most species are native to the tropical regions of Africa, Asia and South America. Monkeys are the only mammals which, like man, have good stereoscopic vision, that is, they see objects in the solid, not as flat surfaces. The chimpanzee, gorilla and orang-utan are APES and not monkeys.

Below A rhesus monkey, native to the Far East

MONSOON

Word derived from the Arabic *mawsin*, meaning 'season', and describing the winds which, in the northern hemisphere, blow for six months from the north-east and for six months from the south-west. Generally the word is applied to the rainy season from June to September in India and other countries of southern Asia.

MONTAIGNE, Michel de (1533–92)

French writer who created the form of the essay and influenced the work of later English essayists. In his own essays he advocated tolerance, a healthy scepticism and commonsense as a way of life.

MONTESQUIEU, Charles de Secondat, Baron (1689–1755)

French lawyer and philosopher, whose writings on political institutions had a big influence on the shaping of the Constitution of the UNITED STATES OF AMERICA and on the institutions of the FRENCH REVOLUTION.

MONTEVERDI, Claudio (1567–1643)

Italian composer. He was for many years Director of Music at St Mark's Basilica, Venice, and wrote for it some very expressive and dramatic religious music. Venice was also the first city to open public opera houses, and Monteverdi was the first major composer to write OPERAS. These works are noted for their imaginative use of instruments, and for this reason Monteverdi is generally regarded as the founder of the orchestra.

MONTGOLFIER, Joseph Michel (1740–1810)

French pioneer of air travel. He and his brother Jacques Étienne were the inventors of the hot-air balloon, which made its first successful ascent in 1783.

MONTGOMERY of Alamein, Field Marshal Viscount (1887–1976)

British soldier who played a leading role in WORLD WAR II. The important part of his career began with his appointment in 1942 as commander of the British Eighth Army in

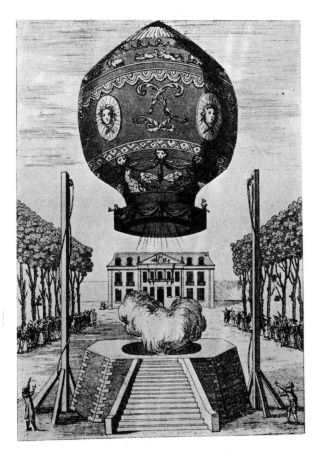

The ascent of the Montgolfier balloon, 1783

North Africa. Later that year he won a famous victory against a German and Italian force at El Alamein in Egypt, and continued the offensive across North Africa and into Tunisia. In 1944 he commanded the Allied land forces in the invasion of German-occupied France and the following year accepted the surrender of the German armies in the West. After World War II he was appointed Chief of the Imperial General Staff, and later, Deputy Supreme Commander of NORTH ATLANTIC TREATY ORGANIZATION forces in Europe. He was much respected by men under his command.

MOON

The satellite of our planet. Its mean distance from the Earth is approximately 384,400 km (238,860 miles). It is approximately 3,476 km

(2,160 miles) in diameter, and its sidereal revolution in $27\frac{1}{3}$ days. Because of its motion only one face is ever seen from the Earth, but in 1959 the far side of the moon was photographed by *Lunik* III, a Soviet spacecraft. In 1969 American astronauts in the Apollo 11 spacecraft landed on the moon. They found it a silent, lonely place with no atmosphere. The sky is always black. At night the surface is colder than anywhere on Earth. During the day the ground is too hot to touch.

MOORE, Henry (born 1898)

English artist. His chief fame is as a sculptor, in which field of art he has been much concerned with the relationship between internal and external spaces of large abstract shapes. Institutions all over the world have commissioned examples of his work. However, during WORLD WAR II he was a British war artist, producing many drawings of sleeping figures which he observed during the London blitz.

The King and Queen, bronze by Henry Moore

MOORS

Race of people of North Africa, closely related to the other ARAB races, and followers of ISLAM. From the eighth to the fifteenth centuries they occupied almost the whole of SPAIN and in this way influenced many aspects of European art, architecture and science.

MOOSE. *See* ELK

MORALITY PLAY

Form of drama during the Middle Ages in which actors impersonated virtues and vices. The plays developed from religious pageants. Originally they aimed to teach a lesson, but the crowds enjoyed the acrobatics of the Devil and imps so much that the character of the plays gradually changed.

MORE, Sir Thomas (1478–1535)

English statesman, politician and writer. He was at first admired by HENRY VIII, and rose to be Speaker of the House and Lord Chancellor. However, More was a very religious man and would not approve of Henry's divorce from Catherine of Aragon, which led to his retirement. Later he refused to recognize Henry as supreme head of the English Church, was charged with treason and beheaded. His best known book is *Utopia*, a political essay about an imaginary land where there is freedom of worship and universal education.

MORMONS

American religious sect founded in 1831 by Joseph Smith, who wrote *The Book of Mormon*. Under the leadership of Brigham Young a settlement was made in 1847 in Utah, which grew into Salt Lake City. For many years the settlement was opposed by the American government because of Young's idea that a man could have more than one wife. There are more than half a million mormons in the United

States. The correct name for the sect is 'Church of Jesus Christ of Latter-day Saints'.

MOROCCO

ARAB kingdom of North Africa with an area of 446,550 sq km (172,423 sq miles) and 20 million people. Large cities include Casablanca, Rabat, the capital, and Marrakesh. The Atlas Mountains run through Morocco. Most people live by farming, but phosphates are the main export. Morocco was ruled by France from 1912 but it gained independence in 1956. In 1976 Morocco and Mauritania divided neighbouring Western (formerly Spanish) Sahara between them. But many Saharans wanted independence. Mauritania withdrew in 1979 and Morocco claimed all of Western Sahara. But the Saharans fought on.

MORRIS, William (1834–96)

English designer, craftsman and artist who reacted against what he saw as the ugliness and de-humanizing aspects of the INDUSTRIAL RE-VOLUTION by designing fabrics, wallpapers, stained glass and furniture intended to restore the beauty of earlier times. He also wrote a number of books and essays that showed his hostility to machinery, for he believed that working life could only be improved by handicraft.

MORSE, Samuel (1791–1872)

American creator of the telegraph and radio code which bears his name. Each letter of the alphabet, plus numerals, is represented by a sequence of signals, either long (a dash) or short (a dot) in duration.

MOSAIC

Art form in which pictures or designs are composed by joining together small pieces of glass, stone or other material of different colours. They are usually set in cement and used as a wall or floor decoration. The art of mosaics

Mosaic of Christ from Ravenna, Italy

was known to the Romans. Evidence that Latin American Indians also knew the art has been found in the ruins of ancient temples.

MOSES

Jewish political and religious leader and lawgiver, whose life is described in the Old Testament of the BIBLE. He freed the Jewish people from Egyptian captivity and provided the Ten COMMANDMENTS as the moral and religious basis of JUDAISM.

MOSLEM. See ISLAM

MOSQUITO

INSECT belonging to the FLY family and found in most parts of the world. Its eggs are laid and hatched in stagnant water. One species of tropical mosquito transmits MALARIA. Another is similarly responsible for yellow fever.

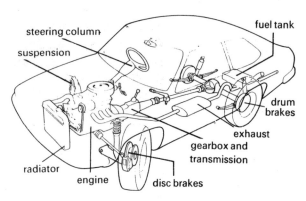

The main components of a motor car

MOTOR CAR

Road vehicle powered by an engine. In 1770 the French engineer Nicholas Cugnot built a three-wheeled cart powered by steam; and in 1829 the Englishman Sir Goldsworthy Gurney built a much more elaborate steam carriage that could travel at a speed of 24 km/h (over 16 mph). Versions of the INTERNAL COMBUSTION ENGINE were introduced into motor cars towards the end of the nineteenth century. One of the first in this field was the German inventor Dr Nikolaus Otto. Another was the Austrian engineer Siegfried Markus who adapted the Otton engine to run on petrol gas. The Englishman Edward Butler produced an engine with electric ignition and a carburettor to supply a mixture of air and petrol vapour to the cylinders – principles that have not changed in nearly a hundred years.

Other important pioneers of the internal combustion engine were Gottlieb Daimler and Karl BENZ in Germany, René Panhard in France, Frederick Lanchester, Henry Royce and Charles Rolls in England, and Henry FORD in the United States. By 1900 the motor car had become an accepted means of transport in Western countries; and by 1910 the petrol-driven bus and taxi had largely replaced the horse-drawn carriage and hansom cab.

MOUSE. *See* RODENT

MOZAMBIQUE

East African republic, formerly Portuguese East Africa, with an area of 783,030 sq km (302,346 sq miles) and a population of about 10 million. The capital is Maputo (called Lourenço Marques before independence in 1975).

MOZART, Wolfgang Amadeus (1756–91)

Austrian composer. He was a child prodigy and toured the courts of Europe, including London, with his father and sister. But he later quarrelled with his first employer, the Archbishop of Salzburg (his birthplace), and was dismissed. From then on Mozart found it increasingly difficult to earn a living, being finally buried in a pauper's grave. From his youth onwards Mozart could write charming music for any occasion. As he grew older he combined his mastery of classical eighteenth-century forms with music that was sometimes very dramatic and expressive. Works of this mature period include the OPERAS *The Marriage of Figaro, Don Giovanni* and *The Magic Flute;* the last three SYMPHONIES, nos. 39, 40 and 41 ('Jupiter' Symphony); some of the piano CONCERTOS; string quartets and other CHAMBER MUSIC compositions. Mozart's output – over 600 works – was later catalogued by a scholar named Ludwig Koechel, and individual pieces are often referred to by their 'K' number.

MULE

Offspring of an ass (male) and a horse (mare). Mules cannot be bred from other mules as they are sterile.

MUNCH, Edvard (1863–1944)

Norwegian painter who strongly influenced modern German painting. His style of painting developed from that of Paul GAUGUIN and other Post-Impressionists and is violent or neurotic in character.

MUSCLE

Fibrous bands of animal tissue that expand or contract to produce movement in the body. Skeletal muscles are attached to bones and control their movement. Smooth muscles act independently of the bones. They help the movement of internal organs, such as the stomach. Cardiac muscles operate the heart.

MUSHROOM. *See* FUNGUS

MUSIC

Organized sound, traditionally considered to consist of three basic ingredients, used separately or in combination: RHYTHM, melody and HARMONY. Some scholars contend that in its origins music is the oldest form of human communication or expression, ritualized shouts and dances probably being practised long before men could speak or draw. The ancient Greeks believed that music had divine properties. PYTHAGORAS was one of many who sought a mystical connection between numbers, as they related to his ideas about the universe, and musical pitch (highness or lowness of a note). The beginnings of Western music are regarded as medieval plainsong; while the best-known musical forms, OPERA, ORATORIO, SYMPHONY, CONCERTO, SONATA, all developed during the seventeenth and eighteenth centuries. Other important forms, styles, or techniques of music dealt with in this encyclopedia are: CONDUCTING, DANCE, JAZZ and SONG. The work of individual composers is discussed under their own entries.

MUSICAL INSTRUMENT

For thousands of years musical instruments have been designed to produce sounds either by being struck, by being blown into or across, or by having a tightened string plucked or scraped with a bow. The quality and volume of their basic sounds have then been largely determined by matters of size and shape.

The scientific classification of musical instruments is as follows: *idiophones* (those made of a single material that vibrates when struck, such as the blocks of a xylophone, cymbals, gongs and bells); *membranophones* (instruments which have a stretched skin as their source of sound, including all drums); *aerophones* (instruments that have a tube of some kind and are blown into); *chordophones* (instruments with stretched strings).

The more familiar classification, based on the arrangement of instruments in an ORCHESTRA, is as follows: *strings* (violin, viola, cello, double bass, harp, guitar); *woodwind* (flute, oboe, clarinet, bassoon, recorder); *brass* (trumpet, trombone, horn, tuba); *percussion* (kettledrum, bass drum, xylophone, tubular bells, cymbals, gongs, triangle). There are a few instruments, such as the human voice, organ, piano and saxophone, that cannot easily be classed according to this second set of headings. Also, during this century electronic instruments have been invented that produce their sounds from totally different sources.

Stringed instruments of the early 17th century

MUSK OX

MAMMAL that in appearance is a cross between a sheep and an ox, native to the Arctic regions of Canada and Greenland. It has downward curving horns and thick brown fur.

MUSSOLINI, Benito (1883–1945)

Italian politician and dictator. As a young man he was a member of the Italian socialist party, but was expelled when he supported his country's entry into WORLD WAR I. Soon after the war he founded the Italian Fascist Party, and after a daring march on Rome with his supporters in 1922 bluffed the King into appointing him as Prime Minister. Mussolini gradually assumed the powers of a dictator. He rallied the people with such slogans as 'Obey, Believe, Fight', and within the country he did stimulate industry and create new jobs. His foreign policy was ultimately disastrous. A desire for military glory led him to take Italy into WORLD WAR II on Germany's side. His armies in North Africa were defeated and Italy itself invaded. In 1943 the King had him arrested. HITLER then had him rescued and placed at the head of a puppet state in northern Italy. He was finally captured by partisans and shot, being put on public display hanging by his feet.

MUSSORGSKY, Modest (1835–81)

Russian composer, and member of the group of Russian musicians, called The Five, dedicated to creating a national school of music. His own output was small but distinguished, including the opera *Boris Godunov*, the piano suite *Pictures at an Exhibition* (later orchestrated by RAVEL) and some remarkable songs.

MUSTANG

When the Spanish invaded Central America many of their horses (Arab breed) escaped to form herds. These roamed the plains of Mexico and Texas, and were greatly prized by the Indians. A partly wild horse of this origin is called a mustang, and one completely untamed a bronco.

MYTH

The creation of stories and characters, usually both supernatural and cosmic, to explain the forces of nature. All societies have had their myths, centred round a pantheon of gods and goddesses who represent the natural elements or some basic human instinct or need. Most famous are the characters of Greek and Roman mythology, including the chief god (Zeus/Jupiter), the god of the sea (Poseidon/Neptune), the god of fertility (Demeter/Ceres), the goddess of love (Aphrodite/Venus), the god of war (Ares/Mars), the god of fire (Hephaestus/Vulcan), and the god of wine and plenty (Dionysus/Bacchus).

Venus, the Roman goddess of love

N

NAMIBIA

Territory until recently known as South West Africa, with an area of 824,292 sq km (318,278 sq miles) and a population of 1,008,000. The capital is Windhoek. Much of the country is desert, but it is rich in minerals. Germany ruled Namibia before World War I. It was then governed by South Africa under a League of Nations mandate. But, in 1946, South Africa refused to accept a UN trusteeship for Namibia. South Africa's government of Namibia has been condemned by the U.N. which has sought to negotiate independence for the territory.

NANSEN, Fridtjof (1861–1930)

Norwegian scientist and polar explorer. He was the first man to cross the Greenland ice cap.

NAPIER, John (1550–1617)

Scottish mathematician. He devised logarithms and prepared the first logarithmic tables. He also invented a calculating device, the forerunner of the slide rule.

NAPOLEON I (Napoleon Bonaparte, 1769–1821)

French emperor and military leader. Born in Ajaccio, Corsica, he received his military education in France and was a captain by the age of twenty. His first military success was the

Napoleon in his coronation robes

capture of Toulon from a force of royalists in 1793. Three years later he was a general and commanded military campaigns in Italy and Egypt. In 1799 he returned to France, was elected First Consul and virtual ruler of the country, and devoted himself to a period of widespread social reform which made France the first truly modern state in terms of law, finance and administration. In 1804 Napoleon had himself crowned Emperor, and embarked upon the conquest of Europe with a series of spectacular victories against a coalition of royalist countries at Ulm, Austerlitz, Jena and Friedland. He was not so successful in his campaign against a British force in Spain and Portugal in what is called the Peninsular War. And in 1812 he led his armies to disaster when attempting a winter withdrawal from Moscow. Two years later another coalition of European powers, including Britain, forced Napoleon to abdicate, and he was exiled to the Mediterranean island of Elba. He escaped, returned to France in triumph and gathered a new army, but was defeated by a British and Prussian force at Waterloo (1815). He was finally exiled to the remote South Atlantic island of St Helena where he died. *See also* Admiral Horatio NELSON and Duke of WELLINGTON.

NARCOTIC

By definition, a narcotic is any substance producing sleep or stupor and today the term covers a wide range of drugs, though some are not directly taken for this effect. Alcohol is the commonest narcotic. The anaesthetics, such as ether, chloroform, and cylopropane, belong to this group, as do sleeping pills. There is also the group of alkaloids containing morphine and Indian hemp. Narcotics act by slowing up activity of the cortex of the cerebrum.

NATIONAL DEBT

The money which the State borrows on the security of the taxes it can raise and upon future sources, such as North Sea Oil in Britain. This was done in Norman times, but the National Debt of today was a system adopted in the reign of William III. In recent years money has been received from the INTERNATIONAL MONETARY FUND (IMF).

NATIONAL HEALTH SERVICE

This was created in 1948 to provide a nationwide medical service for all in need. It included dental, pre- and post-natal treatment. The original intention was that the service should be entirely free, in the sense that patients would not pay directly for treatment, which would be financed from taxation and NATIONAL INSURANCE contributions. However, a direct contribution towards some forms of treatment and medicines was soon introduced, and this practice has continued. *See also* Aneurin BEVAN and LABOUR PARTY.

NATIONAL INSURANCE

State insurance scheme, now operated by the Department of Health and Social Security, whereby regular contributions from all wage-earners are used to give financial support to the unemployed, the sick, or the handicapped. Old Age Pensions are a part of the service. Many other countries have similar arrangements.

NATIONAL PARK

Area of outstanding natural beauty or of some other special interest, which is preserved by legislation for public use. Many countries have national parks, including Canada, South Africa, Tanzania. In Great Britain many such areas have been preserved by the National Trust.

Pony trekking on Exmoor, a National Park

NATO. *See* NORTH ATLANTIC TREATY ORGANIZATION

NATURAL HISTORY

The study of plant and animal life in all its aspects. The two main branches of this vast subject are BOTANY (plant life) and ZOOLOGY (animal life). Another big aspect of the subject is EVOLUTION, relating to both plants and animals. In this encyclopedia natural history is considered under these basic headings. There are also many entries devoted to the principal classifications of plant and animal life; to groups of individual species of animal; and to the many scientists (natural historians) who have contributed to our knowledge of the subject. *See also* ANATOMY, ANIMAL KINGDOM, GENETICS and PALAEONTOLOGY.

NAURU

Very small island republic in the Central Pacific Ocean with an area of only 21 sq km (8 sq miles) and a population of less than 10,000. It is entirely dependent on its export of phosphate.

NEANDERTHAL MAN

Species of prehistoric man who lived between 100,000 and 35,000 years ago in parts of Europe, Asia and Africa. The first fossil evidence of this extinct type of man was found in the Neander Gorge near Düsseldorf, West Germany, hence the name.

NEBULA

The word *nebula* is the Latin for 'cloud', and in ASTRONOMY is the term used to describe huge clouds of gas or dust far out in space. Many of these are faintly illuminated by the light from other stars. Some are dark areas which obscure the stars lying beyond them. However, the term is also now used to describe other patches of light which are not gas or dust clouds but the faint image of other complete star systems, similar to our own galaxy of the Milky Way, and existing at unimaginable distances out in space.

NEHRU, Jawaharlal (1889–1964)

Indian statesman. Before WORLD WAR II he was imprisoned by the British for his part in political movements aimed at achieving Indian independence. After the granting of independence in 1947 he became the first Prime Minister of India and a world leader due to his policy of non-alignment during the most acute period of ideological dispute between the communist and non-communist worlds, known as the Cold War.

Nelson on the eve of Trafalgar

NELSON, Admiral Horatio, Viscount (1758–1805)

English naval officer. Born in Norfolk, he was a fragile looking young man but was a captain by the age of twenty and soon recognized as a brave and dashing commander. He lost his right eye in operations against the French off Corsica and his right arm during an engagement near the Canary Islands. Nelson's two greatest triumphs were his victory against a French Fleet at Aboukir Bay in 1798, which forced NAPOLEON's withdrawal from Egypt; and the even more significant victory he won against a combined French and Spanish fleet off Cape Trafalgar in 1805. It was just before this battle that he sent the celebrated message to his fleet, from the flagship *Victory*, 'England expects that every man will do his duty'; and it was during the engagement that he was killed by a French sharp-shooter.

NEON

Chemical ELEMENT and one of the so-called INERT GASES. It was discovered by the British chemists Sir William Ramsay and Morris Travers. It is widely used in electric lamps and display signs.

NEPAL

Asian kingdom north of India with an area of 140,797 sq km (54,365 sq miles) and a population of about 14 million. The capital is Kathmandu. The country runs along the line of the HIMALAYAS and the highest mountain in the world, Everest, stands just within its frontiers. The Gurkhas, famed for their toughness and bravery as soldiers, come from Nepal.

NEPTUNE

PLANET of the SOLAR SYSTEM with an equatorial diameter of 45,000 km (28,200 miles) and an average distance from the SUN of 4,500 million km (2,800 million miles). Neptune is the second outermost planet in the solar system and is one of the 'gas giants' (so called because they contain a high proportion of hydrogen), along with Jupiter, Saturn and Uranus.

NERO (AD 37–68)

Roman emperor. Soon after his accession in AD 54 he murdered both his mother Agrippina and his wife Octavia and from then on his rule was marked by folly and brutality. He is supposed to have played his lyre while fire swept through Rome, then accused the Christians of the disaster and had hundreds of them put to death. The generals in the army revolted against his rule and had him deposed. He committed suicide.

NETHERLANDS (Holland)

Kingdom in Western Europe with an area of 40,844 sq km (15,771 sq miles) and a population

Tulip fields in the Netherlands

of about 14 million. The seat of government is The Hague, but the chief city and capital is Amsterdam and the chief port is Rotterdam. In the south the river Rhine (called the Waal) flows east to west and enters the North Sea. Further north, large areas have been reclaimed from the sea and remain below sea level, protected by dykes and other engineering works. The most ambitious land reclamation scheme is in the area once known as the Zuider Zee, a former inlet of the North Sea, now divided by a dam into Ijsselmeer to the south and Waddenzee to the north. The reclaimed areas are called polders. There are virtually no hills. Rotterdam is now the busiest port in Europe and a major industrial centre; elsewhere the chief activities are dairy farming and horticulture (especially tulip cultivation).

In the fifteenth century the Netherlands were part of the kingdom of Burgundy, which also encompassed most of northern and eastern France. Then they became a Spanish province, and there followed widespread religious persecution. In the seventeenth and eighteenth centuries the Dutch navy grew to rival those of Britain and France, and there was intermittent war with England up to 1689, when WILLIAM of Orange became the English king. As a result of the Napoleonic Wars the Netherlands and Belgium were created as one nation. This union did not last, but the neutrality of both was guaranteed by the major European powers right up to WORLD WAR I. In WORLD WAR II the Netherlands was occupied by Germany. After the war the country modernized its industry, granted independence to its overseas territories in the Far East and South America, and became one of the original six members of the EUROPEAN ECONOMIC COMMUNITY. Since World War II, two Dutch monarchs have abdicated. First, in 1948, Queen Wilhelmina was succeeded by her daughter who became Queen Juliana. The Queen Juliana herself abdicated in favour of her daughter Crown Princess Beatrix in 1980. *See also* BENELUX.

NEUTRON

Fundamental part of the nucleus of the ATOM, so called because it is electrically neutral, that is, carries no electrical charge. It was first identified by Sir James CHADWICK in 1932. *See also* PROTON.

NEWCOMEN, Thomas (1663–1729)

English engineer. He was the first to design and build a steam engine, technically called an atmospheric steam engine because the rapid condensation of steam in the cylinder created a vacuum which drew the piston downward. It was a stationary machine, used for pumping water out of Cornish tin mines.

NEW GUINEA

Large island in the Pacific Ocean, just north of Australia, with an area of 831,000 sq km (321,000 sq miles). Politically it is divided into two areas, the western half, Irian Jaya, belonging to INDONESIA and the eastern half PAPUA NEW GUINEA.

NEW HEBRIDES. *See* VANUATU

NEWTON, Sir Isaac (1642–1727)

English mathematician and scientist. He was born in the village of Woolsthorpe, Lincolnshire, had a brilliant career as a student, and at twenty-six was already Professor of Mathematics at Cambridge University. Newton's most celebrated achievement was his formulation of the laws of GRAVITY and motion as applied to the movement of the planets in relation to each other and to the Sun. He also discovered that LIGHT could be split up into the coloured bands called the SPECTRUM, invented a new type of TELESCOPE, the reflecting telescope, and created the branch of mathematics called CALCULUS. His book *Principia Mathematica* was one of the most significant and far-reaching works of science ever to be written.

NEW ZEALAND

Dominion of the BRITISH COMMONWEALTH comprising two large islands (North and South Islands) and several smaller ones in the South Pacific Ocean. It has a total area of 268,676 sq km (103,742 sq miles) with a popula-

Tattooed Maori chief from New Zealand

tion of about 3¼ million. The capital is Wellington, and other important towns are Auckland, Dunedin and Christchurch. The North Island has a warm temperate climate and some spectacular scenery, including regions of geysers and hot springs. The South Island has a range of mountains, the Southern Alps, and extensive pasture lands, ideal for both sheep and cattle.

The country was first discovered by the Dutch navigator Abel Tasman in 1642, but was more thoroughly explored by Captain James COOK in 1769. The islands became a British possession in 1840. There was some conflict with the original inhabitants, the Maoris, but colonization was generally peaceful. New Zealand was granted Dominion status in 1907. For the next sixty years the vast bulk of the country's meat and dairy products were exported to Britain. Since British entry into the EUROPEAN ECONOMIC COMMUNITY these exports have declined, and New Zealand has had to create new outlets for its products. It has a number of dependencies among the Pacific Islands, including Cook Island.

NIAGARA FALLS

North American waterfalls situated between Lakes Ontario and Erie, and marking the border between the United States and Canada. There are two distinct falls. The American Falls are on the United States side; 59 m (193 ft) high and about 335 m (1,100 ft) wide. The more famous Horseshoe Falls are in Canada; 57 m (186 ft) high and 640 m (2,100 ft) across. They are a great tourist attraction, and are also used to generate hydro-electric power.

NICARAGUA

Central American republic, 130,000 sq km (50,196 sq miles) in area, with a population of about 2½ million. The capital is Managua. The chief exports are cotton, coffee, bananas and sugar.

NICHOLAS II (1868–1918)

The last tsar of Imperial Russia. During his reign Russia suffered humiliating defeat at the

Tsar Nicholas II with his family

hands of JAPAN, and further defeats in the field after entry into WORLD WAR I. Due to these events, to the influence of the monk Rasputin over the Empress, and to mounting social discontent, Nicholas was forced to abdicate in 1917. Soon after he was taken into custody by the Bolsheviks and executed with all his family. *See also* RUSSIAN REVOLUTION.

NICKEL

Metallic ELEMENT widely used in steel alloys because of its resistance to corrosion. The chief mineral ore from which it is extracted is pentlandite.

NIETZSCHE, Friedrich Wilhelm (1844–1900)

German philosopher. His most famous work is *Thus Spake Zarathustra,* in which he argued that the driving force in human affairs is the desire for some sort of power, and spoke of a new breed of supermen needed to transform society. *See also* ZOROASTER.

NIGER

North African republic with an area of 1,267,000 sq km (489,218 sq miles) and a population of about 5¼ million. The capital is Niamey. The country takes its name from the River Niger which flows across the south-western corner. The remainder of the land is within the SAHARA DESERT and virtually uninhabited. It was formerly a part of French West Africa, and gained its independence in 1960.

NIGERIA

West African federal republic with an area of 923,768 sq km (356,668 sq miles) and a population of about 84 million – the largest in Africa. The capital is Lagos. The River Niger and its tributaries create a delta region of mangrove swamp as they flow into the Gulf of Guinea. Inland the country is grassland and

Decorated doorway of a clay house, Kano, Nigeria

tropical forest. The chief products are cocoa, cotton and palm oil. Nigeria was formerly a British colony, gaining its independence in 1960. It remains a member of the BRITISH COMMONWEALTH. The country's history since independence has been marred by a civil war in 1967–70 and by several military coup d'états. Oil production, however, has brought Nigeria much wealth and civilian government was restored in 1979.

NIGHTINGALE

Small BIRD of the thrush family, native to parts of Europe, Asia and North Africa. It is noted for its beautiful song, which it delivers more or less continually, day and night, from spring-time up to about the end of June.

NIGHTINGALE, Florence (1820–1910)

English nurse and hospital reformer. She became famous at the time of the CRIMEAN WAR when she and a small party of other nurses went to the battle zone and set up hospital units at Balaclava and Scutari. Her strict new standards of hygiene and organization greatly reduced the mortality rate among the wounded and were soon copied elsewhere. She later founded a nurses' training school at St Thomas's Hospital, London. To the wounded soldiers under her care she was known as 'The Lady with the Lamp'.

NILE

African river and the world's longest, rising in Lake Victoria and flowing northwards for a distance of 6,690 km (4,160 miles) into the MEDITERRANEAN SEA. This is the White Nile. It is joined by its principal tributary, the Blue Nile, at Khartoum in the SUDAN. For much of its length it flows through desert. Its waters were literally life-giving to such ancient civilizations as that of EGYPT, whose people regarded it as sacred. Its annual flooding is now controlled by such engineering works as the Aswan Dam, in Egypt, which have brought large tracts of land under permanent irrigation.

NITROGEN

Chemical ELEMENT, usually in the form of a colourless, odourless gas and constituting about three-quarters of the Earth's ATMOSPHERE. It plays a vital part in the food chain of plants and animals, and is also widely used in industry, especially in the manufacture of ammonia, explosives, fertilizers and dye-stuffs.

NOBEL, Alfred Bernhard (1833–96)

Swedish chemist. He invented the explosive dynamite, and from this and other sources amassed a huge fortune. This money he bequeathed to the annual award of five prizes, in the fields of physics, chemistry, medicine, literature and the cause of peace. The Nobel prizes have been awarded since 1901. Their individual value is about £60,000.

NORMAN CONQUEST

The Normans came originally from SCANDINAVIA and were of VIKING descent. During the tenth century they invaded and conquered the part of northern France which is still called Normandy. In the next century, under WILLIAM the Conqueror, they invaded and subdued England. This event brought about the end of SAXON England and saw the start of a new era of English history, with new styles of ARCHITECTURE and a new form of social and political order called the FEUDAL SYSTEM. It is interesting to note that while William was conquering England, other Norman chiefs sailed down the coasts of France and Spain, entered the Mediterranean Sea and conquered Sicily and some parts of southern Italy. Norman knights from France and Italy also played a leading role in the CRUSADES.

NORTH ATLANTIC TREATY ORGANIZATION (NATO)

International military defence organization, created in 1949, with the following member states: Belgium, Canada, Denmark, France, Iceland, Italy, Luxembourg, Netherlands, Norway, Portugal, United Kingdom and the United States. Greece, Turkey and West Germany joined later. The original European headquarters were in Paris, but were transferred to Brussels in 1967.

NORWAY

North European kingdom, classed as part of SCANDINAVIA, with an area of 324,219 sq km (125,188 sq miles) and a population of about 4 million. The capital is Oslo; other towns are Bergen and Stavanger. The country extends well beyond the Arctic Circle and covers a large part of the region known as LAPLAND. It is nearly all mountainous, the mountains running straight down into the sea to create the long flooded valleys called fiords, or fjords. Fishing is the most important industry. Hydro-electricity has been the chief source of energy; but oil from the North Sea started flowing into the country in the early 1970s.

Norway was the original home of the VIKINGS, who created a united kingdom during the ninth century. The country was united with DENMARK from the fourteenth to the nineteenth centuries, and then, for a short time, with SWEDEN. During WORLD WAR II it was occupied by Germany.

NOVEL

Literary form, a work of fiction with characters and some type of worked out theme or plot. The first novel to be generally recognized as such was Miguel de CERVANTES' *Don Quixote*, though this and other examples of prose fiction, like John BUNYAN's *Pilgrim's Progress* and the works of Daniel DEFOE, carried strong moral or religious overtones. The great age of novel writing started in the mid-eighteenth century with the work of Richardson, FIELDING and Smollett. Important nineteenth-century novelists include Charles DICKENS, Sir Walter SCOTT, Jane AUSTEN, the BRONTË sisters, George ELIOT, Thomas HARDY, Gustave FLAUBERT, Nikolai GOGOL and Leo TOLSTOY. In the twentieth century the traditional form of the novel was greatly altered and influenced by the works of James JOYCE and Virginia WOOLF. Most novels contain at least 50,000 words. Works of fiction much shorter than this are usually classed as short stories.

NUCLEAR ENERGY

An ATOM is a minute particle of matter, consisting of a nucleus surrounded by electrons. The nucleus is itself a minute part of the whole, perhaps as little as a million-millionth part of the volume of the complete atom. Yet the two parts of the nucleus, the PROTON and the NEUTRON, are bound together by forces of enormous strength. When they are separated this force is released in the form of heat energy. This is the principle of nuclear energy. Separation of the atomic nucleus is achieved by bombarding it with other nuclear particles. This can be done artificially by so-called 'atom smashers' such as the CYCLOTRON. It can also be done with naturally RADIOACTIVE ELEMENTS which are constantly shooting out atomic particles of their own. One such substance is uranium. In this element individual atoms are being broken up, that is, their nuclei are being 'split', all the time. Left to itself the process continues indefinitely. But it can be speeded up by the creation of a 'chain reaction', whereby the splitting of the nucleus of one uranium atom causes the splitting of two more, both of which then split the nuclei of two more atoms, and so on. In this way the energy from the split or fractured nuclei of countless millions of atoms can be released in a fraction of a second. If uncontrolled, the process leads to an atomic explosion. If controlled, as it is in an atomic pile, or reactor, the energy can be released as a steady flow of heat. In a nuclear power station the heat is used, instead of fuels like coal or oil, to produce steam to drive electric generators.

The process of splitting the atomic nucleus is called fission. It is also possible to obtain atomic energy by forcing atoms together. This is called fusion, and can only take place at very high temperatures. If four hydrogen atoms are forced to unite, to make one helium atom, an enormous amount of atomic energy is released. This process is used in the hydrogen bomb. It is also thought to be the source of energy in the SUN. So far, however, no way has been discovered of controlling this thermo-nuclear fusion (unlike fission), so that the energy can be put to practical use. *See also* ATOM, ISOTOPE, LINEAR ACCELERATOR, Niels BOHR, Sir John COCKCROFT, Albert EINSTEIN, Enrico FERMI, Otto HAHN, Ernest RUTHERFORD.

NUCLEIC ACID

A compound or a group of compounds that exist, mainly in association with proteins, in the nucleus of living cells and control their function. There are two types: deoxyribonucleic acid (DNA), which is the chief material in CHROMOSOMES, and ribonucleic acid (RNA).

NYLON

Name for a group of synthetic fibrous materials, known technically as polyamides. They were first produced in the United States in the 1930s. They are strong, long-lasting, elastic, and are used extensively in clothing, and in industry and engineering.

O

OASIS

Area in a desert region with enough water to make it fertile. This may range from a simple water hole surrounded with date palms, to large areas with crops of fruits, cereals and vegetables. The water may be supplied by an ARTESIAN WELL or irrigation.

OBELISK

Pointed four-sided pillar, used as a monument, especially by the ancient Egyptians. The most famous obelisks today are known as Cleopatra's needles. There is one each in London, Paris and New York.

OBSERVATORY

Building used in ASTRONOMY for observation of the moon, sun, stars and planets. One of the earliest observatories in Europe was founded by the Danish astronomer Tycho BRAHE in 1576. For a long time the chief equipment of observatories was optical TELESCOPES, through which objects in space were literally observed. Today an observatory can contain, or consist of, radiotelescopes which operate on an entirely different principle. Three of today's most famous observatories are the Hale Observatory (including Mount Palomar), in California; JODRELL BANK in Cheshire; and the Royal Greenwich, now at Herstmonceux, Sussex.

OCEANOGRAPHY

The study of the oceans: the contours and composition of the ocean floor; the strength, direction and temperature of the ocean currents; and the variety and distribution of marine plant and animal life. This latter aspect of oceanography is becoming increasingly important as the seas and oceans are now viewed as a major source of world food supplies in the future.

OCEANS AND SEAS

Large bodies of salt water (although the word 'sea' is sometimes applied to freshwater lakes). Seas are usually defined by the proximity of land, and may be almost surrounded by land. Oceans are the great areas of water separating the continents – PACIFIC, ATLANTIC, Indian and ARCTIC Oceans. The water of the oceans and seas covers almost three-quarters of the EARTH'S surface.

Hale Observatory, California

OCEANIA

Collective name for the island groups of the central and southern regions of the Pacific. These groups are themselves divided into three main regions: Melanesia (SOLOMON ISLANDS, VANUATU and FIJI); Micronesia (MARSHALL ISLANDS, KIRIBATI and NAURU); Polynesia (HAWAII, PITCAIRN ISLAND, TONGA, TUVALU, SAMOA and SOCIETY ISLAND).

OCELOT

Wild CAT of Central and South America with a distinctive coat similar in colouring to that of a leopard, and valued for its fur.

OCTANE

A colourless, liquid HYDROCARBON that occurs in petrol. The higher the grade of petrol the more octane it contains.

OCTOPUS

Sea creature related to the squid and cuttlefish, and classified as a MOLLUSC. It has eight arms, the true tentacles found in the squid being absent. The common octopus of European waters inhabits shallows where it hunts for

An octopus paralyses its prey with poison.

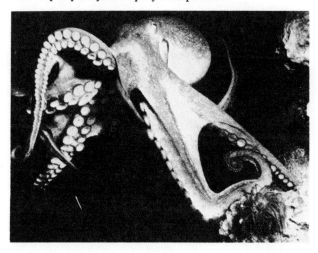

crabs. The giant ocean octopus can attain a total span of about 9.6 m (32 ft).

ODE

Type of poem which originated in ancient Greece, usually written to celebrate a victory or some religious festival, and also often set to music. Pindar (522–442 BC) was a great writer of this type of ode. The general spirit of the ode, as a poem for ceremonial occasions, survived until the early nineteenth century, when it became a much freer form of expression in the hands of the Romantic poets.

OERSTED, Hans Christian (1777–1851)

Danish scientist. He was a pioneer in the field of electro-magnetism, and was also the first to isolate the element aluminium.

OFFENBACH, Jacques (1819–80)

German-born composer who spent most of his life in Paris. He wrote many successful OPERETTAS, including *La Belle Hélène* and *Orpheus in the Underworld* from which comes the famous 'can-can'. His last work was *The Tales of Hoffman,* more serious in tone and closer to true opera.

OHM, Georg Simon (1787–1854)

German scientist. His main work was concerned with electricity, and he discovered the law of conduction. This Ohm's Law states that volts = current (amps) × resistance. The unit of electrical resistance is named after him.

OIL. *See* PETROLEUM

OKAPI

MAMMAL related to the GIRAFFE, but not so big and without the same long neck. Its coat, however, is distinctive; reddish-brown with black and white stripes on the legs. It is native to the tropical forests of central Africa, but it is a rare animal and is now protected.

OKINAWA

Volcanic island in the western Pacific Ocean, and the scene of bitter fighting between the United States and Japan in WORLD WAR II. After the war it became an American protectorate, but was restored to Japan in 1972.

OLYMPIC GAMES

International sports and ATHLETICS competition. The Games originated in ancient Greece, being held every fourth year at Olympia in honour of the god Zeus, from 776 BC to AD 394. They were revived in 1896, the first series of modern games being held at Athens. Today the Olympic Games embrace many sports, including winter sporting events. However, it is the athletics which remain the most important part of the Games. Since WORLD WAR I these have been held in the following cities: Antwerp (1920), Paris (1924), Amsterdam (1928), Los Angeles (1932), Berlin (1936), London (1948), Helsinki (1952), Melbourne (1956), Rome (1960), Tokyo (1964), Mexico City (1968), Munich (1972), Montreal (1976), Moscow (1980).

OMAN

Independent sultanate of south-eastern Arabia, with an area of 212,457 sq km (82,035 sq miles) but only 893,000 people. The capital is Muscat. The main product is oil.

OMAR KHAYYÁM (*c*. 1050–1123)

Persian poet, astronomer and mathematician. He helped to revise the calendar, compiled astronomical tables and developed algebra. However, he is now remembered for his poem *The Rubáiyát* which was first translated into English in 1859 by Edward Fitzgerald.

OMBUDSMAN

Government official who investigates complaints made against public authorities. The idea of such an official started in Sweden, and the word is Swedish, meaning 'legal representative'.

The flame lit for the 1976 Montreal Olympics

O'NEILL, Eugene Gladstone (1888–1954)

American dramatist whose plays are noted for the intense personal relationships they portray. Best known are the three related plays (trilogy) *Mourning Becomes Electra, The Iceman Cometh* and *Long Day's Journey into Night*.

OPERA

Combination of MUSIC and DRAMA. The two art forms had been combined in one way or another by the ancient Greeks, and in such medieval entertainments as the MIRACLE and MORALITY plays. But opera, as it is thought of today, started among a group of seventeenth-century Italian poets and musicians who called themselves the *Camerata* (Society). Their object, in fact, was to revive what they thought was the form and style of ancient Greek theatre. From these beginnings developed opera as consisting basically of sung dialogue (recitative) interspersed with individual songs (arias) or pieces for groups of singers (ensembles). Special types of opera, developed during the seventeenth and eighteenth centuries, were the Italian *opera buffa* (comic opera) and *opera seria* (serious or tragic opera); and the German *Singspiel* type of opera with spoken dialogue. During the nineteenth century there was grand opera, noted for its spectacle and its use of large choruses; also the special type of opera created by Richard WAGNER, and called by him music drama, which consisted of one continuous, unfolding stream of dramatic and musical ideas. The other principal operatic composers discussed in this encyclopedia are Vincenzo BELLINI, Benjamin BRITTEN, Gaetano DONIZETTI, Christoph Willibald GLUCK, George Frideric HANDEL, Leoš JANÁČEK, Jean-Baptiste LULLY, Claudio MONTEVERDI, Wolfgang Amadeus MOZART, Giacomo PUCCINI, Henry PURCELL, Jean-Philippe RAMEAU, Gioacchino ROSSINI, Richard STRAUSS, Giuseppe VERDI, and Carl Maria von WEBER.

OPERETTA

The word means 'little opera', and describes an entertainment generally much lighter both in spirit and in musical treatment than true opera. Operetta developed during the nineteenth century. Most examples of the form have spoken dialogue, and from them grew the stage musical which first became popular in the 1920s and 1930s. Composers of operettas discussed in this encyclopedia are Jacques OFFENBACH, Johann STRAUSS and Sir Arthur SULLIVAN.

OPOSSUM

Small group of MAMMALS, classed as MARSUPIALS, native to the American continent. They have the habit of rolling on to one side and feigning death when disturbed.

OPTICS

Branch of PHYSICS dealing with the subject of LIGHT and vision. The principles and development of the TELESCOPE and MICROSCOPE are two of the most important aspects of optics.

ORATORIO

Musical form similar in some respects to an OPERA, but nearly always dealing with a religious theme and not intended for performance in a theatre. The name is derived from the Oratory of St Philip Neri in Rome, where the first oratorios were performed early in the seventeenth century. The Passion is a special type of oratorio, setting to music the events leading to Christ's crucifixion as recounted in the New Testament gospels.

ORBIT

The path of an object in space which is controlled by gravitation. The Earth and other planets orbit round the sun. The moon, and satellites, orbit round the Earth. The orbit's curve is known as an ellipse. The nearest point of one orbiting body to another is known as the perigee, and the farthest point the apogee.

ORCHESTRA

A fairly large ensemble of musical instrumentalists. The orchestra, and the history of orchestral music, is considered to have started with the operas of Claudio MONTEVERDI. Its familiar composition, divided into the four basic groups of instruments – strings, woodwind, brass and percussion – dates from the second half of the eighteenth century and is especially connected with the work of Joseph HAYDN. The orchestra grew dramatically in size during the nineteenth century, from an ensemble of about thirty-five players to a company of well over a hundred. During the same period the composition of orchestral music, and the particular use made of individual instruments or groups of instruments, became increasingly the hallmark of a composer's own particular style. *See also* MUSICAL INSTRUMENTS.

ORE

Mineral mined or quarried for the extraction of a metal. Many ores, like those yielding iron and copper, occur in massive layers like beds of rock (strata). Others take the form of crystals lining fissures and cavities in the rocks. Such crystals are usually deposited by percolating water, but are sometimes derived from vapours and liquids of volcanic origin. Fissures thus filled with mineral ores are called 'veins' or 'lodes'. Among the metals obtained from them are tin and lead. Most ores consist of a combination of the metal with either sulphur or oxygen (and sometimes carbon as well).

ORGAN

Musical instrument which can be classed as a wind instrument, because the sounds are produced by the passage of air across pipes of varying sizes. At the same time, it has keyboards, which operate the flow of air to the pipes, so giving it a feature in common with all other KEYBOARD INSTRUMENTS. One of the earliest types of organ was the hydraulus, or

The grouping of instruments of the orchestra

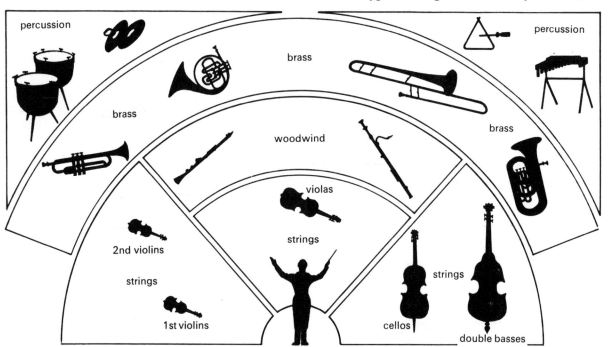

water organ, examples of which date back to the third century BC. Exactly how such an instrument worked is now a mystery. In the Middle Ages organs were often small enough to be carried about, but were tough to operate, the heavy, broad keys needing to be struck with the fist, while air was supplied through one or more sets of bellows. The standard organ has two basic sets of pipes, flue pipes and reed pipes. The choice between one set of pipes and the other, or between various combinations of the two, is determined by sets of levers called stops; while two or more keyboards actually operate the pipes. Most organs also have a pedal keyboard. Pedals, manual keyboards and stops constitute the organ console. The modern electric organ produces its sounds by electrical impulses, though these are usually designed to imitate a conventional organ.

ORKNEY ISLANDS

Group of islands lying just north of the Scottish mainland. They have a total area of 975 sq km (376 sq miles) and a population of about 17,000. The stretch of water within them called Scapa Flow was a naval base during WORLD WAR I and WORLD WAR II.

ORWELL, George (1905–50)

English writer, whose real name was Eric Arthur Blair. Many of his books are about the poor and down-trodden, but the two best-known are *Animal Farm,* a satire on communism, and *1984,* a prophetic book about political and technological control.

OSCILLOGRAPH

Electrical instrument for recording the patterns of electrical currents or sound waves.

OSMIUM

Metallic ELEMENT with the greatest density of all elements, and twice as heavy as lead. It is used to tip fountain pen nibs, and for electric light filaments.

OSMOSIS

Name given to the mingling of two fluids through porous membrane. It is the way oxygen enters the blood through the lungs, or the way that water is absorbed by the roots of a plant.

OSPREY

Large predatory bird of the HAWK family that feeds on fish. It has nested in Scotland in recent years.

OSTRICH

Flightless BIRD, also the largest, standing as high as 2.4 m (8 ft) and weighing 156 kg (345 lb). It is native to parts of Africa and Arabia. The South American rhea is similar to the ostrich, but has three toes to each foot while the ostrich has only two.

OTTER

MAMMAL belonging to the WEASEL family, but specially adapted for life in the water. It feeds

North American otter

on fish and eels. The freshwater otter is found in many parts of the world, including Great Britain. The sea otter is a heavier-built creature, now in danger of extinction after years of being hunted and killed for its fur.

OTTOMAN EMPIRE

Islamic empire founded by the Turkish sultan Osman I (1259–1326). By the sixteenth century, at the time of Suleiman the Magnificent, it covered much of the coastal region of North Africa, much of the Middle East, and the whole of south-eastern Europe almost as far as Vienna. The Ottoman navy suffered a serious defeat at the Battle of Lepanto (1571), and during the next three hundred years the empire gradually declined, both in size and power, being finally dissolved just after WORLD WAR I.

OVERTURE

Musical composition for the ORCHESTRA, taking its name from the French *ouverture* ('opening'), and usually written to open or commence an OPERA. But in the nineteenth century composers sometimes wrote concert-overtures as orchestral pieces in their own right.

OVID (Publius Ovidius Naso, 43 BC–AD 17)

Roman poet. Many of his poems, such as *Ars Amatoria* and *Metamorphoses*, are fanciful and far less serious than the work of other Roman poets like VIRGIL. But he had a big influence on many later writers of the Middle Ages and the RENAISSANCE.

OWL

Group of predatory BIRDS who usually hunt their prey at night. They have very distinctive faces, the large, round eyes both being in the front, enabling them to see clearly in the dark and to focus accurately on their prey. Two of the most familiar species are the barn owl (with

Short-eared owl with young

its evocative hoot) and the tawny owl. There is also the eagle owl, which is capable of catching a small antelope; and the beautiful snowy owl of the Arctic regions.

OXYGEN

ELEMENT usually in the form of a colourless gas; an essential ingredient of both air and water, and essential also for the respiration of all animals. It combines with most of the other elements and forms nearly 50% of the Earth's crust. Discovered by Joseph Priestley (1733–1804) and independently by Karl Scheele (1742–86).

OYSTER

Shellfish classed as a MOLLUSC and valued as a sea food. The pearl-bearing oyster is found in tropical and sub-tropical waters, the pearl being formed inside the shell as a result of some irritant action.

OZONE

Form of OXYGEN, created naturally by strong sunlight, which has 3 instead of 2 atoms to each MOLECULE. It can kill some germs and is a food preservative, but can also be dangerous in high concentrations.

P

PACIFIC OCEAN

The largest ocean, extending from the Bering Sea in the north to ANTARCTICA, and from the coasts of North and South AMERICA almost half way round the world to AUSTRALIA, the islands of south-east Asia, CHINA and JAPAN. Its total area is 165,200,000 sq km (63,800,000 sq miles). It also has a number of very deep trenches, the deepest being the Marianas Trench, east of the Philippines, which has a depth of 11,033 m (36,198 ft) – the deepest point in the world's oceans. The Pacific Ocean was given its name by Ferdinand MAGELLAN, because his first impression of it was one of peace and calm.

PAINTING

The application of some coloured pigment to a surface. It can be for purely practical purposes, such as the protection of the material beneath; but is generally understood to mean a form of decorative or expressive art. Prehistoric cave paintings have been found at places like LAS-CAUX in France, estimated to be 20,000 years old. Among the ancient civilizations the Egyptians were enthusiastic painters, most of their work being rendered on stone walls and pillars, either in tombs, or as pure decoration in their palaces and homes. European painting of the BYZANTINE period was religious and formal, and still mostly confined to walls. Paint pigments of this time were usually mixed with white of egg, and called tempera. When applied to wet wall plaster, which they often were in order to obtain a particular effect, the result was a fresco. The use of certain vegetable oils instead of tempera, which came about during the RENAISSANCE period, revolutionized painting techniques and styles. From then on portrait and landscape painting became more important than religious subjects, progressing through such styles as IMPRESSIONISM to the various expressionist, surrealist and abstract painting styles of this century.

Most oil painting is done on a prepared canvas or wooden board. Oil paints take several days to dry, and can be worked and re-worked on the canvas or other surface. Water colour painting requires a totally different technique. As the name implies, water is the fluid mixed with the pigments, while paper is the only suitable surface for the paints. Because the water quickly dries into the paper, the work itself has to be done quickly, and it is difficult to correct mistakes. Gouache paints are also water-soluble but stronger in colour and tone than true water colours. In this encyclopedia the work of the many artists who have produced great paintings is discussed under their individual entries.

Society Islands in the Pacific Ocean

PAKISTAN

Independent republic of southern Asia with an area of 803,943 sq km (310,421 sq miles) and a population of about 80 million. The capital is Islamabad; other cities are Karachi and Lahore. The River Indus flows north to south the entire length of the country, the ruins of the ancient Indus Valley civilization still to be seen in its vicinity. Despite the presence of this river, much of the land is dry and hard to cultivate in the hot climate, and the general standard of living is low. Pakistan was formerly joined with INDIA at the time of the British Empire. When India secured independence in 1947 Pakistan was created as a separate, Moslem state. In fact, it consisted of two provinces, West Pakistan and East Pakistan, separated by 1,600 km (1,000 miles) of Indian territory. In 1971 East Pakistan broke away from this union and the following year, after a period of civil strife, became the independent state of BANGLADESH.

PALAEONTOLOGY

Study of the evolution and structure of plants and animals through the evidence of FOSSIL

The Piltdown skull, found in 1913

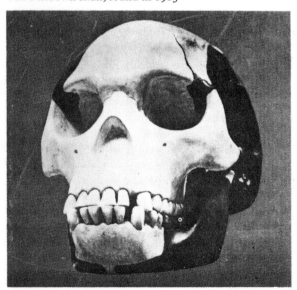

remains. Before the nineteenth century fossils were treated largely as curios and little serious thought was given to their origins or significance. The most exciting period of palaeontological research was in the second half of the nineteenth century, when fossil remains of many of the great DINOSAURS first came to light. There have also been some celebrated hoaxes, such as the case of Piltdown Man, a classification of prehistoric man based on the fossil remains of a skull, which was later found to be bogus.

PALESTINE

Name given to the ancient Biblical lands which, since 1947, have been divided between ISRAEL and JORDAN. The problem of re-settling the Arab inhabitants of the region, uprooted by the creation of the state of Israel, has been one of the causes of conflict between Israel and its Arab neighbours.

PALESTRINA, Giovanni Pierluigi da (c. 1526–94)

Italian composer, noted for the purity of his choral church music as expressed in such works as the *Missa Papae Marcelli* (Mass for Pope Marcellus). He also composed many motets and hymns, also some secular MADRIGALS.

PANAMA

Central American republic, 75,650 sq km (29,210 sq miles) in area with a population of nearly 2 million. The capital is Panama City. The most famous feature of the country is the Panama Canal which links the ATLANTIC and PACIFIC OCEANS at the narrowest point of the Central American isthmus. It is 80 km (50 miles) long, with 12 locks, and is used each year by about 15,000 ships. The Canal was opened in 1914. It is owned by the Panama Canal Company, although a treaty signed in 1977 has ensured that the United States will control the Canal until 1999.

PANCREAS

Organ in the body of most VERTEBRATES, including man, which produces digestive juices and the hormone INSULIN. In man the pancreas is about 18 cm (7 in) long and is situated behind and below the stomach.

PANDA

Small group of bear-like MAMMALS, native to parts of China, including Tibet. The giant panda is the celebrated member of the group, distinguished by its face of white fur with dark patches round the eyes. The creature lives almost entirely on bamboo shoots and is very difficult to rear in captivity. There is also the lesser panda, or cat bear, similar in appearance to a RACCOON.

The giant panda, found only in China

PANGOLIN

Small group of ant-eating MAMMALS native to parts of Africa and southern Asia. They have a protective coating of large spiny scales, hence another name for them is scaly anteater. When attacked they roll up like a hedgehog. They are nocturnal in habit.

PANTHER

Name sometimes given to various members of the CAT family, including the puma and the leopard.

The Babes in the Wood, from a pantomime of 1898

PANTOMIME

Originally a type of mimed drama based on the Italian *commedia dell'arte* with such traditional characters as Harlequin, Pantaloon and Columbine. Now a type of musical comedy show based on classic stories such as Cinderella and specially associated with the Christmas season.

PAPER

Substance made from fibrous plant material or basic wood pulp. The Chinese had produced a type of paper by the second century AD, although before this the Egyptians used strips of papyrus grass to make a somewhat similar material. Paper was introduced into Europe during the fourteenth century. Before this time the principal material for written work was dried animal skin called parchment.

PAPUA NEW GUINEA

The Independent State of Papua New Guinea includes the eastern part of NEW GUINEA and various smaller islands. The total area is 461,691 sq km (178,270 sq miles) and a population of 3,072,000. The capital is Port Moresby. The country became independent from Australia in 1975.

PARAGUAY

South American republic with an area of 406,752 sq km (157,056 sq miles) and a population of about 3 million. The capital is Asunción. The Paraguay river flows across the centre of the country. Cattle rearing, rice, cotton and tobacco cultivation are the main occupations.

PARLIAMENT

The word is derived from the old French *Parlement,* or speaking place, and is applied to many kind of legislative assembly, usually composed of elected representatives. Hence the West German *Bundestag* and the French National Assembly are types of parliament. The Parliament of Great Britain consists of the House of Commons and the House of Lords, nominally headed by the Monarch. The House of Commons is the important assembly. Its members are elected by universal SUFFRAGE, each member representing a constituency, or voting area. The political party which secures a majority of members at a general election (or a larger number of members than any other single party) forms the Government. Members of the Government are invariably also elected members of the House of Commons. Under the general leadership of the PRIME MINISTER, Government members propose matters of policy which are debated by the House of Commons. Proposed new laws have also to be debated by the House of Commons and then approved or rejected by a majority vote. The Chairman of the House of Commons, presiding

The Parliament of Edward I

over debates, is the SPEAKER. The corresponding post in the House of Lords is held by the LORD CHANCELLOR.

The history of the British Parliament has been a long story of its gradual ascendancy over the power of the Monarchy; and also of the ascendancy of the elected House of Commons over the non-elected House of Lords. Significant events in this process were Simon de Montfort's Parliament of 1265, which contained some elected representatives; and the execution of CHARLES I in 1649, which established the sovereign right of Parliament to order its own affairs. During the nineteenth and early twentieth centuries a series of electoral reforms extended the suffrage to new groups of people and also re-arranged constituencies so that each roughly represented the same number of electors. Other reforms increasingly curtailed the power of the House of Lords to oppose or reject legislation, until its role became one of modification and advice.

Parliament meets in a building called the Palace of Westminster. The previous premises were destroyed by fire in 1834. The present

Palace of Westminster dates from 1867. See also BALLOT, BIG BEN, CHANCELLOR OF THE EXCHEQUER, CONSERVATIVE PARTY, LAW, LABOUR PARTY, LIBERAL PARTY. The work of important British parliamentarians is discussed under individual entries.

PARSEC

Unit in ASTRONOMY adopted from the words *parallax* and *second* to measure the enormous distances between the stars. It is 3.26 light-years or 30,900,000,000,000 kilometres (19,200,000,000,000 miles) in length.

PARTHENON

Greek temple to the goddess Athena, on the Acropolis at Athens, built between 447 BC and 432 BC, under the supervision of the architect Pheidias. It was constructed of marble and is generally regarded as one of the world's greatest works of ARCHITECTURE. Parts of its frieze can be seen in the British Museum. These were acquired by Lord Elgin in 1806 and are usually referred to as the Elgin Marbles.

PASCAL, Blaise (1632–62)

French mathematician, scientist and philosopher. He contributed to the development of CALCULUS and to the mathematics of probability. As a philosopher his most famous work is his *Pensées*.

PASSION PLAY

Dramatic representation of the events leading up to the crucifixion of Jesus Christ. The most celebrated presentation of a Passion Play is that given at the village of Oberammergau in southern Germany.

PASSOVER

Jewish feast commemorating the deliverance of the ancient Israelites from Egyptian bondage, as recounted in the Old Testament of the BIBLE.

PASTEUR, Louis (1822–95)

French chemist. He investigated BACTERIA and developed the process of 'pasteurization' to sterilize foodstuffs against harmful bacteriological action. He also introduced vaccines to combat anthrax and rabies. The Pasteur Institute in Paris is one of the world's leading research centres.

PATHOLOGY

Branch of MEDICINE concerned with diseases, their symptoms and effects upon the body.

PAVLOV, Ivan Petrovich (1849–1936)

Russian physiologist. He conducted a famous series of experiments with dogs in connection with his work on that aspect of PSYCHOLOGY called the conditioned reflex. He rang a bell each time his dogs received food. After a time the dogs started to salivate as soon as they heard the bell even when food was not forthcoming.

Pavlov conducting an experiment with one of his dogs

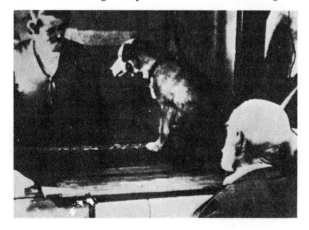

PEACOCK

BIRD native to India and other regions of southern Asia, but now kept in parks and zoos in many parts of the world on account of the male of the species which displays a magnificent fan-shaped tail in the mating season.

PEARY, Robert Edwin (1856–1920)

American arctic explorer. He led several expeditions to GREENLAND, and was the first man to reach the North Pole in 1909.

PEEL, Sir Robert (1788–1850)

He was PRIME MINISTER twice, but is best remembered today for his earlier work as Home Secretary when he established the Metropolitan Police Force, one of the first properly organized police forces anywhere. Its members were popularly known as 'Peelers'.

PENDULUM

Weight suspended from a fixed point by a string or rod and caused to swing to and fro. The time required for a complete swing is determined by the length of the string or rod and is independent of the size of the weight. The French scientist Jean FOUCAULT used a type of pendulum to demonstrate the rotation of the Earth.

PENGUIN

Group of flightless sea BIRDS native to the southern hemisphere and especially to Antarctic regions. There are fifteen species, ranging from the emperor penguin to the little penguin of Australia and New Zealand.

PENICILLIN. *See* ANTIBIOTICS

PEPYS, Samuel (1633–1703)

English diarist, born in London. Fame came to him posthumously in 1825 when his diary, written in cipher, was discovered amongst the papers that he bequeathed to Magdalene

Samuel Pepys with his diary

College, Cambridge. It is a most valuable source of information about social customs and habits of the RESTORATION period.

PERICLES (*c.* 490–429 BC)

Greek statesman and greatest leader of the city state of Athens. Though he was an able general during the wars with SPARTA, his finest achievements were domestic. He reformed the constitution and beautified Athens with many splendid buildings, including the PARTHENON.

Pericles

PERIODIC LAW

Dmitri MENDELEYEV in 1869 stated that properties of the ELEMENTS recurred in regular cycles in a list starting with the element of lowest atomic weight and progressing in consecutive order of atomic weight. Henry G. J. Moseley in 1913 showed that the important thing was atomic number, not atomic weight. On this basis all the elements can be arranged in order of increasing atomic number, i.e., number of protons in the nucleus, with elements of similar chemical properties in the same vertical columns. This is known as the periodic table and the theory on which it is based as the Periodic Law. The easiest example of the working of this law is that of the elements called HALOGENS – fluorine, chlorine, bromine, iodine, astatine – which are found in the same vertical column and have atomic numbers 9, 17, 35, 53 and 85 respectively.

PERU

South American republic with an area of 1,285,216 sq km (496,252 sq miles) and a population of about 17¾ million. The capital is Lima. It produces coffee, cotton, rice and sugar; there are also big deposits of coal, copper, iron ore, zinc, gold and petroleum. Peru was the home of the INCA civilization which was destroyed by Spanish conquest during the sixteenth century, though many Peruvians are of Inca descent.

PETER the Great (1672–1725)

Russian tsar. As a young man he toured Western Europe, including England, and encouraged cultural and commercial contacts between Russia and the West. Through war with Sweden he then secured a strip of land on the Baltic Sea and built there a new port and capital city – St Petersburg, now Leningrad. The city is noted for its spacious squares and splendid buildings, dating from Peter's time.

PETRARCH (Francesco di Petracco, 1304–74)

Italian poet and scholar. His lyrical love poems, the *Canzoniere,* and other poetic works had a

great influence on RENAISSANCE literature. Indeed, his poetic gifts were well recognized by his contemporaries and he was crowned as poet-laureate in Rome.

PETROLEUM

Mineral oil found trapped below the surface of the ground by a layer of dense rock. Bore-holes sunk through this layer release the oil, which then squirts up in 'gushers'. Crude petroleum is a thick, black oil, but it is refined into petrol, paraffin, lubricating oil and grease.

Drilling platform for oil in the North Sea

PETROLOGY

Branch of GEOLOGY which studies the origins of rocks. The description of the rocks themselves is usually termed petrography. Three main groups of rocks have been classified according to their origin, namely: igneous rocks, sedimentary rocks, and metamorphic rocks. Igneous rocks are of volcanic origin and are formed from consolidated magma. Sedimentary rocks are formed from materials broken down by such agents as running water, frost and changes of temperature. The resulting fragments are carried by water or wind to new places where they are deposited as sediments. Sedimentary rocks are also formed from such materials as shells and plants, and amongst the common forms of rock are sandstone, limestone and shale, as well as coal. Metamorphic rocks form large portions of the Earth's crust. They originated under conditions of great pressure or heat.

PHARAOH

The title of the kings of ancient EGYPT. The name actually describes the royal palace, and means 'great house'.

PHILIP II (1527–98)

Spanish king. He married the English queen Mary Tudor and after her death hoped for some time to marry her sister ELIZABETH I. His ambition was to restore Europe to the Catholic faith by becoming its most powerful monarch. For some years he successfully moved towards this goal, but dispersal of his ARMADA against England in 1588 was one of several events which marked the beginning of Spain's decline as a world power.

PHILIPPINES

Large group of islands in the Pacific Ocean with a total area of 300,000 sq km (115,837 sq miles) and a population of about 48 million. The largest islands are Luzon and Mindanao. The capital and chief port is Manila. Manila and the old capital, Quezon City, are on the island of Luzon. The chief products are coconuts, rice, sugar and mahogany which grows abundantly in the tropical forests. Ferdinand MAGELLAN reached the Philippines in 1521 and they became a Spanish colony until 1898. They then became a possession of the U.S.A. Independence was gained in 1946.

PHILOSOPHY

The word comes from the Greek and means 'love of wisdom'. The aims of philosophy are generally defined as inquiry into the principles of knowledge and awareness. Western philosophy has its roots in Greek systems of thought. The main branches are *ontology*, theory of the reality of existence; *epistemology*, theory of human knowledge; *aesthetics*, theory of beauty; *logic*, theory of accurate thinking; *ethics*, theory of human conduct. Ideas of science, religion, history and politics are all encompassed by these basic philosophical disciplines. In this encyclopedia the ideas of many great philosophers are discussed under their individual entries.

PHOENICIA

Ancient kingdom which flourished about 1000 BC and was centred on the eastern Mediterranean. The Phoenicians were great traders and established the city states of Tyre, Sidon and Byblos. They also founded such other famous cities as Carthage and colonies in Crete, Malta, Rhodes, Sicily and Spain.

PHOSPHOROUS

Chemical ELEMENT that is essential for plant and animal growth. White phosphorus combines with other elements and will easily ignite, therefore it is stored in water.

PHOTO-ELECTRIC CELL

Type of cell, usually in the form of a valve, which will conduct electrically when exposed to light. Modern photo-electric cells use thin films of potassium and other metals which also emit electrons under the action of light.

PHOTOGRAPHY

As long ago as the sixteenth century it was known that light had a peculiar action on silver chloride. It was also known that a small hole pierced in the darkened window of a room would admit rays of light to reproduce on a screen the view outside. The camera is a combination of these two scientific principles. Three men who played an important part in its development during the nineteenth century were W. H. Fox Talbot, Louis DAGUERRE and Joseph Nièpce.

Modern photography is based on the fact that when an optical image is thrown on to a plate or film coated with a suspension of silver

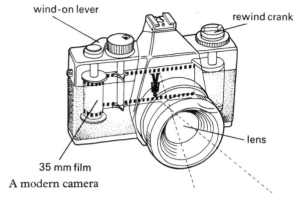

wind-on lever

rewind crank

lens

35 mm film

A modern camera

bromide in gelatine, a latent image is formed in the emulsion. This is result of the action of the light on the silver atoms. When the plate or film is immersed in what is termed a 'developer' the latent image is fixed, that is, further action on the silver atoms by light is stopped. Fixing is simply the removal of surplus bromide. The image which remains is the 'negative'. By taking a photo-copy of this on light-sensitive paper the process is reversed. The result, called a 'positive', is similar in all respects (except colour) to the original image.

There are two main types of colour photography. In the additive process the photograph is taken through a fine network of tiny filters, red, green and blue. In the subtractive process the film is made up of three layers sensitive to blue, green and red. After exposure each layer is processed to its complementary colour, dye being absorbed in proportion to the amount of silver deposited by the action of light.

PHOTOSYNTHESIS

Essential process of PLANT life in which water and carbon dioxide gas from the air are absorbed and converted into glucose sugar. Some of this is used immediately to help the plant grow. Some is stored in the leaves as starch. The process involves CHLOROPHYLL and takes place in the presence of sunlight. The word itself, derived from the Greek, means 'building up with light'. One other important feature of photosynthesis is the production of oxygen which the plant returns to the air.

PHYSICS

The science of matter and ENERGY and the relationship between them. In a broader sense, physics is concerned with the behaviour of matter, while CHEMISTRY is concerned with its composition. The main branches of physics, as they are dealt with in this encyclopedia, are ELECTRICITY, HEAT, LIGHT, MAGNETISM, MECHANICS and NUCLEAR ENERGY. The work of many great physicists is also discussed under their individual entries.

PIANO

Musical instrument classed as a KEYBOARD INSTRUMENT. The Italian Bartolommeo Cristofori is credited with the invention, during the early part of the eighteenth century, of the device which makes the piano different from other keyboard instruments – a hammer which can strike the appropriate string and bounce straight back, allowing the sound to be sustained. He called his early instruments of this type the *pianoforte* (soft-loud) to distinguish them from existing keyboard instruments like the HARPSICHORD. The piano – to use its usual abbreviated name – did not develop into the type of instrument we know today until towards the end of the nineteenth century. The two main types of modern piano are the grand piano, where the strings lie horizontally, and the upright piano, where instead the strings are

A Steinway concert grand piano

positioned vertically and are thus much more economical of floor space.

PICASSO, Pablo (1881–1973)

Spanish artist. His painting progressed through a number of distinctive styles, from such early styles as the so-called 'blue period', through CUBISM to near abstraction. The same developments can be seen in his ceramics and sculpture; and his influence on twentieth-century art has been profound. After the Spanish Civil War and the establishment of the FRANCO regime, Picasso went into voluntary exile, living mainly in the south of France. The bombing of the town of Guernica during the war inspired his most famous painting.

PICCARD, Auguste (1884–1962)

Belgian scientist. He made a number of balloon ascents into the stratosphere to investigate COSMIC RAYS. More recently his studies of deep-sea life, made in a bathysphere, aroused great interest.

PIERO della Francesca (c. 1420–92)

Italian artist. He painted frescoes in Florence and at Loretto, and was one of the first artists to paint in oils. He has been described as the greatest geometrician of his day, making many advances in the use of perspective in painting. Thus he exerted a great influence on the development of RENAISSANCE art.

PIG

Group of MAMMALS found in many parts of the world. They are distinguished by their snout, which most species use to dig into the ground for roots. Varieties of wild pig include the warthog of southern Africa and the European boar, once widely distributed but now mainly limited to wildlife reserves. There are several varieties of domestic pig, bred in many countries for their meat (pork, ham and bacon).

The Baptism of Christ by Piero della Francesca

PIGEON

Group of BIRDS, widely distributed throughout the world, and including doves. Varieties include the wood pigeon, pouter pigeon, racing pigeon, turtle dove and collared dove. The most familiar variety of all, the feral pigeon, seen in towns and cities almost everywhere, is descended from a wild species called the rock pigeon.

PISSARRO, Camille (1830–1903)

French artist. He was born in the West Indies, but moved to Paris as a young man, becoming a leading exponent of the Impressionist school of painting.

PITCAIRN ISLAND

Remote island in the South Pacific Ocean administered by Britain and New Zealand. The mutineers from HMS *Bounty* landed there in 1790 and some of their descendants are among the tiny population of about 100.

PITMAN, Sir Isaac (1813–97)

He developed the best-known system of shorthand, based on phonetics (the sounds of words) and therefore adaptable to many languages.

PITT, William, 1st Earl of Chatham (1708-78)

English statesman. He was known as the 'Great Commoner' for his championship of constitutional rights for the House of Commons. As PRIME MINISTER he presided over triumphant British campaigns in India and Canada. His son, William Pitt the Younger (1759–1806), was also Prime Minister, first instituting many domestic reforms then leading his country during some periods of the Napoleonic Wars.

William Pitt the Younger

PLANCK, Max (1858–1947)

German scientist. His QUANTUM THEORY about the nature of energy places him with Albert EINSTEIN as one of the founders of modern physics.

PLANET

Small, solid body which revolves round the sun. Unlike stars, planets do not make their own light but reflect that of the sun. There are nine planets of different sizes circling at varying distances from the sun: MERCURY, VENUS, EARTH, MARS, JUPITER, SATURN, URANUS, NEPTUNE and PLUTO. *See also* SOLAR SYSTEM.

PLANETARIUM

A dome-like building on to whose ceiling is projected, by means of a special optical device, a replica of the northern or southern night sky. The apparatus can show not only the positions of stars and planets, but also their movements.

PLANKTON

Minute plant and animal organisms found in water, a source of food for many species of fish, and also for whales. During the past few years research has been carried out to increase the quantity of plankton as a fish food and to find out if it can also be used as a food for human beings.

PLANT

Living organism that conforms to some or all of the following characteristics: manufactures its own food by PHOTOSYNTHESIS; continues growing in size up to its death due to the fact that old tissue remains and new tissue is constantly added; has CELLS with rigid or semi-rigid walls; has no means of independent locomotion except by growth. The main groups of plant are: *thallophytes* (BACTERIA, FUNGI, ALGAE and SEAWEEDS); *bryophytes* (mosses and liverworts);

pteridophytes (ferns); *spermatophytes* (TREES, shrubs and GRASSES, which includes all flowering plants). *See also* BOTANY.

PLASTIC

Man-made material mainly produced from PETROLEUM derivatives and the by-products of coal. Moulding of one sort or another is an essential part of the manufacturing process. There are two main groups. *Thermoplastics* soften when heated and harden when cooled without undergoing further chemical change. They include cellulose acetate and acrylic resins such as 'perspex', NYLON, polythene and polystyrene. *Thermosetting* plastics do undergo change when subjected to heat or pressure. The most important plastic of this group is phenol formaldehyde resin which is moulded into such items as telephone receivers and electric light switches. The first plastic material, celluloid, was produced by the British chemist Alexander Parkes in 1865. *See also* POLYMER.

Moulding plastic cups

PLATINUM

Heavy silver-white metal that is more costly than gold, first discovered in 1557. It makes a valuable alloy, especially with iridium.

PLATO (427–347 BC)

Greek philosopher, born in Athens. He studied under SOCRATES and travelled in Italy, Sicily and Egypt. About 388 BC he opened his ACADEMY in Athens. Among his students was ARISTOTLE. Plato wrote many works, all in the form of dialogues. The most important of these is the *Republic*, in which he put forward his ideal state. In this, men were to be permanently divided into three social classes – the guardians who would rule, the soldiers and the workers.

PLATYPUS, Duckbilled

MAMMAL native to rivers and streams in parts of Australia and Tasmania. Although classed as a mammal, it has many unique features, including a duck-like beak and webbed feet. Also, it lays eggs.

PLEBISCITE

Type of national consultation, involving a BALLOT, on some particular issue; not the same as an election. Another name for it is referendum.

PLIMSOLL LINE

Another name for this is the 'loading line'. It is a line or lines on the side of a ship to show the depth she may be loaded to safely. It takes its name from Samuel Plimsoll (1824–98).

PLUTARCH (*c.* AD 46–120)

Greek historian and biographer. His most famous work, the *Parallel Lives*, gives biographical details of twenty-three Romans and twenty-three Greeks, arranged in pairs. They have provided the sources for the plots of many well-known dramas, including some of SHAKESPEARE'S plays.

PLUTO

PLANET of the SOLAR SYSTEM with an equatorial diameter of about 6,000 km (3,700 miles) and an average distance from the SUN of 5,900 million km (3,700 million miles). It has a very elliptical orbit. Pluto is the outermost planet of the solar system and was only discovered this century. Some astronomers think that Pluto may be an escaped moon of NEPTUNE; but in fact very little is known about Pluto.

PNEUMATICS

Branch of MECHANICS as applied to the behaviour of gases.

POETRY

Literature in which special techniques are employed to give sound patterns. Lyrics are usually short and are songs without music. BALLADS are stories in verse. Idylls and epics are long narrative poems usually with heroic themes. ODES are lyrics with strong feeling and are often addressed to a person or object. Elegies are melancholy poems, often mourning someone's death. The rhythm of a poem depends on the metre. Rhymes are the repetition of sounds at the ends of lines. *See also* SONNET.

POLAND

East European republic with an area of 312,677 sq km (120,732 sq miles) and a population of about 35½ million. The capital is Warsaw; other important cities are Lodz, Krakow and Gdansk (Danzig). The River Vistula flows right across the country from south to north, and most of the land is a gently undulating plain. Poland is still largely agricultural, with substantial crops of wheat, barley, sugar beet and potatoes; but since WORLD WAR II there has been a big increase in heavy industry. In the seventeenth century Poland was a powerful country, occupying territory that included the Ukraine. During the eighteenth century, however, the land was divided between Russia, Austria and Prussia, and Poland ceased to exist as an independent state. Independence was restored after World War I. The German attack on Poland in September 1939 was the opening event of World War II. After that war, new frontiers were defined for Poland which incorporated a good deal of former German territory. The country then adopted a Communist form of government and in 1949 it became a founder member of the Council for Mutual Economic Assistance (COMECON).

POLAR BEAR. *See* BEAR

POLECAT

MAMMAL related to the WEASEL and the ferret, and native to Europe and parts of Asia. It has a dark brown coat with white on the underside and white tips to the ears. It is savage and kills poultry.

POLITICS

The word comes from the Latin *politia*, meaning 'policy', and politics is generally defined as the science or art of government. Politics have played an increasing part in human affairs since men and women first organized themselves into societies, and most of history is an account of politics in one form or another. There were brief periods of relatively free or representative government during the Greek and Roman eras. But until the seventeenth century, politics was mostly the concern of absolute monarchs or other people in positions of high authority such as church leaders. Often they indulged in little more than personal struggles for power. The rise of political parties during the seventeenth and eighteenth centuries heralded the concept of government by consent rather than force. However, political parties can still be used to project people into positions of absolute authority, as was demonstrated by the rise of the National Socialist German Workers' Party (Nazi Party) which carried Adolf HITLER to power. Countries with some form of representative (democratic) government, such as Great Britain, France and the United States, try to guard against such abuses of power, through written constitutions or long established traditions. But the control of political power is always difficult. *See also* CONGRESS, CONSERVATIVE PARTY, DEMOCRACY, DEMOCRATIC PARTY, LABOUR PARTY, LIBERAL PARTY, PARLIAMENT, PRESIDENT, REPUBLICAN PARTY.

POLO

There are two games called polo. The first is played on horseback, but is otherwise similar to the game of HOCKEY. The other is water polo, played in a swimming pool, with rules similar to those of BASKETBALL.

POLYMER

Chemical compound composed of chains of interlocking MOLECULES, almost like one giant molecule. PLASTICS are made from polymers.

POPE

The Bishop of Rome and head of the ROMAN CATHOLIC CHURCH. He is regarded by Catholics as the spiritual successor of St Peter and the true representative of Christ on earth. The traditional home of the Papacy (the office of Pope) is the Vatican City in Rome, though there was a period, during the fourteenth century, when the Papacy moved to Avignon in southern France for political reasons; and another brief period soon after when there were two rival claimants to the office. The Pope is now elected by a college of cardinals. An outstanding Pope of modern times was John XXIII (held office from 1958–63) who convened the Second Vatican Council and heralded a great period of reform within the Church. *See also* GREGORY I.

POPE, Alexander (1688–1744)

English poet and essayist. He was a leading exponent of the Classical style in English literature, modelling much of his work on the poets of Greek and Roman times. The mock epic and satirical *The Rape of the Lock* is his most celebrated work. He also undertook translations of Homer's own two great epics *Iliad* and *Odyssey*.

PORCELAIN

Form of pottery which is the finest kind of chinaware. It is white throughout and seems to be translucent. A kind of porcelain has been made in China for the last three thousand years, and by AD 700 it had reached perfection. It was not produced in Europe until about AD 1500. Famous porcelain factories are Chelsea, Spode, Wedgwood, Worcester and Derby in England, Limoges in France, and Meissen in Germany. *See also* POTTERY.

PORPOISE

Sea MAMMAL related to the WHALE. Porpoises travel in 'schools', and make long, curving leaps out of the water. They are sometimes confused with DOLPHINS, but they do not possess the latter's beak.

PORTUGAL

European republic on the western side of the Iberian peninsula with an area of 92,082 sq km (35,555 sq miles) and a population of about 10 million. The capital is Lisbon, and the chief port is Oporto. The most famous product of the country is port wine. During the fourteenth and fifteenth centuries Portuguese navigators, such as Bartholomew DIAZ and Vasco da Gama, were some of the greatest explorers of their time, and Portugal was an important maritime power with a large overseas empire. BRAZIL remained a colony until 1820. For much of this century the country was governed by a form of dictatorship. In 1974 there was a revolution, and a more democratic type of republic came into being. At the same time, Portugal granted independence to its remaining colonies, mostly in Africa. The MADEIRA ISLANDS and the Azores, however, remain Portuguese provinces.

POTASH

Name given to potassium carbonate when it is used commercially. It is prepared from the mineral ore *sylvite*, a compound of potassium and chloride, and is used as a fertilizer and for making glass.

POTASSIUM

Silver-white metallic ELEMENT. It is a valuable fertilizer and is also used in medicines. As caustic potash (potassium hydroxide) it is used in the manufacture of ceramics, soaps, dyes, glass and detergents.

POTTERY

General term for objects made from baked clay. Pottery is one of mankind's oldest crafts, examples of which have been found dating back more than 6,000 years. Some interesting examples of early pottery are clay tablets found in the region of MESOPOTAMIA bearing written inscriptions. This ancient pottery had to be modelled by hand. The craft was revolutionized by the invention of the potter's wheel, again probably in Mesopotamia, about 4,000 BC. From then on it became very much easier to shape clay into drinking vessels, vases and other containers. The traditional way of making pottery is to mould the clay to the required shape and to bake it in a special type of oven called a kiln; then to dip the objects into a specially prepared glaze and bake again. The finest type of pottery is PORCELAIN. The simplest examples are sometimes called earthenware.

PREHISTORY

The entire period of the Earth's history before the first written records; more especially the age of man's direct ancestors, starting about 2 million years ago and continuing up to the time of the earliest human inscriptions which date from about 5,000 BC.

Potter throwing a jug

PRE-RAPHAELITE BROTHERHOOD

Name adopted by a group of nineteenth-century British artists who wished to revive styles of painting, decoration and literature before the time of the Italian artist RAPHAEL. To a large extent they were reacting against what they saw as the ugliness produced by the INDUSTRIAL REVOLUTION. Their chief sources of inspiration were Gothic architecture and stained glass, and medieval legends such as the Arthurian legends with their mixture of chivalry and mysticism. The leading members of the group were Dante Gabriel Rossetti,

Holman Hunt, Ford Maddox Brown and Edward Burne-Jones.

The Golden Stairs by Burne-Jones

PRESIDENT

Title given to the head of state or chief executive of most political republics. In some cases a president may be a virtual dictator. In others, he merely represents his country, as does the monarch in a constitutional monarchy. In other cases again, the president will exercise real political power, as defined by a constitution. This is the case with the President of the UNITED STATES. Unlike the British PRIME MINISTER, the American President is elected directly to office. The period of office is four years, and no president may hold office for more than two consecutive periods.

PRIMATE

The highest order of MAMMALS, which includes *homo sapiens* (man). APES, MONKEYS, LEMURS and tarsiers are included in this order.

PRIME MINISTER

The leading member of the government in some republics (with a president as head of state) and in most constitutional monarchies. The first British Prime Minister to be so named was Sir Robert Walpole (1676–1745) who presided over the ministerial CABINET in place of George I, who could speak no English. However, the official title of the leading government minister continued to be First Lord of the Treasury up until 1917. The British Prime Minister is not elected directly to office, like the Presidents of France or the United States. He is first the elected leader of a political party, and only assumes office when his party obtains a majority of seats in the House of Commons (*see* PARLIAMENT). The monarch remains head of state, while the Prime Minister assumes overall responsibility for government policy. A government, and therefore a Prime Minister, may not remain in office for more than five years without a general election. However, an election may be held within that period if he so decides.

PRINTING

The transfer of an image from one surface to another. As early as 2500 BC the Sumerians had devised a way of printing on soft clay with engraved rollers. Another early printing device, widely used by the Chinese, was the wooden block, whose carved surface image was inked and then transferred to paper or some other similar surface. But printing as the term is generally understood today dates back to the fifteenth century and the invention of movable type – little blocks of individual letters which could be assembled into words and sentences for printing, then broken up and re-assembled into a new text. The first printer to use movable type was the German Johann GUTENBERG, and his techniques were soon taken up by others, including the Englishman William CAXTON. Printing from movable type revolutionized the spread of knowledge and information. This type of printing, where the raised image of the letter (or illustration) comes into direct contact with the paper (or other printing surface) is called letterpress; and with various modifications and improvements, letterpress printing has continued to the present day. However, there are other important printing techniques, including LITHOGRAPHY; and today a great deal of printing is done with the aid of photo-setting techniques, which dispense entirely with movable type.

The design of letters for printing, called typefaces, is an important aspect of the subject. Many famous printers or typographers have designed typefaces which they considered clear and pleasing to the eye; and an essential part of newspaper, magazine and book production is the selection of a typeface, or combination of typefaces, suitable for the work in question. This encyclopedia is set in Plantin.

The machine on which this book was printed

PRIVY COUNCIL

Originally this was a council of advisers to the monarch. When PARLIAMENT grew in size and importance the Council then met with the monarch separately and in private, hence the name. The monarch still formally presides over some of the Council meetings, but most of the real work is done by individual Council committees, presided over the the Lord President of the Council. All members of the CABINET are members of the Privy Council, but others may also be recruited. They are addressed as Right Honourable.

PROKOFIEV, Sergei (1891–1953)

Soviet Russian composer and pianist. For some years after the RUSSIAN REVOLUTION he lived abroad, writing music that was generally regarded as advanced for its time. Then he returned to the Soviet Union and started to compose in a more 'popular' style, works from this period of his career including the ballet *Cinderella* and the orchestral piece with narrator *Peter and the Wolf*.

PROTEIN

Chemical compound containing nitrogen, essential to the cells of animals and plants. Proteins have an important job to do in the maintenance of tissues and cells of the body. Lean meat, fish, cheese and eggs all provide proteins to the human diet.

PROTON

Part of the nucleus of the ATOM that carries one unit of positive electricity.

PROTOPLASM

Living substance that is the basis of life and is contained in all plant and animal cells.

PROTOZOA

Simplest kind of animal. Some scientists do not class this one-celled member of the sub-kingdom *Protozoa* as an animal at all, but put it with one-celled plants in the kingdom *Protista*.

PROUST, Marcel (1871–1922)

French writer whose work consists almost entirely of a series of novels which are called collectively *À la recherche du temps perdu* (Remembrance of Things Past). These represent a deep and detailed recollection of childhood and have influenced the work of many other twentieth-century writers.

PSYCHOANALYSIS

Method of discovering and treating the causes of mental sickness or abnormality, founded by Sigmund FREUD. It is largely a painstaking process, continued over a period of a year or more, of question and answer between psychoanalyst and patient until certain troublesome thoughts or feelings in the unconscious mind are revealed. The belief is that the revelation of such thoughts and feelings will bring mental relief.

PSYCHOLOGY

Science of the mind. Among the ancient Greeks ARISTOTLE gave thought to the condition of the mind as something distinct from the rest of the physical body; though from his day and continuing for hundreds of years, 'mind' was usually thought of more in the spiritual sense of soul and was not considered in a very scientific light. True psychological studies do not date back much more than two hundred years, but they play a big role in society today, as applied to education, industry and advertising. In these fields psychologists are usually considering people's minds in the context of general and collective behaviour. The branch of psychology that studies mental illness and abnormality is psychiatry. Sigmund FREUD was a pioneer in this field of research, devising a form of treatment called PSYCHOANALYSIS. Two early disciples of Freud who went on to create their own schools of psychiatry were Alfred Adler and Carl JUNG.

PTOLEMY (c. AD 170)

Greek-Egyptian astronomer and mathematician. In his work *Almagest* ('The Great System'), he placed the spherical planet Earth at the centre of a universe of stars, planets, sun and moon, and so provided the basis for astronomical thought up to the time of COPERNICUS.

PUERTO RICO

Island of the West Indies, 8,897 sq km (3,435 sq miles) in area with a population of about 3½ million. The capital is San Juan. It was a Spanish possession for 400 years; then ceded to the United States in 1898. It has local self-government.

PUCCINI, Giacomo (1858–1924)

Italian composer, almost exclusively of operas, including *La Bohème, Madame Butterfly* and *Tosca*. He also contributed to a type of Italian opera called *verismo* (realism), in the sense that it presented a true picture of some aspects of life rather than a theatrical fabrication.

PULSAR

Objects that may be small stars composed of neutrons, that send out radio waves in a regular rhythm. Some of them may also send out X-RAYS and light waves. Pulsars were first discovered in 1967.

PUMICE

Light-weight porous stone that results when lava from a volcano cools and is used as an abrasive cleaner.

PUNIC WARS

Series of wars covering the period 264–146 BC between Rome and Carthage. In the Second Punic War, HANNIBAL made use of elephants when he crossed the ALPS with his armies to attack Rome from the north. The eventual outcome of these conflicts was victory for Rome.

PURCELL, Henry (1659–95)

English composer. He wrote the first great English opera, *Dido and Aeneas,* and much other music for the stage, including incidental music to *The Fairy Queen* which was an adaptation of Shakespeare's *A Midsummer Night's Dream.* He was also organist at Westminster Abbey.

PURITANS

Protestant religious group or sect which advocated extreme simplicity in matters of worship and a strict moral code. The movement began during the reign of ELIZABETH I, and it was persecution by CHARLES I that led some of them, now known as the Pilgrim Fathers, to sail to America in the *Mayflower.* Puritan support helped Oliver CROMWELL and the Parliamentarians to victory in the Civil War; after the restoration of CHARLES II persecution was resumed for some time. Two famous Puritan writers were John BUNYAN and John MILTON.

PUSHKIN, Alexander (1799–1837)

Russian writer, and the first to be widely recognized outside his own country. His best-known works are the drama *Boris Godunov,* the romantic novel *Eugene Onegin* and the heroic poem *Russlan and Ludmilla.* He had a big influence on Russian writers who came after him, and was also a major source of inspiration to Russian composers.

PYRAMID

Building constructed according to basic geometric principles. Pyramid-shaped buildings have been constructed in various places, but the most celebrated are those in Egypt built between about 2700 and 1900 BC as tombs for the PHARAOHS. The biggest is the Great Pyramid of Cheops which covers an area of 52,500 sq m (13 acres) and is 146 m (481 ft) high.

The Great Pyramids, Egypt

PYRENEES

Range of mountains stretching from the Bay of Biscay to the Mediterranean Sea and providing a perfect natural frontier between France and Spain. The highest point is Mt Aneto, 3,405 m (11,170 ft).

PYTHAGORAS (*c.* 582–*c.* 507 BC)

Greek mathematician and philosopher. He is best known for his contributions to geometry, especially his famous theorem. He also studied the theory of numbers in his search for an explanation of the universe, and by so doing discovered a significant relationship between mathematics and musical pitch.

Q

QATAR

Independent Arab sheikdom on the Persian Gulf with an area of 11,000 sq km (4,247 sq miles) and a population of about 247,000. The capital is Doha. The country's economy depends almost entirely on oil.

Iohn the Quaker
Le Trembleur de Londre.

QUAKERS, or The Society of Friends

Protestant religious sect, similar in aims and origins to the PURITANS, and founded by the Englishman George Fox. The name Quaker was first used as a term of derision, but was soon generally accepted, though Society of Friends remains the official title. The basic Quaker belief is in an 'inner light' that can guide the individual to spiritual understanding without any ritual or established form of worship. Another celebrated Quaker was William Penn who established a community in America during the seventeenth century and gave his name to the state of Pennsylvania.

QUANTUM THEORY

Theory postulated by Max PLANCK that radiant energy does not exist as a continuous stream but in tiny sections or units, each called a quantum. This theory, developed by Albert EINSTEIN, Niels BOHR and others has proved to be one of the foundations of atomic physics.

QUARTZ

Crystalline form of SILICA and one of the main constituents of such rocks as GRANITE. It forms about 35% of the Earth's crust. Fused quartz is used to make lenses.

QUASAR

A source of intense radio activity, estimated to exist at an immense distance away in space. The first was detected in 1961, and several more have been registered since, but their exact nature remains uncertain.

QUININE

A bitter tasting medicine taken from the bark of the cinchoda tree. It is the traditional treatment for MALARIA and other fevers.

A Quaker in the 18th century

R

RABBIT

Group of MAMMALS similar to RODENTS but not strictly belonging to that order. Instead they are classed with hares as lagomorphs. The rabbit is both a domestic pet and regarded as a pest by farmers in many countries. The long-haired angora is bred for its wool.

RABELAIS, François (c. 1490–1553)

French writer. He was a theological student and medical doctor and a man of great learning, but his two stories of fantasy, *Gargantua* and *Pantagruel* are works of satire and robust humour. The title of the first has produced the adjective 'gargantuan', while the spirit of both has inspired the adjective 'Rabelaisian' to describe a full-blooded love of life.

RACCOON

MAMMAL native to North America, about the size of a large cat, with distinctive dark stripes of fur across its eyes and a large striped tail. It eats practically anything, hunting mostly at night, and has the other distinctive feature of washing its food in water before eating. A slightly different species, the crab-eating raccoon, is found in South America.

RACHMANINOV, Sergei (1873–1943)

Russian composer and pianist, best known for his symphonies and piano concertos, plus the *Rhapsody on a Theme of Paganini,* written in a generally late-Romantic, melancholy style.

RACINE, Jean (1639–99)

French dramatist. He modelled his plays on stories and legends of Classical antiquity, developing a style that paid special attention to the delivery of the French language.

RADAR

The word is made up from the original title *Radio Detection and Ranging,* and is a system involving the transmission and reflection of radio waves. By directing a radio wave along a particular beam and registering its return, converted into visible pulses on a screen by a CATHODE RAY TUBE, the presence of any object along its path can be located. Radar was developed by a team of British scientists led by Robert Watson-Watt before WORLD WAR II and first used during the Battle of Britain to locate the approach of enemy aircraft. Today it has been adapted for navigational use by aircraft and ships, and can also give warning of approaching storms.

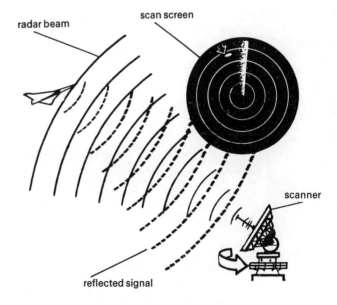

A radar screen picks up an incoming aircraft

RADIOACTIVITY

The splitting up or disintegration of the nucleus of an ATOM, which causes the emission of a shower of electron particles, called radiation. These consist of alpha, beta and gamma rays. Some substances are naturally radioactive, one of these, and the first to be discovered, being radium. In such cases, once the nucleus of the atom has split and lost some of its original material, it becomes the nucleus of a different element. In radium the atomic nuclei thus change from one element to another until all radioactivity has ceased. With radium the final result of the process is non-radioactive lead. Radioactivity can be induced artificially by the bombardment of atomic nuclei by other nuclear particles in such a device as the CYCLOTRON, and in this way elements can be converted into other artificial elements called ISOTOPES. These have widespread use in medicine, agriculture and many other fields of research. *See also* NUCLEAR ENERGY and GEIGER COUNTER.

Remote controls for handling radioactive material

RADIOASTRONOMY

Branch of ASTRONOMY which investigates RADIO WAVES from space. The most powerful optical telescopes can just perceive objects an estimated 2,000 million light years away; but specially designed radio receivers, or radio telescopes, can receive radio signals from sources which are an estimated 10,000 million light years distant, or five times as far. At the same time, radio telescopes can detect the existence of objects, or clouds of inter-stellar dust or gas, which emit no light and are therefore invisible to an optical telescope. Certain NEBULAE have been identified in this way. Also, radio telescopes have detected the presence of stars and other matter previously obscured by dark nebulae or dust clouds. The most powerful source of radio waves yet received comes from two galaxies in collision. This source, known as Cygnus-A, is an estimated 270 million light years away (not so distant by radioastronomy standards) and is emitting the equivalent of 1,000 million, million, million, million, million kilowatts. Thus the many discoveries of radio astronomy have completely revolutionized ideas about the size, the nature and the age of the universe. *See also* COSMOLOGY, PULSAR, QUASAR.

RADIO-CARBON DATING

Method of assessing the age of dead organic matter from the proportion of the carbon-14 ISOTOPE it contains. This radioactive isotope is created quite naturally by COSMIC RAYS in living matter. When the plant or animal dies, the isotope begins to disintegrate, or 'decay'. By measuring the extent of this decay, in relation to the known rate of carbon-14 decay, it is possible to assess with accuracy the age of the plant or animal. This method is of great value in assessing the age of such items as papyrus scrolls (made from plant matter) or mummified bodies. It is not so reliable for objects which are known to be more than 20,000 years old. *See also* ARCHAEOLOGY, RADIOACTIVITY.

RADIOLOGY

Use of various forms of radiation in the diagnosis and treatment of injuries and disease. An important type of radiation employed is that of X-RAYS. In diagnostic radiology X-rays reveal bone fractures, the presence of foreign bodies in the anatomy, or the development of diseases like tuberculosis or cancer. This diagnostic use of X-rays can take the form either of radioscopy, whereby a fluorescent screen registers the passage of X-rays through the body under examination; or of radiography, which records a photographic plate of the X-ray examination. In radiotherapy X-rays and other forms of radiation are used to combat disease, especially to destroy the abnormal cells of cancer.

RADIO-SONDE

High-altitude balloon carrying radio equipment which broadcasts signals during its ascent. The pressure, temperature and humidity of the atmosphere are calculated from the frequency of the radio signals. A separate waveband is used for determining the speed and altitude of the balloon.

RADIO WAVES

Radio waves are waves of electromagnetic energy which travel through space at the speed of LIGHT. They were predicted by James Clerk MAXWELL. The possibility of transmitting radio signals through space and receiving them again at another point was first demonstrated in 1887 by the German scientist Heinrich Hertz. The first transmission of a message by radio was achieved by the Italian Guglielmo MARCONI in 1897 when he transmitted morse signals over a distance of about 5 km (3 miles). In 1901 Marconi succeeded in transmitting a similar morse signal from Cornwall to Newfoundland.

Radio waves, like SOUND waves, operate on many different frequencies, and are divided into long and short waves, depending on their wavelength. Hence many radio transmissions can be made simultaneously, and without mutual interference, each occupying its own frequency, or waveband.

Radio waves transmit broadcasts to listeners

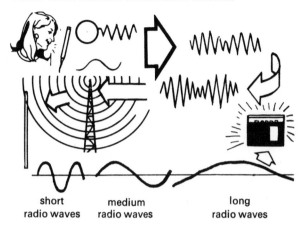

short radio waves   medium radio waves   long radio waves

RAILWAYS

System of transportation involving movement along a raised track. Before the construction of relatively smooth and even road surfaces, and the invention of the pneumatic tyre, trucks or carriages designed to run along a specially prepared track provided an efficient form of transport. As early as the sixteenth century stretches of wooden track were built in many parts of Europe, mostly in the vicinity of mines, along which men pushed or horses pulled trucks laden with coal or mineral ore. However, railways as we generally think of them began in Great Britain. In 1801 the Surrey Iron Railway, with horse-drawn trucks, was opened for the transport of goods. In 1809 Richard Trevithick opened a circular section of track near the present Euston station in London to demonstrate his steam locomotive *Catch Me Who Can*. In 1813 the steam locomotive *Puffing Billy* was used in a Durham colliery. And in 1825 was opened the Stockton and Darlington Railway, the world's first steam-hauled public railway company for passengers and goods. The steam engine used was called *Locomotion*, designed by George STEPHENSON who a few years later was joint designer of the more celebrated *Rocket*. The first railway to be opened in France was in 1828; in the United States in 1830; and in Germany in 1835.

Great Britain also led the way with underground railways. The very first section of underground track, from Bishop's Road, Paddington, to Farringdon Street in London, was opened in 1863, with steam locomotives and open trucks.

The first electric locomotive, designed by the German Werner von Siemens, was demonstrated in 1879, and electric traction, especially for the underground, was introduced soon after. However, most railways continued to be steam-hauled until the 1950s when wholesale conversion to electric or diesel motive power was made. There have been many experiments with monorail (single railtrack) units, but none have yet come into general use. The longest single stretch of railway, begun in 1891, is the Trans-Siberian Railway—from Moscow to Nakhodka near Vladivostok, a distance of 9,335 km (5,800 miles). The all-time speed record for a steam locomotive was set by the British London and North Eastern Railway Company engine *Mallard* in 1938 with a speed of 201 km/h (126 mph). The speed record for an electric locomotive was set up by the US Federal Railroad in 1974 with a speed of 376.9 km/h (234.2 mph).

RAINBOW

Multi-coloured arc seen in the sky when sunlight passes through raindrops and is split up into the colours of the visible SPECTRUM. Sometimes there appears a second image of the rainbow, reflected by the raindrops. In this case the order of the colours is reversed.

RALEIGH, Sir Walter (*c*. 1552–1618)

English explorer. During the reign of ELIZABETH I he organized expeditions to North America, which resulted in the introduction to Britain of tobacco and potatoes. He also named one of his new colonies Virginia in honour of the Queen. With the accession of James I he fell

An early steam locomotive

THE PLANET LOCOMOTIVE, 1830

Sir Walter Raleigh

from favour, was tried for treason and condemned to death. He was reprieved on condition that he should find the fabled city of El Dorado in South America and return with its treasures. The expedition failed, Raleigh fought with the Spanish at a time when the King was trying to improve relations between England and Spain, and upon his return he was beheaded.

RAMEAU, Jean-Philippe (1683–1764)

French composer and organist. He composed much keyboard music, but also operas and opera-ballets noted for their vivid stage effects and descriptive music. In addition he wrote several important books of musical theory.

RAMSAY, Sir William (1852–1916)

Scottish chemist, famous for his discovery of the INERT GASES helium, argon, neon, krypton and xenon.

RAPHAEL (Raffaello Sanzi, 1483–1520)

Italian artist and architect. He is generally regarded, with LEONARDO da Vinci and MICHELANGELO, as one of the three greatest painters of the Italian Renaissance. His best-known work was done in Rome where he decorated the Vatican Library with a series of frescoes, including his most famous painting, *The School of Athens*. He also designed a series of tapestries for the Vatican, the cartoons (detailed sketches) for which are in the Victoria and Albert Museum, London.

RASPUTIN, Gregory (1872–1916)

Russian monk who secured a position of power in Imperial Russia due to his influence over the Tsarina. She believed he could cure her son of the rare blood disorder haemophilia. His general unpopularity was one of the many causes leading to the RUSSIAN REVOLUTION of 1917, although he was assassinated the previous year.

RAT

Group of RODENTS found in most parts of the world. They are noted for their intelligence, but also classed as vermin because they can spread disease. The bubonic plague (BLACK DEATH) was spread by the Asian black rat. The brown rat is now far more common.

RATTLESNAKE

Group of poisonous SNAKES native to North America, which produce a distinctive rattling noise with the tail when disturbed. The most dangerous type is the diamondback. Rattlesnakes are also known as pit vipers.

RAVEL, Maurice (1875–1937)

French composer. He shared DEBUSSY's interest in musical impressionism, and developed an individual harmonic style of his own. But he also wrote other pieces, mostly for piano or orchestra, which have some special connection with the past, or are inspired by some theme of fantasy. His works include the ballets *Mother Goose* and *Daphnis et Chloé*; the opera *L'Enfant et les sortilèges* ('The Bewitched Child'); and his re-creation of the old Spanish court dance *Bolero*.

RED CROSS

International organization concerned especially with the care of the wounded, and of prisoners, in time of war. It was founded by the Swiss Henri DUNANT, and has derived its name, and its symbol – a red cross on a white background – from the Swiss flag (a white cross on a red background). In Moslem countries the symbol is a red crescent. Many countries have their own Red Cross societies, but the organization itself is always neutral. Therefore in wartime its symbol on any person, building, vehicle, aircraft or ship indicates the care of war wounded and should act as a guarantee against attack.

REFORMATION

Religious movement which started in Germany in the sixteenth century with Martin LUTHER. It involved a break with the ROMAN CATHOLIC CHURCH, caused originally by what were seen as abuses among the priesthood, and hence the need for reform. Luther's Protestant ideas spread quickly to the countries of Scandinavia, but in Germany itself dispute between the Protestants and Catholics led to the THIRTY YEARS WAR. In Switzerland the Reformation was led by Ulrich Zwingli and Jean CALVIN, and their ideas spread to France (whose Protestants were called HUGUENOTS), to the Netherlands and to Scotland (through the preaching of John KNOX). In England also there was a break with the Roman Catholic Church, but this was due in the first place to HENRY VIII's personal dispute with the Pope; and the subsequent establishment of the CHURCH OF ENGLAND was a compromise between the Catholic and Protestant faiths. There was, however, Protestant activity, producing such religious groups as the PURITANS.

REFRACTION

In PHYSICS the change in direction of a ray of LIGHT as it passes from one medium to another.

Demonstration of refraction

A simple example of this is the way a stick appears to bend as it breaks the surface of a pool of water.

REFRIGERATION

Process of reducing the temperature of a substance. It is based on the second law of THERMODYNAMICS, which states that heat will always pass from a warmer body to a colder one. For centuries this could only be achieved artificially with ice. A modern form of refrigeration uses liquid ammonia which is very cold and can be continually circulated round a refrigerated compartment. Traditionally refrigeration has been used for the storage of quickly perishable foods like meat and fish. Today it is also extensively used in medicine, to preserve vaccines, blood or organs of the body.

REINCARNATION

Belief held by some religions, including HINDUISM, that a soul returns to many physical existences. The word means 'return to the body'. Another name for it is metempsychosis.

REINDEER

Small group of MAMMALS, native to the Arctic regions of Europe, North America and Asia. They are members of the deer family, but are

Right Late Roman Temple of Bacchus at Baalbek

Northern European reindeer

Early prehistoric burial sites often reveal objects, or the remains of items of food, buried with the corpse, suggesting a belief that the spirit of the dead person might live on and somehow still need such things. Religions then went on to try and rationalize the forces of nature – the elements, fertility, life and death – with a belief in many gods and spirits. The ancient Egyptians believed in life after death and preserved their dead, leaving them with food, weapons and jewels to accompany them in the next world. In Greek mythology the gods that lived on Mount Olympus were formidable tyrannical beings, and some of them were later adopted by the Romans.

The world's most important religions began in the East. JUDAISM is the oldest religion to teach that there is only one God, and its history is contained in the Hebrew Bible. CHRIST-IANITY is the most widespread religion in the world, founded upon a belief in the divinity of Jesus Christ, and its teachings are contained in the Bible. ISLAM is widely believed in Africa and Asia. It was founded by the prophet MOHAMMED, and its followers, Moslems, believe in the one God, Allah. HINDUISM is the traditional religion of India and BUDDHISM is also widespread in the East. Other important religions include Confucianism, based on the teachings of CONFUCIUS, TAOISM and Sikhism (*see* SIKHS).

the only species in which antlers grow on the heads of both sexes. The caribou is the North American species.

RELATIVITY

Name for two theories of PHYSICS, presented by Albert EINSTEIN, in 1905 and 1915 respectively, as the Special and General Theories of Relativity. Through them he showed that speed and position are relative things and that there are no absolute measurements for time and space. He also stated that matter and energy are interchangeable, a concept that has had a considerable bearing on the development of nuclear physics. In this century Einstein's theories of Relativity have revolutionized ideas about the nature of matter and of the universe, as Sir Isaac NEWTON's laws of gravity revolutionized scientific thinking two hundred years before.

RELIGION

Belief in a power or spirit beyond the observable world of the ordinary senses which offers some special purpose to life. There are many different religions throughout the world, but most attempt to explain the origin and nature of the universe. Most religions involve prayer and worship and belief in a life after death.

Left The helmet from the Saxon Sutton Hoo ship-burial, early 7th century

REMBRANDT (Rembrandt Harmenszoon van Rijn, 1606–69)

Dutch artist. He was born in Leyden and soon established himself as a successful portrait painter. But after the death of his wife in 1642 he began to turn away from this profitable type of work with the result that he became destitute. One of the first paintings which represents the big change in his artistic outlook is the celebrated *The Night Watch*, a work of great drama and power which none the less displeased those who had commissioned it because it was not a straightforward group portrait in which everybody could be clearly seen. Some

Belshazzar's Feast by Rembrandt

of his greatest paintings from then on were self-portraits, revealing a treatment of paints and brushwork and a depth of spiritual feeling hitherto unknown in art. As well as his 700 paintings, Rembrandt produced a large number of etchings.

RENAISSANCE

The word is French for 'rebirth', and in this sense describes the revival of interest in the art and culture of Classical Greece and Rome that came about in the fifteenth century. In a broader sense it is the name given to the tremendous flowering of the arts and sciences, of commerce and exploration, that started in Italy and spread to most parts of western and central Europe during the fifteenth and six-teenth centuries. It included such religious movements as the REFORMATION, which began as a challenge to the established order and authority of the Church. Indeed, before the period of the Renaissance, religion and the Church dominated European affairs. During and after the Renaissance there was increasing freedom in scientific thinking, in scholarship and in all the means of artistic expression.

RENOIR, Pierre Auguste (1841–1919)

French artist. He was a leading member of the Impressionist school of painting, producing many paintings, often of groups of people in an outdoor summer setting, noted for their impression of flickering light and shade.

REPRODUCTION

Process by which all living things produce new individuals. There are two main types of reproduction – asexual and sexual.

Simple plants and animals reproduce asexually, either by splitting into two (like the amoeba) or by producing special cells or buds which then form new plants (like the yeast fungus).

Sexual reproduction involves a male and a female 'parent'. In animals the male produces sperms and the female produces eggs. Fertilization takes place when the sperm and egg join to form a single cell known as a zygote, which then develops into a new animal. Sexual reproduction also occurs in seed-bearing plants. The male sex cell is stored in a pollen grain, which may be transferred to the female part of the flower by wind, water or insects.

In animals there are two types of fertilization – internal and external. External fertilization occurs with most fish. The female fish lays her eggs in water and the male fish then fertilizes the eggs by covering them with sperm. Fertilization in birds and reptiles takes place inside the female. She then lays eggs, which are protected by shell. The new organism inside, the embryo, lives on the food materials stored in the egg until it is ready to hatch.

Most MAMMALS give birth to live young. The male sperms fertilize the female's eggs inside the body and the embryo then develops inside the mother's body. The period of development is known as gestation. In most advanced mammals there is an additional organ called the placenta. This develops inside the mother's uterus, or womb, and the embryo feeds on materials that pass into the placenta from the mother's blood. After a period of gestation or pregnancy the young mammal is born. It is like the adult, but smaller. *See also* GENETICS.

REPTILE

Group of VERTEBRATES which are cold-blooded and have a skin composed of scales. One way in

Reptile: land iguana from the Galapagos Islands

which reptiles differ anatomically from FISHES is that they all breathe air. There are about 3,000 species, classified under the three main orders of CROCODILES and alligators, tortoises and TURTLES, SNAKES and LIZARDS. There is also the TUATARA.

REPUBLICAN PARTY

Political party of the UNITED STATES, founded in 1854 as an anti-slavery party, and gaining the office of President with the election of Abraham LINCOLN in 1860. In this century the Republicans have drawn their support chiefly from business interests, the agricultural West and the more conservative-minded sections of the population. They have been in general opposition to the DEMOCRATIC PARTY.

RESPIRATION

All plants and animals depend on oxygen in order to grow and live. This gas is taken in during the process known as breathing or external respiration. Simple organisms are able to absorb oxygen through the surface of their bodies, but most larger animals require a special area, which in mammals, for example, is situated in the lungs. Fish are equipped with gills, where oxygen is extracted from the water taken in and passed into the bloodstream. Some other animals which live near water, such as frogs, have thin moist skins through which the gas is able to penetrate.

The use made of the oxygen taken in is

known as internal or chemical respiration. Here, the oxygen combines with food to make energy as well as the waste products of carbon dioxide and water which are then rejected.

All animals rely on plants and other animals to supply the food necessary for internal respiration. Plants, however, are able to manufacture both the food and oxygen they require for respiration during a process known as PHOTOSYNTHESIS, in which carbon dioxide combines with water using the energy of sunlight. Nearly all the oxygen present in the air has been made by photosynthesis. Without plants, animals could not eat nor breathe.

RESTORATION

Period of English history following the return to the throne of CHARLES II in 1660 after the Civil War and Oliver CROMWELL'S republican Commonwealth. In general it heralded a time of social relaxation after the strict moral tone of Cromwell and the PURITANS. The term is especially applied to the plays of the period which are mostly comedies and rather bawdy in spirit.

REYNOLDS, Sir Joshua (1723–92)

English artist who painted portraits of many of the most famous people of his time and was appointed first President of the Royal Academy when it was founded in 1768.

RHEA

Large flightless South American BIRD. It is very similar to the OSTRICH but has three toes on each foot instead of the ostrich's two.

RH FACTOR

Substance found in the blood of human beings and some other mammals. People who have this factor are known as RH-positive. It was first identified in Rhesus monkeys, hence the name.

RHINE

European river which rises in the Swiss ALPS and flows northwards for a distance of 1,320 km (820 miles), entering the North Sea just south of the port of Rotterdam in the NETHERLANDS (in which country it is called the Waal). It is navigable all the way from the sea to Basle in SWITZERLAND and for this reason is of great commercial importance, serving the industrial region of the Ruhr and such inland ports as Köln (Cologne), Mannheim and Strasbourg. It is connected by canal with the DANUBE and the Rhône. Its most celebrated stretch is the Rhine Gorge, the steep sides being given over to vineyards. Politically, too, the Rhine has played a big part in European history, providing a natural frontier between the French-speaking people to the west and the Germanic peoples to the east.

RHINOCEROS

Group of MAMMALS classed as UNGULATES, native to parts of Africa and Asia. Rhinoceroses are distinguished by one or two horns on their snout, though these are composed of tough matted hair and are not true horns. They are vegetarian and generally quite timid creatures, but if aroused will charge at great speed despite their bulk. Largest species is the African white rhino.

East African rhinoceros

RHODES, Cecil John (1853–1902)

English financier and administrator. He made a fortune from diamond and gold mining in South Africa, became Prime Minister of what was then Cape Province and acquired for the British Empire Bechuanaland (now Botswana), and the territory named after him, of Rhodesia, which was renamed ZIMBABWE in 1980. His involvement in a plot to overthrow the Boer republic of the Transvaal which led to the BOER WAR forced him to resign his premiership in 1896.

RHODESIA. *See* ZIMBABWE

RHÔNE

European river which rises in Switzerland and flows eastwards and then south for more than 800 km (500 miles) through France to the Mediterranean Sea. From its source in the Rhône glacier, the river enters Lake Geneva. It then flows through narrow gorges into France. At the city of Lyons, it is joined by the river Saône. It then turns south between the Massif Central and the French Alps. South of Avignon, it divides into two, the Grand and Petit Rhône. These two streams enclose a delta called the Camargue which faces the Mediterranean Sea. The Rhône-Saône valley has been a major historic route between the Mediterranean Sea and northern France.

RHYTHM

Basic beat or pulse of a piece of MUSIC. It can be thought of as the 'backbone' to a piece, while melody and HARMONY provide the 'flesh'. Rhythm is of great significance in much tribal dancing, where it can have a hypnotic effect; and also in much JAZZ, whose own origins lie in the tribal songs and dances of black Africans. In most Western music the rhythm of a piece of music is divided up into regular sections called bars, the most common rhythms being three or four beats to the bar. In much twentieth-century music, however, the number of beats to the bar can vary considerably, often within the same composition. Indian and other oriental music also has complex rhythmic patterns.

RICE

Important staple food for about half the world's population. It grows well in wet soil and warm conditions, and is often grown in paddies, which are small areas surrounded by dykes. The leading rice-growing countries are China, India, Indonesia, Bangladesh, Japan and Thailand.

Richard I and the crusader castle of Krak in Syria

RICHARD I (1157–99)

English king. In fact, he spent less than a year in England during his entire reign, his energies being given over to the Third CRUSADE and disputes with Philip Augustus of France. In his absence England was ruled by his brother John. He earned his nickname of *Coeur de Lion* (Lionheart) for his bravery in battle.

RICHELIEU, Armand Jean-Duplessis, Duc de (1585–1642)

French cardinal and statesman. He became minister of state to the weak and indecisive Louis XIII and dominated French politics. At home he persecuted the HUGUENOTS and captured their stronghold at La Rochelle. Abroad he involved France in the THIRTY YEARS WAR and greatly increased its power and influence in European affairs. He founded the French Academy.

RIFLE

Type of firearm in which the bore of the barrel is spirally grooved to impart a spinning movement to the bullet, and so increase its speed and accuracy of aim. Typical calibres are .303 (service rifle), .500 (game rifle) and .22 (miniature rifle); 'calibre' means the diameter of the bore measured in inches. Well-known makes are the Springfield, Winchester, Remington and B.S.A. The leading event in rifle shooting is held yearly at Bisley.

RIMSKY-KORSAKOV, Nicolai (1844–1908)

Russian composer. He was trained as a naval officer but became the most influential member of the group of Russian nationalist composers known as 'The Five'. He is especially noted for his brilliant orchestration in such works as *Sheherazade,* based on tales from the Arabian Nights, and his opera *The Golden Cockerel.*

ROBESPIERRE, Maximilien (1758–94)

French revolutionary. During the FRENCH REVOLUTION he became leader of the radical JACOBIN Party, then head of the Committee of Public Safety and the man chiefly responsible for the numerous executions carried out during the so-called Reign of Terror between 1793 and 1794. For a short while he was virtual dictator of France, but was then denounced by the National Convention, tried and executed.

ROCK. *See* PETROLOGY

ROCKET

Type of projectile or missile that operates on the same scientific principle as JET PROPULSION,

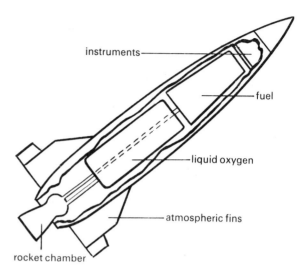

instruments

fuel

liquid oxygen

atmospheric fins

rocket chamber

The main parts of a liquid-fuel rocket

namely that to every action there is an equal and opposite reaction. Thus, as the gases of combustion inside the rocket escape at one end, so the rocket will be propelled forward with an equivalent force in the opposite direction. This propulsion has nothing to do with the pressure of escaping gases against the outside atmosphere. Indeed, rockets operate best in a vacuum where there is no atmosphere to offer resistance either to the escaping gases or to the forward motion.

The Chinese used gunpowder rockets more than 700 years ago, but for many years after rockets were used only for signalling purposes. Serious rocket development began in the early years of this century with the theories and experiments of the Russian Konstantin Tsiolkovsky, the German Hermann Obert, and the American Robert Goddard who in 1926 fired the first liquid-propelled rocket. A dramatic step forward in rocketry was the German V2, developed by Wernher von Braun, which bombarded London from sites in the Netherlands and France during WORLD WAR II. Subsequent rocket development by the Soviet Union and the United States has led to SPACE TRAVEL AND EXPLORATION. Up to the present, most rockets have been classified according to whether they operate on a solid or a liquid fuel propellant, plus an oxidant to aid combustion (as distinct from a jet engine which obtains oxygen from the outside air). Also, those used in space research have mostly been designed in 'stages', each stage or section falling away as its fuel is exhausted. Nuclear-powered rockets are now contemplated.

ROCKY MOUNTAINS

Mountain range covering a large area of the western half of the North American continent, extending from Mexico, across the United States and into Canada. The highest peak is Mt Whitney, 4,419 m (14,495 ft). Mt McKinley, 6,195 m (20,320 ft) in Alaska is much higher but is not technically a part of the Rocky Mountain range.

RODENT

Largest order of MAMMALS, distinguished by their teeth which are specially designed for gnawing. Included in this order are RATS and mice, SQUIRRELS, HAMSTERS, voles, BEAVERS, and porcupines.

Rodent: North American Prairie dog

RODIN, Auguste (1840–1917)

French sculptor who specialized in bronze figures and portrait busts, creating at the same time a powerful individual style with an emphasis placed on contrasting areas of light and shade. *The Kiss* and *The Thinker* are two of his most famous figure studies. His greatest portrait study is the full-length impression of the French writer Honoré de Balzac.

ROENTGEN, Wilhelm Konrad (1845–1923)

German scientist, most famous for his discovery of X-RAYS, so called by him because he did not at first understand their true nature.

ROMAN CATHOLIC CHURCH

Major Christian church. The Pope, as its spiritual leader, is regarded by Catholics as being in direct line of spiritual succession from the Apostle Peter (Apostolic Succession), and the true representative of Christ on Earth. Despite the split with the Eastern Orthodox Church in 1054, the Roman Catholic Church remained the exclusive church for most of Europe up to the time of the REFORMATION. As a strong social and political as well as spiritual institution, it provided employment for the majority of scholars, artists and musicians, and established the various monastic orders which continue to this day. Recently the Church has introduced many internal reforms, notably in the use of the vernacular (the normal language of the congregation in question) in place of the traditional Latin liturgy. It remains the dominant church in the 'Latin' countries of Europe (Italy, France, Spain, Portugal), and in most of South and Central America. It also retains a strong following in other European countries, such as Austria, Belgium, Germany, Poland, the Republic of Ireland and other parts of the British Isles, and in the United States. With about 500 million adherents it is the largest Christian church. *See also* CHRISTIANITY.

The Markets of Trajan and the Tower of the Militia, adjacent to the Imperial Forum, Rome

ROMAN EMPIRE

The city of Rome, according to legend, was founded by Romulus in 753 BC. A Roman republic was established in 509 BC; and by 272 BC, after prolonged conflict with neighbouring peoples, such as the ETRUSCANS and Sabines, and with the Greek colonies which existed in the southern part of the country, Rome controlled the whole of Italy. There followed the struggle with Carthage, known as the PUNIC WARS, during which the Romans acquired Sicily and provinces in present-day Spain, Yugoslavia, Tunisia and Greece. In the next hundred years they added to their possessions Asia Minor, Syria, Judaea, and Gaul (France). Egypt was annexed in 30 BC, and the conquest of Britain began in AD 43. The Empire reached its zenith in the second century AD, extending from Britain in the north-west to the Caspian Sea and Persian Gulf in the east, and encompassing the entire Mediterranean region. Soon after that its power started to decline. There were increasing invasions by the barbarian races from central and eastern Europe, and in AD 410 Rome itself was captured by the Visigoths.

The Roman Empire endured for over five hundred years. Its laws, literature and language have had a tremendous influence on European culture right up to the present; while many of its buildings and other structures – arenas, aqueducts, triumphal arches – remain largely intact, as evidence of brilliant Roman engineering and architectural skill. *See also* AUGUSTUS CAESAR, CLAUDIUS, JULIUS CAESAR, MARCUS AURELIUS and NERO.

ROMANIA

Eastern European republic with an area of 237,500 sq km (91,704 sq miles) and a population of about 22 million. The capital is Bucharest. The River DANUBE forms most of Romania's southern frontier with Yugoslavia and Bulgaria. The country itself contains the Transylvanian Alps and the Carpathian Mountains, also a broad plain extending to the Black Sea. It is mainly agricultural, producing cereal crops and some wines. Most of the country was originally a part of the province of Dacia within the ROMAN EMPIRE. More recently it was a part of the Turkish OTTOMAN EMPIRE and did not become independent until 1878. After WORLD WAR I Romania gained territory from Austro-Hungary; and after WORLD WAR II it became a Communist republic and a member of the East European Soviet Bloc.

ROMMEL, Erwin (1891–1944)

German soldier and the most publicized German military commander of WORLD WAR II. As commander of the *Afrika Korps* he almost drove the British from North Africa before halting through lack of supplies and then being defeated by General MONTGOMERY at El Alamein. Later he was made responsible for building up the coastal defences in northern France, Belgium and the Netherlands in anticipation of Allied invasion. When this invasion succeeded he decided the war was lost for Germany and became involved in a plot to kill HITLER. The plot failed and Rommel committed suicide.

ROOSEVELT, Franklin Delano (1882–1945)

American statesman. He was elected Democratic President in 1933, and re-elected in 1936, 1940 and 1944. Before WORLD WAR II he carried through a policy of large-scale public works, called the 'New Deal', to combat economic depression and unemployment in the United States. After the Japanese attack on Pearl Harbor in 1941 he directed his country's war effort, dying within a few weeks of the German surrender. Roosevelt was a polio victim and largely confined to a wheel chair throughout his political career.

ROSETTA STONE

Large fragment of a stone inscription in three scripts, Greek, demotic and HIEROGLYPHICS, dating from about 200 BC. It was discovered by a French soldier in Egypt in 1798, and the hieroglyphics were deciphered by the French Egyptologist Jean-François Champollion who was able to compare them with the Greek and demotic versions above. The Stone is now in the British Museum, London.

A Customs Post, Paris by Henri Rousseau

ROSSETTI, Dante Gabriel (1828–82)

English poet and painter and a leading member of the PRE-RAPHAELITE BROTHERHOOD. His sister, Christina Georgina, was also an active member of the Pre-Raphaelites, confining herself to poetry.

ROSSINI, Gioacchino (1792–1868)

Italian composer, almost exclusively of operas, including *The Barber of Seville* and *William Tell*. He was considered a noisy composer in his own day and earned the nickname 'Signor Crescendo'. Nevertheless, he was very successful, made a fortune, and virtually retired at the age of thirty-seven, though he lived for another thirty-nine years, enjoying the life in Paris – especially good food.

ROSTAND, Edmond (1868–1918)

French poet and dramatist, best known for his play *Cyrano de Bergerac* about a hero with an abnormally long nose.

ROUSSEAU, Henri (1844–1910)

French artist, often called *le Douanier* as he was also a customs official. He is described as a 'primitive' painter because he was largely self-taught. At the same time his paintings, usually of an exotic and dream-like character, had a considerable influence on the work of other artists and are very popular today, partly because of their naïve quality, but also because of our deeper understanding of psychology.

ROUSSEAU, Jean-Jacques (1712–78)

Swiss thinker and writer. He was much concerned with the freedom and rights of the common man and greatly influenced the leaders of the FRENCH REVOLUTION. His most important work was *The Social Contract*, while his *Confessions* is considered a notable work of autobiography.

ROWLANDSON, Thomas (1756–1827)

English artist. He produced hundreds of water colours and drawings of contemporary life and manners, which are exuberant, humorous and display masterful draughtsmanship. One of his best-known series is the set of illustrations to *Dr Syntax*.

ROYAL SOCIETY

Most important scientific society in Great Britain. It was started by a group of learned men for the purpose of discussing science. It received its royal charter in 1662 when it was known as the Royal Society of London for Improving Natural Knowledge. A similar society was formed in Edinburgh in 1783. Members, or Fellows, of the two societies carry the initials F.R.S. or F.R.S.E. after their names.

RUBBER

Gummy substance exuded by a wide variety of trees and plants, especially the trees *Hevea brasiliensis,* and several other species of *Hevea* which are native to Amazon, but are grown chiefly in the East Indies, particularly the Malay Peninsula. Rubber is also obtained from the large tree *Castilla elastica,* found in Mexico. So-called dandelion rubber is derived from the roots of various species of dandelion plant grown in Turkestan, USSR.

Rubber trees are tapped (i.e. cuts are made in the bark) and the latex, a milk-like juice, containing about 30–40% rubber, is coagulated by exposing it to heat and wood smoke, or by mechanical means, so as to separate the rubber from the water, mineral salts, sugars, resins, and protein matters. The rubber obtained in this way is known as 'crude'. Latex is also extensively used in industry for making foam rubber products, footwear, dolls, etc. Untreated crude rubber is naturally soft and lacks the requisite strength for making into manufactured articles. To improve its strength and usefulness it is vulcanized or heated with sulphur, the proportion of sulphur used determining the hardness and elasticity of the rubber. Fillers such as carbon black or channel black are also vital constituents of rubber, particularly tyre rubber. About 75% of the rubber produced goes into the manufacture of tyres, the remainder being utilized for cable sheathing, wire covering, footwear, flooring, the proofing of clothing, upholstery material and hose. Latest developments include bullet-proof tyres, non-tear rubber for fuel tanks, flame-proof hose, and suits for frogmen.

RUBENS, Sir Peter Paul (1577–1640)

Flemish artist. He travelled to Italy as a young man, became court painter to the Duke of Mantua and returned home rich and successful. From then on he was in great demand all over Europe, often delegating work on large canvasses to assistants. In England he was knighted by CHARLES I. Nearly all his work is generous in scale and executed in strong, exuberant colours.

RUNES

Old Norse and Teutonic script dating from about AD 300 and consisting chiefly of straight lines at various angles. Many runic stone inscriptions survive, mainly in SCANDINAVIA.

RUSKIN, John (1819–1900)

English writer and art critic. He was a strong supporter of the PRE-RAPHAELITE BROTHERHOOD and other artists of his time, though not of the American artist James NcNeill Whistler who brought a famous libel action against him. His own books were mostly on ARCHITECTURE or the morality of art.

RUSSELL, Bertrand Arthur William, Earl (1872–1970)

English philosopher. In collaboration with A. N. Whitehead he wrote *Principia Mathematica,* one of the most important philosophical works of this century, concerned chiefly with mathematics and logic. Bertrand Russell was also a well-known public speaker and an outspoken pacifist.

RUSSIA. *See* UNION OF SOVIET SOCIALIST REPUBLICS

RUSSIAN REVOLUTION

The long-term causes of the Revolution were autocratic or tyrannical rule by a succession of tsars (kings or emperors), lack of social reform and great extremes of poverty and wealth. The immediate causes were Russian entry into WORLD WAR I followed by humiliating defeats at the hands of the Germans, and the apparent corruption and indifference of the imperial Russian court as epitomized in the person of the monk RASPUTIN and his influence over the Tsarina. Widespread mutinies in the armed forces led to the abdication of Tsar NICHOLAS II early in 1917 and the formation of a government by Alexander Kerensky, whose aim was to introduce democratic institutions while continuing the war. However, the Germans helped Vladimir Lenin, who had been living in exile, to return to Russia in the expectation that if he and the extreme left-wing Bolsheviks came to power they would sue for peace. Lenin swiftly gained support among the soldiers and workers councils, or soviets, in Petrograd (formerly St Petersburg, now Leningrad), Moscow and elsewhere, and in October 1917 in Petrograd itself he and his military colleague Leon TROTSKY organized an armed uprising which overthrew Kerensky's government. Lenin and the Bolsheviks (or majority party) took immediate control of affairs, bring the war swiftly to a close and establishing in Russia the world's first Communist state. Opposition to the regime, supported by arms and men from many other foreign countries, including Great Britain, led to a period of civil war which was won by the newly created Red Army under Trotsky's direction. Meanwhile, the Tsar and

Red Guards with an armoured car in Moscow, 1917

his family had been arrested, held in captivity for some time and then shot.

RUTHERFORD, Ernest, Lord (1871–1937)

New Zealand scientist whose researches into RADIOACTIVITY led to new discoveries about the structure of the ATOM. His work at the Cavendish Laboratory, Cambridge was continued by many of his distinguished students.

RWANDA

Central African republic with an area of 26,338 sq km (10,170 sq miles) and a population of about 4¾ million. The capital is Kigali. This poor country was once ruled by Belgium. It became fully independent in 1962.

RYUKYU ISLANDS

String of islands in the north-western Pacific between Taiwan and Japan, with a total population of about 973,000. The largest island is OKINAWA. They were occupied by the United States after WORLD WAR II and returned to Japan in 1953.

S

SABLE

MAMMAL belonging to the WEASEL family, native to parts of Siberia and valued for its fur. It is specially reared in the Soviet Union.

SABLE ANTELOPE

Large, dark coloured ANTELOPE, native to South Africa, and closely related to the oryx, with strong ringed horns.

SABRE-TOOTHED TIGER

Extinct MAMMAL of the CAT family, similar in general appearance to a tiger but with two very large, tusk-like upper teeth. It lived about 10 million years ago.

SACCHARIN

White crystalline powder made from permanganate of potash and nearly three hundred times as sweet as cane sugar. It is widely used as a sugar substitute in foodstuffs.

SAGA

Type of EPIC poem, especially associated with the ancient history, myths and legends of SCANDINAVIA and ICELAND. The *Heimskringla,* a history of the ancient kings of Norway, probably first written down in the twelfth century, and the *Njals Saga* are two of the most famous examples of the form.

The Sahara Desert

SAHARA

Desert of northern Africa which stretches eastwards from the Atlantic to the Red Sea and southwards from the Mediterranean to the grasslands and tropical forests of equatorial Africa. It has an area of about 8 million sq km (3 million sq miles), and is the world's largest desert region. There are two very ancient groups of mountains, the Tibesti and the Ahaggar. The world's highest temperatures have been recorded in the Western Sahara. The traditional inhabitants have been the nomadic Berbers and Arabs, moving from OASIS to oasis; but vast areas remain totally uninhabited. There is the evidence of recent severe droughts in parts of NIGERIA and neighbouring countries to suggest that the Sahara is expanding southwards. On the other hand, there are plans to irrigate some areas; also, the desert has valuable mineral deposits of oil, iron ore, phosphates and uranium.

ST HELENA

Remote volcanic island and British colony in the South ATLANTIC OCEAN, famous as the place to which NAPOLEON Bonaparte was finally exiled and where he died. Today it has about 5,000 inhabitants. St Helena has itself two other island dependencies, Ascension Island and TRISTAN DA CUNHA.

St Lambert lock on the St Lawrence Seaway

ST LAWRENCE SEAWAY

North American inland waterway for ocean-going ships, comprising the St Lawrence river itself and numerous canals and locks. It connects the North Atlantic Ocean to the region of the GREAT LAKES and extends for a total distance of 3,060 km (1,900 miles). Work on the project began at the end of the last century, and the complete system was opened in 1959. As well as linking large areas with the sea, the system provides abundant hydro-electricity.

ST LUCIA

West Indian island nation in the BRITISH COMMONWEALTH, independent since 1979, with an area of 616 sq km (238 sq miles) and 125,000 people. The capital is Castries.

SAINT-SAËNS, Camille (1835–1921)

French composer. He wrote a large quantity of music in practically every established form – symphonies, operas, concertos, church music, songs. Two of his best-remembered pieces today are the *Danse Macabre* and the humorous *Carnival of the Animals* for two pianos and orchestra.

ST VINCENT

West Indian island group in the BRITISH COMMONWEALTH, independent in 1979, with an area of 388 sq km (150 sq miles) and 108,000 people. The capital is Kingstown.

SALADIN (1137–93)

Sultan of Egypt and Syria. During the CRUSADES he won a crushing victory over the Christians at Tiberias in 1187 and recaptured Jerusalem for ISLAM. This led to the launching of the Third Crusade. RICHARD I of England and Philip Augustus of France then captured the city of Acre, but Richard on his own could not reach Jerusalem. Richard and Saladin entered upon a truce; Richard departed and Saladin died soon after.

SALAMANDER

Group of AMPHIBIANS, similar in appearance to some lizards, but with a scaleless, moist skin. Largest species is the giant salamander of China and Japan which is about $1\frac{1}{2}$ m (5 ft) in length. Another species is the European fire salamander with strong yellow markings. Newts are also salamanders.

SALT

Mineral crystalline compound of sodium and chlorine. It is a constituent of sea water but is obtained mostly from salt flats and lakes, and from rock salt. It is an essential item of the human diet, has been used for thousands of years as a food preservative.

SALVATION ARMY

International religious organization, founded in 1865 by William Booth. As its name implies, it is organized in a military manner, with uniforms and ranks, and military-type bands. Though it holds services of a kind, its main concern is with welfare work among the destitute and others in special need.

SAMOA

Group of volcanic islands in the South PACIFIC OCEAN. The islands of Western Samoa form an independent state within the BRITISH COMMONWEALTH, formerly administered by New Zealand. The capital is Apia. The remaining islands of the group are administered by the United States. Their capital is Pago Pago.

SAND, George (1804–76)

French writer, whose real name was Aurore Dupin. Her work as a novelist has been overshadowed by her unconventional way of life.

SAN MARINO

Very small independent republic in the Apennine mountains of ITALY with a population of about 20,000.

SANSKRIT

Language of ancient INDIA from which most modern Indic languages have grown. Many sacred and literary texts of India, dating back to about 1500 BC, are written in Sanskrit.

SÃO TOMÉ & PRINCIPE

Island republic, independent since 1975, off the west coast of central Africa, with an area of 964 sq km (372 sq miles) and 110,000 people. The capital is São Tomé.

SAPPHO (born c. 650 BC)

Greek poetess of the island of Lesbos. Only fragments of her work have survived, these being parts of lyrical love poems.

SARGASSO SEA

Region of the North ATLANTIC OCEAN, northwest of the WEST INDIES, which is the comparatively calm centre of several ocean currents.

SARTRE, Jean Paul (1905-80)

French writer and philosopher. He has been an influential exponent of the existential philosophical movement, which places personal decision and responsibility above any doctrine or set of rules. In World War II he was a leading member of the French Resistance.

SATIRE

Type of literature designed to expose some human weakness or hypocrisy in a humorous way, rendering its targets ridiculous.

SATURN

PLANET of the SOLAR SYSTEM with an equatorial diameter of 120,500 km (75,300 miles) and an average distance from the SUN of 1,427 million km (891 million miles). Saturn spins on its axis so fast that it is markedly flattened at the poles. The most spectacular feature of Saturn is its sequence of rings, thin layers spun out around its equator and consisting of tiny rocky particles. Saturn has seventeen moons. Its atmosphere is probably similar to that of Jupiter, and very cold.

The planet Saturn

SAUDI ARABIA

Independent kingdom that occupies most of the Arabian peninsula. It has an area of 2,149,690 sq km (830,045 sq miles) and a population of about 9 million. The capital is Riyadh. The country's wealth is derived almost exclusively from oil. The country also contains the two holy cities of ISLAM, Mecca and Medina.

SAXONS

Tribesmen originally from northern Germany whose name is probably derived from the *seax*, a short sword which was their favourite weapon. They invaded parts of Gaul (France) and Italy itself. They also started raiding the shores of Roman Britain from about the third century AD, often with another north European race, the Angles. By the end of the sixth century most of England was in the hands of these ANGLO-SAXONS.

SCANDINAVIA

Regional name for the large north European peninsula which comprises FINLAND, NORWAY and SWEDEN; and by historical and cultural extension, DENMARK and ICELAND also.

SCARLATTI, Alessandro (1660–1725) and Domenico (1685–1757)

Italian composers. Alessandro composed many operas, oratorios and masses which influenced other eighteenth-century composers, including HANDEL. His son Domenico wrote over 500 keyboard sonatas which pioneered development of the true Classical SONATA and SONATA FORM.

SCHEELE, Karl Wilhelm (1742–86)

Swedish chemist who discovered OXYGEN independently of Joseph Priestley. He also discovered chlorine and investigated many other chemical compounds.

SCHILLER, Johann Christoph Friedrich (1759–1805)

German dramatist and poet. He wrote several historical dramas, including *William Tell*, which provided the basis for ROSSINI's opera of the same name. Another composer, BEETHOVEN, was inspired to set to music his poem *Ode to Joy* as the last movement of the 'Choral' Symphony.

SCHOENBERG, Arnold (1874–1951)

Austrian composer. He created a new harmonic basis for music called twelve-tone composition, which replaced the traditional twenty-four major and minor keys with a new kind of scale. He also developed a special style of singing called *Sprechgesang*, or 'Speech-Song'. Thus Schoenberg was one of the most original musical thinkers of this century. His works include the strange, dream-like song-cycle *Pierrot Lunaire* ('Moonstruck Pierrot'), and the cantata *A Survivor from Warsaw* in memory of fellow Jews who had died in Nazi concentration camps.

SCHOPENHAUER, Arthur (1788–1860)

German philosopher. In his most famous book, *The World as Will and Idea*, he claimed that a person's own will and power to act is governed by a much greater force of will controlling the universe. Therefore, he argued, the will of the individual can never be really satisfied or know any peace.

SCHUBERT, Franz (1797–1828)

Austrian composer. During his tragically short life of thirty-one years he composed nine symphonies, including the well-known 'Unfinished' Symphony (No 8), and many sonatas, string quartets and other chamber music works. Most celebrated of all are his hundreds of songs. Schubert established a special type of German song (or *Lied*), crowning his achievements with two of the greatest of all song-cycles (groups of related songs), *Die schöne Müllerin* ('The Fair Maid of the Mill') and *Die Winterreise* ('The Winter Journey'). Almost none of

Franz Schubert

this music was published or publicly performed in the composer's own lifetime.

SCHUMANN, Robert (1810–56)

German composer. He wrote some of the finest early Romantic piano music, including *Carnival* and *Scenes of Childhood;* and some of the most beautiful *Lieder* (songs) after SCHUBERT. He also wrote four symphonies and a very popular piano concerto. In addition, Schumann was a noted musical journalist and critic. His marriage to the pianist Clara Wieck was one of the happiest in music. Tragically he later lost his reason and died in an asylum.

SCHWEITZER, Albert (1875–1965)

French (Alsatian) doctor, missionary and musician. He was a noted organist and author of several religious and philosophical books. But he is best remembered for his missionary and medical work in equatorial Africa, and especially for the hospital at Lambaréné which he founded.

SCILLY ISLES

Group of islands 40 km (25 miles) off the south-west coast of England. The main island is St Mary's. They have the mildest climate of any part of Great Britain and export flowers and vegetables to the mainland throughout the year.

SCIPIO (Publius Cornelius Scipio, *c.* 237–*c.* 183 BC)

Also known as *Africanus Major,* he invaded Carthage and defeated HANNIBAL during the PUNIC WARS. His adopted grandson, Publius Cornelius Scipio Aemilianus (185–129 BC), also known as *Africanus Minor,* completed the destruction of Carthage in 146 BC.

SCORPION

Group of ARACHNIDS, native to many warm and tropical regions. They are distinguished by two large claws and by their long tails which carry a poisonous sting. However, only some large tropical species are really dangerous to man. They are most active at night.

SCOTLAND

Most northerly country of GREAT BRITAIN with an area of 79,000 sq km (30,000 sq miles) and a population of just over 5 million. It includes several groups of islands off the west coast, chiefly the Inner and Outer HEBRIDES; and the ORKNEY and SHETLAND ISLANDS to the north. The capital is Edinburgh, but the largest city is Glasgow. Other towns and cities are Aberdeen, Dundee, Perth and Inverness. The principal industries have long been shipbuilding and heavy engineering; but the arrival of North Sea oil is bringing big changes to the Scottish economy. The country's other famous product is whisky. The Scottish Highlands and Islands are also noted for their beauty. Included is Ben Nevis, 1,343 m (4,406 ft), the highest point in the British Isles.

Scotland became a united kingdom in the ninth century AD and embarked upon a long

Right Fire-footed squirrel from Sierra Leone

period of conflict with England. In the thirteenth century William Wallace first defeated the English at Stirling, then was captured, taken to London and executed. In the fourteenth century Robert BRUCE inflicted a serious

Loch Awe, near Dalmally, Argyllshire, Scotland

defeat on an English army at Bannockburn in 1314. There were also close ties with France, and several attempts to establish a line of Catholic Scottish kings and queens on the English throne. However, the introduction of Protestant ideas into the country by John KNOX, and the establishment soon after of a Presbyterian CHURCH OF SCOTLAND, changed the situation. The Act of Union of 1707 between England and Scotland brought to an end the centuries of rivalry and struggle, although there were two JACOBITE rebellions against English rule, in 1715 and 1745, the second led by CHARLES EDWARD STUART, known also as 'Bonnie Prince Charlie'. In the nineteenth century Scotland played a big part in the INDUSTRIAL REVOLUTION. This century has seen a decline in the traditional heavy industries, but a recent revival of the economic climate, closely linked to the discovery and exploitation of North Sea oil, much of which will come ashore in Scotland. Also linked to the matter of North Sea oil are the political moves

Left Girl with guitar by Jan Vermeer

towards a greater degree of self-government for Scotland.

SCOTT, Captain Robert Falcon (1868–1912)

English explorer. He organized and led two expeditions to ANTARCTICA, in 1900 and again in 1910. It was on this second expedition that he reached the South Pole, shortly after the Norwegian explorer Roald AMUNDSEN. On his return journey Scott and his small party perished in a blizzard, when they were only a few miles from safety.

Captain Scott before he left for the South Pole

SCOTT, Sir Walter (1771–1832)

Scottish poet and novelist, born in Edinburgh. He was greatly interested in the folklore and history of the Border country and published several collections of poems and ballads as a result. His famous novels followed later, including *Waverley*, *The Heart of Midlothian*, *Quentin Durward* and *Redgauntlet*.

SCOUTS AND GUIDES

World-wide movements for boys and girls founded by Lord BADEN-POWELL in 1908 and 1910 respectively. The general aim of the movements is to encourage a sense of personal pride and responsibility.

SCULPTURE

Art or craft of creating shapes out of stone, or by carving wood, modelling clay, or casting metal. For thousands of years sculpture has been closely associated with ARCHITECTURE; and for such ancient civilizations as those of Egypt and Greece the two activities were often combined. Sculpture generally has always been produced on a large scale, often seen at its best in the open, although there are numerous pieces of sculpture specially designed for rooms. In this encyclopedia the work of the world's greatest sculptors is discussed under their individual entries.

SEAL

Group of marine MAMMALS, found in nearly all seas and oceans, distinguished by flippers instead of arms or legs. There are several species, including the Atlantic or grey seal, which frequents the coasts of north-western Europe; and the giant elephant seal of Antarctica which can grow to a length of 6 m (20 ft) and weigh 2,500 kg (5,500 lb). Closely related are sea-lions and the walrus. Walruses live in Arctic regions. The male grows two very long teeth, usually called tusks, which he uses to pull shellfish off rocks or to haul himself on to dry land.

SEAWEED

Group of marine PLANTS classed as ALGAE. The larger and more developed seaweeds contain CHLOROPHYLL and produce food by PHOTO-SYNTHESIS like most land plants; but their strong pigments often give them a red or brown colour instead of the more familiar green. Some seaweeds are gathered for food, especially in China and Japan.

SECOND WORLD WAR. *See* WORLD WAR II

SEMAPHORE

System of signalling employing two mechanical arms on a post placed in different positions to represent letters of the alphabet. Once widely used in the navy, with a man holding a flag in each hand. It can also describe the old system of railway signalling, where coloured arms moved to and from a horizontal position on a post to indicate whether or not a train could proceed down the track.

SENEGAL

West African republic with an area of 196,192 sq km (75,754 sq miles) and a population of over 5½ million. The capital is Dakar. Senegal became independent from France in 1960 and it achieved stability under its president Léopold Senghor, who retired in 1980.

SEURAT, Georges (1859–91)

French artist. He is often classed with the Impressionist painters, but developed an individual style of his own, called Pointillism, in which he represented colour as tiny dots or points of paint.

SEVEN WONDERS OF THE ANCIENT WORLD

These were the Pyramids of Egypt, the Hanging Gardens of Babylon, the Temple of Diana at Ephesus, the Mausoleum at Halicarnassus, the Colossus of Rhodes, the Statue of Zeus at

Olympia, and the Pharos or Lighthouse at Alexandria.

SEVEN YEARS WAR

Conflict between France, Austria and Russia on the one side, and Britain and Prussia on the other. It was mainly a continuation of the overseas colonial rivalry between France and Britain, and of the territorial disputes between Austria and Prussia. The main areas of conflict were in North America, where General WOLFE's eventual capture of Quebec secured Canada for Britain; and in Germany, where FREDERICK the Great of Prussia fought a long, hard but eventually victorious struggle against Austria and Russia for the territory of Silesia. The Treaty of Paris ended the war in 1763.

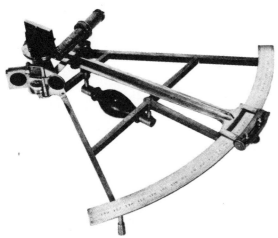

An 18th-century sextant

SEXTANT

Instrument used for measuring the angle between two distant objects, and especially in navigation for measuring the angle of the sun above the Earth. It was invented by the Englishman John Hadley during the eighteenth century.

SEYCHELLES

Island republic in the Indian Ocean, independent since 1976, with an area of 280 sq km (108 sq miles) and a population of 67,000. The capital is Victoria.

SHACKLETON, Sir Ernest Henry (1874–1922)

British explorer. He was a member of SCOTT's Antarctic expedition of 1900. He commanded two later expeditions to Antarctica, during which he was the first to reach the South Magnetic Pole.

SHAFTESBURY, Anthony Ashley Cooper, 7th Earl of (1801–85)

English social reformer who introduced laws limiting the working hours in some industries and banning the employment of women and children in mines. He also interested himself in housing and education for the poor.

SHAKESPEARE, William (1564–1616)

English dramatist and poet. He was born in Stratford-upon-Avon, married Anne Hathaway, and worked as an actor and theatre manager in London. Beyond this little is known for certain about his life, which has led people to question the authorship of some or all of his

Ophelia from Shakespeare's *Hamlet*, painting by Millais

plays. Nevertheless, the authorship is generally accepted, and the plays of Shakespeare are universally acknowledged as the greatest ever written, with regard both to their poetry and their insight into human behaviour and states of mind.

It is usual to classify them according to content and style. Thus there are the comedies, including *The Two Gentlemen of Verona*, *As You Like It*, *Twelfth Night* and *A Midsummer Night's Dream;* the historical plays, *Richard* II, *Richard* III, *Henry* IV (parts I and II), *Henry* V; the Roman plays, *Coriolanus*, *Julius Caesar* and *Anthony and Cleopatra;* the tragedies, *Romeo and Juliet*, *Hamlet*, *Macbeth*, *Othello* and *King Lear*; and those plays, written towards the end of Shakespeare's career, which are neither true comedies nor tragedies, notably *The Tempest*. In addition, Shakespeare wrote a large number of sonnets; once again, mystery surrounds the circumstances of their composition.

SHARK

Group of FISH, found in most tropical and warm seas and oceans, and sometimes round the north-west coasts of Europe. Species include the blue shark and the curious hammer-headed shark. Largest is the whale shark, which can grow to over 12 m (40 ft). Sharks can be dangerous, but do not usually attack swimmers unless provoked; and some species are quite harmless.

SHAW, George Bernard (1856–1950)

Irish dramatist and critic. Shaw was interested in ideas more than people, and so his plays generally are arguments about certain moral, social or political issues. An important part of most of them is the Preface, which can be read as an essay. Best-known are *Arms and the Man*, *The Devil's Disciple*, *Man and Superman*, *Major Barbara*, *Pygmalion* and *Saint Joan*. Shaw was also a leading music critic for some years; and a member of the intellectual, politically left-wing Fabian Society.

SHEEP

Group of MAMMALS, classed as ruminants (cud-chewers). There are still a few species of wild sheep; but most are reared domestically for their wool or their meat (mutton or lamb). Among domestic breeds are the Cotswold, Wensleydale, Dorset, Hampshire and Suffolk varieties.

SHELLEY, Percy Bysshe (1792–1822)

English poet, and a leading member of the Romantic group of poets. He wrote some long works, but best remembered today are some of his shorter pieces, including *Ode to the West Wind* and *Ode to a Skylark*. His wife, Mary Shelley, wrote the celebrated Gothic horror novel *Frankenstein*.

SHERIDAN, Richard Brinsley (1751–1816)

Irish dramatist and author of several of the wittiest plays in the English language include *The Rivals* and *The School for Scandal*. He also took a prominent part in British politics and was a successful theatre manager.

SHETLAND ISLANDS

Group of about 100 islands, the most northerly part of the British Isles, being situated 80 km (50 miles) north of the ORKNEYS. They are officially known as the county of Zetland. The population is about 20,000, and the chief town is Lerwick. They are famous for their small breed of pony; and today are an important base for North Sea oil.

SHINTO

Japanese religion. The word means 'way of the gods', and the basic Shinto belief is that the gods were ancestors of the Japanese people. At one time this led to the cult of ancestor worship among individual families, and to a belief in the divinity of the emperor. This latter aspect of the religion was officially abandoned in 1946.

SHIP

The name was originally applied to a sailing vessel with three or more masts, but now describes any sea-going vessel. Sailing ships of different kinds date back thousands of years. By the end of the eighteenth century they had reached their maximum size, especially with the building of such warships as HMS *Victory* (NELSON's flagship at the Battle of Trafalgar) which carried 100 guns; and achieved their greatest speed in the design of merchant clippers. The big change from wooden sailing ships to iron- or steel-built steamships took place during the nineteenth century, a notable example being I. K. BRUNEL's *Great Eastern*, the largest ship built during that century. Warships also became increasingly heavy-armoured, and were known as 'iron-clads'. This century has witnessed a second dramatic change, from steam to diesel- or nuclear-powered ships. Nuclear power has particularly influenced the design and efficiency of SUB-MARINES, which can now remain submerged for long periods of time and travel through the water at great speeds.

SHORTHAND

Name given to any system of writing by brief signs and abbreviations, usually based on word sounds. There were forms of shorthand in Roman times, and in England a type of short-hand was introduced during the time of Elizabeth I. Several shorthand systems are used today, notably that devised by Sir Isaac PITMAN. Another name for shorthand is sten-ography, meaning 'narrow writing'.

SHOSTAKOVICH, Dmitri (1906–75)

Soviet Russian composer. As a young man he wrote some very advanced music for the time, but later tried to follow the political doctrine of

his country that music, like all the arts, should be understandable to most people and generally optimistic in tone. Best known are his fifteen symphonies, especially the seventh symphony which he wrote in Leningrad while the city was under siege from the Germans during World War II.

SHREW

Group of MAMMALS. A few species live in water, but most are land animals, living on insects, worms and snails. The common shrew of Europe and Asia is about the size of a mouse.

The shrew, a small mammal

SIBELIUS, Jean (1865–1957)

Finnish composer. His best-known work is *Finlandia,* which is almost like a national anthem to the Finns themselves. However, Sibelius expressed the character of his home-land more deeply in his seven symphonies, violin concerto, and such tone-poems, based on Finnish folklore and legend, as *The Swan of Tuonela* and *Tapiola*.

SIERRA LEONE

West African republic with an area of 71,740 sq km (27,700 sq miles) and a population of about 3½ million. The capital is Freetown. The chief exports are diamonds, coffee and cocoa. The country became independent from Britain in 1961 and a republic in 1971 but it remains within the BRITISH COMMONWEALTH.

SIKHS

Indian religious community whose homeland is in the Punjab. Their founder was Baba Nanak who lived in the fifteenth century, and one of their aims has been to unite Hindus and Moslems. Under the leadership of Ranjit Singh they became a strong military force which opposed the British in the Sikh Wars of 1845 to 1849. They wear distinctive turbans over their uncut hair.

SIKKIM

A former Asian kingdom, Sikkim became the 22nd state of the Indian Union in 1975. It has an area of about 7,300 sq km (2,800 sq miles) and a population of about 250,000. The capital is Gangtok.

SILICON

Non-metallic ELEMENT, most commonly found in the form of silicon dioxide, or silica. This substance exists in many sands and rocks and as such forms about 60% of the Earth's crust. Silica is the main constituent of glass.

SILICONE

Name of various man-made POLYMERS of silicon and oxygen, widely used for lubrication and in water-resistant seals and polishes.

SILK

Natural fibre produced by silk worms, the larva of which spins a silken cocoon on mulberry leaves. The Chinese discovered how to use silk about 2,700 BC, and for thousands of years it remained one of the finest materials for clothing and linen. During this century it has been largely replaced by NYLON and other synthetic fibres.

SILVER

Metallic ELEMENT. It is the best conductor of heat and electricity among the metals. It is widely used in photography and metal processing; while silver coins and jewelry are often highly prized.

SINGAPORE

South-east Asian republic at the southern end of the Malay peninsula. It has an area of 581 sq km (224 sq miles) and a population of 2,404,000. The capital city of Singapore is a large sea port. Before World War II it was also an important British naval base, and during the war was occupied by the Japanese. Singapore gained internal self-government in 1959 and was part of Malaysia from 1963 to 1965, when it became an independent republic in the BRITISH COMMONWEALTH.

SKELETON

A rigid framework which supports and protects the soft tissue of an animal's body. It is the most durable part of an animal, for whereas the rest of the body decays rapidly after death, the skeleton can be preserved for thousands of years.

In vertebrate creatures such as man this framework is internal. In some animals, however, it appears on the outside. The skeleton of insects and shellfish, for example, is in the form of a hard outer case enclosing the vulnerable soft organs. In most instances this case is shed from time to time to allow the body inside to grow.

The skeleton of an adult human being consists of 206 bones, fitting together at the joints, and richly supplied with blood which nourishes the living cells of which they are composed. This framework is able to prevent the soft flexible body collapsing and protects it. Thus the brain is enclosed by the skull, the spinal cord by the backbone and the heart and lungs by the rib cage. The muscles needed for movement are also attached to the skeleton. *See also* BONE and VERTEBRATES.

The human skeleton

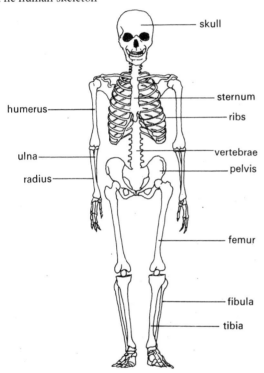

SKIN

Flexible covering of the body of many animals, though some of its functions vary from one class or group of animals to another. In human beings skin consists of an outer layer, the epidermis; and an inner layer, the dermis, which contains nerve endings, hair follicles and various glands. The sweat glands exude waste matter through skin pores and by so doing also help to regulate internal body heat. The sebaceous glands produce oily substances to prevent the skin from drying up.

SKUNK

MAMMAL related to the WEASEL, and native to North America. It has a large bushy tail; a distinctive coat of fur with a broad white stripe running down the back; and an even more distinctive and offensive smell which it discharges from special glands when alarmed or attacked.

SKYLARK

Small brown-and-white-feathered bird native to Europe and Asia, usually found in open stretches of countryside, and noted for its almost continuous song in flight.

SLOTH

MAMMAL native to the tropics of Central and South America. It lives its entire life in trees, hanging from branches by the hook-shaped toes or claws on each of its four legs. There are two basic species, the two-toed and three-toed sloth, both strictly vegetarians.

SMETANA, Bedřich (1824-84)

Czech composer, generally regarded as the founder of a Czech national style or school of music. His two best-known works are the opera *The Bartered Bride* and the group of orchestral tone-poems, depicting various scenes from Czech life and legend, called collectively *Ma Vlast* (My Country). Smetana, like Beethoven, went deaf.

SMITH, Adam (1723–90)

Scottish economist. His book *The Wealth of Nations* was the first to establish the true principles of political economy, and had a big influence on the course of British trade and industry during the period of the INDUSTRIAL REVOLUTION.

SMITH, Captain John (1580–1631)

English colonizer. After an eventful youth, during which he served in the Imperial Army and was captured by the Turks, he joined the company of colonists which journeyed out to Virginia, founding Jamestown in 1607. During an expedition into Indian territory he was captured. His life, it is said, was saved by the Indian princess Pocahontas. Smith later returned to England and published maps and pamphlets about America.

Captain Smith, saved by Pocahontas

King Powhatan comands C.Smith to be slayn, his daughter Pokahontas beggs his life his thankfullness and how he Subiected 39 of their kings reade ‡ history

SNAIL

Group of INVERTEBRATE animals classed as MOLLUSCS. There are over eighty species, adapted to life either in the sea, in fresh water or on land. All are protected by a spiral shell; some have been eaten since Roman times.

SNAKE

Large group of REPTILES, closely related to LIZARDS, but limbless. Snakes move by means of muscles attached to the ribs which pull the skin backwards and forwards in a kind of wave motion, the scales on the underside of the body gripping the ground or branches of a tree. Alternatively, some snakes move by twisting their bodies sideways and wriggling along. There are over 2,000 species, many confined to tropical regions, but some widely distributed. The largest species, such as the boa and python, can grow to a length of 9 m (30 ft). They do not have a poisonous bite but kill their prey by crushing it within their coils. Some snakes are very poisonous, including the cobras, RATTLESNAKES and mambas. They strike with poison-injecting fangs and not with their tongues which are used to catch particles of scent and help the snake to test its surroundings. The only poisonous British snake, found in many other parts of Europe, is the adder; but this will only strike if disturbed. The much larger grass snake is harmless.

SOCIETY ISLANDS

Group of volcanic islands in the Central Pacific Ocean, forming a part of French Polynesia. They cover an area of 1,700 sq km (650 sq miles); the largest island is Tahiti; and the total population is about 90,000.

SOCIOLOGY

Study of human behaviour related to society and general environment, encompassing aspects of HISTORY, economics, POLITICS and PSYCHOLOGY.

SOCRATES (470–399 BC)

Greek philosopher. He committed nothing to writing, and our knowledge of him comes from the accounts of some of his pupils, especially PLATO. Socrates was concerned with probing the meaning and truth of ideas by a technique of question and answer, and by so doing laid the foundations of systematic philosophical thought. At the same time, he called into question the institutions of state. This made him enemies; he was brought to trial on a charge of corrupting the minds of the young, condemned to death and elected to take his own life by drinking poison.

SODIUM

Soft, silvery-white metallic ELEMENT, found in many compounds, including SALT, but never in a pure form. Soda is the name given to some of these compounds, including sodium bicarbonate, familiar as a baking powder and a medicine.

SOLAR SYSTEM

Name for the SUN and the group of planets, with their own satellite moons, that revolve around it; also including the asteroids, which constitute a belt of several thousand minor planets or planetoids, and various COMETS and METEORITES. Nicolas COPERNICUS was the first to suggest the basic arrangement of the solar system, in contradiction to the previously held belief that the Earth was the centre of the universe. Most astronomers now believe that if our sun can support a system of planets, then it is mathematically probable that many other suns or stars also have solar systems.

The solar system

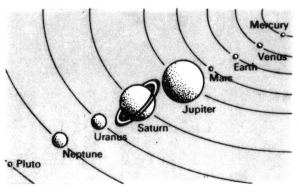

SOLENOID

In PHYSICS a coil of wire which produces a magnetic field when an electric current is passed through it. Used in many electrical devices, including starter-motors and magnetic brakes.

SOLOMON ISLANDS

An island nation in the PACIFIC OCEAN east of the island of New Guinea. The Solomon Islands are either mountainous, volcanic islands or low-lying coral formations. They have an area of 28,446 sq km (10,984 sq miles) and a population of about 227,000. The capital is Honiara, which is situated on Guadalcanal, the largest island. Two islands which are geographically part of the Solomon Islands, Buka and Bougainville, became part of PAPUA NEW GUINEA when it became independent in 1975. The chief exports are copra, fish, palm oil and cocoa.

SOLSTICE

The two days in each year when the sun is directly overhead along the line of the Tropics of Cancer and Capricorn. In Great Britain these correspond to the longest (21 June) and shortest (21 December) days of the year respectively.

SOMALI REPUBLIC

East African republic with an area of 637,657 sq km (246,214 sq miles) and a population of about 4 million. The capital is Mogadishu. It was created from a union of Italian Somalia and British Somaliland in 1960.

SONAR

System of underwater detection using sound waves, and similar in principle to RADAR. Sound waves are sent out at regular intervals. If they encounter any near-by object or surface they will be reflected back to source. The interval of time between the departure of a sound impulse and its return indicates the distance away of the object. Asdic was a type of sonar used for submarine detection during WORLD WAR II.

SONATA

Type of musical composition. The word comes from the Italian *suonare,* 'to sound', and describes a piece for instruments, as distinct from a cantata (from *cantare,* 'to sing'), which is a piece for voices. Early sonatas of the seventeenth century were often pieces for several instruments; but the word is usually applied to a type of composition, frequently in three movements (separate pieces), for the solo piano or piano and one other instrument, as developed during the Classical period of the eighteenth century.

SONATA FORM

Special way of constructing a single piece of music, comprising an *exposition* (presentation of themes), a *development* (development and extension of the themes) and *recapitulation* (return to opening section with some modifications). In strict sonata form the exposition is supposed to be repeated before proceeding to the development section. It was introduced during the Classical period of the eighteenth century and provides the basis of many individual movements in symphonies, concertos, sonatas and chamber music works.

SONG

Musical composition usually for solo voice, with or without instrumental accompaniment. Most songs are musical settings of existing poems or other lyrics, though in the case of folk songs words and music are often created together. In European music, the first great period for songs was that of the troubadours and other minstrels of the Middle Ages; a little later there was a distinctive type of English song called an ayre. During the nineteenth century special styles or traditions of song writing developed according to nationality and language, notably the German LIED. Most songs take the form of verses, with the melody repeated for each verse. The technical name for this is strophic. A song-cycle is a group of songs with a related theme or idea, written in a certain order and intended to be performed in that way.

SONNET

One of the best-known forms of POETRY. It is a poem of fourteen lines, almost always concentrating on one image or idea. There are several different types of rhyming sequence. The form was introduced to England from Italy during the sixteenth century.

SOPHOCLES (496–406 BC)

Greek dramatist. He introduced many new ideas and styles into Greek DRAMA, and the themes of some of his plays have been a source of inspiration to many other writers, and to some composers. Most famous of his tragedies are *Antigone, Oedipus Rex* and *Electra.*

SOUND

Form of ENERGY that travels through air at 1,222 km/h (764 mph), with slight variations for temperature and atmospheric pressure. It travels through water and other materials at a variety of different speeds. Sound is a succession of pulses or vibrations, usually described as waves. When these sound waves reach the ear they make the eardrum vibrate at the same rate, and these vibrations are then transmitted to the brain and interpreted as sound. The speed or rapidity of sound waves is called the frequency, measured in cycles per second; and the faster the frequency, the higher will be the pitch of the sound. People with good hearing can detect sounds with a frequency as low as 20 cycles per second, and as high as 20,000; though some other animals, such as BATS, can emit and hear higher-pitched sounds than these. In MUSIC the note A above middle C is tuned, by international agreement, to a frequency of 440. Also of great importance in music is the quality or tone of a sound. This is determined by overtones – a whole range of differently pitched sounds which accompany the note actually interpreted as such by the brain. Overtones make it possible to tell the difference in tonal quality between the notes of, say, a violin and a trumpet, or the individual sounds of our own voices. The scientific study of sound is called acoustics.

SOUTH AFRICA

Republic with an area of 1,221,037 sq km (471,471 sq miles) and a population of about 29 million. There are two capitals, Cape Town for legislation and Pretoria for administration; other important towns and cities are Johannesburg, Durban and Port Elizabeth. Most of South Africa is a high plateau, with a range of mountains, the Drakensberg, in the east. Another famous and beautiful point is Table Mountain, near Cape Town. The country is rich in mineral deposits, above all diamonds; in agriculture it produces abundant crops of maize, wheat and other cereals, and citrus fruits.

The first European settlers in South Africa were the Dutch who colonized the region of the Cape in the seventeenth century. Early in the nineteenth century the British took possession of the Cape region and most of the Dutch, or Boer settlers moved north to found their own republics of the Transvaal and the Orange Free State. At the end of the nineteenth century dispute between the Boers and the British led to the BOER WAR, after which the whole of South Africa came under British rule. The Union of South Africa within the British Empire and Commonwealth was created in 1910, but Boer influence remained strong. After WORLD WAR II the nation adopted a

Lion's Head Mountain near Cape Town, South Africa

policy of apartheid, which sought to separate, as far as possible, the minority white community from the many native black communities. Foreign criticism of this led South Africa to withdraw from the British Commonwealth and declare itself an independent republic in 1961. Overseas criticism of apartheid has continued, and the policy is slowly being modified.

SOUTHERN YEMEN

Republic in southern Arabia, officially the People's Democratic Republic of Yemen. It has an area of 332,968 sq km (128,567 sq miles) and a population of 1.8 million. The capital is Aden. The Yemen P.D.R. was a British protectorate until 1967.

SOUTH POLE. *See* ANTARCTICA

SOUTH-WEST AFRICA. *See* NAMIBIA

SPACE TRAVEL AND EXPLORATION

The first problem of space flight is to escape sufficiently from the gravitational pull of the Earth to go into orbit around it, or to escape from its gravitational field entirely in order to proceed further into space. There is also the problem of re-entry into Earth's ATMOSPHERE from space, which creates conditions of great heat due to the speed of re-entry and consequent friction with the atmospheric gases. In space itself men have to operate in weightless or near-weightless conditions, which requires very special training.

The age of space exploration opened on 4 October 1957 when the Soviet Union placed in orbit round the Earth the first artificial satellite, *Sputnik I*, weighing 83 kg (183 lb). A month later they launched *Sputnik II*, weighing 500 kg (1,100 lb). and carrying aboard the first space traveller, a dog called Laika. The first man in space was the Soviet cosmonaut Yuri Gagarin, who completed one orbit of the Earth in the spacecraft *Vostok I*, on 12 April 1961. The Soviet Union continued to take the lead in such space accomplishments until 1967, when the United States embarked upon its programme, called Apollo, of landing a man on the MOON. This object was achieved on 21 July 1969 when Neil Armstrong stepped down from the spacecraft of *Apollo 11* on to the moon's surface. The United States has also placed in orbit many satellites for telecommunications or weather research purposes; both the United States and the Soviet Union have launched unmanned space probes to other planets; and there are plans to maintain a space station or laboratory in orbit round the Earth.

Up to the present satellites and spacecraft have been launched by ROCKETS using quickly exhaustible fuels. Also, existing rockets cannot reach the speeds necessary to carry men on long journeys into space. Hence new methods of propulsion are being considered.

SPAIN

Kingdom of south-west Europe occupying most of the Iberian peninsula. It has an area of 504,782 sq km (194,908 sq miles) and a population of about 38 million. The capital is Madrid; other important cities include Barcelona, Bilbao, Valencia, Seville and Granada. Also administered by Spain are the BALEARIC

The Bull Ring, Madrid, Spain

and CANARY ISLANDS. Most of Spain is a high plateau, hot and dry in summer, cold in winter; but along the Atlantic coast and the Bay of Biscay there is a moister, more temperate climate; while along the Mediterranean coast and in the southern province of Andalusia, the climate is warm and mild, or sub-tropical. The chief products are wine, especially Sherry, olives, citrus fruits and cereals; but there are textile, chemical and engineering industries. Also, the tourist industry along the Mediterranean coast and in the Balearic islands is of great importance.

Spain was a province of the ROMAN EMPIRE for 500 years. During the Middle Ages the country was conquered by the MOORS of North Africa, and some regions were ruled by them for many centuries. In the fifteenth and sixteenth centuries came the great age of Spanish exploration, especially of Central and South America, making the country one of the wealthiest and most powerful European nations. This power declined from the sixteenth century onwards, and during the nineteenth century Spain lost most of its American possessions. This century the country suffered a terrible civil war, followed by a long period of dictatorial rule by General FRANCO. With his death in 1975 there was a period of civil disturbance; but Prince Juan Carlos was restored to the throne, and democratic institutions are being established. Spain has applied for membership of the EUROPEAN ECONOMIC COMMUNITY. *See also* ARMADA and PHILIP II.

SPARTA

City-state of ancient Greece covering much of the southern part of the country called Peloponnisos. Its great rivalry with the city-state of Athens led to the Peloponnesian Wars (431–404 BC) which ended with Spartan victory. The nation fell, with the rest of Greece, under Roman power during the second century BC. The traditional Spartan qualities were physical fitness and strict discipline.

SPEAKER

Name given to the Chairman of the House of Commons *(see also* PARLIAMENT). He is a Member of Parliament, but once elected to the position by his fellow MPs takes no further part in party politics. His duty is to maintain order and to give a fair hearing to all MPs during debates.

SPECIFIC GRAVITY

Ratio of the density of any material to that of water at 4° centigrade.

SPECIFIC HEAT

Ratio of the quantity of HEAT required to raise the temperature of 1 gramme of a material by 1° centigrade to the quantity required to raise the temperature of 1 gramme of water by the same amount.

SPECTRUM

In PHYSICS the term originally given to the range of colours produced by sunlight passing through a prism (red, orange, yellow, green, blue, indigo, violet); now applied to the entire range of electromagnetic waves which extends beyond each side of the visible part of the spectrum. In RADIOASTRONOMY an instrument called a spectroscope is used to analyse the light from stars and so provide much valuable information about their physical nature. *See also* Sir Isaac NEWTON and RAINBOW.

SPENSER, Edmund (1552–99)

English poet. He modelled much of his work on the styles of CHAUCER, created a new form of the SONNET, and built up a poetic vocabulary from words both old and new. His greatest work, *The Faerie Queen,* is a romantic epic based on episodes from the Arthurian legends.

The cross or garden spider building its web

SPIDER

Large group of INVERTEBRATE animals classed as ARACHNIDS. They differ from INSECTS in several respects, having eight legs instead of six, and a body divided into two sections only (head and thorax combined, plus abdomen). Also, nearly all spiders spin a delicate kind of silken thread, either to capture their prey or to line the inside of their nests. Spiders are graded according to the way they use their thread, from the most primitive species that simply pounce on their prey, to the group called the orb-spinning spiders which spin an elaborate web. A few species live in water, but most are land animals. The largest types live in the tropics, can grow to a length of about 23 cm (9 in) and are able to capture small mammals and birds. They are often mistakenly called tarantulas. The true tarantula lives in the Mediterranean region. Its bite was once believed to cause madness, and the only cure was thought to be a kind of dancing designed to sweat out the poison. The dance called the tarantella is named after this old belief. In fact, few species of spider are dangerous to man. One of these is the North American black widow spider.

SPINNING

The drawing out and twisting of cotton, wool or flax fibres into thread or yarn. For thousands of years this was a cottage industry, in which the yard was spun by a spindle. In the latter part of the eighteenth century new types of spinning machine were designed by James Hargreaves, Richard Arkwright and Samuel Crompton, and these turned the process into a manufacturing industry.

SPINOZA, Baruch (1632–77)

Dutch philosopher. He applied the methods of rationalism developed by René DESCARTES to his own philosophical theory that all matter and all events are indivisible and all equally a part of the same divine essence (God). His principal work is called, simply, *Ethics*.

SPONGE

Primitive group of INVERTEBRATE marine animals belonging to the group *Porifera*, so called because of the large pores that occur over the surface of the body. Most sponges attach themselves to the sea bed or to rocks. The common bath sponge is a skeleton from which the flesh has been removed.

SQUIRREL

Group of MAMMALS belonging to the RODENT family. Most species of squirrel are excellent climbers and spend much of their time in trees; others keep to the ground and live in burrows, such as the American CHIPMUNK. There is also the so-called flying squirrel, though this actually glides with the aid of membranes between the outstretched legs. In Europe there is the red squirrel and the far more common grey squirrel introduced from America.

SRI LANKA

Island republic, formerly Ceylon, south and east of the Indian mainland, with an area of 65,610 sq km (25,334 sq miles) and a population of about 15 million. The capital is Colombo. The chief products are tea, rubber, coffee, rice and precious stones, especially sapphires and rubies. It became a self-governing dominion within the BRITISH COMMONWEALTH in 1948, and the first country to have a woman prime minister when Mrs Sirimavo Bandaranaika succeeded to that post in 1960.

STALACTITE

Mineral deposit of calcium carbonate or similar matter on the roof of a limestone cave. It hangs from the roof like an icicle, and consists of fine, sparkling crystals. The water which filters

Stalactites and stalagmites in a cave in New Zealand

down from above and creates the stalactite then drips to the floor beneath where a second deposit, called a stalagmite, is built upwards in the form of a pillar. Sometimes a stalactite and its corresponding stalagmite join up.

STALIN, Joseph Vissarionovitch (1879–1953)

Soviet Russian political leader. He was born Joseph Dzhugashvili in the Caucasus region of Georgia and became a local Communist and Bolshevik leader in the years before the RUSSIAN REVOLUTION. By 1924, when LENIN died, he was General Secretary of the Soviet Communist Party and quickly assumed a position of supreme power. He introduced a series of ruthlessly prosecuted Five Year Plans to build up Soviet industry and agriculture. When Germany invaded the Soviet Union in 1941, thus bringing the country into WORLD WAR II on the side of the Allies, Stalin became supreme military commander. At the end of the war Soviet forces occupied most of the countries of eastern Europe, and he ensured that Communist regimes were established in them. A few years after his death, Stalin was denounced by the new Soviet leader Nikita Krushchev for political crimes.

STANLEY, Sir Henry Morton (1841–1904)

British explorer. After an adventurous early life, which included service in the American Civil War, he became a journalist and was sent by his newspaper to Africa to search for David LIVINGSTONE who was missing. Stanley found Livingstone and together they explored the northern end of Lake Tanganyika. On later African expeditions Stanley was the first white man to explore the Congo (now Zaïre) river.

STAR

All stars are probably similar in composition and chemical action to our SUN, though some

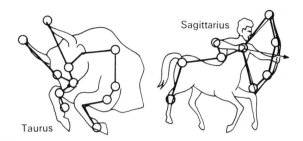

Signs of the Zodiac: Sagittarius and Taurus

are much larger or smaller, brighter or dimmer. The nearest star, after the sun, is Proxima Centauri, which is just over 4 light-years (40 million million kilometres) away. Beyond that are the remaining millions of stars of our galaxy of the MILKY WAY. And at infinitely greater distances beyond the Milky Way are other galaxies containing many more millions of stars.

The stars, as distinct from our planetary neighbours in the SOLAR SYSTEM, are often called the 'fixed' stars because they appear never to move from their particular position in the firmament. In fact, most of them are moving away from us at incredible speeds. Also, it has been discovered that some stars are double, or binary stars, revolving round each other; there can be triple or multiple stars also.

Astronomers now believe that most, if not all, stars go through a similar cycle of development. They start as a huge cloud of hydrogen gas and dust which gradually gets packed tighter and tighter together under its own gravitational attraction, getting hotter and hotter in the process. At a high enough temperature the hydrogen molecules join up to make molecules of helium, thus creating the same kind of conditions as those of a hydrogen bomb (*see* NUCLEAR ENERGY). Then comes a time when the hydrogen is almost used up; the star begins to cool but at the same time swells up to become what is known as a red giant. Finally it contracts again, becoming hotter as it becomes smaller, until all energy within it is exhausted and it exists as a tiny point of light, or white dwarf. *See also* PULSAR, QUASAR and RADIO-ASTRONOMY.

STEAM ENGINE

Any machine which uses steam as its motive power. Experiments in steam power date back to about 130 BC, but one of the first steam engines to be put into practical operation was designed by Thomas NEWCOMEN in the late seventeenth century. It was a stationary engine which helped to pump water out of mines, and did not work on the same principle as most later models. James WATT, in the next century, improved upon Newcomen's ideas and designed much more efficient stationary engines to drive machinery. In the early nineteenth century, Richard Trevithick, George STEPHENSON and others developed steam power for locomotive purposes on railways, and the steam engine assumed its most common and popular form for the next 100 years. Early in the nineteenth century steam engines were also introduced into ships. Steam power was used to propel some early road vehicles, but development in this direction was curtailed by the introduction of the INTERNAL COMBUSTION ENGINE. Today new types of steam engine are being considered, especially steam TURBINES, which can extract maximum power from the steam before any of it condenses back into water.

STEEL

Steel is iron plus a small quantity of carbon. It is characterized by its strength, resilience, and resistance to corrosion. Stainless steel is made by adding chromium and nickel. *See also* Sir Henry BESSEMER.

Steel works at Newport, Wales

STEPHENSON, George (1781–1848)

English engineer and pioneer of steam locomotion. One of his first railway steam engines was, in fact, called *Locomotion,* and first ran on the Stockton and Darlington Railway in 1825, with George Stephenson at the controls. More celebrated was his locomotive *Rocket* of 1829. His son Robert became an equally illustrious railway engineer, specializing in bridge and viaduct construction. *See also* RAILWAYS.

STEROIDS

Chemical compounds that have an important function in the development of most animals. They play a part in METABOLISM, which is the process of changing food into energy, and include bile acids and sex HORMONES.

STETHOSCOPE

Familiar device used by doctors for sounding a patient's heart and lungs. It is a simple sound amplifier, invented by the French physician R. Laennec (1781–1826).

STEVENSON, Robert Louis (1850–94)

Scottish novelist. He developed one of the finest narrative styles in English literature, and wrote some of the most popular classics, including *Treasure Island, Kidnapped* and *The Strange Case of Dr Jekyll and Mr Hyde,* the latter being an early masterpiece in the style of a psychological thriller. An invalid for much of his life, he travelled a great deal and finally settled in Samoa.

STOAT

MAMMAL closely related to the WEASEL, and native to many parts of the world. In winter its light brown fur changes to white and is valued as ermine.

STOCK EXCHANGE

Building where stocks and shares in commerce and industry are bought and sold. The first European stock exchange was founded in Antwerp, Belgium, in 1531. The London Stock Exchange is in Throgmorton Street, in the City of London. The New York Stock Exchange is in Wall Street. In Paris the same institution is known as the Bourse.

STRATOSPHERE. *See* ATMOSPHERE

STRAUSS

Family name of two famous Viennese composers. Johann Strauss the elder (1804–49) wrote some waltzes, polkas and other popular dances of his day, but is chiefly remembered today for the *Radetzky March*. His son, Johann Strauss the younger (1825–99), wrote most of the famous waltzes, including *The Blue Danube* and *Tales from the Vienna Woods*. He also wrote many equally tuneful operettas, notably *Die Fledermaus* ('The Bat').

STRAUSS, Richard (1864–1949)

German composer, and no relation to the Strauss family of Vienna. He was a brilliant orchestrator, and followed a series of symphonic poems, including *Don Juan* and *Till Eulenspiegel's Merry Pranks*, with a succession of operas. The most famous of his operas include *Der Rosenkavalier*, the one-act *Salome* and *Elektra*.

STRAVINSKY, Igor (1882–1971)

Russian-American composer. He was born in Russia, but left in 1914 and after living for some years in France settled in the United States and became an American citizen. His three famous scores for the Diaghilev Ballet, *The Firebird*, *Petrushka* and *The Rite of Spring* established him as an outstanding new composer. From then on he progressed through a number of different styles, but remained throughout his long creative career a leading figure in twentieth-century music.

SUBMARINE

Underwater vessel. A very early type of submarine was built by the American Robert Fulton (1765–1815), but the submarine was not used extensively until WORLD WAR I, when the Germans built a fleet of U-boats, as they called them, to attack British merchant ships. In WORLD WAR II the Germans build an even more formidable fleet of U-boats. A type of one-man or midget submarine was also developed. Today's submarines are powered by nuclear energy, are much larger, faster and can stay submerged for an indefinite period of time. Many are equipped with ballistic missiles which they can fire at targets from beneath the waves.

Submarine

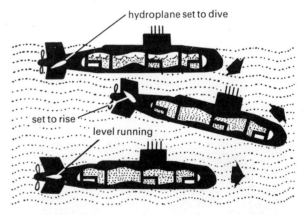

SUDAN

African republic with an area of 2,505,813 sq km (967,553 sq miles) and a population of about 18 million. The capital is Khartoum. The River NILE flows northwards across the entire length of the country and provides water for the irrigation of land that would otherwise be arid desert. One of the principal crops is cotton. The Sudan also produces about 80% of the world's gum arabic. The country was administered jointly by Britain and Egypt from 1899 to 1955, and secured its independence the following year.

SUEZ CANAL

It is 160 km (100 miles) long and connects the Mediterranean and Red Seas, thus shortening the sea route from Europe to India and the Far East by nearly 10,000 km (6,000 miles). It was constructed by the French engineer Ferdinand de Lesseps and opened in 1869. Then it passed into British ownership until nationalized by Egypt in 1956. This caused the so-called Suez Crisis, during which Britain and France attacked Egypt. Their action was condemned by the UNITED NATIONS and they were ordered to withdraw.

SUFFRAGE

The right to vote in elections. Thus the women who campaigned on behalf of their sex for the

Sylvia Pankhurst addressing a meeting, 1918

right to vote were called Suffragettes. They started campaigning in Britain during the early years of this century, under the leadership of Mrs Emmeline Pankhurst, often risking arrest and imprisonment. One suffragette threw herself under the King's horse on Derby Day 1913 to attract attention to the cause. In the event women over thirty secured the vote in Britain in 1918 and in 1928 received the same voting rights as men.

SUGAR

Sweet crystalline substance obtained from sugar cane or sugar beet. Foodstuffs containing sugar are classed as CARBOHYDRATES. Sugar is also an important raw material in the manufacture of ALCOHOL (including beer and wine) and other products.

SULLIVAN, Sir Arthur (1842–1900)

English composer. He wrote an opera and several works for the concert hall, but is chiefly remembered today for his long collaboration with the librettist W. S. GILBERT to produce such operettas as *HMS Pinafore, The Pirates of Penzance, Iolanthe, The Mikado* and *The Gondoliers*. These are usually referred to as the Gilbert and Sullivan operas.

SULPHUR

Non-metallic ELEMENT existing naturally as a yellow crystalline rock, often found in the region of VOLCANOES and hot springs. It is used in the manufacture of gunpowder, in fertilizers, and as the basis of some medicines and drugs. Sulphuric acid is a thick, colourless liquid and very corrosive. Sulphates is the general name for salts of sulphuric acid. Sulphate compounds are found in many forms, including calcium sulphate or gypsum, and magnesium sulphate or epsom salts.

SUMATRA. *See* INDONESIA

SUMER

Ancient civilization of southern MESOPOTAMIA which flourished between the fourth and second millennia BC. Known as the Land of the Two Rivers, watered by the Tigris and the Euphrates, it included the city-states of Kish, Lagash and Ur, and produced some fine pottery and metalwork.

SUN

The STAR at the centre of our SOLAR SYSTEM. Its diameter is about 1,390,000 km (864,000 miles), or 109 times that of the EARTH; is estimated to be 333,000 times more massive but to have only one-quarter of the density of our planet. The average distance between sun and Earth is 150 million km (94 million miles). At its surface, or photosphere, the sun has a temperature of about 6,000^7 centigrade. At its centre or core, the temperature may be more than 14 million degrees centigrade. Its immense light and energy are produced by the constant coversion of hydrogen into helium, which is similar to the process that takes place to create a hydrogen bomb explosion. The

Sun spot photographed from Greenwich Observatory

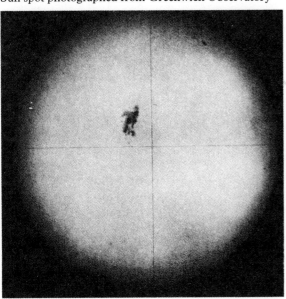

outer ring of the sun's atmosphere is called the corona, or crown. There are also the sunspots which literally appear as dark spots on the photosphere. They are areas of swirling gases, somewhat cooler than the surrounding areas. They grow and contract in area at fairly regular intervals. Associated with them are eruptions of incandescent gas called solar flares; and periods of so-called sunspot activity can affect radio communications on Earth.

The sun rotates about its own axis, and it moves in orbit round the centre of the MILKY WAY galaxy (of which it is a member), just as the planets of the solar system move in orbit around it.

SURINAM

South American republic with an area of 163,265 sq km (63,040 sq miles) and a population of about 403,000. The capital is Paramaribo. It was called Dutch or Netherlands Guiana until independence in 1975.

SURREALISM

Artistic and literary movement, officially founded by the French poet André Breton in 1924. It is based on dreams and the workings of the unconscious mind, and aims to present images and ideas beyond the world of everyday reality. Many artists and writers of this century have been influenced by it.

SWAZILAND

South African kingdom with an area of 17,363 sq km (6,704 sq miles) and a population of about 554,000. The capital is Mbabane. It was formerly a British protectorate, but was created an independent kingdom in 1967, while remaining within the BRITISH COMMONWEALTH.

SWEDEN

North European kingdom, occupying a large part of SCANDINAVIA, with an area of 449,964 sq km (173,742 sq miles) and a population of about 8¼ million. The capital is Stockholm, other important towns and cities are Gothenburg and Malmö. The country extends from the southern tip of the Scandinavian peninsula northwards beyond the Arctic Circle, where it forms a part of the region of LAPLAND. There are many lakes and forests, and timber is an important export. Mineral resources include iron ore, lead, zinc and sulphur. The principal industries are shipbuilding and motor manufacture. Sweden first became a kingdom in the tenth century. During the sixteenth century it grew into a major European power and became involved in a number of wars, including the THIRTY YEARS WAR. Early in the nineteenth century, however, it adopted a foreign policy of neutrality, which it has pursued up to the present day.

SWIFT, Jonathan (1667–1745)

Irish writer. He was a poet and prolific letter-writer, but is famous above all as the author of *Gulliver's Travels*. The first two parts of the book have become regular reading for children, but the entire work was written not as entertainment but as an angry attack on the follies and, as Swift saw them, crimes of the men and women of Gulliver's country – that is, England.

SWITZERLAND

European federal republic with an area of 41,288 sq km (15,942 sq miles) and a population of about 6⅓ million. The capital is Berne; other towns and cities are Zürich, Basle and Geneva. The ALPS cover more than half the area of the country, and Switzerland has long been an international resort for skiing and winter holidays. However, there are good pastures, and dairy farming is important. Switzerland has no heavy industries, but is famous for its manufacture of precision instruments, notably clocks and watches. Its geographical position, between the three much larger countries of France, Germany and Italy, has led to distinct French-, German-, and Italian-speaking areas. It has also led to Switzerland's long-standing neutrality, making it a centre of international banking and of many international organizations.

SYMPHONIC POEM

Musical composition for orchestra intended to depict some story or scene. It was created by LISZT and became popular with other nineteenth- and early twentieth-century composers. Some orchestral compositions, very similar in character, are called tone-poems.

SYMPHONY

Type of musical composition. The word comes from the Greek, meaning 'sounding together', and there have been instrumental compositions called symphonies since the RENAISSANCE. In the seventeenth and early eighteenth centuries a symphony was often an instrumental interlude in some larger work, such as the so-called 'Pastoral' symphony from HANDEL'S *Messiah*. However, the symphony as we know it today developed during the Classical period of the eighteenth century as a self-contained orchestral composition, usually in four separate movements; and during the nineteenth century, largely due to BEETHOVEN, it became the most important type of orchestral work, sometimes with a chorus and soloists as well. Many twentieth-century composers have continued to write symphonies.

SYRIA

Middle East republic with an area of 185,180 sq km (71,502 sq miles) and a population of over 8½ million. The capital is Damascus, one of the oldest cities in the world. Syria became an independent republic in 1944, and was a member of the United Arab Republic between 1958 and 1961. Its proximity to ISRAEL has also involved it in the Arab disputes with that country.

T

TACITUS, Cornelius (*c.* AD 55–117)

Roman historian. His father-in-law was Gnaeus Julius AGRICOLA, the Roman soldier and governor of Britain, and his *Life of Agricola* is generally regarded as the first true work of biography.

TAHITI. *See* SOCIETY ISLANDS

TAIWAN

Island republic, formerly the island of Formosa, off the Chinese mainland with an area of 35,989 sq km (13,896 sq miles) and a population of over 17 million. The capital is Taipei. From 1895 to 1945 the island was under Japanese rule. In 1949 it became the refuge for the Chinese Nationalists after the creation of the People's Republic of CHINA, with military and political support from the United States. But in 1971 the Nationalists lost their membership of the UNITED NATIONS to the Chinese People's Republic. In 1981 mainland China made approaches to Taiwan aimed at achieving closer ties between the countries.

TAJ MAHAL

Palatial Moslem tomb in Agra, India, built by the Shah Jahan for his wife Mumtaz Mahal between 1630 and 1650. With its surrounding gardens it is considered to be one of the most beautiful buildings in the world, and is constructed entirely of marble.

TALLIS, Thomas (*c.* 1505–85)

English composer, mostly of choral church music in a rich, solemn style. His most famous piece, a Latin motet called *Spem in alium*, has forty separate vocal parts.

TAMERLANE (Timur the Lame, (*c.* 1336–1405)

Mongol warrior and a direct descendant of GENGHIS KHAN. By a series of military conquests he extended the Mongol Empire to Moscow in the north, Egypt in the south-west, and as far as the mouth of the River Ganges in the east. He died while preparing to invade China.

TANK

Heavily armoured and armed military vehicle. The first tanks were introduced by the British in WORLD WAR I during the Battle of the

The Taj Mahal, Tagra, India

Somme in 1916. In WORLD WAR II the Germans, with their panzer divisions, and the Russians employed the most powerful tanks, especially during the great tank battle of Kursk on the eastern front in 1943.

TANZANIA

East African republic with an area of 945,087 sq km (364,920 sq miles) and a population of about 18 million. The capital is Dar es Salaam, but Dodoma will become the capital in the 1980s. Mt Kilimanjaro in northern Tanzania, 5,895 m (19,340 ft), is Africa's highest mountain. The chief exports are coffee, cotton, cloves, sisal and diamonds. Tanzania was formed when the former British Territories of Tanganyika (independent in 1961) and Zanzibar (independent 1963) united in 1964, remaining within the BRITISH COMMONWEALTH.

Coffee harvesting on the slopes of Kilimanjaro, Tanzania

TAOISM

Chinese philosophy or way of life, probably founded by Lao-Tzu. Little is known about him, but he may have lived at the same time as CONFUCIUS. *Tao* means the changeless reality of natural things. The follower of *tao* leads a quiet, passive life so that he may feel himself to be a part of this changeless reality and so become wise.

TAPE RECORDER

Instrument which uses magnetized plastic tape to record sound waves as magnetic patterns and then reproduce them as sounds. Tape recorders were introduced during the 1950s, and some composers became interested in them as new ways of processing and re-creating sounds. Early musical experiments of this type were called *musique concrète*. Today there are videotape recorders which register and play back both sound and vision.

TAPESTRY

Fabric in which yarns of different colours are threaded to make patterns or to illustrate scenes. Most famous is the Bayeux Tapestry, depicting events leading up to WILLIAM the Conqueror's invasion of England, and the Battle of Hastings. This tapestry, dating from the eleventh century, is embroidered on linen and is about 70 m (230 ft) long. It is preserved in the town of Bayeux, Normandy, France.

TAPIR

MAMMAL classed as an UNGULATE. One species is native to parts of Central and South America; the other, larger species lives in Malaya. Tapirs are vegetarian, nocturnal and timid. They are also good swimmers.

TASMANIA

Island off the south-east mainland of Australia, with an area of 68,000 sq km (26,000 sq miles) and a population of about 400,000. The capital is Hobart. Tasmania is one of the six states of the Commonwealth of Australia.

TASMANIAN DEVIL

Small, bear-like MAMMAL, classed as a MARSUPIAL, once found in part of Australia but now limited to the island of Tasmania. It lives on other small animals.

TCHAIKOVSKY, Peter Ilich (1840–93)

Russian composer. He began his career as a civil servant, but once he had turned to music he quickly created a colourful and dramatic orchestral style. For many years he was helped financially by Madame Nadejda von Meck, a rich widow who admired his work, though they never met. Tchaikovsky wrote six symphonies, several concertos, symphonic poems and operas. His most popular works today are the Piano Concerto no. 1 in B flat minor, the fantasy-overture *Romeo and Juliet,* the three ballet scores, *Swan Lake, The Sleeping Beauty* and *The Nutcracker,* and the overture *1812,* inspired by NAPOLEON's invasion of Russia.

TEETH

Most vertebrate animals are equipped with teeth. These project from the jaws and are used for breaking down the food taken in the mouth into small pieces, to make it easier to digest. They vary considerably in shape, according to the type of food which different creatures consume. Animals known as herbivores, such as cows, which feed only on plants and vegetables have teeth for crushing and grinding, whereas carnivores like dogs and tigers, which feed from other animals, have the sharp and pointed teeth necessary for tearing flesh. Since a human's diet is very varied and can be

Tasmanian devil

composed of both meat and vegetable matter, he is equipped with four different kinds of teeth. The incisor and canine teeth at the front of his jaw are for cutting and tearing, while the premolars and molars at the back are able to crush and grind food. During his lifetime the human being has two sets of teeth. The first set of twenty, called the milk teeth, appear when the baby is about six months old. Approximately six years later these begin to be replaced by the adult set, which when complete will number thirty-two.

Each tooth is composed mainly of calcium, with a soft central pulp containing nerves, lymph and blood vessels which nourish it. The outer exposed surface is protected by enamel, a very hard substance, which is nevertheless subject to decay from prolonged contact with sweet and starchy foods.

TELEGRAPHY

Method of sending messages of some sort by means of electrical impulses along a wire, or by RADIO WAVES. A pioneer in electric telegraphy was the Englishman Charles Wheatstone, who took out a patent for a type of telegraphy apparatus in 1837. More famous was the work of Samuel MORSE who transmitted his first message in his own newly invented code along 16 kilometres (10 miles) of cable in 1838. The principles of the telephone were first applied to a novelty electric violin invented by the German Philip Reis about 1860; but the first true telephone apparatus was built by Alexander Graham BELL in 1876. The possibility of using radio waves as a means of communication was first demonstrated by the German Heinrich Hertz in 1887, and ten years later Guglielmo MARCONI transmitted the first radio message.

TELESCOPE

Instrument for enlarging the appearance of distant objects. The most famous telescopes are those used in ASTRONOMY. There are two types of optical telescope, the refracting and the reflecting telescope. GALILEO made one of the first successful models of the former type; while Sir Isaac NEWTON was the first to build one of the latter. Today's most powerful reflecting telescope is installed in the OBSERVATORY at Mount Palomar in the United States. It can detect objects about 2 billion light-years away. However, there are also radio telescopes, such as the one at JODRELL BANK, Cheshire, which listen in to the immense amount of radio activity in the universe and can receive signals from objects far more distant in space than any that could actually be seen.

TELEVISION

The transmission and reception of visual images by electromagnetic waves. The images received by the camera are converted into a pattern of electrical impulses, transmitted as radio waves, and reconverted into the original image by the receiver. The pioneer of television was John Logie BAIRD who produced the very first televisual image in 1924, and two years later demonstrated his invention to the Royal Institution of Great Britain. His system was adopted for further development by the BRITISH BROADCASTING CORPORATION in 1929, and was used when the BBC opened the world's first television service in 1936. However, it was later superseded by a different and more reliable system perfected by the Russian-American scientist Vladimir Zworykin.

TELL, William

Legendary hero of the Swiss struggle for independence from Austria in the fourteenth century. According to legend, he shot an apple from his son's head with his crossbow in order to gain a pardon from the death sentence. His adventures inspired a play by the German dramatist Johann SCHILLER and later ROSSINI's opera.

TENNIS

Game played between two or four players. There is a marked-out area, the court, with a long net drawn across the centre. The opposing

Filming a television serial

Swedish tennis champion Bjorn Borg

players hit a ball to each other with rackets. They concede points to their opponent each time they hit the ball into the net, or place it outside the limits of the court. In other words, one player (or pair) wins by the other's mistakes. The game is played on grass (lawn tennis) or on a hard court. Its origins go back to the sixteenth century, and the modern form of the game dates from 1873. Two of today's most important international tennis competitions are the Wimbledon Championships in London, and the Davis cup for men's teams. The indoor game of table tennis has similar, though simpler rules.

TENNYSON, Alfred, 1st Baron (1809–92)

English poet and one of the leading literary figures of the Victorian age. He wrote several long lyric poems, including *Idylls of the King*, based on the Arthurian legends; though most popular of his works at one time was his poem celebrating the Charge of the Light Brigade at Balaclava during the Crimean War. Tennyson was one of the best-known poets to hold the post of Poet Laureate.

TERMITE

Group of INSECTS similar to but not the same as ANTS, though they are sometimes called white ants. They live mainly in tropical and subtropical regions of Africa, Australia and South America. Some species build hard mud nests which can be up to 6 m (20 ft) high. They feed on wood and can do serious damage to buildings and furniture.

THACKERAY, William Makepiece (1811–63)

English novelist. His best-known work, *Vanity Fair*, is a satire upon the sentimentality and pretensions of English Victorian society, the title being taken from John BUNYAN's *Pilgrim's Progress*. Other novels by Thackeray are *Pendennis* and *The History of Henry Esmond*.

THAILAND

South-east Asian kingdom with an area of 514,000 sq km (198,467 sq miles) and a population of about 46 million. The capital is Bangkok. The chief products are rice and rubber. For most of its history the country was called Siam, and it remained largely isolated from the outside world until the nineteenth century.

THEATRE

Place for the performance of drama. The ancient Greeks built open-air theatres, usually on a hillside, with semi-circular rows of seats overlooking a circular space called the orchestra. The restored theatre at Epidaurus, dating from about 350 BC, is a good example of a Classical Greek theatre. The Romans altered this plan by introducing a raised platform for the performers. A fine example of this type of theatre, restored and still regularly used, is at Orange in southern France. The first theatre in London was erected in Shoreditch by Richard Burbage, a colleague of SHAKESPEARE; a little

Shakespeare's Globe Theatre, London

later, in about 1590, he built the more famous Globe theatre across the River Thames at Southwark. However, the first theatre in the modern sense was built at Parma, Italy in 1618, with the familiar plan of an auditorium with a raised state and a curtain. This type of theatre, and opera house, is still the most usual design; but during this century there have been built theatres in which the seats almost surround the stage, the idea being to create a closer sense of participation between audience and performers. Such designs are called 'theatre in the round'.

THEOLOGY

The study of religious doctrines and beliefs, mainly about the nature of God. It could be called the philosophy of religion, and many philosophers have included theological ideas in their thinking.

THERMODYNAMICS

Science of the relationship between HEAT and mechanical energy, and an important part of many branches of PHYSICS and ENGINEERING.

THERMOMETER

Instrument for measuring amounts of HEAT (temperature). Most thermometers consist of a tube containing a liquid, usually mercury or coloured alcohol, which expands or contracts, and thus moves up or down the tube, according to the temperature. There are several different scales of temperature degree. The most widely used today is the centigrade scale, in which 0 degrees and 100 degrees are the freezing and boiling points of water respectively. Another is the KELVIN scale, mostly used for measuring very low temperatures.

THIRTY YEARS WAR

European conflict (1618–48) centred round the rivalry between Protestant and Catholic royal families. It was a confused struggle, fought mainly on German soil. The German Catholic Emperor Ferdinand II aimed to restore the whole of Germany to the Catholic faith, and won many victories with his generals Johann Tilly and Albrecht von Wallenstein. But King Gustavus Adolphus of Sweden then entered the war on the Protestant side, and the tide turned in his favour. Eventually France entered the struggle on the side of Sweden, also declaring war on Spain. The Peace of Westphalia brought the war officially to an end, though the fighting between France and Spain continued until 1659.

THOMAS, Dylan (1914–53)

Welsh poet. His most important work was *Under Milk Wood*, the poetic evocation of a

Execution of prisoners during the Thirty Years War

Welsh village, with various roles as in a play, and originally intended for radio performance.

THUCYDIDES (*c.* 460–400 BC)

Greek historian and general. His longest work is a history of the Peloponnesian War, which is both of historical value and of great literary merit.

TIBET

Autonomous province of CHINA, with an area of 1,222,000 sq km (472,000 sq miles) and a population of about 1½ million. The capital is Lhasa. The whole of Tibet is a part of the HIMALAYAS and the highest country in the world with an average altitude of 4,600 m (15,000 ft). For centuries it remained virtually cut off from the outside world, its people creating a special type of BUDDHISM with lamas as priests. In 1950 the People's Republic of China claimed the country as a province, and a few years later the Dalai Lama, or chief priest, was forced to leave.

TIDE

Regular rise and fall in the sea level, due to the gravitational pull of the MOON, and to a lesser extent of the SUN. When it is high tide in one part of the world it is low tide in another. Spring tides occur when the sun and moon are in a direct line in relation to the EARTH and combine their gravitational pull, causing the greatest rises and falls in sea level. Neap tides occur when the sun and moon are at right angles in relation to the Earth and their gravitational forces cancel each other out, reducing the rise and fall of the sea to a minimum.

TIEPOLO, Giovanni Battista (1696–1770)

Italian artist. He was a master of FRESCO painting, decorating in a light and graceful

Rococo style the ceilings and walls of many churches and palaces, especially in Venice, Würzburg and Madrid.

TIERRA DEL FUEGO

Large group of islands at the southern end of South AMERICA, shared territorially between ARGENTINA and CHILE.

TIGER

Large carnivorous MAMMAL and member of the CAT family, native to parts of Asia. Tigers are distinguished by their yellowish-orange coats with black stripes. They can be ferocious animals but rarely attack people and are now in danger of being hunted to extinction.

Asian tiger

TIME

Measure of duration based on such events as the rotation of the EARTH in relation to the SUN (day and night) and the movement of the Earth about the sun (the seasons of the year). *See also* CALENDAR and CLOCKS AND WATCHES..

TINTORETTO (1518–94)

Italian artist whose real name was Jacopo Robusti. He created an intensely dramatic style of painting and concentrated on Biblical scenes which he executed on a very large scale. One of his most famous paintings is *The Last Supper* in the church of San Giorgio Maggiore, Venice, Italy.

TITANIUM

Metallic ELEMENT, widely distributed in various rocks but difficult to extract. It is added to steel ALLOYS and used in the construction of jet engines and missiles because of its resistance to high temperatures.

TITIAN (*c.* 1487–1578)

Italian artist whose real name was Tiziano Vecelli. During his long career he was the unchallenged leader of the Venetian school of RENAISSANCE painters. He produced a number of large scenes from classical mythology in rich, glowing colours, and also many portraits, notably of PHILIP II of Spain.

TOGO

West African republic with an area of 56,000 sq km (21,623 sq miles) and a population of about 2½ million. The capital is Lomé. Togo became independent from France in 1960. Exports include phosphates, cocoa and coffee.

TOLTEC

Pre-Christian civilization of MEXICO which flourished from about the sixth to the thirteenth centuries. The Toltecs were skilled metal and stone workers, and the ruins of some of their towns and cities are still to be seen.

They were supplanted by the AZTECS who, however, continued to worship their chief god, Quetzalcoatl, 'The Plumed Serpent'.

TOLSTOY, Count Leo Nikolayevich (1828–1910)

Russian novelist. He was an aristocrat with a large country estate, but spent much of his time among his peasant employees, finally renouncing his property and wealth in the name of his Christian beliefs. His two greatest works are the epic *War and Peace*, set at the time of Napoleon's invasion of Russia in 1812 and partly an account of that campaign; and *Anna Karenina*.

TONGA

Kingdom which comprises 150 small islands in the South PACIFIC OCEAN. The population is about 97,000 and the capital is Nuku'alofa on the main island of Tongatapu. It gained independence from Britain in 1970.

TORNADO

Type of whirlwind usually developing a kind of funnel which moves across the surface of the land (or sea) causing great damage along its path. Tornados occur especially in the region of the Mississippi basin in the United States, where they are known as 'twisters'.

TORPEDO

Type of under-water self-propelling shell or bomb, developed during the late nineteenth century and used extensively by German submarines (U-boats) in both WORLD WAR I and WORLD WAR II. Torpedoes can also be launched from surface vessels or from aircraft. Modern types are jet propelled and guided by remote control.

TORTOISE. *See* TURTLE.

TOULOUSE-LAUTREC, Henri de (1864–1901)

French artist. He specialized in drawings and paintings of Paris cafés and cabarets which he executed with a brilliant sense of mood and atmosphere. He also revolutionized the art of graphic design with his many theatre and cabaret posters.

Poster by Toulouse-Lautrec

TRADE UNION

Association whose members work in one particular trade, industry or service, or related trades, industries and services. Its chief aims are to safeguard the jobs of its members and to represent their interests. The modern trade union movement began in Britain in the nineteenth century, when working people were often ruthlessly exploited by their employers. As individuals they were helpless, but as an organized group they could act to improve their conditions. A group of laws, called the Combination Laws, made it illegal for working people to organize themselves, and in 1834 some agricultural workers in the Dorset village of Tolpuddle were deported for trying to form themselves into a trade union. Henceforth they were known as the Tolpuddle Martyrs, and their case so outraged liberal opinion that the formation of trade unions was permitted. The ultimate power of a trade union lies in its right to call a strike of its members, that is, to withhold their labour. However, most trade union activity is much less dramatic, involving day-to-day contact with employers and a peaceful settlement of any problems or disputes. The Trades Union Congress (TUC) is a confederation of British trade unions, and an important political and social institution. Most other Western democracies have similar trade union movements.

TRADE WIND

Tropical ocean wind that blows for most of the year, from the north-east in the Tropic of Cancer and from the south-east in the Tropic of Capricorn. The name dates from the days of merchant sailing ships.

TREE

Large group of PLANTS, and also the largest kinds of plant. A tree is distinguished by its woody supporting stem or trunk. Trees of different types grow on land in most climates and conditions, except for deserts and arctic and antarctic regions. They can be classed as evergreen (those that retain their foliage throughout the year), and deciduous (those that shed their leaves annually, usually in the winter). Another classification is between conifers (including all types of pine) and broad-leaved trees (beech, oak, plane, ash and many more). The largest species are the redwoods, or sequoias, of Northern America, which can grow to a height of 90 m (300 ft). The

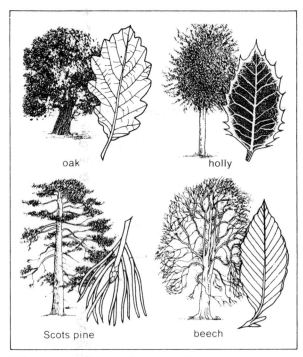

Silhouettes and leaves of common European trees

cultivation of trees for timber, or as a means of protecting land from erosion, is called forestry.

TRIGONOMETRY

Branch of mathematics based on the relationship between the sides and angles of triangles and widely used in navigation and surveying.

TRINIDAD AND TOBAGO

Republic in the WEST INDIES comprising the two islands so named. The former is the much larger island of the two, with an area of 5,130 sq km (1,981 sq miles). The population is about 1,166,000 and the capital is Port of Spain. Oil production is one of the leading industries and an important source of revenue. The chief agricultural products are cocoa and sugar. The islands were discovered by Christopher COLUMBUS. They were a British possession until 1962, and remain within the BRITISH COMMONWEALTH.

TRISTAN DA CUNHA

Remote volcanic island in the south ATLANTIC OCEAN, and a dependency of ST HELENA. Today the few inhabitants maintain important radio and weather stations.

TROJAN WAR

According to Greek mythology, a war waged by the Greeks against the city of Troy, or Ilium, in Asia Minor (now TURKEY). The true circumstances of this war, and its dates, are largely a matter of conjecture. The most famous incident, according to mythology, was the building by the Greeks of the giant Wooden Horse by which they gained entry into Troy.

TROPICS

The Tropics of Cancer and Capricorn are two imaginary lines which represent the limits, north and south of the EQUATOR, of the region where the sun is overhead at noon. The Tropic of Cancer is $23°$ $27'$ north of the Equator, the Tropic of Capricorn the same latitudinal distance south. Within the Tropics the climate is constantly warm or very hot.

TROPISM

Movement or growth of PLANTS according to external conditions. Phototropism is the action of some plants to turn towards the sun. Hydrotropism is the growth of roots towards moisture.

TROTSKY, Leon (1879–1940)

Soviet Russian revolutionary. Trotsky, whose real name was Bronstein, worked closely with LENIN to bring about the RUSSIAN REVOLUTION of 1917, and soon after organized the Red Army and led it to victory in the period of civil war. After Lenin's death he quarrelled with STALIN and eventually went into exile in Mexico where he was assassinated by a Soviet agent.

TUATARA

Last surviving member of a group of REPTILES closely related to DINOSAURS. It resembles a LIZARD but has a beaked face, and is confined to a few lonely islands off the coast of New Zealand.

TUNGSTEN

Metallic ELEMENT with a high melting point. It is a part of many steel ALLOYS and is also widely used in the electrical industry, especially as a lamp filament.

TUNISIA

North African republic with an area of 163,610 sq km (63,174 sq miles) and a population of about 6⅓ million. The capital is Tunis. The region was first settled by the PHOENICIANS in about 1000 BC and was later a part of the ROMAN EMPIRE after the capture and destruction of Carthage, which was near Tunis. It became a French protectorate in the nineteenth century, was fought over during WORLD WAR II and gained its independence in 1956.

TURBINE

Type of ENGINE in which steam or some other hot gas is applied to a kind of rotor or series of blades, which then transfer the heat energy directly into motion.

The turbine engine works on much the same

Turbine engine

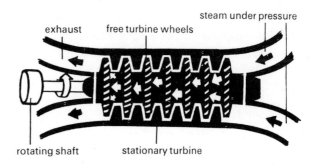

steam under pressure
exhaust   free turbine wheels
rotating shaft   stationary turbine

mechanical principle as the water wheel. The original steam turbine engine was developed late in the nineteenth century by the British engineer Sir Charles Parsons. Because the steam was used within the engine itself, instead of having to be introduced into cylinders, it was much more efficient than conventional steam engines. Steam turbine engines were soon preferred to cylinder and piston engines for ship propulsion, both because of their efficiency and because of their more compact design. They are also widely used in power stations to drive the electric generators.

TURKEY

Republic partly in Europe but mostly in Asia Minor, with an area of 780,576 sq km (301,399 sq miles). The population is about 45 million and the capital is Ankara. The other important city is Istanbul. Much of Turkey is wild, mountainous countryside, but it contains the sites of some of the most famous cities of the ancient world and Biblical times, including Ephesus, Antioch and Tarsus. During the Middle Ages most of present-day Turkey was a part of the BYZANTINE EMPIRE with its capital at Constantinople (now Istanbul). The Ottoman Turks entered the land during the fourteenth century, and two hundred years later had created the OTTOMAN EMPIRE which covered large areas of the Middle East and south-east Europe. This empire declined rapidly during the nineteenth century and was brough to an end after WORLD WAR I, partly because Turkey had entered the war against the Allies. Kemal ATATURK then created the modern Turkish republic. Since WORLD WAR II there have been disputes with GREECE, including the question of the status of the Turkish population of CYPRUS.

TURNER, Joseph Mallord William (1775–1851)

English artist. He painted mainly landscapes, developing a style that had a great influence on

The Fighting Temeraire by Turner

the later French Impressionists. He then proceeded to almost total abstraction. Thus he was far ahead of his time in many ways.

TURTLES AND TORTOISES

Group of REPTILES distinguished by their massive bony shell from which only the head and legs protrude, and into which they can be withdrawn. Different species are adapted for life on land or in the sea. Largest species is the giant tortoise of the GALAPAGOS ISLANDS in the Pacific Ocean, which can grow to a length of 2 m (6 ft) and weigh up to 550 kg (1,200 lb).

TUVALU

A Pacific Ocean island nation north of Fiji, formerly called the Ellice Islands. Tuvalu became an independent member of the BRITISH COMMONWEALTH in 1978. It has an area of 24 sq km (9 sq miles) and a population of 7,000. The capital is Funafuti.

TWAIN, Mark (1835–1910)

American novelist whose real name was Samuel Langhorne Clemens. His best-known books are *The Adventures of Tom Sawyer* and *The Adventures of Huckleberry Finn*.

U

UGANDA

East African republic with an area of 236,036 sq km (91,139 sq miles) and a population of about 13 million. The capital is Kampala. Uganda contains Lake Victoria, the source of the White Nile. Uganda became independent in 1962 and is a member of the BRITISH COMMONWEALTH. From 1971 to 1979 Uganda was ruled by the tyrant General Idi Amin, but he fled when Ugandan exiles and a Tanzanian army force invaded the country.

ULTRASONICS

Branch of the physics of SOUND concerned with sound waves of a very high frequency and beyond the normal range of the human ear. Ultrasonics can be applied to the detection of weaknesses in metal, to the cleaning of very small and complex articles, and to certain kinds of echo-sounding.

ULTRA-VIOLET RAYS

Band of electromagnetic waves just beyond the visible light band of the SPECTRUM. Ultra-violet light, either from the sun, or from sunray lamps, produces vitamin D in the skin and a tan, but over-exposure can be dangerous.

UNGULATE

The word comes from the Latin *unguis*, meaning a hoof, and describes that large group of MAMMALS which have their toes protected by hard, horny pads. Included in the group are HORSES, DEER, cattle, CAMELS and RHINO-CEROSES.

UNION OF SOVIET SOCIALIST REPUBLICS (USSR)

Federation of Communist states of Europe and Asia. It is the largest nation with an area of 22,402,200 sq km (8,650,010 sq miles). The total population is 262,436,000 (1979 census). The federal capital is Moscow.

The largest republic within the federation (Soviet Union) is Russia. Other important Russian cities, apart from Moscow, are Leningrad (formerly St Petersburg, the old Imperial Russian capital), Rostov, Volgograd (formerly Stalingrad), Kuybyshev and Kazan. The principal physical feature is the River Volga which flows west to east and then north to south into the CASPIAN SEA across the Russian plain. The Caucasus mountains form a natural frontier in the south, while the Ural mountains divide European Russia from Siberia in the east. (*See also* CATHERINE the Great, PETER the Great, IVAN the Terrible, NICHOLAS II.)

After Russia, the two most important republics, in terms of population are the Ukraine (capital, Kiev) and Byelorussia (capital,

The position of ultra-violet rays within the spectrum

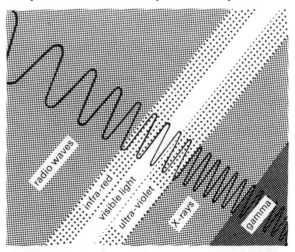

Minsk). The remaining republics are: Armenia, Azerbaidjan, Estonia, Georgia, Kazakstan, Kirghizia, Latvia, Lithuania, Moldavia, Tadzhikistan, Turkmenistan and Uzbekistan. Siberia is a region administered by the Russian federal republic, though it is the largest part of the Soviet Union in area.

The RUSSIAN REVOLUTION of 1917 ended the imperial dynasty of the tsars and heralded the establishment of the first Communist state. The Soviet Union was officially created in 1922. The Ukraine and the great series of plains, or steppes, extending southwards and eastwards into Asia, are the principal regions for cereal crops and cattle-raising. Much of Russia, and of Siberia beyond, is heavily forested, changing to tundra within the Arctic Circle. It is in the field of industry and technology that the Soviet Union has made the most dramatic advances. Its industrial capacity was far behind that of other European nations, and especially that of the UNITED STATES, at the time of the Revolution. Great damage was done to its industry during WORLD WAR II, yet it led the way into the space age in 1957, and has been the only rival of the United States in terms of

St Basil's, Moscow, USSR, built 1555-60

space achievements and armaments. Since World War II new industrial centres have been created in Siberia, and there are big plans to exploit the vast mineral resources of the region. *See also* LENIN, STALIN, TROTSKY.

UNITED ARAB EMIRATES

Federation of seven states in south-east Arabia on the Persian Gulf, with an area of 83,600 sq km (32,280 sq miles) and a population of 961,000. The seven states are Abu Dhabi, Al Fujayrah, Ash Shariqah, Dubai, Ras al Khaymah, Ujman and Umm al Aaywayn. They were formerly the Trucial States and a British protectorate until 1971, when they gained full independence.

UNITED KINGDOM. *See* GREAT BRITAIN, ENGLAND, IRELAND, SCOTLAND, WALES

UNITED NATIONS (UN)

International organization, established in 1945 with the aim of maintaining peace and security by the collective action of member nations, and promoting economic and cultural co-operation throughout the world. Thus it can be seen as a successor to the LEAGUE OF NATIONS, but with far greater areas of interest and action. There were originally 51 member nations; today the number is 154. There is a Secretary-General who controls UN administration and represents the organization to the world as a whole; a General Assembly, at which all member nations have a place and equal voting rights; and the Security Council, comprising Great Britain, France, the United States, the Soviet Union and China. The UN headquarters are in New York, but its many agencies are administered from various other centres. Chief of these agencies are: United Nations Educational, Scientific and Cultural Organization (UNESCO); World Health Organization (WHO); International Monetary Fund (IMF); and Food and Agriculture Organization

The meeting of the United Nations General Assembly

(FAO). There is also the International Court of Justice, which usually sits at The Hague in the Netherlands.

UNITED STATES OF AMERICA (USA)

Federal republic with an area of 9,363,123 sq km (3,615,319 sq miles) and a population of about 226 million. The federal capital is Washington DC. This city occupies the small federal area called District of Columbia, and therefore stands apart from any of the fifty states, each of which has its own legislative capital. Other major cities are New York City, Chicago, Los Angeles, Philadelphia, Houston, Detroit, Dallas, San Diego, Baltimore, San Antonio, Phoenix and Indianapolis. The nation has several important geographical features. From west to east there are the ROCKY MOUNTAINS, the central plains of the Mississippi river and its many tributaries, and the Appalachian Mountains. There are also several distinct climatic zones, ranging from the continental-type climate of the prairies (warm dry summers and cold, severe winters) to the sub-tropical conditions of Florida and other states bordering the Gulf of Mexico.

In 1783 Great Britain acknowledged the independence of the United States of America, comprising the thirteen colonies which had fought against Britain during the AMERICAN WAR OF INDEPENDENCE. These states were distributed along the eastern seaboard of the North American continent. During the nineteenth century many more states were added to the Union, until by the end of that century the nation stretched all the way from the Atlantic to the Pacific Ocean. The AMERICAN CIVIL WAR brought great suffering to many people and economic ruin to some areas; but generally the history of the nation was one of dramatic territorial and economic expansion. An important part of this development was the arrival of millions of immigrants mainly from the nations of Europe; and these, together with the large black population which had originally been imported as slave labour, made the United States the most cosmopolitan nation on Earth. By the beginning of the twentieth century it was also the world's leading industrial power. It entered WORLD WAR I on the side of the Allies. In the late 1920s and 1930s it suffered most from the economic depression, which had started with the crisis in its own New York stock exchange. Entry into WORLD WAR II brought with it new industrial expansion, and, at the end of hostilities, an obligation to aid the

The skyline of New York, USA

economic recovery of Europe, which it did through a programme known as Marshall Aid. It remains the leading nation in industry and technology; has the highest material standard of living; and, in contrast to its general policy of isolationism during the nineteenth century, is deeply involved in world affairs at every level. *See also* CONGRESS, DEMOCRATIC PARTY, Dwight D. EISENHOWER, Abraham LINCOLN, REPUBLICAN PARTY, Franklin D. ROOSEVELT, George WASHINGTON.

UPPER VOLTA

West African republic with an area of 274,200 sq km (105,875 sq miles) but a population of under 6 million. The capital is Ougadougou. This extremely poor country got its name from the Volta river which flows into Ghana, but much of the land is arid. Formerly French, Togo became independent in 1960.

URANIUM

Heavy, metallic, radioactive element which is the main source of nuclear energy. It occurs naturally in pitchblende and other ores.

URANUS

PLANET of the SOLAR SYSTEM with an equatorial diameter of 49,700 km (31,000 miles) and an average distance of 2,868 million km (1,792 million miles) from the SUN. Uranus is very like NEPTUNE.

URUGUAY

South American republic with an area of 176,215 sq km (68,041 sq miles) and a population of about 3 million. The capital is Montevideo. The chief products are meat and wool.

VACCINATION

Form of preventive MEDICINE by the injection of a weakened or dead form of an infectious disease into an animal's bloodstream in order to get the blood to produce antibodies and so combat any attack of the real disease. The English doctor Edward Jenner first used the method in 1796 as a prevention against smallpox. The word 'vaccination' comes from the Latin for 'cow', as it was a vaccine of cowpox that Jenner originally used. Many diseases can now be prevented by this method.

Vaccination against measles

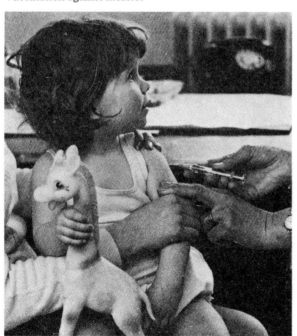

VACUUM

In PHYSICS the term used to describe a state of emptiness, from the Latin *vacuus*, meaning 'empty'. In practice, a complete vacuum can never be obtained, but the state can be approached sufficiently for so-called vacuums to have uses in engineering.

VAN DYCK, Sir Anthony (1599–1641)

Flemish artist. He was a student of RUBENS who specialized in portrait painting. He became Court Painter to Charles I of England.

VAN GOGH, Vincent (1853–90)

Dutch artist. While still in the Netherlands he did many drawings and rather sombre paintings of Dutch peasants, or of miners in the industrial regions of Belgium and northern France. But in Paris he met some French Impressionists, who excited his interest in colour. He went to Arles in Provence where he produced the paintings for which he is most remembered – works of vibrant colour.

VANUATU

The former New Hebrides in the Pacific Ocean became the independent Republic of Vanuatu in 1980. The area is 14,763 sq km (5,700 sq miles) and the population is 108,000. The capital is Vila.

VATICAN CITY

An independent state in Rome, covering only 44 ha. It is the seat of the government of the ROMAN CATHOLIC CHURCH.

VAUGHAN WILLIAMS, Ralph (1872–1958)

English composer. As a young man he took a deep interest in English folk song, developing his own style from it. Much of his music evokes a feeling of the English countryside. In other works, such as the *Fantasy on a Theme of Thomas Tallis,* Vaughan Williams revived interest in the English music of past ages.

VELÁZQUEZ, Diego Rodríguez de Silva y (1599–1660)

Spanish artist. For much of his career Velázquez was painter to the Spanish Court, producing many portraits of the royal family. They, and his other studies of less elevated people, convey a new sense of realism and of sympathy for the subject which influenced the work of many later artists. One of his largest canvases is the famous *Surrender of Breda.* Another famous work is *The Waterseller* in the Wellington Museum, London.

Detail of a painting by Velázquez

VENEZUELA

South American republic with an area of 912,050 sq km (352,164 sq miles) and a population of about 15 million. The capital is Caracas; another important city is Maracaibo. Around the shores of Lake Maracaibo are some of the richest oil wells in the world, and oil has long been the country's principal export. It was in the region of the country's Orinoco river that the fabled city of El Dorado was supposed to have been situated.

VENUS

PLANET of the SOLAR SYSTEM with an equatorial diameter of 12,392 km (7,745 sq miles) and an average distance from the SUN of 107 million km (67 million miles). Venus comes closer to the EARTH than any other planet, and is the brightest object in the sky after the SUN and MOON. It has an atmosphere of thick clouds of carbon dioxide gas, which trap the heat, and, according to information relayed from the Soviet space probe of 1967, a surface temperature almost as high as that of MERCURY.

VERDI, Giuseppe (1813–1901)

Italian composer, almost exclusively of operas. Though Verdi had some failures, he was the unchallenged master of Italian opera for over fifty years, gradually developing his style until it approached WAGNER's ideas of a continuous flow of music. His best-known operas, containing many celebrated arias, are *Rigoletto, Il Trovatore* and *La Traviata. Aida,* one of the most grandly conceived of operas, was written for the opening of the SUEZ CANAL. Verdi's last opera, *Falstaff,* based on the character from Shakespeare, was composed when he was 80 years old.

VERLAINE, Paul (1844–96)

French poet, and a leading member of the group called the Symbolists. As such, he conveyed the subtlest shades of meaning and feeling by the suggestive power of words and images. He led a wretched life and died in poverty, though recognized as a poet of genius.

VERMEER, Jan (1632–75)

Dutch artist whose paintings of the interiors of houses are executed with meticulous care and a very fine sense of colour and light.

VERNE, Jules (1828–1905)

French novelist, and a pioneer in the field of science fiction. His books include *Journey to the Centre of the Earth* and *Twenty Thousand Leagues under the Sea.*

VERONESE, Paolo (1528–88)

Italian artist whose real name was Paolo Cagliari. He was a leading member of the Venetian school of Italian Renaissance painters, his works being rich in colour and elaborate in design. *Marriage at Cana* and *Supper at Emmaeus* are two of his best-known paintings.

VERTEBRATE

One of the two principal groups within the ANIMAL KINGDOM. The word describes an animal having a backbone made up of separate bones called vertebrae. Within this group are all FISHES, AMPHIBIANS, REPTILES, BIRDS and MAMMALS. Such animals are said to rank higher than INVERTEBRATES with regard to the development of their nervous systems and possession of a true brain.

VICTORIA, Queen (1819–1901)

English monarch who reigned for over sixty years and presided over the period of Britain's greatest expansion as a colonial power and greatest period of growth as an industrial nation. In 1840 she married Prince Albert of Saxe-Coburg, to whom she was absolutely devoted. They had nine children, but Victoria never quite recovered from the shock of Albert's sudden death in 1861. For a time she retired from public life, but DISRAELI charmed her out of her seclusion.

VIETNAM

South-east Asian state with an area of 329,556 sq km (127,249 sq miles) and a population of about 55 million. The capital is Hanoi. The country secured independence from France in 1954 after a long and bitter war. It was then divided into North and South Vietnam. North Vietnam had a Communist administration and dispute between the two regions brought increasing involvement of the United States on the side of South Vietnam. This led to another long period of war, ending in 1973 with the complete withdrawal of American forces and victory for the Communists led by Ho Chi Minh. In 1976 the unification of North and South Vietnam took place, to form the Socialist Republic of Vietnam.

VIKINGS

Sea-raiders from SCANDINAVIA. From about AD 800 to 1000 they ventured forth in their longships, first to the shores of Britain, then increasingly farther afield, to Spain, Morocco, Sicily, and from the Baltic down the Russian rivers to the Black Sea. One of the boldest, Eric the Red, discovered Greenland; while his son, Leif Eriksson, reached a place he called Vinland and which was almost certainly North America.

VIOLIN

Stringed musical instrument, usually played with a bow. The violin and its deeper-pitched relatives, the viola, cello and double-bass, gradually replaced the older viol family of bowed stringed instruments during the seventeenth century. The greatest violin makers were several families of craftsmen who lived in the Italian town of Cremona during the seventeenth and eighteenth centuries.

VIRGIL (Publius Vergilius Maro, 70–19 BC)

Roman poet. One of his most important works was *Georgics,* a book of instruction about farming and agriculture. More celebrated is the *Aeneid,* an epic poem about the hero Aeneas, legendary founder of Rome.

VIRGIN ISLANDS

Group of islands in the WEST INDIES. The majority are administered by the United States; the remainder by Great Britain.

VIRUS

Most elemental form of life, smaller than BACTERIA, and capable of multiplying only in another living cell. Nevertheless, they are the cause of such serious diseases as poliomyelitis (infantile paralysis) and smallpox; also of the many different strains of the common cold.

VITAMIN

Group of chemical compounds found in various foodstuffs (though now also manufactured) and essential in small quantities for good health. The basic vitamins are A (found in milk, fish and vegetables, and important to growth); B (found in eggs, some meats and yeast, and important to digestion, appetite and growth); C (found in citrus fruits, tomatoes, potatoes and some vegetables, and important for prevention of some diseases and resistance to others); D (found in fish, and necessary for sound bone development); and K (found in some vegetables and wheat germ, and necessary for the good condition of the blood).

VIVALDI, Antonio (1678–1741)

Italian composer. He was one of the group of Italian musicians who first wrote important music for the VIOLIN family of instruments. He composed nearly 500 works in the concerto grosso style (*see* CONCERTO), best known of these being a group called *The Four Seasons*.

VOLCANO

Mountain formed by the eruption of molten lava from the interior of the Earth. Most have a conical shape due to this action. Some form islands in the sea. Most volcanoes are near the

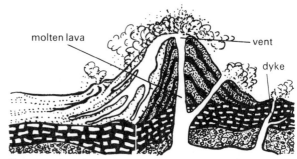

Cross-section through an active volcano

edges of the 'plates' in the Earth's crust, such as along the ocean ridges or near 'subduction zones' where one plate is being pushed down beneath another. The descending plate is melted to form magma. *See also* CONTINENTAL DRIFT.

VOLTA, Alessandro (1745–1827)

Italian scientist. He was the first to demonstrate the actual existence of an electric current as distinct from just some of its effects, and made the first battery, known as the voltaic pile, to produce a continuous current. The unit of force of an electric current, the *volt*, is named after him.

VOLTAIRE (1694–1778)

French writer whose real name was François Marie Arouet. He wrote numerous plays, novels, epic poems, volumes of philosophy and of history; and also spent much time attacking what he saw as the political and social injustices of his age. Several times he was imprisoned for his views, which had a great influence on events leading up to the FRENCH REVOLUTION.

VULTURE

Group of large BIRDS native to many temperate or tropical regions, distinguished by their broad wing-span and featherless head and neck. They rarely kill prey, but feed readily on carrion. Largest species is the condor of the ANDES mountains.

W

WAGNER, Richard (1813–83)

German composer, almost exclusively of operas. His works fall roughly into two categories: those which still generally conform to established operatic standards, including *The Flying Dutchman, Tannhäuser* and *Lohengrin;* and those based on his own theories about the creation of a new art form, which he called music-drama. Chief among these is the huge related group of four operas, based on Teutonic mythology, called *The Ring of the Nibelung.* These music-dramas are characterized by a continuous, unfolding line of music and words, and the use of musical motto themes, called *Leitmotive* (leading-motives) which create a kind of tapestry of sound. The famous 'Ride of the Valkyries' is itself one such *Leitmotiv.* Other works of the composer's full maturity are *Tristan and Isolde* and *The Mastersingers of Nuremburg.* Wagner revolutionized many aspects of music, while his theories about art had a tremendous influence on writers and philosophers as well as other composers.

WALES

Country of GREAT BRITAIN, called a Principality, with an area of 20,760 sq km (8,000 sq miles) and a population of nearly 3 million. The capital is Cardiff; other important towns and cities are Swansea and Newport. South Wales is an industrial region producing much coal, iron and steel, copper, tinplate and zinc. The remainder of the country is mostly moun-

Caerphilly Castle, Wales, built by Edward I

tainous, the highest point being Snowdon, 1,085 m (3,560 ft) in the north. Off the north coast is the island of Anglesey.

Many Welsh people are of Celtic descent, sharing something of the same heritage as the Celts of SCOTLAND, IRELAND, Cornwall and Brittany in France; and the Welsh language is still spoken and taught in schools. The Celts resisted the Romans, ANGLO-SAXONS and Normans, but were conquered by the English during the thirteenth century. A revolt by Owen Glendower in the early fifteenth century did not succeed, and by the Act of Union of 1536 Wales and England were politically united. However, Wales has retained its special culture. About one-fifth of the people speak Welsh as well as English.

WALTON, Sir William (born 1902)

English composer. He quickly developed a vivid and vigorous way of writing for the orchestra which he displayed in the overture *Portsmouth Point* and the music to the ballet *Façade* (originally written for a narrator and small instrumental group). Another well-known work is the dramatic oratorio *Belshazzar's Feast.* He also wrote music to the films of *Henry V* and *Hamlet.*

WARS OF THE ROSES

Series of battles between the royal houses of York (whose emblem was a white rose) and Lancaster (red rose) for the English crown. The opening Battle of St Albans in 1455 brought victory for the House of York. The closing Battle of Bosworth Field in 1485 saw the defeat and death of Richard III (York) and the ascent to the throne of Henry Tudor, the last of the Lancastrian claimants, as Henry VII. By marrying into the House of York he brought the dispute to an end.

WASHINGTON, George (1732–99)

Born in the colony of Virginia, he took command of the colonial army in the AMERICAN WAR OF INDEPENDENCE and led it to final victory against the British in the face of much internal dispute, lack of funds and one very hard winter at a place called Valley Forge when his army nearly starved. After the establishment of the Republic he was unanimously elected in 1789 as the first PRESIDENT of the UNITED STATES, and re-elected in 1792.

WASP

Group of INSECTS related in some respects to both ANTS and BEES, and widely distributed throughout warm and temperate regions. So-called social wasps live in colonies like bees but do not store food; only the young queens survive each winter, creating new colonies in the spring. Hornet is the name given to several species of large wasp, and their sting can be dangerous.

WATER

Chemical compound of OXYGEN and HYDROGEN, and one of the few substances to be found commonly in each of the three states of matter, solid (ice), liquid and gaseous (clouds and steam). The centigrade temperature scale is based upon its freezing point (0°) and boiling point (100°). Sea water contains many compounds, especially sodium chloride (ordinary SALT). So-called 'hard' water contains salts of magnesium and calcium (bicarbonates), chlorides and sulphates.

WATT, James (1736–1819)

Scottish engineer. He greatly improved upon the steam engine of Thomas NEWCOMEN, and so heralded the true age of steam power from the early days of the INDUSTRIAL REVOLUTION into the twentieth century. One of his famous stationary engines, called the 'sun and planet' engine because of its special arrangement of cog wheels, is in the Science Museum, London. The *watt*, as a unit of power, is named after him. In ELECTRICITY this is the product of amps multiplied by volts.

Watt's steam engine

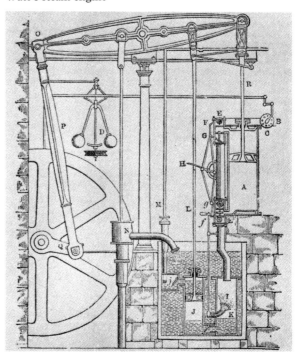

WATTEAU, Antoine (1648–1721)

French artist. He painted pastoral scenes and groups of people with grace, delicacy and a subtle use of colour, and was thus a leading representative of the Rococo style of art and decoration. He also produced many engravings of similar character.

WEASEL

Group of MAMMALS, most being distinguished by long, slender bodies and short legs. The common European weasel hunts rats and mice, while the larger STOAT catches rabbits. Other members of the weasel family are the MINK, WOLVERINE, SABLE, SKUNK, POLECAT (from which has been bred the ferret) and pine marten. The BADGER is also related to the weasel family.

WEATHER. *See* METEOROLOGY

WEBER, Carl Maria Friedrich Ernst von (1786–1826)

German composer who established a type of German Romantic opera which influenced WAGNER. Most successful is *Der Freischütz* (The Marksman) with its exciting touches of the supernatural. Weber also wrote the well-known *Invitation to the Dance.*

WELLINGTON, Arthur Wellesley, 1st Duke of (1769–1852)

British soldier and statesman. The important part of his military career began in 1808 when he went to Spain in command of a British expeditionary force whose task was to aid the Spanish and Portuguese in their revolt against the French. This developed into the Peninsular War, during which he defeated some of NAPOLEON's best generals and finest troops. Following Napoleon's return to France from Elba, Wellington commanded the Allied army which brought about his final defeat at the Battle of Waterloo (1815). After the war he entered politics and served as PRIME MINISTER from 1828 to 1830. He was popularly known as the 'Iron Duke'.

WELLS, Herbert George (1866–1946)

English writer, usually known as H. G. Wells. He is best remembered for his science fiction stories, notably *War of the Worlds* and *The Time Machine,* but wrote other quite different types of novel, including *Kipps* and *The History of Mr Polly.*

WESTERN SAMOA. *See* SAMOA

WEST INDIES

The whole group of tropical and sub-tropical islands between the mainlands of North and South AMERICA, which also separate the Caribbean Sea from the ATLANTIC Ocean. There are three main groups: the BAHAMAS; the Greater Antilles (including CUBA, JAMAICA, Hispaniola – HAITI and the DOMINICAN REPUBLIC – and PUERTO RICO); and the Lesser Antilles (including BARBADOS, TRINIDAD AND TOBAGO).

WHALE

Group of MAMMALS adapted for life in the sea. Largest is the blue whale, which is also the largest of all animals, reaching a length of 30 m (nearly 100 ft) and a weight of 180,000 kg (396,000 lb). Indeed, no other animal, so far as is known, has ever reached this size. Astonishingly, this mighty creature lives on minute, shrimp-like animals called krill, which it filters through a fine curtain of whalebone called balleen. The other principal type of whale, not so large but still very big, is the sperm whale. This has teeth and hunts other large sea creatures like the squid. There is also the killer whale which, in a pack, will attack any sea creature, including the blue whale itself. DOLPHINS and PORPOISES are related to whales.

WHITTLE, Sir Frank (born 1907)

English inventor and pioneer of jet propulsion. He took out his first patent in 1930 and

347

The Bayeux tapestry, record of William I's conquest of England

produced his first jet engine in 1937, although the first successful jet aircraft was the experimental German Heinkel He178 of 1939. The RAF's Gloster *Meteor* and the German Luftwaffe's Messerschmitt Me262, both much faster than propellor-driven aircraft, were in service before the end of WORLD WAR II.

WILBERFORCE, William (1759–1833)

English social reformer. He opposed the Slave Trade, which in his day meant the transportation and sale of black people from Africa to work mainly on the cotton plantations in the United States. As a Member of Parliament Wilberforce negotiated a bill which abolished the British Slave Trade in 1807, then secured the freedom of all slaves in British colonies in 1833.

WILDE, Oscar Fingal O'Flahertie Wills (1854–1900)

Irish writer of such brilliant social comedies as *The Importance of Being Earnest* but also of the strange and sinister novel *The Picture of Dorian Gray*.

WILLIAM I (The Conqueror, 1027–87)

As Duke of Normandy he laid claim to the English throne upon the death of Edward the Confessor. The English chose Harold, Earl of Wessex, as their new king, whereupon William assembled an army and invaded England. He defeated Harold's army near Hastings on 14 October 1066, during which battle Harold was killed, and was himself crowned king on Christmas Day of that year. *See also* NORMAN CONQUEST.

WILLIAM III (William of Orange, 1650–1702)

He was a Dutch prince, and in 1688 was invited to England to take over the throne by a group of influential Protestant Englishmen who feared that the reigning monarch, James II, would restore the Catholic faith as the official religion. William accepted and landed with an army near Torbay. James, unsure of his support, surrendered the throne and eventually fled to France. The following year, 1689, William became king under conditions set out in a Bill of Rights which guaranteed the control of

PARLIAMENT over many aspects of law and administration. These events are known as 'The Glorious Revolution' and mark the true beginning of the British constitutional monarchy. William was married to James II's daughter Mary.

WILLIAMS, Tennessee (born 1914)

American writer and dramatist, whose real name is Thomas Lanier Williams. Most of his plays, notably *A Streetcar Named Desire* and *Cat on a Hot Tin Roof,* deal with what he has seen as the doom and decay of life in the American Deep South. Most of them, also, have been made into films.

WILSON, Thomas Woodrow (1856–1924)

American Democratic President who kept his country out of WORLD WAR I until 1917. His famous 'Fourteen Points' for a just peace then helped to bring about the Armistice of 1918. He also played a leading role in the creation of the LEAGUE OF NATIONS, but could not gain support from Congress for American membership. Lack of this membership was one reason for the League's ultimate failure.

WINDWARD ISLANDS

Group of islands in the WEST INDIES, including French Martinique, and the islands of St Lucia, St Vincent and Grenada. They are so called because they lie in the path of the prevailing wind.

WOLF

Large wild DOG which was once quite common in parts of Europe but is now mostly restricted to the remoter regions of Russia, Asia and Canada. Wolves co-operate by hunting in groups called packs, though their danger to man has been exaggerated. Closely related is the American COYOTE.

WOLFE, James (1727–59)

English soldier. He joined the army as a boy and was a lieutenant-colonel at the age of 22. His greatest triumph was his campaign against the French in CANADA. He was ordered to capture Quebec, which occupied a commanding position on the Heights of Abraham above the St Lawrence river. Under cover of darkness Wolfe and his army approached the city by the river and scaled the Heights. He then led his troops to victory against the French under the command of the Marquis de Montcalm. Both commanders lost their lives in the battle, which secured Canada for Britain.

WOLVERINE

Largest member of the WEASEL group of MAMMALS, native to the northern forests of Canada and Alaska, and distinguished by its thick, blackish fur and bushy tail.

WOMBAT

MAMMAL belonging to the group of MARSUPIALS and native to parts of Australia. It is a stocky animal with coarse, greyish hair, given to burrowing, and is sometimes called a badger in Australia.

WOOL

Fibrous type of hair, usually curly, grown by sheep and some other mammals, and spun into yarn. As a material for clothing it is warm, strong, unaffected by moisture, resistant to creasing and able to hold coloured dyes; and despite the introduction this century of many artificial fibres, wool is still extensively used.

WOOLF, Virginia (1882–1941)

English novelist. In novels like *Mrs Dalloway* she broke away from the conventional narrative novel and experimented in the realm of impressionistic writing, reflecting and penetrat-

Virginia Woolf

ing the thoughts of her characters rather than describing their actions.

WORDSWORTH, William (1770–1850)

English poet and leading figure of the English Romantic movement in literature. Thus he took the unspoilt beauty of nature as his principal theme and inspiration, although one of his best-known poems is the sonnet *Composed Upon Westminster Bridge*. His largest work is the autobiographical *The Prelude*.

WORK

Concept of PHYSICS, and especially of MECHANICS, calculated as the product of force multiplied by the distance, applied to the motion and mass of an object. As long as an object is static (i.e. in a state of equilibrium) no mechanical work is done.

WORLD, The

In this encyclopedia the different countries of the world appear as individual entries. On pages 352-3 is a map of the world, listing countries in alphabetical order. More detailed maps will be found with the entries on the following: Australasia, Africa, Asia (Middle East and Far East), Europe, India, America (North and South).

WORLD WAR I

Conflict primarily between Britain and the Commonwealth, France, Imperial Russia and the United States (the Allies); and Germany and Austro-Hungary (the Central Powers). Technical cause of the war was the assassination at Sarajevo, in June 1914, of the Archduke Franz Ferdinand, heir to the Austro-Hungarian throne. The deeper reasons were long-standing economic and territorial rivalries among the major European powers. Britain entered the conflict in August 1914, in response to Germany's invasion of Belgium, whose neutrality had been guaranteed.

In western Europe the fighting was mainly on French and Belgian soil and proceeded in three phases: the initial German advance on Paris, checked by the French at the Battle of the Marne (1914); the long period of trench warfare, including the Battles of Verdun and the Somme (1916) and the Third Battle of Ypres, or Passchendaele (1917); and the final breaking of the deadlock with the United States' entry into the war in 1917. In eastern Europe, the Russians suffered heavy defeats, notably at the Battle of Tannenberg (1914), leading to the Revolution of 1917 and their withdrawal from the war. There were also diversionary campaigns, including the British Commonwealth landings at Gallipoli in the Dardanelles (1915), which failed. At sea the Germans attacked British merchant ships with their submarines (U-boats), while the British navy attempted a blockade of German ports. There was one important naval engagement, at Jutland (1916),

British troops in the trenches in France in World War I

which was inconclusive. An armistice in November 1918 ended the fighting; the Treaty of Versailles officially ended the war in 1919.

On paper, the Central Powers had lost. In practice, nobody won, and the total death toll was over 10 million. The war had seen the introduction of poison gas, tanks, air raids and food rationing. The chief military commanders were, on the German side, General Erich von Ludendorff and Field Marshal Paul von Hindenburg; on the Allied side Field Marshal Sir Douglas Haig and Marshal Ferdinand Foch. *See also* Georges CLEMENCEAU, David LLOYD GEORGE and Thomas Woodrow WILSON.

WORLD WAR II

Conflict primarily between Britain and the Commonwealth, the United States and the Soviet Union (the Allies); and Germany, Italy and Japan (the Axis); though many more nations were involved. German economic ruin after WORLD WAR I and resentment against the Treaty of Versailles had much to do with the rise to power of Adolf HITLER; and it was his aim to unite all German-speaking people in one nation (Reich) that started the war. Having annexed Austria and occupied Czechoslovakia, Hitler invaded Poland in September 1939. Pledged to support that country, Britain and France declared war, but Germany's victory was swift and complete. German conquests in Europe (including the Fall of France) culminated in the invasion of the Soviet Union in June 1941; and until the autumn of 1942 the only checks to this success were the Battle of Britain (1940), fought between the Royal Air Force and the German Luftwaffe, and a Soviet offensive in the winter of 1941. Destruction of a whole army group by the Red Army at Stalingrad in the winter of 1942 marked the beginning of Germany's defeat on the eastern front;

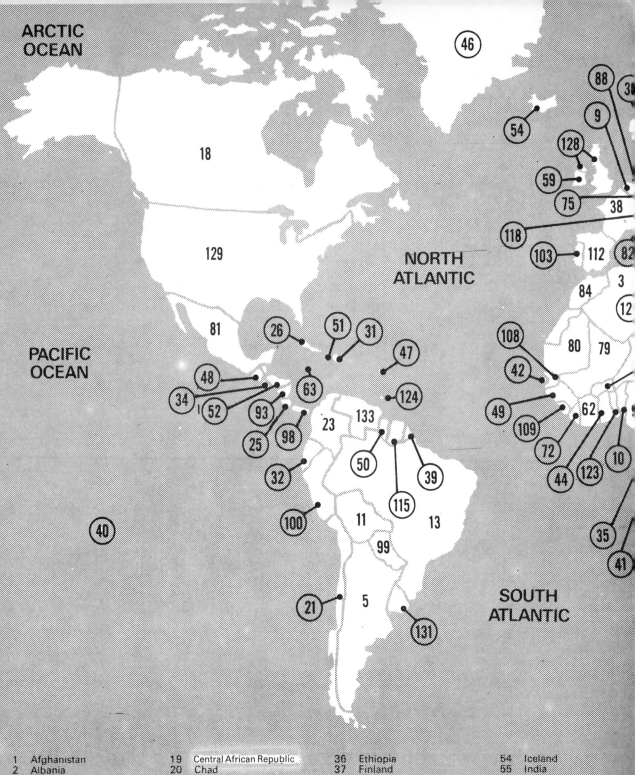

ARCTIC OCEAN

PACIFIC OCEAN

NORTH ATLANTIC

SOUTH ATLANTIC

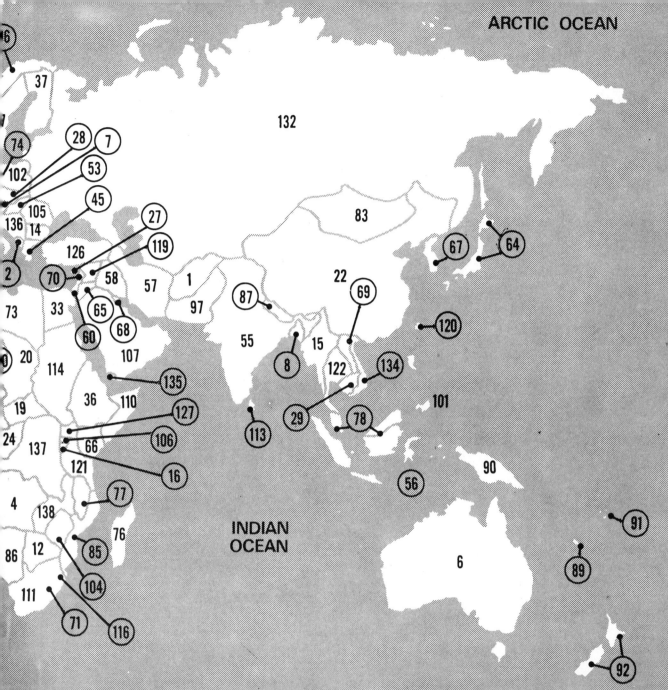

ARCTIC OCEAN

INDIAN
OCEAN

THE WORLD

British children evacuated during the bombing of London in World War II

while British victory at El Alamein, Egypt, in October 1942, followed by Anglo-American invasion, first of Sicily and Italy, then of Occupied France (Normandy Landings, June 1944), led to German defeat in the west. The Red Army entered Berlin in April 1945 and Germany surrendered on 8 May 1945.

Meanwhile, the Japanese attack on the American naval base at Pearl Harbor, Hawaii, in December 1941 (which brought the United States into the war) was followed by rapid advances, westwards towards India and southwards, through Malaya, almost to Australia. These conquests were checked by the naval battles of Coral Sea and Midway (1942). American re-conquest of the Pacific islands, British re-conquest of Burma, and the dropping of atomic bombs on Hiroshima and Nagasaki brought the surrender of Japan on 2 September 1945.

Other major aspects of the war were the German air raids on Britain (the Blitz) and the more devastating British and American bombing of Germany; the German U-boat campaign against Allied shipping and its eventual defeat (Battle of the Atlantic); German use of the first true ballistic missile (V2); and the introduction by both the Luftwaffe and the RAF of jet aircraft.

The total military killed or missing was about 15 million (nearly 8 million suffered by the Soviet Union). In strategic terms the war saw the end of Britain and France as world powers and the rise of the Soviet Union and the United States as superpowers. *See also* Sir Winston CHURCHILL, Charles DE GAULLE,

Dwight D. EISENHOWER, General Douglas MacARTHUR, Field Marshal Bernard MONTGOMERY, Benito MUSSOLINI, Field Marshal Erwin ROMMEL, Franklin D. ROOSEVELT and Joseph STALIN.

WREN, Sir Christopher (1632–1723)

English architect, also mathematician and astronomer. He designed buildings for both Oxford and Cambridge universities, also most of the Royal Naval College at Greenwich (originally a hospital). After the Great Fire of London in 1666, Wren prepared plans for the complete re-building of the city. These were not carried out, but included in them were the new cathedral of St Paul's, which was built, together with about fifty other London churches. Some of these were destroyed during WORLD WAR II, but most have been restored.

WRIGHT BROTHERS, Wilbur (1867–1912) and Orville (1871–1948)

American aviation pioneers. In 1903 at Kittyhawk, North Carolina, they made the world's first flight in a power-driven, heavier-than-air machine, over a distance of 262 m (859 ft); and within two years had accomplished a flight of 39 km (24 miles).

WYCLIFFE, John (c. 1320–84)

English scholar and religious reformer. Over a century before Martin Luther, he attacked the Church for what he saw as abuses among the clergy, and challenged some aspects of doctrine. He inspired a band of preachers, later known as the Lollards, who spread his ideas, while he himself embarked upon a translation of the Bible into English.

The dome of St Paul's Cathedral, built by Wren

X Y Z

high-speed electrons hit an aluminium anode in a CATHODE RAY TUBE. Their radiation is similar to that of visible light, but of a much shorter wavelength, which enables them to pass through solid and opaque substances. They are widely used in medicine to produce special photographs of the inside of the body and to destroy diseased tissue; also in chemistry and industry to examine crystal structures and metals.

XENOPHON (*c.* 430–*c.* 355 BC)

Greek historian and soldier. He was a student of SOCRATES, and produced an account of his life and teachings. Xenophon's historical writings are based largely on his own military experiences, which included fighting with SPARTA against Athens, leading to his banishment.

X-RAYS

Form of electromagnetic radiation contained within the invisible part of the SPECTRUM and discovered by the German scientist Wilhelm ROENTGEN in 1895. X-rays are produced when

YAK

MAMMAL closely related to the ox and native to the HIMALAYAS, especially Tibet. It is a tough, stocky animal with a thick, shaggy brown coat and black horns, and is kept for milk, meat and transportation.

YANGTZE KIANG

Longest river in ASIA. It rises in TIBET and flows in a general easterly direction right across CHINA for a distance of 5,520 km (3,430 miles), entering the East China Sea just north of Shanghai. It is navigable for a length of about 2,400 km (1,500 miles), serving the inland ports of Nanking, Hankow and Chungking.

X-ray photographs of an adult's hand and a child's hands

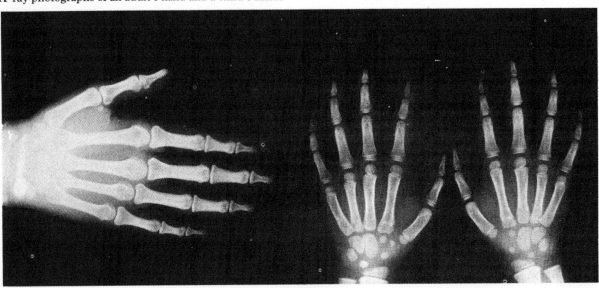

YEAST

Type of microscopic, single-celled FUNGUS. In the production of beer, wine and cider it converts SUGAR into ALCOHOL. In baking it releases carbon dioxide from the dough, thus causing the bread to rise. Yeast is also a valuable source of VITAMIN B.

YEATS, William Butler (1865–1939)

Irish poet and dramatist. He supported the Irish struggle for independence from Britain, and some of his poems express this. Others are an expression of his own mystical feelings, written in a lyrical and gently musical-sounding style.

YEMEN

Republic of south-western Arabia bordering the Red Sea, with an area of 195,000 sq km 75,294 sq miles) and a population of 5,904,000. The capital is San'a. A former monarchy, it became the Yemen Arab Republic in 1962. *See also* SOUTHERN YEMEN.

YIDDISH

Language based on German but with words from other languages, including Hebrew, and written in the Hebrew alphabet; traditionally spoken by many European Jews.

YUGOSLAVIA

Federal republic of south-eastern Europe with an area of 255,804 sq km (98,772 sq miles) and a population of about 22 million. The capital is Belgrade; other towns and cities include Zagreb and Skopje. Much of the country is rugged and mountainous, but the Adriatic coast is beautiful and has become a tourist centre. The main occupations are farming and forestry, but deposits of coal, iron ore and lead have helped to establish some industry. Almost the whole of present-day Yugoslavia was for a long time part

Dubrovnik harbour, Yugoslavia

of the OTTOMAN EMPIRE. The nation was created in 1918 from parts of the old Austro-Hungarian Empire together with the states of Serbia and Montenegro. It was a kingdom until the end of WORLD WAR II, when it adopted a Communist form of government under its wartime leader Marshal Josip Tito but has remained outside the main Soviet sphere of influence.

ZAÏRE

Central African republic with an area of 2,345,409 sq km (905,617 sq miles) and a population of about 28 million. The capital is Kinshasa (formerly Léopoldville). This very large country occupies almost the whole of the Zaïre (Congo) river basin with its vast equatorial forests which are the haven of many rare forms of animals life and of the race of pygmy men and women. On the other hand, the province of Katanga is rich in mineral deposits, especially of copper; and elsewhere there are diamonds and deposits of radium. Zaïre was formerly the Belgian Congo. It gained its independence in 1960, after which there was a period of civil war when Katanga tried to become a separate state. A republic was formally declared in 1964, and the present name was adopted in 1971.

ZAMBIA

Central African republic with an area of 752,614 sq km (290,602 sq miles) and a population of about 5½ million. The capital is Lusaka. The chief agricultural products are cotton, tea and tobacco, but there are also valuable deposits of copper ore, which it exports in large quantities. Formerly called Northern Rhodesia, the country gained its indepence from Britain in 1963 but remains within the BRITISH COMMONWEALTH.

ZANZIBAR. *See* TANZANIA.

ZEBRA

MAMMAL belonging to the same family as the HORSE and the ASS, native to parts of Africa, and distinguished by its black- or brown-and-white striped coat.

ZEBU

Domesticated MAMMAL related to other bovine species, such as the cow, and found in many parts of Africa, India and the Far East. It has a distinctive fatty hump across the shoulders and a large dewlap (fold of loose skin under the jaw).

ZENO of Citium (*c.* 340–*c.* 265 BC)

Greek philosopher. He founded the Stoic school of philosophy, so named because he taught in the Stoa Poikile (Painted Colonnade) market place, Athens. Zeno saw the world as

Zebras by a watering hole, South Africa

The Zeppelin airship under construction

one organic whole and declared that man's duty was to live in peace and harmony with the rest of nature.

ZEPPELIN, Ferdinand, Graf von (1838–1917)

Pioneer in airship design. His airships were used during WORLD WAR I to bomb London.

ZIMBABWE

Southern African republic, called Rhodesia until it achieved full independence in 1980, with an area of 390,580 sq km (150,812 sq miles) and a population of 7,383,000. The capital is Salisbury. The chief exports are tobacco, asbestos, gold and cotton.

ZOLA, Émile (1840–1902)

French writer. In his novels he attempted to portray life with total honesty and realism, and his work had a big influence on many twentieth-century novelists. Zola was also a supporter of Dreyfus in the DREYFUS AFFAIR.

ZOOLOGY

Branch of BIOLOGY concerned with the study of the ANIMAL KINGDOM. ARISTOTLE started a classification of animal life, but the modern scientific classification of animals into species, genus, family etc. started with the work of the Swedish biologist Carl LINNAEUS. In this encyclopedia the thousands of forms of animal life, their features and classification, are discussed under individual entries. *See also* ANATOMY, EMBRYOLOGY and GENETICS.

ZOROASTER (Zarathustra, c. 640–c. 580 BC)

Persian prophet and religious leader. He taught of the existence of one supreme being (Ahura Mazda, or 'Wise Lord'), and of two opposed spirits representing the forces of good and evil. These were very advanced ideas for their time, and some aspects of them were absorbed into other religions, notably JUDAISM and MITHRAISM, and, more indirectly, in CHRISTIANITY. The religion of Zoroastrianism is still practised by the Parsees of India.

TABLE 1   THE SOLAR SYSTEM

name	distance from sun		diameter		rotation on axis			orbit period		satellites or large moons
	in kilometres [approx.]	in miles [approx.]	in kilometres	in miles	days	hours	mins	years	days	
Sun			1,390,000	864,000	25	9				
Mercury	57,000,000	36,000,000	4,980	3,025	59				88	
Venus	107,000,000	67,000,000	12,390	7,600	243				225	
Earth	150,000,000	93,000,000	12,740	7,927		23	56	1		Moon
Mars	228,000,000	142,000,000	6,750	4,200		24	37	1	322	1 Phobos 2 Deimos
Jupiter	777,000,000	465,000,000	142,800	89,200		9	50	11	315	1 Io 2 Europa 3 Ganymede 4 Callisto 5 Amalthea 6 Himalia 7 Elara 8 Pasiphae 9 Sinope 10 Kysithea 11 Carme 12 Ananke 13 Leda
Saturn	1,427,000,000	891,000,000	120,500	75,300		10	14	29	167	1 Mimas 2 Tethys 3 Dione 4 Rhea 5 Titan 6 Hyperion 7 Iapetus 8 Phoebe 9 Enceladus
Uranus	2,868,000,000	1,792,000,000	49,700	31,000		10	48	84	7	1 Miranda 2 Umbriel 3 Ariel 4 Titania 5 Oberon
Neptune	4,500,000,000	2,800,000,000	45,000	28,200		14	0	164	80	1 Triton 2 Nereid
Pluto	5,900,000,000	3,700,000,000	2,414	1,500	6	9	0	248	90	Charon

TABLE 2   COUNTRIES OF THE WORLD

country	capital	area in		population
		square kilometres	square miles	
Afghanistan	Kabul	647,497	250,014	15,416,000
Albania	Tirana	28,748	11,100	2,735,000
Algeria	Algiers	2,381,741	919,646	18,819,000
Andorra	Andorra la Vella	453	175	26,000
Antigua	St John's	442	171	75,000
Angola	Luanda	1,246,700	481,380	7,071,000
Argentina	Buenos Aires	2,766,889	1,068,360	27,088,000
Australia	Canberra	7,686,848	2,968,070	14,595,000
Austria	Vienna	83,849	32,376	7,511,000
Bahamas	Nassau	13,935	5,381	239,000
Bahrain	Manama	622	240	407,000
Bangladesh	Dacca	143,998	55,601	89,396,000
Barbados	Bridgetown	431	166	255,000
Belgium	Brussels	30,513	11,782	9,882,000
Belize	Belmopan	22,965	8,867	132,000
Benin	Porto Novo	112,622	43,486	3,526,000
Bhutan	Thimphu	47,000	18,148	1,295,000
Bolivia	La Paz, Sucre	1,098,581	424,188	5,613,000
Botswana	Gaborone	600,372	231,818	788,000
Brazil	Brasília	8,511,965	3,286,668	126,442,000
Bulgaria	Sofia	110,912	42,826	8,910,000
Burma	Rangoon	676,552	261,232	33,712,000
Burundi	Bujumbura	27,834	10,747	4,110,000
Cameroon	Yaoundé	475,442	183,579	8,429,000
Canada	Ottawa	9,976,139	3,852,019	23,992,000
Cape Verde	Praia	4,033	1,557	312,000
Central African Republic	Bangui	622,984	240,549	1,997,000
Chad	N'Djaména	1,284,000	495,782	4,513,000
Chile	Santiago	756,945	292,274	11,098,000
China	Peking	9,596,961	3,705,610	980,723,000
Colombia	Bogota	1,138,914	439,761	26,723,000
Comoros	Moroni	2,171	838	414,000
Congo	Brazzaville	342,000	132,054	1,535,000
Costa Rica	San José	50,700	19,576	2,217,000
Cuba	Havana	114,524	44,220	10,023,000
Cyprus	Nicosia	9,251	3,572	657,000
Czechoslovakia	Prague	127,869	49,373	15,341,000
Denmark	Copenhagen	43,069	16,630	5,133,000
Djibouti	Djibouti	22,000	8,495	340,000
Dominica	Roseau	751	290	80,000
Dominican Rep.	Santo Domingo	48,734	18,817	5,445,000
Ecuador	Quito	283,561	109,489	8,334,000
Egypt	Cairo	1,001,449	386,683	41,754,000
El Salvador	San Salvador	21,041	8,124	4,552,000
Equatorial Guinea	Malabo	28,051	10,831	362,000
Ethiopia	Addis Ababa	1,221,900	471,804	32,594,000
Fiji	Suva	18,274	7,056	630,000
Finland	Helsinki	337,009	130,127	4,791,000
France	Paris	547,026	211,219	53,767,000
Gabon	Libreville	267,667	103,352	652,000
Gambia	Banjul	11,295	4,361	604,000
German Democratic Rep.	East Berlin	108,178	41,770	16,748,000
Germany, Fed. Rep. of	Bonn	248,577	95,981	61,269,000
Ghana	Accra	238,537	92,104	11,678,000
Greece	Athens	131,944	50,947	9,512,000
Grenada	St. George's	344	133	110,000
Guatemala	Guatemala City	108,889	42,045	7,023,000

country	capital	area in		population
		square kilometres	square miles	
Guinea	Conakry	245,957	94,970	5,422,000
Guinea-Bissau	Bissau	36,125	13,949	791,000
Guyana	Georgetown	214,969	83,005	857,000
Haiti	Port au Prince	27,750	10,715	5,047,000
Honduras	Tegucigalpa	112,088	43,280	3,686,000
Hong Kong	Victoria	1,045	403	4,764,000
Hungary	Budapest	93,030	35,921	10,764,000
Iceland	Reykjavik	103,000	39,771	229,000
India	Delhi	3,287,590	1,269,415	671,504,000
Indonesia	Djakarta	2,042,012	788,468	141,391,000
Iran	Tehran	1,648,000	636,331	37,975,000
Iraq	Baghdad	434,924	167,934	13,073,000
Irish Rep.	Dublin	70,283	27,138	3,292,000
Israel	Jerusalem	·20,770	8,020	3,874,000
Italy	Rome	301,225	116,310	57,280,000
Ivory Coast	Abidjan	322,463	124,510	8,544,000
Jamaica	Kingston	10,991	4,244	2,221,000
Japan	Tokyo	372,313	143,759	117,225,000
Jordan	Amman	97,740	37,740	3,189,000
Kampuchea	Phnom Penh	181,035	69,902	8,992,000
Kenya	Nairobi	582,646	224,973	15,827,000
Kiribati	Tarawa	886	342	58,000
Korea, North	Pyongyang	120,538	46,543	17,962,000
Korea, South	Seoul	98,484	38,027	38,010,000
Kuwait	Kuwait	17,818	6,880	1,344,000
Laos	Vientiane	236,800	91,434	3,437,000
Lebanon	Beirut	10,400	4,016	3,165,000
Lesotho	Maseru	30,355	11,721	1,340,000
Liberia	Monrovia	111,369	43,002	1,863,000
Libya	Tripoli	1,759,540	679,399	2,970,000
Liechtenstein	Vaduz	157	61	26,000
Luxembourg	Luxembourg	2,586	999	356,000
Madagascar	Antananarivo	587,041	226,670	8,726,000
Malawi	Lilongwe	118,484	44,205	6,022,000
Malaysia	Kuala Lumpur	329,749	127,324	14,010,000
Maldives, Rep. of	Malé	298	115	155,000
Mali	Bamako	1,240,000	478,793	6,631,000
Malta	Valletta	316	122	337,000
Mauritania	Nouakchott	1,030,700	397,977	1,632,000
Mauritius	Port Louis	2,045	790	948,000
Mexico	Mexico City	1,972,547	761,646	69,852,000
Monaco	Monaco	1.6	0.6	25,000
Mongolia	Ulan Bator	1,565,000	604,283	1,671,000
Morocco	Rabat	446,550	172,423	20,097,000
Mozambique	Maputo	783,030	302,346	10,458,000
Nauru	Nauru	21	8	7,000
Nepal	Kathmandu	140,797	54,365	14,268,000
Netherlands	Amsterdam	40,844	15,771·	14,098,000
New Zealand	Wellington	268,676	103,742	3,287,000
Nicaragua	Managua	130,000	50,196	2,672,000
Niger	Niamey	·1,267,000	489,218	5,299,000
Nigeria	Lagos	923,768	356,688	84,566,000
Norway	Oslo	324,219	125,188	4,089,000
Oman	Muscat	212,457	82,035	893,000
Pakistan	Islamabad	803,943	310,421	80,804,000
Panama	Panama City	75,650	29,210	1,908,000
Papua New Guinea	Port Moresby	461,691	178,270	3,072,000

country	capital	area in square kilometres	area in square miles	population
Paraguay	Asunción	406,752	157,056	3,074,000
Peru	Lima	1,285,216	496,252	17,777,000
Philippines	Manila	300,000	115,837	48,067,000
Poland	Warsaw	312,677	120,732	35,656,000
Portugal	Lisbon	92,082	35,555	10,046,000
Qatar	Doha	11,000	4,247	247,000
Romania	Bucharest	237,500	91,704	22,251,000
Rwanda	Kigali	26,338	10,170	4,786,000
St. Lucia	Castries	616	238	125,000
St. Vincent	Kingstown	388	150	108,000
San Marino	San Marino	61	24	22,000
São Tomé & Principe	São Tomé	964	372	110,000
Saudi Arabia	Riyadh	2,149,690	830,045	8,792,000
Senegal	Dakar	196,192	75,754	5,669,000
Seychelles	Victoria	280	108	67,000
Sierra Leone	Freetown	71,740	27,700	3,468,000
Singapore	Singapore	581	224	2,404,000
Solomon Islands	Honiara	28,446	10,984	227,000
Somali Republic	Mogadishu	637,657	246,214	3,942,000
South Africa	Pretoria, Cape Town	1,221,037	471,471	29,244,000
Spain	Madrid	504,782	194,908	37,835,000
Sri Lanka	Colombo	65,610	25,334	14,888,000
Sudan	Khartoum	2,505,813	967,553	18,368,000
Surinam	Paràmaribo	163,265	63,040	403,000
Swaziland	Mbabane	17,363	6,704	554,000
Sweden	Stockholm	449,964	173,742	8,298,000
Switzerland	Berne	41,288	15,942	6,325,000
Syria	Damascus	185,180	71,502	8,647,000
Taiwan (Formosa)	Taipei	35,989	13,896	17,480,000
Tanzania	Dar es Salaam	945,087	364,920	18,134,000
Thailand	Bangkok	514,000	198,467	46,760,000
Togo	Lomé	56,000	21,623	2,559,000
Tonga	Nuku'alofa	10	4	97,000
Trinidad and Tobago	Port of Spain	5,130	1,981	1,166,000
Tunisia	Tunis	163,610	63,174	6,356,000
Turkey	Ankara	780,576	301,399	45,367,000
Tuvalu	Funafuti	24	9	7,000
Uganda	Kampala	236,036	91,139	13,181,000
United Arab Emirates	–	83,600	32,280	961,000
United Kingdom	London	244,046	94,232	55,877,000
United States	Washington D.C.	9,363,123	3,615,319	226,505,000
Upper Volta	Ouagadougou	274,200	105,875	5,732,000
Uruguay	Montevideo	176,215	68,041	2,923,000
USSR	Moscow	22,402,200	8,650,010	262,436,000
Vanuatu	Vila	14,763	5,700	108,000
Vatican City	–	0.44	0.17	1,000
Venezuela	Caracas	912,050	352,164	14,891,000
Vietnam	Hanoi	329,556	127,249	55,000,000
Western Samoa	Apia	2,842	1,097	160,000
Yemen	San'a	195,000	75,294	5,904,000
Yemen P.D.R.	Aden	332,968	128,567	1,835,000
Yugoslavia	Belgrade	255,804	98,772	22,341,000
Zaïre	Kinshasa	2,345,409	905,617	28,278,000
Zambia	Lusaka	752,614	290,602	5,638,000
Zimbabwe	Salisbury	390,580	150,812	7,383,000

TABLE 3   RIVERS

river	length in kilometres [approx.]	length in miles [approx.]	country	flows into
Amazon	6,570	4,080	South America	Atlantic Ocean
Amur	4,510	2,800	Mongolia	North Pacific
Brahmaputra	2,700	1,680	Asia	Bay of Bengal
Colorado	3,220	2,000	USA	Pacific Ocean
Columbia	2,250	1,400	North America	Atlantic Ocean
Danube	2,850	1,770	Europe	Black Sea
Darling	1,860	1,160	Australia	Murray River
Dnieper	2,280	1,420	Russia	Black Sea
Don	1,850	1,150	Russia	Sea of Azov
Elbe	1,160	720	Germany	North Sea
Euphrates	2,690	1,670	West Asia	Persian Gulf
Ganges	2,490	1,550	India	Bay of Bengal
Hwang Ho	4,670	2,900	China	Yellow Sea
Hudson	230	144	USA	Atlantic Ocean
Indus	2,740	1,700	Pakistan	Arabian Sea
Irrawaddy	2,290	1,420	Burma	Bay of Bengal
Jordan	100	65	Palestine	Sea of Galilee, on into the Dead Sea
Lena	4,270	2,650	Siberia	Arctic Sea
Limpopo	1,610	1,000	Africa	Mozambique, entering Indian Ocean
Loire	1,010	630	France	Bay of Biscay
Mackenzie	4,240	2,630	North America	Beaufort Sea
Madeira	3,220	2,000	South America	Amazon
Mekong	4,180	2,600	China	China Sea
Missouri-Mississippi	6,210	3,860	USA	Gulf of Mexico
Murray	2,570	1,600	Australia	Indian Ocean
Niger	4,170	2,590	Africa	Gulf of Guinea
Nile	6,690	4,160	Africa	Mediterranean Sea
Oder	900	560	N. Europe	Baltic Sea
Orange	2,090	1,300	Africa	Atlantic Ocean
Orinoco	2,900	1,800	Venezuela	Atlantic Ocean
Rhine	1,320	820	Germany	North Sea
Rhône	810	505	France	Mediterranean Sea
Rio Grande del Norte	3,030	1,880	USA	Gulf of Mexico
Salween	2,890	1,800	Asia	Gulf of Martaban
São Francisco	2,890	1,800	Brazil	Atlantic Ocean
South and North Saskatchewan	1,120 and 1,300	700 and 810	Canada	Lake Winnipeg after uniting
Seine	760	470	France	English Channel
St Lawrence	3,060	1,900	Canada	Gulf of St Lawrence

river	length in kilometres [approx.]	length in miles [approx.]	country	flows into
Thames	330	210	England	North Sea
Tigris	1,770	1,100	Iraq	Euphrates
Tweed	160	98	Scotland	North Sea
Uruguay	1,370	850	South America	Atlantic Ocean
Ural	2,410	1,500	Russia	Caspian Sea
Vistula	1,040	650	Poland	Baltic Sea
Volga	3,690	2,290	USSR	Caspian Sea
Yangtze Kiang	5,520	3,430	China	China Sea
Yenisei	5,310	3,300	Siberia	Arctic Sea
Yukon	2,900	1,800	Canada	Bering Sea
Zaïre (Congo)	4,660	2,900	Africa	Atlantic Ocean
Zambezi	2,630	1,630	Africa	Indian Ocean

TABLE 4   MOUNTAINS AND PEAKS

mountain range	highest peaks	height in metres to nearest 5	height in feet to nearest 10	country of peak
Alps	Mont Blanc	4,810	15,780	France
	Monte Rosa	4,635	15,220	Italy/Switzerland
	Dom	4,555	14,940	Switzerland/Italy
	Matterhorn	4,475	14,690	Switzerland
	Finsteraarhorn	4,275	14,030	Switzerland
	Breithorn	4,160	13,690	Switzerland
	Jungfrau	4,155	13,670	Switzerland
	Weisshorn	4,505	14,600	Switzerland
Andes	Aconcagua	6,960	22,830	Argentina
	Huascurán	6,770	22,210	Peru
	Sorata	6,555	21,500	Bolivia
	Sajama	6,540	21,460	Bolivia
	Illimani	6,400	21,000	Bolivia
	Chimborazo	6,310	20,700	Ecuador
	Llullaillaco	6,725	22,060	Argentina/Chile
	Cotopaxi	5,895	19,340	Ecuador
	Antisana	5,705	18,850	Ecuador
	Tolima	5,215	18,320	Colombia
Apennines	Mount Corno	3,275	10,740	Italy
Atlas Mountains	Tizi-n-Tamjurt	4,420	14,500	Morocco
Australian Alps	Mount Buller	1,800	5,910	Australia
Barisan Mountains	Koerinji	3,945	12,940	Sumatra
Cantabrians	Pena Vieja	2,665	8,740	Spain
Carpathians	Tatra	2,665	8,740	Czechoslovakia
Cascade Range	Mount Rainer	4,395	14,420	USA
	Mount Hood	3,430	11,250	USA
Caucasus Range	Mount Ararat	5,165	16,950	Turkey
Colorado Plateau	Humphrey's Peak	3,900	12,800	USA
Cordillera de los Andes	Tupungato	6,800	22,310	Chile
	Maipo	5,290	17,460	Chile
Elburz Range	Demavend	5,605	18,550	Iran
Front Range	Mount Evans	4,345	14,260	USA
Great Basin	Boundary Peak	4,010	13,150	USA
Great Dividing Range	Kosciusko	2,355	7,730	Australia
Great Rift Valley	Kilimanjaro	5,895	19,340	Tanzania
Himalayas	Nanga Parbat	8,125	26,660	Tibet
	Mount Everest	8,850	29,030	Tibet
	K.2	8,610	28,250	Tibet
	Kanchenjunga	8,600	28,210	Tibet
Iran Mountains	Kinabalu	4,100	13,450	Borneo
Kunlun Mountains	Godwin Austin	8,610	28,250	Tibet
Owen Stanley Range	Mount Victoria	4,000	13,120	New Guinea
	Mount Simpson	3,040	9,970	New Guinea
Pindus Mountains	Mount Olympus	2,911	9,790	Greece
Pyrenees	Pic de Aneto	3,405	11,170	Spain
	Mount Perdu	3,350	10,990	Spain
Rocky Mountains	Mount Elbert	4,400	14,430	USA
	Mount Massive	4,395	14,420	USA
Salmon River Mountains	Borah Peak	3,860	12,660	USA
Sierra Nevada	Mount Whitney	4,415	14,500	USA
Snowdon	Snowdon	1,085	3,560	Wales
Southern Alps	Mount Cook	3,765	12,350	New Zealand
	Mount Tasman	3,500	11,480	New Zealand
Taurus Mountains	Ala Dagh	3,355	11,000	Turkey

TABLE 5 OCEANS AND SEAS

sea or ocean	area in		greatest depth	
	square kilometres	square miles	in metres (approx.)	in feet (approx.)
Adriatic Sea	135,000	52,000	1,230	4,030
Aegean Sea	179,000	69,000	1,830	6,000
Andaman Sea	780,000	300,000	3,050	10,000
Antarctic Ocean			8,580	28,150
Arabian Sea	390,000	150,000	5,300	17,390
Arctic Ocean	14,056,000	5,427,000	5,450	17,880
Atlantic Ocean	82,217,000	31,744,000	8,380	27,500
Baffin Bay	476,000	184,000	2,740	9,000
Baltic Sea	422,000	163,000	439	1,440
Banda Sea	738,000	285,000	6,400	21,000
Bay of Bengal	1,189,000	459,000	914	3,000
Beaufort Sea	466,000	180,000	3,050	10,000
Bering Sea	2,269,000	876,000	5,120	16,800
Black Sea	461,000	178,000	2,240	7,360
Caribbean Sea	1,943,000	750,000	7,490	24,580
Coral Sea	2,644,000	1,021,000		
English Channel	91,000	35,000	91	300
East China Sea	1,248,000	482,000	3,000	9,840
Great Australian Bight	409,000	158,000		
Greenland Sea	562,000	217,000	4,846	15,900
Gulf of Mexico	1,544,000	596,000	4,380	14,360
Gulf of St. Lawrence	260,000	100,000	122	400
Gulf of Tonkin	1,165,000	450,000		
Hudson Bay	1,233,000	476,000	259	850
Indian Ocean	73,481,000	28,371,000	8,050	26,400
Java Sea	310,000	120,000		
Ligurian Sea	2,100,000	800,000	2,830	9,300
Mediterranean	2,505,000	967,000	4,850	15,900
North Sea	575,000	222,000	661	2,170
Pacific Ocean	165,384,000	63,855,000	11,030	36,200
Persian Gulf	230,000	90,000		
Red Sea	438,000	169,000	2,250	7,370
Sea of Japan	1,008,000	389,000	3,743	12,280
Sea of Okhotsk	1,528,000	590,000	3,480	11,400
South China Sea	2,318,000	895,000	5,510	18,090
Tasman Sea	2,330,000	900,000		
Timor Sea	34,000	13,000		
Weddell Sea	1,990,000	770,000		
Yellow Sea	1,243,000	480,000	91	300

ACKNOWLEDGMENTS

The publisher would particularly like to thank Alan Blackwood of James Moore Associates for his help in the preparation of the text. They would also like to thank those listed below for permission to reproduce photographs in the book.

Albertina, Vienna 114 (photo Mansell Collection)
Angel, Heather 47*l*, 76, 130, 142, 163, 209*r*, 287, 317
Ardea 155, 257
J. W. Arrowsmith Ltd 277
Ashmolean Museum, Oxford 60*t*
Australian Information Service 35*b*, 37*t*, 225*l*, 327
Barnaby's Picture Library 357 (photo Dick Huffman)
BBC 90, 328
BOAC 166
Bodleian Library, Oxford **201**
British Industrial Plastics Ltd 272
British Museum 46 (photo Mansell Collection) 49, 78, 122*t*, 131 (photo Mansell Collection)
British Museum (Natural History) 137
British Steel Corporation 320
British Tourist Authority 123, 305*l*
Camera Press 84, 254, 300, 354, *jacket 9*
Canonbury Service Arts 279 (photo Carolyn Clarke)
Cash, J. Allan 115
Coleman, Bruce *jacket 6*
Commissioners of Public Works in Ireland 74
Courtauld Institute 222 (photo Country Life), 295
Cranham, Gerry *jacket 8*
Crown Copyright Reserved 233, 345
Danish Tourist Board 108
De Beers 109*t*
Elisabeth Photo Library 200
Mary Evans Picture Library 6, 69*t*, 103, 106, 140, 150, 212, 262, 302, 312, 330, 346
Werner Forman Archive **65, 167** (Egyptian Antiquities Museum), 157, 176*r*, 186, 227, 232, 249, 259, 325
French Government Tourist Office 22, 118, 138, 207
Hale Observatories 231*r*
Michael Holford **134** and **270** (Courtesy of the Trustees of the British Museum), **168**
Hornak, Angelo **133, 269,** 355
Hosking, Eric **100**, 113, 135, 176*l*, 198, 258, **303**
IBM 120
Israel Government Tourist Office 193
Italian State Tourist Department (ENIT) 42, 195
Japan National Tourist Organization 190
Kenwood House **304** (photo Cooper-Bridgeman)
Kenya Public Relations Office 10
Keystone Press 153, 154, 191, 226
King's College Hospital, London 356
London Festival Ballet 41 (photo Anthony Crickmay)
Mansell Collection 7, 31*b*, 32, 47*r*, 60*b*, 63*l*, 7*b*, 105, 139, 143, 158, 228*l*, 231*l*, 237, 239, 242, 243, 245, 261*tr*, 280, 342, 359

MGM 83*r*
Museo Etrusca Guarnacci Volterra 128
National Coal Board 87
National Film Board, Ottawa 45*b*, 70, 299
National Gallery, London 19, 56, 71, 209*l*, **236**, 268, 288, 336
National Gallery of Art, Washington **202** (photo Cooper-Bridgeman)
National Maritime Museum *jacket 5*
National Portrait Gallery, London 54, 72, 189, 271, 350
National Trust 161
Netherlands National Tourist Office 246, *jacket 4*
Phaidon 348
Picturepoint *jacket 2, 3* and *10*
Popperfoto 23 (Ashmolean Museum), 51*t*, 97, 104, 144, 187, 196, 208, 220, 221, 223, 248, 287, 298, 305*r*, 315, 318, 322, 329, 340
Radio Times Hulton Picture Library 260
RKO 83*l*
Royal Greenwich Observatory 323
Royal National Lifeboat Institution 211*l*
RSPB 52 and 152 (photos David and Katie Urry)
SATOUR 358
Science Museum, London (Crown Copyright) 27*t*, 57, 284, 307*l*
Scout Association 39*b*
SCR Photo Library 263, 338
Shell International Petroleum Company 265
Society of Apothecaries **66** (photo Cooper-Bridgeman)
Spectrum 125*t* (photo Howard W. Bracewell) **235, 275,** *jacket 1*
Steinway & Sons 267*tr*
Swiss National Tourist Office 15
Tate Gallery, London 102, 107, 276, 307*r*
Trans-Antarctic Expedition 20
Trinity College, Dublin 185
United Kingdom Energy Authority 282
United Nations 339 (photo M. Tzovaras)
US Signal Corps 180
Victoria and Albert Museum, London (Crown Copyright) 286*b*, 170, 333
Wallace Collection, London 160
Walt Disney Productions 110*r*
Warren, Peter M. 341
Wilson, Reg (Royal Ballet, Covent Garden) **99**, *jacket 7*

The diagrams and line drawings were prepared by: Gordon Davies, Peter Dennis, Annette Olney, Jim Robins, Peter Robinson, Malcolm Ward.